D0855925

the best of
Southern Living®

the best of
Southern Living®

Compiled and Edited by
Susan Hernandez Ray

Oxmoor House®

© 2007 by Oxmoor House, Inc.
Book Division of Southern Progress Corporation
P.O. Box 2262, Birmingham, Alabama 35201-2262

All rights reserved. No part of this book may be reproduced in any form or by any means without the prior written permission of the publisher, excepting brief quotes in connection with reviews written specifically for inclusion in a magazine or newspaper.

ISBN: 13: 978-0-8487-3188-5
ISBN: 10: 0-8487-3188-3

Printed in the United States of America
First printing 2007

To order additional publications, call 1-800-765-6400.

Cover: Blackberry Cobbler, page 343

Page 1: Fried Green Tomato Stack, page 274
Page 2: Two-Step Pound Cake, page 327

Southern Living ®

Executive Editor: Scott Jones
Foods Editor: Shannon Sliter Satterwhite
Senior Writers: Donna Florio, Andria Scott Hurst
Associate Foods Editors: Charla Draper, Shirley Harrington,
  Holley Johnson, Kate Nicholson, Mary Allen Perry,
  Vicki A. Poellnitz
Assistant Foods Editors: Natalie Kelly Brown, Marion McGahey
Assistant Recipe Editor: Ashley Leath
Test Kitchens Director: Lyda Jones Burnette
Assistant Test Kitchens Director: James Schend
Test Kitchens Specialist/Food Styling: Vanessa McNeil Rocchio
Test Kitchens Professionals: Marian Cooper Cairns,
  Kristi Michele Crowe, Rebecca Kracke Gordon, Pam Lolley,
  Angela Sellers
Administrative Assistant: Sandra J. Thomas
Production and Color Quality Manager: Katie Terrell Morrow
Creative Director: Jon Thompson
Copy Chief: Paula Hunt Hughes
Copy Editor: Cindy Riegle
Senior Foods Photographer: Ralph Anderson
Photographers: Mary Margaret Chambliss, William Dickey,
  Beth Dreiling
Senior Photo Stylist: Buffy Hargett
Photo Stylists: Lisa Powell Bailey, Rose Nguyen
Photo Production Manager: Larry Hunter
Photo Librarian: Tracy Duncan
Photo Assistant: Catherine Carr
Assistant Production Manager: Jamie Barnhart
Production Coordinators: Christy Coleman, Paula Dennis,
  Brooke Krannich

Oxmoor House, Inc.

Editor in Chief: Nancy Fitzpatrick Wyatt
Executive Editor: Susan Carlisle Payne
Managing Editor: Allison Long Lowery

The Best of Southern Living ®

Editor: Susan Hernandez Ray
Copy Editor: Jacqueline Giovanelli
Proofreader: Donna Baldone
Editorial Assistant: Amelia Heying
Director of Production: Laura Lockhart
Production Manager: Terri Beste
Production Assistant: Faye Porter Bonner

Contributors

Designer: Nancy Johnson
Indexer: Mary Ann Laurens
Editorial Assistant: Laura K. Womble
Proofreader: Amy Edgerton

contents

welcome

We've published tens of thousands of recipes over our 40-plus-year history—many developed in our Test Kitchens, some from chefs, but the overwhelming majority coming from great cooks in home kitchens all over the South. That said, you can imagine how daunting a task it was to select our top picks, which is just what we've done in *Best of Southern Living*®. (Take a quick glance at "Some of My Favorite Recipes" on the opposite page for a tempting preview.)

What's so great about this cookbook is that we're featuring over 500 of the Foods Staff's all-time favorite recipes, along with more than 250 mouth-watering photographs (which also include simple ideas for plating and garnishing). Be sure to reference cook and prep times for each recipe. They'll help you plan your schedule, minimize your time in the kitchen, and maximize time with family and friends.

One of the cookbook's most exciting features is the Menus for All Occasions special section. A virtual feast for the eyes and palate, this collection of special occasion ideas showcases, among other things, a Wine and Cheese Sampling Party, a Halloween Block Party, a Southwestern-Style Thanksgiving, and a Christmas Appetizer Buffet (and just about everything in between). So whether you need a dish for an easy weeknight meal or casual weekend get-together, let this cookbook be your guide to the very best *Southern Living* has to offer.

Happy cooking!

Scott Jones
Executive Editor

some of my favorite recipes

Sweet Lemon Baby Cakes *(page 331):* Perfect for bridal parties, baby showers, and birthday celebrations, these moist little goodies begin with a cake mix.

Ham-Stuffed Biscuits With Mustard Butter *(page 369):* A slightly spicy, buttery spread enlivens tender ham encased in savory biscuits.

Pumpkin Cheese Ball *(page 393):* There are only 5 ingredients in this cheese ball, and it tastes so good. The broccoli stalk makes it look authentic and festive.

Cornbread Dressing Cakes *(page 398):* A flavorful spin on a traditional Thanksgiving dish, this mouthwatering side can be made ahead.

Pecan Pie Cheesecake *(page 324):* This divine dessert won the grand prize in our first-ever cook-off.

Double-Chocolate Brownies *(page 347):* Satisfy your chocolate cravings with this rich bar cookie with pecan crunch.

 ◄**Caramel Sticky Buns** *(page 71):* Wake up to the aroma of these melt-in-your-mouth treats that are extra simple to make with hot roll mix.

 ◄**Baby Blue Salad** *(page 176):* The Balsamic Vinaigrette and Sweet-and-Spicy Pecans put this salad in a category of its own.

 ◄**Peppery Chicken-fried Chicken** *(page 147):* With its crispy golden crust and to-die-for gravy, this dish will remind you of your favorite diner.

 ◄**Caramelized Sweet Onions** *(page 256):* Get to know this recipe. You'll find this side dish appearing as an ingredient in several recipes throughout this book. Here, it's shown in a tart.

 ◄**Fresh Fruit Trifles** *(page 330):* This refreshing summer dessert is great for parties—everyone gets their own individual trifle. You can make the vanilla custard ahead.

 ◄**Lamb Chops With Mint Aïoli** *(page 124):* Celebrate any occasion with tender lamb chops kissed with mint-tinged aïoli.

7

appetizers & beverages

Double-Berry Milk Shake, page 41

Hot Smoky Pecans

Serve these pecans at a holiday party.

MAKES 2 CUPS
PREP: 5 MIN., BAKE: 25 MIN.

¼ cup butter or margarine, melted
2 tablespoons soy sauce
½ teaspoon hot sauce
1 tablespoon Worcestershire sauce
2 cups pecan halves

1. Stir together all ingredients; spread pecans in a single layer in a 15- x 10-inch jelly-roll pan.
2. Bake at 300°, stirring often, 25 minutes or until toasted. Let cool; store in airtight container up to 5 days.

Orange Pecans

These tasty snacks pair well with an assortment of Cheddar cheeses.

MAKES ABOUT 5 CUPS
PREP: 10 MIN., COOK: 10 MIN.

1 cup sugar
1¼ cups fresh orange juice
1 tablespoon grated orange rind
1 teaspoon ground cinnamon
4 cups pecan halves, toasted

1. Bring first 4 ingredients to a rapid boil in a heavy saucepan over medium heat. Stir in pecan halves; cook, stirring constantly, until pecans are coated and syrup is absorbed. Remove from heat; stir just until pecans separate. Spread in a single layer onto wax paper; cool. Store in airtight containers up to 5 days.

Starry Nibbles

MAKES 15 CUPS
PREP: 10 MIN.

2 (8-ounce) packages crispy cereal squares snack mix
1 (16-ounce) package raisins
1 (12-ounce) jar honey-roasted peanuts
1 (9.5-ounce) package fish-shaped Cheddar cheese crackers

1. Stir together all ingredients. Store in an airtight container for up to 1 week.
Note: For testing purposes only, we used Bold Party Blend Chex Mix for crispy cereal squares snack mix and Goldfish Crackers for fish-shaped Cheddar cheese crackers.

Easy-as-Pie Cheese Straws

MAKES 5 DOZEN
PREP: 15 MIN., CHILL: 1 HR., BAKE: 8 MIN. PER BATCH

1 (11-ounce) package piecrust mix
1 (5-ounce) jar sharp processed cheese spread
½ teaspoon ground red pepper
¼ teaspoon dry mustard

1. Process all ingredients in a food processor 30 seconds or until mixture forms a ball, stopping twice to scrape down sides.
2. Use a cookie press fitted with a bar-shaped disc to shape dough into 2½-inch straws, following manufacturer's instructions. Or divide dough in half, and shape each portion into a 7-inch log; wrap in plastic wrap, and chill 1 hour. Cut logs into ¼-inch slices.
3. Place cheese straws on greased baking sheets. Bake at 375° for 8 minutes or until golden. Remove to wire racks to cool. Store in an airtight container for up to 1 week.

Honey-Nut Snack Mix

Honey-Nut Snack Mix

Try this flavorful mix over yogurt for a quick breakfast or snack. You can also substitute cashews for pecans.

MAKES 7 CUPS
PREP: 10 MIN., COOK: 5 MIN., BAKE: 25 MIN.

4 cups toasted oat bran cereal
2 cups uncooked quick-cooking oats
1 cup coarsely chopped pecans
¼ teaspoon salt
1½ teaspoons ground cinnamon
½ cup butter or margarine
½ cup firmly packed brown sugar
½ cup honey
1 (6-ounce) package sweetened dried cranberries

1. Combine first 5 ingredients in a large bowl; set aside.
2. Stir together butter, brown sugar, and honey in a small saucepan over low heat, stirring until butter melts and sugar dissolves.
3. Pour butter mixture over cereal mixture, stirring to coat. Spread evenly on an aluminum foil-lined 15- x 10-inch jelly-roll pan. Bake at 325° for 20 minutes, stirring once. Stir in cranberries; bake 5 minutes. Spread immediately on wax paper; cool. Store in an airtight container up to 1 week.
Note: For testing purposes only, we used Quaker Oat Bran cereal.

Curried Party Mix

Whip up this zesty snack for something with extra bite. The curry powder and red pepper spice up this mix.

MAKES 10 CUPS
PREP: 15 MIN., BAKE: 1 HR.

1/4 cup butter or margarine, melted
2 teaspoons curry powder
3/4 to 1 teaspoon seasoned salt
1/2 teaspoon ground cumin
1/8 teaspoon ground red pepper
5 cups bite-size crispy corn squares cereal
2 cups small pretzels
1 1/2 cups whole almonds
1 1/2 cups salted peanuts

1. Stir together first 5 ingredients in a small bowl. Combine cereal and remaining 3 ingredients in a large bowl. Stir butter mixture, and pour evenly over cereal mixture. Stir cereal mixture until coated.
2. Spread mixture in a greased roasting pan or 15- x 10-inch jelly-roll pan. Bake at 250° for 1 hour, stirring every 15 minutes. Spread mixture in a single layer on paper towels; cool completely. Store in an airtight container for up to 1 week.
Note: For testing purposes only, we used Corn Chex cereal.

Blue Cheese Crisps

MAKES 6 DOZEN
PREP: 10 MIN., CHILL: 2 HRS., BAKE: 15 MIN.

2 (4-ounce) packages crumbled blue cheese
1/2 cup butter or margarine, softened
1 1/3 cups all-purpose flour
1/3 cup poppy seeds
1/4 teaspoon ground red pepper

1. Beat cheese and butter at medium speed with an electric mixer until creamy. Add flour, poppy seeds, and pepper; beat until blended.
2. Divide dough in half; shape each portion into a 9-inch log. Cover and chill 2 hours.
3. Cut each log of dough into 1/4-inch-thick slices, and place on ungreased baking sheets.
4. Bake at 350° for 13 to 15 minutes or until golden. Transfer to wire racks to cool completely.

Rosemary Popcorn With Pine Nuts

Give the usual popcorn an upscale twist with a double infusion of rosemary. Use leftover herb-flavored oil in salad dressings, marinades, or sauces.

MAKES 14 CUPS
PREP: 5 MIN., STAND: 48 HRS., COOK: 7 MIN.

1 cup olive oil
1/2 cup unpopped popcorn kernels
12 (6-inch) rosemary sprigs, cut into 2-inch pieces
1 1/2 teaspoons sea salt, divided
1/2 cup pine nuts, toasted
2 tablespoons coarsely chopped fresh rosemary

1. Heat olive oil in a small saucepan over low heat 3 minutes. Add popcorn kernels, rosemary sprigs, and 1 teaspoon sea salt. Remove mixture from heat; cover and let stand at room temperature 48 hours.
2. Drain kernels, reserving oil; discard rosemary sprigs.
3. Place 3 tablespoons herb-flavored oil and popcorn kernels in a Dutch oven. Cook kernels, covered, over high heat, shaking the pan often 4 minutes or until popping begins to slow. Remove popcorn from heat, and let stand until the popping stops.
4. Place popcorn in a large bowl. Add remaining salt, pine nuts, and chopped rosemary, and toss. Serve immediately.

Quick-and-Easy Asian Popcorn: Omit steeping kernels step. Substitute 2 1/2 tablespoons dark sesame oil plus 1/2 tablespoon hot chili oil for olive oil, garlic salt for sea salt, and roasted cashew pieces for pine nuts.

Garlicky Basil-Parmesan Popcorn: Substitute basil for rosemary and 1/2 cup grated garlic-and-herb Parmesan cheese for pine nuts.
Note: For testing purposes only, we used Kraft Parm Plus Garlic Herb.

Rosemary Popcorn
With Pine Nuts

Cream Cheese-and-Olive Biscuits With Tapenade

You can substitute 1 (3-ounce) package of cream cheese for the goat cheese, if desired.

MAKES 30 APPETIZERS
PREP: 30 MIN., BAKE: 10 MIN. PER BATCH

2¼ cups all-purpose baking mix
1 (3-ounce) package cream cheese, softened
⅓ cup buttermilk
½ cup pimiento-stuffed olives, chopped
1 (6-ounce) jar pitted kalamata olives
1 tablespoon capers, drained
1 garlic clove, minced
1 tablespoon chopped fresh parsley
2 tablespoons balsamic vinegar
2 tablespoons olive oil
¼ teaspoon pepper
1 (3-ounce) log goat cheese

1. Pulse first 4 ingredients in a food processor 3 or 4 times or until combined. Turn dough out onto a lightly floured surface. Pat the dough to a ½-inch thickness; cut with a 2-inch round cutter. Place rounds on ungreased baking sheets.
2. Bake at 425° for 10 minutes.
3. Pulse kalamata olives and next 6 ingredients in a food processor until combined. Split biscuits in half, and spread cut sides with goat cheese; top with olive mixture.

Cream Cheese-and-Olive Biscuits With Sun-Dried Tomato Spread and Bacon: Omit kalamata olive mixture and goat cheese. Spread the biscuit halves with 1 (8-ounce) container sun-dried tomato-basil spreadable cheese. Top with cooked and crumbled bacon.
Note: For testing purposes only, we used Alouette spreadable cheese; substitute any flavor, if desired.

Chicken-Chile Quesadillas

Quesadillas lend themselves to a variety of fillings, so have fun and experiment.

MAKES 8 APPETIZER SERVINGS
PREP: 20 MIN., COOK: 6 MIN. PER BATCH

10 (6-inch) flour tortillas
2 cups chopped cooked chicken
2 cups (8 ounces) shredded Mexican four-cheese blend
1 (4.5-ounce) can chopped green chiles, drained
5 green onions, thinly sliced
⅓ cup chopped fresh cilantro
Toppings: salsa, sour cream

1. Sprinkle 5 tortillas evenly with chicken and next 4 ingredients. Top with remaining 5 tortillas.
2. Cook quesadillas, in batches, in a lightly greased skillet or griddle over medium heat 2 to 3 minutes on each side or until browned. Cut each quesadilla into wedges. Serve with toppings.

Curried Chicken Pâté

MAKES 3 CUPS
PREP: 15 MIN., CHILL: 8 HRS.

2 cups chopped cooked chicken breast
½ Granny Smith apple, peeled and quartered
1 large shallot, quartered
½ cup butter or margarine, softened
½ teaspoon salt
½ teaspoon curry powder
1 teaspoon lemon juice
Garnishes: Italian parsley sprig, chopped pimiento
Hot mango chutney
Crackers or beaten biscuits

1. Process first 3 ingredients in a food processor until smooth, stopping to scrape down sides. Add butter and next 3 ingredients; process until smooth.
2. Spoon mixture into a lightly greased 6- x 3-inch loaf pan. Cover and chill 8 hours. Unmold, and garnish, if desired. Serve with hot mango chutney and crackers or beaten biscuits.

Parmesan-Artichoke Crostini

Parmesan-Artichoke Crostini

MAKES 12 APPETIZER SERVINGS
PREP: 20 MIN., BAKE: 5 MIN.

1 (14-ounce) can artichoke hearts, drained and
    chopped
1 (4.5-ounce) can chopped green chiles
2 garlic cloves, minced
1 cup grated Parmesan cheese
1 cup light mayonnaise
½ cup chopped pecans, toasted
40 (¼-inch-thick) French baguette slices, toasted
Garnish: Chopped fresh chives

1. Stir together first 6 ingredients. Spread 1 tablespoon artichoke mixture evenly on each bread slice, and place on ungreased baking sheets.
2. Bake at 400° for 3 to 5 minutes or until thoroughly heated. Garnish, if desired. Serve crostini immediately.

Parmesan-Shrimp Crostini: Omit chopped artichoke hearts and chopped green chiles. Add 2 cups chopped cooked shrimp and 6 sliced green onions; proceed with recipe as directed.

Layered Spinach-Tomato Spread

Layered Spinach-Tomato Spread

MAKES 12 APPETIZER SERVINGS
PREP: 30 MIN., STAND: 5 MIN., CHILL: 8 HRS.

1 (9-ounce) package frozen creamed spinach
2 (8-ounce) packages cream cheese, softened
1/8 teaspoon garlic powder
1/8 teaspoon ground red pepper
1/2 (7-ounce) jar sun-dried tomatoes in oil, drained
　　and chopped
1/8 teaspoon salt
1 green onion, chopped
French baguette slices

1. Microwave spinach according to package directions.
Let spinach stand 5 minutes.
2. Beat spinach, 1 package cream cheese, garlic powder,
and red pepper at medium speed with an electric mixer
until smooth. Set aside.
3. Beat remaining 1 package cream cheese, tomatoes,
and salt at medium speed with an electric mixer until
blended. Stir in green onion.

4. Spread half of tomato mixture in a plastic wrap-
lined 4-cup glass bowl; top with half of spinach mixture. Repeat procedure with remaining tomato mixture
and spinach mixture. Cover and chill 8 hours.
5. Invert chilled mixture onto a serving plate; remove
plastic wrap. Serve with baguette slices.

LET'S FREEZE, PLEASE

Many appetizer spreads made with cream
cheese can be frozen. Just prepare the recipe
as directed, omitting any garnish, and place
in an airtight container. Freeze up to one
month. Thaw in the refrigerator for eight
hours before serving.

Shrimp Rounds

MAKES 1½ DOZEN
PREP: 30 MIN., COOK: 5 MIN., BAKE: 15 MIN.

2¼ cups water
¾ pound unpeeled, medium-size fresh shrimp
18 (¼- to ½-inch-thick) baguette slices
½ cup (2 ounces) shredded Cheddar cheese
2 tablespoons minced celery
1 tablespoon minced onion
2 tablespoons mayonnaise
1 teaspoon chopped fresh dill
⅛ teaspoon salt
Dash of ground pepper

1. Bring 2¼ cups water to a boil in a large saucepan; add shrimp, and cook 3 to 5 minutes or just until shrimp turn pink. Drain and rinse with cold water.
2. Peel shrimp; devein, if desired. Cut 9 shrimp in half lengthwise; set aside. Dice remaining shrimp.
3. Bake baguette slices on a baking sheet at 350° for 5 to 10 minutes or until lightly toasted.
4. Stir together diced shrimp, cheese, and next 6 ingredients; spread mixture on baguette slices.
5. Bake at 350° for 5 minutes or until lightly browned. Top each with a shrimp half.

Smoked Salmon Spread

Spoil your party guests with this extra-rich and spicy salmon spread.

MAKES 1 CUP
PREP: 10 MIN., CHILL: 2 HRS.

6 ounces smoked salmon
1 (3-ounce) package cream cheese, softened
2 tablespoons butter or margarine, softened
½ teaspoon hot sauce
1 teaspoon lemon juice
2 tablespoons coarsely chopped red onion
Garnishes: chopped red onion, green onion tops

1. Pulse first 6 ingredients in a food processor until smoked salmon is coarsely chopped, stopping to scrape down sides. Chill 2 hours. Garnish, if desired. Serve with celery sticks or assorted crackers.

Black Pepper-Goat Cheese Log

MAKES 6 TO 8 APPETIZER SERVINGS
PREP: 5 MIN.

2 tablespoons cracked black pepper
1 (11-ounce) goat cheese log
2 tablespoons extra-virgin olive oil
Garnish: fresh rosemary sprigs

1. Sprinkle pepper on a square of wax paper. Roll goat cheese log over pepper to coat. Drizzle with olive oil. Serve with toasted baguette slices. Garnish, if desired.

Pinecone Cheese Ball

MAKES 16 SERVINGS
PREP: 20 MIN., CHILL: 2 HRS.

1 (8-ounce) container garden vegetable cream cheese
1 (8-ounce) container roasted garlic cream cheese
1 cup (4 ounces) shredded sharp Cheddar cheese
3 green onions, chopped
2 cups pecan halves, toasted
Fresh rosemary sprigs

1. Stir together first 4 ingredients. Shape into an oval; chill 2 hours.
2. Arrange pecan halves over cheese oval in overlapping rows, beginning at bottom and working upward. Arrange rosemary sprigs at top of pinecone. Serve with crackers.

Blue Cheese Rolls

MAKES 4 (7-INCH) LOGS
PREP: 15 MIN., CHILL: 1 HR.

2 (8-ounce) packages cream cheese, softened
1 (8-ounce) package sharp Cheddar cheese slices,
      cut up
2 (4-ounce) packages crumbled blue cheese
½ small onion, diced
1½ tablespoons Worcestershire sauce
½ teaspoon ground red pepper
1½ cups finely chopped toasted pecans, divided
1½ cups finely chopped fresh parsley, divided

1. Place first 6 ingredients in a food processor; pulse 1 to 2 minutes, stopping to scrape down sides.
2. Stir together cheese mixture, 1 cup pecans, and ½ cup parsley. Cover and chill 1 hour.
3. Shape cheese mixture into 4 (7-inch-long) logs.
4. Combine remaining ½ cup pecans and 1 cup parsley. Roll logs in parsley mixture; cover and chill. Serve with crackers.
Note: For testing purposes only, we used Old English cheese slices. Cheese rolls may be prepared ahead and frozen, if desired. Thaw in refrigerator overnight.

Blue Cheese Rolls

Goblin Dip With Bone Crackers

Gather with friends and family to enjoy the chills and thrills of Halloween. Your guests will love the bold Southwest flavor of this festive dip that's simple to make. Add a spooky touch with bone-shaped crackers.

MAKES 6 CUPS
PREP: 10 MIN., COOK: 15 MIN.

1 (16-ounce) can chili without beans
1 (16-ounce) can refried beans
1 (8-ounce) package cream cheese
1 (8-ounce) jar chunky pico de gallo
1 (4.5-ounce) can chopped green chiles, undrained
½ teaspoon ground cumin
Toppings: shredded Cheddar or Monterey Jack cheese with peppers, chopped black olives, sliced green onions
Bone Crackers

1. Cook first 6 ingredients in a heavy saucepan over low heat, stirring often, 15 minutes or until cream cheese is melted. Sprinkle with desired toppings, and serve warm with Bone Crackers.

Bone Crackers:

MAKES 60 CRACKERS
PREP: 20 MIN., BAKE: 30 MIN.

2 (13.5-ounce) packages 9-inch flour tortillas
½ cup butter or margarine, melted
¼ teaspoon garlic salt

1. Cut tortillas with a 3½-inch bone-shaped cutter, and place on baking sheets. Stir together butter and garlic salt; brush mixture on cutouts.
2. Bake at 250° for 30 minutes or until crisp.
Note: Flour tortillas can be cut into bone shapes using kitchen shears.

Hot Spinach Dip

Serve this dip with a Mexican-style meal.

MAKES 8 CUPS
PREP: 15 MIN., BAKE: 30 MIN.

2 (10-ounce) packages frozen chopped spinach, thawed
2 (8-ounce) packages cream cheese, cubed
2 cups (8 ounces) shredded Monterey Jack cheese
1 cup freshly grated Parmesan cheese
1 small onion, chopped
1 (14-ounce) can artichoke hearts, drained and chopped
2 (10-ounce) cans diced tomatoes and green chiles, undrained
2 teaspoons ground cumin
2 teaspoons chili powder
1 teaspoon garlic powder

1. Drain spinach; press between layers of paper towels to remove excess moisture.
2. Combine spinach, cream cheese, and next 8 ingredients, stirring well. Spoon mixture into a greased 2½-quart baking dish. Bake, uncovered, at 350° for 30 minutes or until bubbly. Serve with Melba toast rounds or corn chips.

Hummus

Hummus

MAKES 2 CUPS
PREP: 10 MIN., CHILL: 1 HR.

1 (16-ounce) can chickpeas, rinsed and drained
3 garlic cloves, chopped
1/3 cup tahini
1/4 cup fresh lemon juice
1/2 teaspoon salt
1/4 cup extra-virgin olive oil

1. Process first 5 ingredients in a food processor until smooth, stopping to scrape down sides. With processor running, pour olive oil through food chute in a slow, steady stream; process until smooth. Chill 1 hour. Serve hummus with carrot and celery sticks, asparagus spears, sugar snap peas, and red bell pepper strips.

Creamy Tomato-Pesto Dip With Tortellini

MAKES 20 APPETIZER SERVINGS
PREP: 30 MIN., COOK: 15 MIN., STAND: 20 MIN.

4 quarts water
1 (9-ounce) package refrigerated mushroom tortellini
1 (9-ounce) package refrigerated spinach tortellini
1 (9-ounce) package refrigerated tomato tortellini
12 dried tomatoes
1 (8-ounce) package cream cheese, softened
1 (7-ounce) jar roasted sweet red peppers, drained
1/2 cup shredded Parmesan cheese
2 garlic cloves, minced
6 fresh basil leaves
2 tablespoons olive oil
1 tablespoon lemon juice
3/4 teaspoon salt
1/4 teaspoon dried crushed red pepper
Green and ripe olives (optional)

1. Bring 4 quarts water to a boil in a stockpot. Add pasta, and cook over medium-high heat 5 minutes. Rinse with cold water. Drain and chill, if desired.
2. Place dried tomatoes in a bowl, and cover with boiling water. Let stand 20 minutes. Drain.
3. Process tomatoes, cream cheese, red peppers, and next 7 ingredients in a food processor or blender until smooth, stopping to scrape down sides. Spoon into a bowl, and sprinkle with olives, if desired. Serve with tortellini.

Quick Fiesta Dip

MAKES 1 1/2 CUPS
PREP: 5 MIN., COOK: 10 MIN., STAND: 5 MIN.

1 (9-ounce) package frozen corn niblets
1 (12-ounce) jar thick-and-chunky mild salsa
1 cup (4 ounces) shredded colby or Cheddar cheese

1. Cook corn according to package directions; drain.
2. Pour salsa into a 9-inch glass pieplate; stir in corn. Cover with plastic wrap, and fold back a small section of wrap to allow steam to escape. Microwave at HIGH 2 minutes or until bubbly. Sprinkle cheese over salsa; cover with plastic wrap. Let stand 5 minutes or until cheese is melted. Serve with chips.

Blue Cheese-Bacon Dip

This rich, creamy dip can be baked in individual cups or a 1-quart dish.

MAKES 12 TO 15 SERVINGS
PREP: 20 MIN., BAKE: 15 MIN.

7 bacon slices, chopped
2 garlic cloves, minced
2 (8-ounce) packages cream cheese, softened
1/3 cup half-and-half
4 ounces crumbled blue cheese
2 tablespoons chopped fresh chives
3 tablespoons chopped walnuts, toasted
Grape clusters
Flatbread or assorted crackers
Garnish: chopped fresh chives

1. Cook chopped bacon in a skillet over medium-high heat 10 minutes or until crisp. Drain bacon, and set aside. Add minced garlic to skillet, and sauté 1 minute.
2. Beat cream cheese at medium speed with electric mixer until smooth. Add half-and-half, beating until combined. Stir in bacon, garlic, blue cheese, and chives. Spoon mixture evenly into 4 (1-cup) individual baking dishes.
3. Bake at 350° for 15 minutes or until golden and bubbly. Sprinkle evenly with chopped walnuts, and serve with grape clusters and flatbread or assorted crackers. Garnish, if desired.

Warm-and-Spicy Salsa

Warm-and-Spicy Salsa

Serve leftover salsa on burgers and taco salads.

MAKES 3 CUPS
PREP: 18 MIN., COOK: 32 MIN.

1 cup white vinegar
1 large onion, diced
2 celery ribs, diced
3 garlic cloves, finely chopped
3 (10-ounce) cans diced tomatoes and green chiles,
    undrained
1 (15-ounce) can crushed tomatoes, undrained
1 teaspoon sugar
1 teaspoon salt
½ teaspoon pepper
½ teaspoon ground cumin
⅓ cup chopped fresh cilantro

1. Bring first 4 ingredients to a boil in a large saucepan over medium-high heat; add tomatoes and green chiles and next 5 ingredients. Return to a boil; reduce heat, and simmer 25 minutes, stirring occasionally. Stir in cilantro. Serve warm with tortilla chips.

Avocado-Mango Salsa

This fresh-flavored salsa tastes great the minute it's made. It's delicious with quesadillas or tortilla chips.

MAKES ABOUT 5 CUPS
PREP: 20 MIN.

¼ cup jalapeño pepper jelly
¼ cup fresh lime juice
1 (26-ounce) jar refrigerated mango pieces, drained
    and diced*
2 large avocados, diced
1 large red bell pepper, diced
¼ cup chopped fresh cilantro

1. Whisk together jelly and lime juice in a large bowl.
2. Add mango and remaining ingredients; stir until blended.
*2 large peeled and diced mangoes may be substituted.

Fruit Salsa With Cinnamon Crisps

Flour tortillas toasted with cinnamon and sugar on them make great dippers for this sweet fruit salsa. Serve it for an appetizer or a dessert.

MAKES 4 SERVINGS
PREP: 35 MIN., CHILL: 1 HR., BAKE: 8 MIN.

1 pint fresh strawberries, chopped
1 large banana, chopped
1 red delicious apple, chopped
1 kiwi fruit, peeled and chopped
¼ cup fresh lemon juice
¼ cup sugar
¼ teaspoon ground nutmeg
1¼ teaspoons ground cinnamon, divided
4 (7½-inch) flour tortillas
Vegetable cooking spray
2 tablespoons sugar

1. Combine first 4 ingredients. Stir together lemon juice, ¼ cup sugar, nutmeg, and ½ teaspoon cinnamon; toss with fruit. Chill at least 1 hour.
2. Cut each tortilla into eighths. Arrange pieces on baking sheets. Lightly coat with cooking spray. Combine remaining ¾ teaspoon cinnamon and 2 tablespoons sugar. Sprinkle over tortilla chips.
3. Bake at 350° for 6 to 8 minutes or until lightly browned. Serve with fruit salsa.

Grilled Tomatillo 'n'
Green Tomato Salsa

Grilled Tomatillo 'n' Green Tomato Salsa

MAKES ABOUT 5 CUPS
PREP: 20 MIN., GRILL: 20 MIN., COOL: 10 MIN., CHILL: 2 HRS.

1½ pounds fresh tomatillos, husks removed
3 medium-size green tomatoes, stems removed
1 jalapeño pepper
½ medium-size red onion, sliced
½ cup fresh cilantro leaves
1 garlic clove
2 tablespoons fresh lime juice
½ teaspoon ground cumin
½ teaspoon pepper
1¼ teaspoons salt
Tortilla chips
Lime wedges

1. Spray cold grill cooking grate with cooking spray; place grate on grill over high heat (400° to 500°). Place tomatillos and next 3 ingredients on cooking grate; grill, covered with grill lid, 10 to 15 minutes or until tomatillos look charred, turning often. Remove tomatillos and jalapeño pepper. Grill tomatoes and onion 5 more minutes or until tomatoes look charred and blistered and onion is tender, turning often. Cool 10 minutes. Slice jalapeño; discard seeds, if desired. Combine jalapeño slices, tomatillo, tomatoes, and onion.
2. Process grilled tomatillo mixture, cilantro leaves, and next 5 ingredients in a food processor 10 seconds or until mixture is coarsely chopped, stopping to scrape down sides. Cover salsa, and chill at least 2 hours. Serve with tortilla chips and lime wedges.

Chunky Black-eyed Pea Salsa

MAKES 2 CUPS
PREP: 20 MIN., BROIL: 10 MIN., STAND: 10 MIN.

1 large poblano chile pepper
1 (15.8-ounce) can black-eyed peas, rinsed and
    drained
1 ripe mango, peeled and chopped
½ small sweet onion, chopped
½ small red bell pepper, chopped
¼ cup chopped fresh cilantro
½ teaspoon grated lime rind
3 tablespoons fresh lime juice
2 teaspoons olive oil
¼ to ½ teaspoon salt
¼ to ½ teaspoon black pepper
Tortilla chips

1. Broil poblano pepper on an aluminum foil-lined baking sheet 5 inches from heat about 5 minutes on each side or until pepper looks blistered.
2. Place pepper in a zip-top plastic bag; seal and let stand 10 minutes to loosen skin. Peel pepper; remove and discard seeds. Chop pepper.
3. Stir together pepper, peas, and next 9 ingredients. Cover and chill. Serve with tortilla chips.

Chunky Black-Eyed Pea Salsa

Avocado-and-Leek-Stuffed
Portobello Mushrooms

Avocado-and-Leek-Stuffed Portobello Mushrooms

If you can't find baby portobellos, use 6 large or 8 medium-size portobello mushrooms.

MAKES 12 APPETIZER SERVINGS (ABOUT 2 PER SERVING)
PREP: 25 MIN., BAKE: 10 MIN.

2 (8-ounce) packages fresh baby portobello
    mushrooms
2 tablespoons butter
2 leeks, sliced
1 garlic clove, pressed
2 large avocados, peeled and chopped
1 teaspoon chopped fresh or dried rosemary
1 tablespoon fresh lime juice
¼ teaspoon salt
4 ounces goat cheese
3 tablespoons chopped walnuts
2 tablespoons olive oil

1. Remove brown gills from the undersides of mushrooms using a spoon; discard gills.
2. Melt butter in a large skillet over medium heat; add leeks and garlic, and sauté until tender. Remove from heat, and let cool.
3. Stir together avocados and next 3 ingredients in a medium bowl; stir in leek mixture.
4. Divide and press goat cheese evenly into mushroom caps; top evenly with avocado mixture. Sprinkle evenly with chopped walnuts, and drizzle with olive oil. Place on a rack in a broiler pan.
5. Bake mushrooms at 400° for 5 minutes; cover loosely with aluminum foil, and bake 5 more minutes or until walnuts are golden brown and mushrooms are tender. Serve immediately.

Grilled Eggplant Appetizers

Melted Parmesan cheese adds a great finishing touch to this finger food.

MAKES 40 APPETIZERS
PREP: 30 MIN., BROIL: 3 MIN., STAND: 30 MIN., GRILL: 20 MIN.,
CHILL: 8 HRS.

2 (1-pound) eggplants, peeled and cut into ½-inch
    slices
½ teaspoon salt
½ cup coarsely chopped fresh basil
2 garlic cloves, minced
1 tablespoon olive oil
¼ teaspoon ground red pepper
1 (22-inch) French baguette, cut into ½-inch slices
4 plum tomatoes, each cut into 10 slices
⅓ cup freshly grated Parmesan cheese

1. Sprinkle eggplant with salt, and let stand 30 minutes. Combine basil, garlic, and olive oil; set aside. Rinse eggplant slices, and pat dry.
2. Coat food rack with cooking spray, and place rack on grill over medium coals (300° to 350°). Place eggplant slices on rack in a single layer.
3. Cook, without grill lid, 8 to 10 minutes on each side. Place half of eggplant slices in an airtight container, and sprinkle with basil mixture; top with remaining eggplant slices. Cover and chill 8 hours.
4. Position knife blade in food processor bowl; add eggplant mixture and red pepper. Process until smooth, stopping once to scrape down sides.
5. Spread about 1½ teaspoons eggplant mixture on each of 40 baguette slices, and top each with a tomato slice. Sprinkle tomato slices evenly with cheese.
6. Broil 5½ inches from heat 2 to 3 minutes or until cheese melts. Serve immediately.

Vegetable Platter With Creamy Honey-Herb Dip

To get a head start, wash rinse, pat dry, and wrap in paper towels. Refrigerate in a zip-top plastic bag. Vegetables can be steamed 8 hours ahead and chilled.

MAKES 8 SERVINGS
PREP: 15 MIN., COOK: 30 MIN.

6 new potatoes, halved
2 sweet potatoes, peeled and cubed (optional)
½ pound small fresh green beans, trimmed
2 cups fresh cauliflower florets
2 cups fresh broccoli florets
Lettuce leaves
Creamy Honey-Herb Dip

1. Arrange new potato and, if desired, sweet potato in a steamer basket over boiling water. Cover and steam 20 minutes or until tender. Rinse with cold water to stop the cooking process.
2. Arrange green beans in steamer basket over boiling water. Cover and steam 4 minutes or until crisp-tender. Plunge into ice water to stop the cooking process; drain. Repeat procedure with cauliflower, and then broccoli.
3. Place vegetables on a lettuce-lined platter; cover and chill. Serve with Creamy Honey-Herb Dip.

Creamy Honey-Herb Dip:

If you don't have time to steam vegetables, serve this dip with a deli vegetable tray from the supermarket.

MAKES 1¼ CUPS
PREP: 5 MIN.

2 green onions
1 garlic clove
1 (8-ounce) container sour cream
1½ tablespoons stone-ground mustard
1 tablespoon honey
1 tablespoon cider vinegar
1 teaspoon dried tarragon
1 teaspoon anchovy paste (optional)

1. Process first 7 ingredients and, if desired, anchovy paste in a food processor or blender until smooth; cover and chill.

Crab Cakes With
Maui Sauce

Crab Cakes With Maui Sauce

MAKES 4 SERVINGS
PREP: 25 MIN., COOK: 12 MIN.

8 ounces lump crabmeat, drained
¼ cup soft breadcrumbs
2 tablespoons minced shallots
2 tablespoons minced fresh parsley
1 tablespoon minced fresh basil
2 tablespoons Dijon mustard
1 tablespoon lemon juice
1 teaspoon minced fresh ginger
1 teaspoon dark sesame oil
½ teaspoon salt
½ teaspoon coarsely ground pepper
1 large egg, lightly beaten
¼ cup butter or margarine, divided
6 cups loosely packed fresh spinach leaves
Maui Sauce
Garnish: shredded fresh spinach leaves

1. Stir together first 12 ingredients, and shape into 12 patties.
2. Melt 2 tablespoons butter in a large nonstick skillet over medium heat. Add crab cakes, and cook 5 minutes on each side or until golden. Remove crab cakes from skillet, and keep warm.
3. Add spinach leaves to skillet, and sauté 1 to 2 minutes or until wilted. Stir in remaining 2 tablespoons butter.
4. Spoon Maui Sauce onto 4 individual plates, and top evenly with crab cakes. Spoon spinach mixture around crab cakes. Garnish, if desired. Serve immediately.

Maui Sauce:

MAKES ¾ CUP
PREP: 5 MIN., COOK: 10 MIN.

1 cup pineapple juice
¼ cup rice wine vinegar
1 teaspoon soy sauce
3 tablespoons mayonnaise

1. Bring pineapple juice and vinegar to a boil in a small saucepan over medium-high heat. Boil 8 to 10 minutes or until mixture is reduced by half. Stir in soy sauce; cool slightly.
2. Whisk in mayonnaise until smooth. Serve warm.

Grilled Zucchini-Wrapped Shrimp

Add a thin slice of pickled jalapeño pepper to each shrimp appetizer for extra heat.

MAKES 6 APPETIZER SERVINGS
PREP: 30 MIN., CHILL: 15 MIN., COOK: 2 MIN., GRILL: 6 MIN.

1 pound unpeeled, large fresh shrimp
½ cup fresh lime juice
8 tablespoons vegetable oil, divided
2 garlic cloves, pressed
¾ teaspoon salt
½ teaspoon ground red pepper
2 large zucchini
Fresh cilantro sprigs (optional)

1. Peel shrimp, and devein, if desired.
2. Combine lime juice, 3 tablespoons vegetable oil, and next 3 ingredients in a zip-top freezer bag, gently squeezing to blend; add shrimp. Seal and chill mixture 15 minutes.
3. Remove shrimp from marinade, reserving marinade.
4. Bring reserved marinade to a boil in a small saucepan; remove from heat.
5. Cut zucchini lengthwise into thin slices with a vegetable peeler. Wrap each shrimp with a zucchini slice, and secure with a wooden pick. Brush rolls with remaining 5 tablespoons vegetable oil.
6. Grill rolls, without grill lid, over medium-high heat (350° to 400°) about 4 minutes.
7. Brush with reserved marinade; turn and brush again. Grill 2 more minutes or just until shrimp turn pink. Serve hot or at room temperature on a cilantro-lined platter, if desired.

Coconut Shrimp

These pleasantly sweet and crunchy gems from the sea rival any you've enjoyed at a restaurant.

MAKES 4 APPETIZER SERVINGS
PREP: 30 MIN., CHILL: 1 HR., COOK: 4 MIN. PER BATCH

1 pound unpeeled, large fresh shrimp
½ cup cream of coconut
3 tablespoons cornstarch
1 tablespoon mayonnaise
1 tablespoon lemon juice
1 teaspoon Worcestershire sauce
1 cup cornstarch
1¼ cups flaked coconut
½ cup fine, dry breadcrumbs
Vegetable oil

1. Peel shrimp, leaving tails intact; devein, if desired.
2. Stir together cream of coconut and next 4 ingredients until mixture is smooth.
3. Coat shrimp with 1 cup cornstarch; dip in cream of coconut mixture, and drain on a wire rack.
4. Dredge shrimp in coconut; dredge in breadcrumbs. Place on a baking sheet; cover and chill 1 hour.
5. Pour oil to a depth of 2 inches into a Dutch oven; heat to 375°. Fry shrimp, in batches, 4 minutes or until golden. Drain.

Shrimp 'n' Grits Tarts

Shrimp 'n' Grits Tarts

MAKES 3 DOZEN
PREP: 40 MIN., COOK: 25 MIN., BAKE: 35 MIN.

3½ cups chicken broth, divided
1 cup milk
¼ cup butter or margarine, divided
½ teaspoon white pepper
1 cup uncooked coarse-ground or regular grits
⅔ cup shredded Parmesan cheese
⅔ cup diced smoked ham
3 tablespoons all-purpose flour
3 tablespoons chopped fresh parsley
¾ teaspoon white wine Worcestershire sauce
36 medium-size shrimp, peeled and cooked
Garnish: chopped fresh parsley

1. Bring 2 cups chicken broth, milk, 2 tablespoons butter, and white pepper to a boil in a large saucepan over medium-high heat. Gradually whisk in grits; return to a boil. Reduce heat, and simmer, stirring occasionally, 5 to 10 minutes or until thickened. Add Parmesan cheese, and whisk until melted and blended.
2. Spoon 1 rounded tablespoonful of grits mixture into each lightly greased muffin cup of 3 (12-cup) miniature muffin pans.
3. Bake at 350° for 20 to 25 minutes or until lightly browned. Make indentations in centers of warm grits tarts, using the back of a spoon. Let tarts cool completely in pans. Remove tarts from muffin pans, and place on a 15- x 10-inch jelly-roll pan.
4. Melt remaining 2 tablespoons butter in a medium saucepan over medium-high heat; add ham, and sauté 1 to 2 minutes. Sprinkle 3 tablespoons flour evenly over ham, and cook, stirring often, 1 to 2 minutes or until lightly browned. Gradually add remaining 1½ cups chicken broth, stirring until smooth.
5. Reduce heat, and cook, stirring often, 5 to 10 minutes or until thickened. Stir in 3 tablespoons chopped parsley and white wine Worcestershire sauce, and spoon evenly into tarts. Top each with 1 shrimp.
6. Bake at 350° for 5 to 10 minutes or just until warm. Garnish, if desired.
Note: For testing purposes only, we used Cumberland Gap Diced Ham.

Chicken Wontons With Peanut Dipping Sauce

MAKES 3 DOZEN
PREP: 30 MIN., COOK: 10 MIN. PER BATCH

1 cup diced cooked chicken
4 green onions, diced
1 cup finely shredded cabbage
2 tablespoons diced fresh cilantro
2 teaspoons brown sugar
1 tablespoon hoisin sauce
1 teaspoon sesame oil
36 wonton wrappers
Peanut oil
Peanut Dipping Sauce

1. Stir together first 7 ingredients. Spoon 1 teaspoon mixture in center of each wonton wrapper. Moisten wonton edges with water. Bring corners together, pressing to seal.
2. Pour oil to a depth of 3 inches into a Dutch oven; heat to 375°. Fry wontons in batches until golden, turning once. Drain on wire racks over paper towels. Serve immediately with Peanut Dipping Sauce.

Peanut Dipping Sauce:

MAKES ABOUT ¾ CUP
PREP: 10 MIN., COOK: 2 MIN.

½ cup chicken broth
2 tablespoons hoisin sauce
2 tablespoons sesame oil
2 tablespoons soy sauce
1 tablespoon creamy peanut butter
1 teaspoon cornstarch

1. Bring all ingredients to a boil in a small saucepan, whisking constantly; boil 1 minute.

Fried Chicken Fingers With
Come-Back Sauce

Fried Chicken Fingers With Come-Back Sauce

MAKES 16 APPETIZER SERVINGS
PREP: 12 MIN., CHILL: 4 HRS., FRY: 6 MIN. PER BATCH

8 skinned and boned chicken breasts
2 cups milk
2 teaspoons salt
½ teaspoon lemon pepper
½ teaspoon black pepper
2 cups all-purpose flour
Vegetable oil
Come-Back Sauce

1. Cut each chicken breast half into 4 strips.
2. Combine chicken strips, milk, and next 3 ingredients in a shallow dish or zip-top freezer bag. Cover or seal, and chill 4 hours.
3. Remove chicken, discarding marinade; dredge in flour.
4. Pour oil to depth of 2 inches into a large Dutch oven; heat to 350°. Fry chicken, in batches, 5 to 6 minutes or until golden. Drain on paper towels. Serve chicken fingers with Come-Back Sauce.

Come-Back Sauce:

MAKES 3 CUPS
PREP: 10 MIN., CHILL: 1 HR.

1 tablespoon sugar
1 cup mayonnaise
½ cup olive oil
⅓ cup chili sauce
⅓ cup ketchup
2 tablespoons water
4 teaspoons Worcestershire sauce
4 teaspoons prepared mustard
2 teaspoons coarsely ground pepper
⅛ teaspoon paprika
¼ teaspoon hot sauce
1 medium onion, minced
2 garlic cloves, minced

1. Stir together all ingredients. Cover and chill 1 hour.

Sesame-Maple Chicken Wings

MAKES 8 TO 10 APPETIZER SERVINGS
PREP: 20 MIN., CHILL: 2 HRS., COOK: 6 MIN., BAKE: 54 MIN.

⅓ cup maple syrup
¼ cup soy sauce
3 tablespoons sesame oil
1 tablespoon chopped fresh ginger
1 tablespoon chili oil
3 garlic cloves
4 pounds chicken wing pieces
2 tablespoons sesame seeds

1. Process first 6 ingredients in a blender or food processor until smooth, stopping to scrape down sides. Place chicken in a shallow dish or large zip-top freezer bag; pour marinade over chicken. Cover or seal, and chill 2 hours.

2. Remove chicken from marinade, reserving marinade. Arrange chicken in a single layer on a lightly greased 15- x 10-inch jelly-roll pan.

3. Bring reserved marinade to a boil in a small saucepan; boil 1 minute, and remove from heat.

4. Bake chicken at 375° for 25 minutes; turn chicken, and bake 15 more minutes. Baste chicken with marinade; bake 7 more minutes. Turn chicken, and baste with remaining marinade; sprinkle with sesame seeds, and bake 7 more minutes or until sesame seeds are golden.

Sesame-Maple
Chicken Wings

Hot 'n' Spicy Chicken Wings

MAKES 10 APPETIZER SERVINGS OR 4 TO 6 MAIN DISH SERVINGS
PREP: 20 MIN., CHILL: 3 HRS., GRILL: 30 MIN.

4 to 5 pounds chicken wings*
1/3 cup Melvyn's Seasoning Mix
1 cup hot sauce

1. Cut off wing tips, and discard; cut wings in half at joint, if desired.
2. Stir together Melvyn's Seasoning Mix and hot sauce.
3. Place chicken wings in a large shallow dish or large zip-top freezer bag. Pour half of hot sauce mixture over wings. Cover or seal; chill 3 hours, turning occasionally. Cover and chill remaining hot sauce mixture.
4. Remove wings from marinade, discarding marinade.
5. Grill chicken, covered with grill lid, over medium-high heat (350° to 400°) 15 minutes on each side or until done, basting occasionally with reserved hot sauce mixture.
*1 (4-pound) package frozen party-style chicken wings, thawed, may be substituted.
Note: For testing purposes only, we used Red & White Louisiana Hot Sauce.

Spicy Party Meatballs

MAKES 4 DOZEN
PREP: 5 MIN., COOK: 45 MIN.

1 (12-ounce) jar cocktail sauce
1 (10.5-ounce) jar jalapeño jelly
1/2 small sweet onion, minced
1/2 (3-pound) package frozen cooked meatballs

1. Cook first 3 ingredients in a Dutch oven over medium heat, stirring 5 minutes or until jelly melts and mixture is smooth.
2. Stir in meatballs. Reduce heat, and simmer, stirring occasionally, 35 to 40 minutes or until thoroughly heated.

Teriyaki Pork Tenderloin Saté With Spicy Peanut Sauce

Saté is the Indonesian version of kabobs. Following tradition, our recipe is served with a peanut sauce, that gets a kick from red pepper.

MAKES 8 TO 10 APPETIZER SERVINGS
PREP: 30 MIN., SOAK: 30 MIN., GRILL: 8 MIN.

15 (6-inch) wooden skewers
1 1/2 pounds teriyaki pork tenderloin, cut into 3/4-inch cubes
2 bunches green onions, cut into 3/4-inch pieces
Vegetable cooking spray
Garnish: green onion curls
Spicy Peanut Sauce

1. Soak wooden skewers in water 30 minutes.
2. Thread pork and green onions onto 15 (6-inch) skewers; coat with cooking spray.
3. Grill, covered with grill lid, over medium-high heat (350° to 400°) 3 to 4 minutes on each side or until done. Garnish, if desired, and serve with Spicy Peanut Sauce.

Spicy Peanut Sauce:

MAKES ABOUT 1 CUP
PREP: 5 MIN.

1/2 cup creamy peanut butter
1/4 cup water
2 tablespoons rice wine vinegar
2 tablespoons soy sauce
2 tablespoons honey
1 teaspoon ground ginger
1/2 teaspoon dried crushed red pepper

1. Whisk together all ingredients in a bowl until blended. Cover and chill until ready to serve.

Raspberry-Brie Tartlets

Raspberry-Brie Tartlets

MAKES 5 DOZEN
PREP: 1 HR., BAKE: 17 MIN.

20 white bread slices
Melted butter
1 (8-ounce) wedge Brie, cut up
1 (13-ounce) jar raspberry jam

1. Remove crusts from bread slices with a serrated knife. Flatten each bread slice with a rolling pin. Cut 3 circles out of each bread slice with a 1¾-inch fluted or round cookie cutter.
2. Brush muffin cups in miniature muffin pans with melted butter. Press bread circles on bottom and up sides of muffin cups; brush bread cups with melted butter.
3. Bake at 350° for 7 minutes or until lightly toasted.
4. Remove bread cups from muffin pans, and place on ungreased baking sheets. Fill cups evenly with cheese pieces; top each with ¼ teaspoon raspberry jam.
5. Bake at 300° for 10 minutes or until cheese is melted.
To Make Ahead: Freeze toasted bread shells up to 1 month in advance. Thaw at room temperature about 30 minutes. Assemble tartlets, and bake as directed.

Mexican Pinwheels

MAKES 5 DOZEN
PREP: 15 MIN., CHILL: 2 HRS.

1 (8-ounce) package cream cheese, softened
½ cup sour cream
2 cups (8 ounces) shredded Cheddar cheese
1 (4-ounce) can chopped green chiles, drained
1 (2¼-ounce) can sliced ripe olives, drained
⅔ cup chopped green onions
1 garlic clove, minced
¼ teaspoon seasoned salt
6 (8-inch) flour tortillas

1. Beat cream cheese and sour cream in a large bowl at medium speed with an electric mixer until smooth. Stir in Cheddar cheese and next 5 ingredients.
2. Spread ½ cup cheese mixture over each tortilla, and roll up. Wrap each tortilla in plastic wrap. Chill at least 2 hours.
3. Cut each tortilla wrap into 10 (½-inch-thick) slices with a serrated knife.

Creamy Maple Coffee

MAKES ABOUT 6 SERVINGS
PREP: 5 MIN., COOK: 10 MIN.

2 cups half-and-half
¾ cup maple syrup
3 cups hot strong brewed coffee

1. Stir together 2 cups half-and-half and maple syrup in a saucepan over medium heat 8 to 10 minutes or until thoroughly heated, stirring often. (Do not boil.) Stir in coffee, and serve immediately.

Creamy Almond Coffee: Substitute ½ to ¾ cup almond liqueur for maple syrup. Proceed as directed.

Praline Coffee

MAKES 5 SERVINGS
PREP: 5 MIN., COOK: 5 MIN.

3 cups hot brewed coffee
⅔ to ¾ cup firmly packed light brown sugar
¾ cup half-and-half
¾ cup praline liqueur
Topping: sweetened whipped cream

1. Cook first 3 ingredients in a large saucepan over medium heat, stirring constantly, until thoroughly heated. (Do not boil.)
2. Stir in liqueur; top each serving with sweetened whipped cream.

Mexican Coffee

MAKES 6 SERVINGS
PREP: 12 MIN., COOK: 5 MIN.

½ cup ground dark roast coffee
1 tablespoon ground cinnamon
¼ teaspoon ground nutmeg
5 cups water
1 cup milk
⅓ cup chocolate syrup
¼ cup firmly packed dark brown sugar
1 teaspoon vanilla extract
Toppings: whipped cream, ground cinnamon

1. Place coffee in filter basket of coffeemaker; add 1 tablespoon ground cinnamon and ground nutmeg. Add 5 cups water to coffeemaker; brew coffee according to manufacturer's instructions.
2. Combine milk, chocolate syrup, and sugar in a large saucepan; cook over low heat, stirring constantly, until sugar dissolves.
3. Stir in brewed coffee and vanilla extract. Pour immediately into mugs, and top each serving with a dollop of whipped cream and ground cinnamon.

White Chocolate Latte

MAKES ABOUT 4 SERVINGS
PREP: 5 MIN., COOK: 7 MIN.

2 cups milk
1 cup half-and-half
⅔ cup white chocolate morsels
2 tablespoons instant coffee granules
1 teaspoon vanilla extract
¼ teaspoon almond extract
Whipped cream (optional)
Garnish: cinnamon sticks

1. Stir together first 4 ingredients in a small saucepan over low heat 5 to 7 minutes or until white chocolate morsels are melted. Stir in vanilla and almond extracts; pour evenly into 4 mugs. Top with whipped cream, if desired. Garnish, if desired, and serve immediately.

Chocolate Latte: Substitute ⅔ cup semisweet chocolate morsels for ⅔ cup white chocolate morsels, and proceed as directed.

White Chocolate Latte

Minted Tea Punch

Minted Tea Punch

MAKES 9 SERVINGS

PREP: 20 MIN., STEEP: 3 MIN., CHILL: 2 HRS.

4 cups boiling water

4 family-size decaffeinated tea bags

½ cup loosely packed fresh mint leaves

¾ cup sugar

1 (6-ounce) can frozen lemonade concentrate, thawed and undiluted

4 cups cold water

Garnishes: lemon slices, fresh mint sprigs

1. Pour 4 cups boiling water over tea bags and mint leaves. Cover and steep 3 minutes; remove and discard tea bags and mint.

2. Stir in sugar until dissolved. Stir in lemonade concentrate and 4 cups cold water; chill 2 hours. Serve punch over ice. Garnish, if desired.

Eggnog-Coffee Punch

MAKES ABOUT 12 SERVINGS
PREP: 10 MIN.

1 quart eggnog
2 cups brewed coffee
1/2 cup coffee liqueur*
1/2 cup bourbon (optional)
1 quart coffee ice cream, slightly softened
1 quart vanilla ice cream, slightly softened
Ground nutmeg (optional)

1. Stir together first 3 ingredients and bourbon, if desired, in a chilled punch bowl or large bowl. Stir in coffee and vanilla ice creams. Top with ground nutmeg, if desired.

*1/2 cup strong brewed coffee may be substituted.

Chocolate Iced Coffee

To keep the drink from diluting, freeze cubes of half-and-half and brewed coffee to use in place of ice.

MAKES 8 SERVINGS
PREP: 15 MIN., STAND: 10 MIN., CHILL: 2 HRS.

3 1/2 cups water
1 cup ground coffee
2 tablespoons sugar
3/4 teaspoon ground cinnamon
2 cups half-and-half
1/3 cup chocolate syrup

1. Bring 3 1/2 cups water and coffee to a boil in a saucepan; remove from heat, and let stand 10 minutes. Pour mixture through a fine wire-mesh strainer into a bowl, discarding coffee grounds.
2. Stir sugar and cinnamon into coffee until sugar dissolves; let cool. Stir in half-and-half and chocolate syrup; chill 2 hours. Serve over ice.

Fruit Punch

For additional mint flavor, freeze chopped mint leaves with water in ice-cube trays.

MAKES 28 SERVINGS
PREP: 7 MIN., STAND: 30 MIN., CHILL: 8 HRS.

1 cup loosely packed fresh mint leaves
2 cups hot water
2 1/2 cups sugar
2 cups water
1 1/2 cups lemon juice
1/2 cup lime juice
1 pint fresh strawberries, quartered
2 (46-ounce) cans pineapple juice, chilled
3 cups orange juice, chilled
1 (1-liter) bottle ginger ale

1. Stir together mint and 2 cups hot water; let stand 25 to 30 minutes. Pour through a wire-mesh strainer into a 2-quart container, discarding mint.
2. Stir in sugar and next 3 ingredients. Chill 8 hours. Pour mixture into a large punch bowl. Stir in strawberries and remaining ingredients just before serving. Serve over ice.

Mulled Cranberry Tea

MAKES 6 SERVINGS
PREP: 10 MIN., COOK: 15 MIN.

4 to 6 (5-inch) cinnamon sticks
1 tablespoon whole cloves
2 cups sugar
2 quarts water
1 (32-ounce) bottle cranberry juice
1/4 cup lemon juice
1 cup orange juice

1. Place cinnamon sticks and whole cloves in a 4-inch square of cheesecloth; tie with string. Bring spice bag, sugar, and next 3 ingredients to a boil in a large saucepan. Reduce heat; simmer 10 minutes.
2. Remove and discard spice bag; stir in orange juice. Serve hot or cold.

Double-Berry
Milk Shake

Double-Berry Milk Shake

MAKES 4 SERVINGS
PREP: 5 MIN.

1 pint fresh strawberry halves, frozen
¾ cup milk
¼ cup powdered sugar
½ teaspoon vanilla extract
1 pint strawberry ice cream
Garnishes: whipped cream, strawberries

1. Process first 4 ingredients in a blender until smooth. Add ice cream, and process until blended. Garnish, if desired.

Three-Fruit Yogurt Shake

MAKES 5 SERVINGS
PREP: 10 MIN.

2 cups low-fat vanilla yogurt
1 cup fresh blueberries, frozen
1 cup fresh peach slices, frozen
1 (8-ounce) can unsweetened pineapple chunks, drained and frozen

1. Process all ingredients in a blender until smooth, stopping to scrape down sides. Serve immediately.

Café Latte Slush

MAKES 7 SERVINGS
PREP: 15 MIN., FREEZE: 8 HRS.

½ to ¾ cup sugar
2 cups hot strong brewed coffee or espresso
2 cups milk or half-and-half, divided

1. Combine sugar and hot coffee in a large mixing bowl, stirring until sugar dissolves; stir in 1 cup milk. Cover and freeze 8 hours.
2. Let thaw slightly in refrigerator; add remaining 1 cup milk. Beat at medium speed with an electric mixer until smooth. Serve immediately.
To Lighten: Substitute fat-free milk or fat-free half-and-half for regular milk or half-and-half.

Chocolate-Yogurt Malt

MAKES 5 SERVINGS
PREP: 5 MIN.

4 cups low-fat frozen vanilla yogurt
1 cup 1% chocolate low-fat milk
¼ cup chocolate-flavored instant malted milk

1. Process all ingredients in a blender until smooth, stopping to scrape down sides. Serve immediately.
Note: For testing purposes only, we used Ovaltine for chocolate-flavored instant malted milk.

Apricot Bellinis

Apricot Bellinis

MAKES 4 SERVINGS

PREP: 10 MIN.

6 fresh apricots, halved (about ½ pound)*
1 (11.5-ounce) can apricot nectar
¼ cup sugar
1½ cups Champagne**
Crushed ice
Garnishes: fresh apricot slices, fresh mint sprigs

1. Process first 3 ingredients in a blender until smooth, stopping to scrape down sides. Stir in Champagne, and serve immediately over crushed ice. Garnish, if desired.
*1 (17-ounce) can apricot halves, drained, may be substituted for fresh.
**1 (12-ounce) can ginger ale may be substituted for Champagne.

Pineapple Wassail

MAKES 8 SERVINGS

PREP: 5 MIN., COOK: 25 MIN.

4 cups unsweetened pineapple juice
1 (11.5-ounce) can apricot nectar
2 cups apple cider
1 cup orange juice
1 teaspoon whole cloves
3 (6-inch) cinnamon sticks, broken

1. Bring all ingredients to a boil in a Dutch oven; reduce heat, and simmer 20 minutes.
2. Pour through a wire-mesh strainer, discarding spices. Serve hot.

Southern Breeze Punch

Raspberry ice cubes can be made in advance and stored in freezer bags in the freezer until ready to serve.

MAKES 12 SERVINGS
PREP: 10 MIN., FREEZE: 8 HRS.

1 cup sugar
1 (0.22-ounce) envelope unsweetened blue raspberry
    lemonade mix
7 cups water
1 (6-ounce) can frozen lemonade concentrate, thawed
1 (46-ounce) can unsweetened pineapple juice, chilled
1 (2-liter) bottle ginger ale, chilled

1. Stir together first 4 ingredients in a 2-quart pitcher; pour evenly into 5 ice-cube trays, and freeze at least 8 hours.
2. Combine pineapple juice and ginger ale; serve over raspberry ice cubes.
Note: For testing purposes only, we used Kool-Aid Twists Ice Blue Raspberry Lemonade Unsweetened Soft Drink Mix.

Southern Breeze Punch

Garden Sangría

Garden Sangría

MAKES 24 SERVINGS
PREP: 10 MIN., CHILL: 8 HRS.

1 gallon dry white wine
2 cups brandy
1 cup orange liqueur
4 oranges, sliced
1 bunch fresh mint leaves
1 (1-liter) bottle club soda, chilled*
1 quart whole strawberries
2 lemons, thinly sliced
2 limes, thinly sliced
Garnishes: fresh mint sprigs, strawberries, red
    seedless grapes, orange and lime slices

1. Stir together first 5 ingredients in a large container;
cover and chill 8 hours.
2. Add club soda and next 3 ingredients just before
serving; serve over ice, if desired. Garnish, if desired.
*Substitute ginger ale for club soda.

Oklahoma Sunrise

MAKES 16 SERVINGS
PREP: 10 MIN., CHILL: 1 HR.

1 (12-ounce) can frozen orange juice concentrate,
    thawed and undiluted
1 (11.5-ounce) can apricot nectar
3 cups water
1½ pints strawberry or raspberry sorbet, softened
1 (750-milliliter) bottle Champagne, chilled
3 cups crushed ice

1. Stir together first 3 ingredients in a large container;
cover and chill at least 1 hour.
2. Spoon sorbet into a punch bowl; pour chilled orange
juice mixture over sorbet. Add Champagne and ice; stir
gently to blend. Ladle into stemmed glasses.

White Sangría Fizz

*Stir up this fruity beverage ahead, and add sparkling water just
before serving.*

MAKES 8 SERVINGS
PREP: 5 MIN., CHILL: 8 HRS.

1 cup fresh orange juice
½ cup sugar
1 (750-milliliter) bottle dry white wine
1½ cups sparkling water, chilled
Garnishes: lime, orange, and lemon wedges

1. Stir together orange juice and sugar in a large
pitcher until sugar dissolves. Stir in wine; cover and
chill 8 hours.
2. Stir sparkling water into wine mixture just before
serving. Garnish, if desired.

Rio Grande Limeade

MAKES 12 SERVINGS
PREP: 10 MIN., CHILL: 8 HRS.

2 (12-ounce) cans frozen limeade concentrate,
    thawed and undiluted
3 cups tequila
3 cups water
2 cups orange liqueur
1 cup fresh lime juice
Garnish: lime slices

1. Stir together first 5 ingredients. Chill 8 hours. Serve
over ice, and garnish, if desired.

Ginger Beer

MAKES 5 SERVINGS
PREP: 10 MIN., CHILL: 4 HRS.

1 quart water
1 cup sugar
⅓ cup grated fresh ginger
1½ teaspoons grated lime rind
2 tablespoons fresh lime juice

1. Stir together all ingredients until sugar dissolves.
Cover and chill 4 hours.
2. Pour ginger mixture through a wire-mesh strainer
into a large pitcher, discarding solids. Serve over
crushed ice.

breads

Italian Bread, page 68

Toasted Oat Scones

Slather these crusty gems with Strawberry-Almond Cream Cheese.

MAKES 1 DOZEN
PREP: 20 MIN., BAKE: 14 MIN.

1 1/4 cups uncooked quick-cooking oats
1 1/2 cups all-purpose flour
1/2 cup sugar
2 teaspoons baking powder
1/2 teaspoon salt
1/2 teaspoon ground cinnamon
1/4 teaspoon baking soda
1/4 cup butter or margarine, cut up
1/2 cup sweetened dried cranberries
1/2 cup fat-free buttermilk
1/2 cup applesauce
1 teaspoon vanilla extract
2 teaspoons butter or margarine, melted
1 teaspoon sugar

1. Place oats on a lightly greased baking sheet.
2. Bake at 450° for 3 minutes or until lightly toasted, stirring once. Cool completely.
3. Combine 1 cup toasted oats, 1 1/2 cups flour, and next 5 ingredients; cut in 1/4 cup butter with a pastry blender until crumbly. Add dried cranberries, and toss well. Add buttermilk, applesauce, and vanilla, stirring just until dry ingredients are moistened.

4. Turn dough out onto a lightly floured surface; knead dough lightly 4 times. Pat dough into a 9-inch circle on a lightly greased baking sheet. Brush with melted butter; sprinkle with remaining 1/4 cup toasted oats and 1 teaspoon sugar.
5. Bake at 450° for 11 minutes or until golden. Serve scones warm.

Strawberry-Almond Cream Cheese:

Serve this hearty cream cheese as a sweet topping for scones, bagels, or English muffins.

MAKES APPROXIMATELY 1 1/4 CUPS
PREP: 10 MIN., CHILL: 1 HR.

1 (8-ounce) package cream cheese, softened
3 tablespoons powdered sugar
3/4 teaspoon almond extract
1/2 cup chopped fresh strawberries (about 8 large strawberries)

1. Process first 3 ingredients in a food processor just until blended. (Do not overprocess or mixture will be thin.)
2. Add strawberries; process just until blended. Cover; chill at least 1 hour.

Bacon Biscuit Cups

Enjoy these cheesy biscuits an extra day. To reheat, wrap biscuit cups in foil. Bake at 350° for 10 minutes or until warm.

MAKES 10 SERVINGS
PREP: 15 MIN., BAKE: 22 MIN.

2 (3-ounce) packages cream cheese, softened
2 tablespoons milk
1 large egg
½ cup (2 ounces) shredded Swiss cheese
1 green onion, chopped
1 (10-ounce) can refrigerated flaky biscuits
5 bacon slices, cooked and crumbled

1. Beat first 3 ingredients at medium speed with an electric mixer until blended. Stir in cheese and green onions. Set aside.
2. Separate biscuits into 10 portions. Pat each portion into a 5-inch circle, and press on bottom and up sides of 10 greased muffin cups, forming a ¼-inch edge. Sprinkle evenly with half of bacon; spoon cream cheese mixture evenly on top.
3. Bake at 375° for 22 minutes or until set. Sprinkle biscuits with remaining bacon, lightly pressing into filling. Remove biscuits immediately from pan, and serve warm.

Sweet Potato Biscuits

MAKES 14 BISCUITS
PREP: 15 MIN., BAKE: 15 MIN.

4 cups all-purpose flour
2 tablespoons baking powder
2 teaspoons salt
1 cup butter or margarine
1 cup cooked mashed sweet potato
¾ to 1 cup buttermilk

1. Combine first 3 ingredients. Cut in butter with a pastry blender until crumbly.
2. Stir together sweet potato and buttermilk; add to dry ingredients, stirring just until moistened.
3. Turn dough out onto a lightly floured surface, and knead 3 to 4 times. Pat or roll to ½-inch thickness. Cut dough with a 3-inch round cutter, and place biscuits on a lightly greased baking sheet.
4. Bake at 425° for 10 to 15 minutes or until golden.

Dried Cherry and Cream Scones

These pale scones have a light texture due to the abundance of whipping cream in the dough.

MAKES 8 SCONES
PREP: 15 MIN., BAKE: 23 MIN.

2 cups all-purpose flour
1 tablespoon baking powder
½ teaspoon salt
¼ cup sugar
¾ cup chopped dried cherries
1 tablespoon grated lemon rind
1¼ cups whipping cream
2 tablespoons unsalted butter, melted
2 tablespoons sugar
1 teaspoon grated lemon rind

1. Combine first 4 ingredients in a large bowl. Stir in cherries and 1 tablespoon lemon rind. Add whipping cream, stirring with a fork just until dry ingredients are moistened.
2. Turn dough out onto a lightly floured surface; knead lightly 4 or 5 times, just until dough holds together. Pat dough into an 8-inch circle on an ungreased baking sheet. Cut dough into 8 wedges; separate wedges slightly. Brush with melted butter. Combine 2 tablespoons sugar and 1 teaspoon lemon rind; sprinkle over dough.
3. Bake at 400° for 23 minutes or until golden. Remove from pan. Serve warm, or cool on a wire rack.

Peppered Cheddar
Muffins

Hot Cheesy Biscuits

This is the perfect recipe if you want to make biscuits and don't own biscuit cutters. You drop these lumpy favorites onto baking sheets just like cookie dough.

MAKES 2 DOZEN
PREP: 10 MIN., BAKE: 9 MIN.

2 cups all-purpose flour
2 teaspoons baking powder
½ teaspoon salt
½ teaspoon ground red pepper
1 cup (4 ounces) shredded sharp Cheddar cheese
¼ cup shortening
1 cup buttermilk

1. Combine first 4 ingredients in a bowl; cut in cheese and shortening with a pastry blender until mixture is crumbly. Add buttermilk, stirring just until dry ingredients are moistened.
2. Drop by heaping tablespoonfuls onto greased baking sheets. Bake at 450° for 9 minutes or until golden.

Peppered Cheddar Muffins

The extra punch in these spicy muffins will wake you up in the morning. Serve them warm or at room temperature with butter or apple butter.

MAKES 1 DOZEN
PREP: 5 MIN., BAKE: 20 MIN., COOL: 2 MIN.

2 cups all-purpose flour
1 tablespoon sugar
1 tablespoon baking powder
½ teaspoon salt
½ to 1 teaspoon coarsely ground pepper
1 cup (4 ounces) shredded sharp Cheddar cheese
1¼ cups milk
1 large egg
2 tablespoons vegetable oil

1. Stir together first 6 ingredients in a large bowl; make a well in center of mixture.
2. Stir together milk, egg, and vegetable oil until blended. Add to dry ingredients, stirring just until moistened. Spoon batter into greased muffin pans, filling two-thirds full.
3. Bake at 400° for 18 to 20 minutes or until tops are golden. Cool muffins in pans 2 minutes; remove from pans, and serve.

Sunrise Canadian Bacon Muffins

For a fiery flavor, try Monterey Jack cheese with peppers in place of Swiss.

MAKES 15 MUFFINS
PREP: 9 MIN., COOK: 26 MIN., BAKE: 20 MIN.

1 teaspoon butter or margarine
1 (6-ounce) package Canadian bacon slices, chopped
2⅓ cups all-purpose baking mix
¾ cup (3 ounces) shredded Cheddar cheese, divided
½ cup (2 ounces) shredded Swiss cheese
2 tablespoons chopped fresh parsley
1 cup milk
⅓ cup mayonnaise
1 large egg, lightly beaten

1. Melt butter in a large nonstick skillet over medium-high heat. Add bacon; cook 5 minutes or until browned. Set aside.
2. Combine baking mix, ½ cup Cheddar cheese, Swiss cheese, and parsley in a large bowl; make a well in center of mixture. Add milk, mayonnaise, and egg, stirring just until dry ingredients are moistened. Stir in bacon. Spoon into lightly greased muffin pans, filling two-thirds full. Sprinkle with remaining ¼ cup Cheddar cheese.
3. Bake at 400° for 20 minutes or until edges are lightly browned. Remove from pan, and serve warm.
Note: For testing purposes only, we used Bisquick All-Purpose Baking Mix.

Breakfast Muffins

Breakfast Muffins

MAKES 3½ DOZEN
PREP: 30 MIN., COOK: 12 MIN., BAKE: 18 MIN.

8 bacon slices
½ small sweet onion, finely chopped
2 cups all-purpose baking mix
1 cup white cornmeal mix
½ (10-ounce) block extra-sharp Cheddar cheese,
    shredded
1 tablespoon sugar
1 cup milk
2 large eggs

1. Cook bacon in a large skillet until crisp; remove bacon, and drain on paper towels, reserving 2 table-spoons drippings in skillet. Crumble bacon; set aside.
2. Sauté onion in hot drippings 2 to 3 minutes or until tender. Set aside.
3. Combine baking mix and next 3 ingredients in a large bowl; make a well in center of mixture.
4. Whisk together 1 cup milk and eggs; add to cheese mixture, stirring just until dry ingredients are moistened. Stir in bacon and onion. Spoon batter into lightly greased miniature muffin pans, filling two-thirds full.
5. Bake at 425° for 18 minutes or until muffins are golden. Remove muffins from pans. Serve muffins warm, or let them cool on wire racks.
Note: For testing purposes only, we used Bisquick All-Purpose Baking Mix.
To Make Ahead: Place baked muffins in zip-top freezer bags, and freeze up to 1 month. Thaw overnight in re-frigerator, and reheat at 350° for 5 minutes or until warm.

Lemon Muffins

MAKES 2½ DOZEN
PREP: 20 MIN., BAKE: 12 MIN., COOL: 5 MIN.

1¾ cups all-purpose flour
1 teaspoon baking powder
¾ teaspoon baking soda
¼ teaspoon salt
1 tablespoon grated lemon rind
¾ cup sugar
1 large egg, lightly beaten
1 (8-ounce) container lemon yogurt
6 tablespoons butter or margarine, melted
1 tablespoon fresh lemon juice
Glaze

1. Combine first 6 ingredients in a large bowl; make a well in center of mixture.
2. Stir together egg and next 3 ingredients until blended. Add to dry ingredients, stirring just until moistened. Spoon into lightly greased miniature muf-fin pans, filling three-fourths full.
3. Bake at 400° for 10 to 12 minutes or until lightly browned. Cool in pans 5 minutes. Prepare Glaze.
4. Spoon warm Glaze evenly over warm muffins. Remove from pans, and cool completely on wire racks.
To Make Ahead: Place unglazed baked muffins in zip-top freezer bags, and freeze up to 1 month. Thaw; re-heat, if desired.

Glaze:

MAKES ⅓ CUP
PREP: 5 MIN., COOK: 5 MIN.

¼ cup sugar
2 teaspoons grated lemon rind
⅓ cup fresh lemon juice

1. Cook all ingredients in a small saucepan over medium heat, stirring constantly, just until sugar dissolves.

Whole Wheat Quick Bread

MAKES 1 LOAF
PREP: 5 MIN., BAKE: 1 HR.

2 cups whole wheat flour
1½ cups all-purpose flour
1 teaspoon salt
1 teaspoon baking soda
1½ cups buttermilk
1 large egg
3 tablespoons honey
2 tablespoons butter or margarine, melted
¾ cup chopped pecans, toasted (optional)
3 tablespoons uncooked regular oats (optional)

1. Combine first 4 ingredients in a large bowl. Combine buttermilk and next 3 ingredients; add to dry ingredients, stirring until blended. Stir in pecans, if desired. Pour batter into a well-greased 9- x 5-inch loaf pan. Sprinkle with oats, if desired.
2. Bake at 375° for 1 hour or until a wooden pick inserted in center of bread comes out clean. Cool in pan on a wire rack 10 minutes. Remove from pan, and cool completely on wire rack.

Easy Parmesan Cheese Breadsticks

MAKES 12 BREADSTICKS
PREP: 15 MIN., BAKE: 10 MIN.

½ cup freshly grated Parmesan cheese
¼ teaspoon paprika
⅛ teaspoon ground cumin
1 (11-ounce) can refrigerated breadsticks
3 tablespoons melted butter or margarine

1. Combine grated Parmesan cheese, paprika, and ground cumin in a shallow dish.
2. Unroll breadstick dough, and separate into 12 strips at perforations. Gently pull each strip to a length of 12 inches. Brush both sides of each strip with butter; dredge in cheese mixture. Twist each strip, and place 2 inches apart on lightly greased baking sheets.
3. Bake at 400° for 8 to 10 minutes or until golden. Serve warm or at room temperature.

Spiced Applesauce Bread

Warm and toasty spices give this applesauce quick bread its sweet, homespun character. A generous amount of chopped pecans tucked inside and a crunchy pecan and brown sugar topping ensure nutty flavor in every bite.

MAKES 1 LOAF
PREP: 10 MIN., BAKE: 1 HR., COOL: 10 MIN.

1¼ cups applesauce
1 cup granulated sugar
½ cup vegetable oil
2 large eggs, lightly beaten
3 tablespoons milk
2 cups all-purpose flour
½ teaspoon baking powder
1 teaspoon baking soda
¼ teaspoon salt
½ teaspoon ground cinnamon
¼ teaspoon ground nutmeg
¼ teaspoon ground allspice
1½ cups pecans
¼ cup firmly packed light brown sugar
½ teaspoon ground cinnamon

1. Combine first 5 ingredients in a large bowl; stir well.
2. Combine flour and next 6 ingredients; add to applesauce mixture, stirring well. Fold in ½ cup pecans. Pour batter into a greased 9- x 5-inch loaf pan. Combine remaining cup pecans, brown sugar, and ½ teaspoon cinnamon; sprinkle over batter in pan.
3. Bake at 350° for 1 hour or until a wooden pick inserted in center comes out clean. Cool in pan on a wire rack 10 minutes. Remove from pan, and cool completely on wire rack.

Banana-Nut Bread

Macadamia nuts add a tropical flair to this banana bread, but you can substitute an equal amount of any type of nut. Toast the nuts to flaunt their flavor.

MAKES 1 LOAF
PREP: 10 MIN., BAKE: 1 HR., COOL: 10 MIN.

2¼ cups all-purpose flour
1 tablespoon plus ½ teaspoon baking powder
½ teaspoon salt
¾ cup firmly packed light brown sugar
¼ cup granulated sugar
1½ teaspoons ground cinnamon
1¼ cups mashed ripe banana
⅓ cup milk
3 tablespoons vegetable oil
1 large egg
1 teaspoon white vinegar
1 cup macadamia nuts, coarsely chopped

1. Combine first 6 ingredients in a large bowl; make a well in center of mixture. Combine banana, milk, oil, egg, and vinegar; beat with a wire whisk until blended. Add to dry ingredients, stirring just until moistened. Stir in macadamia nuts.

2. Spoon batter into a greased 9- x 5-inch loaf pan. Bake at 350° for 1 hour or until a wooden pick inserted in center comes out clean. Cool in pan on a wire rack 10 minutes. Remove from pan, and cool completely on wire rack.

Banana-Nut Bread

Buttermilk Hush Puppies

MAKES 5 DOZEN
PREP: 20 MIN., COOK: 7 MIN. PER BATCH

2 cups self-rising white cornmeal
2 cups self-rising flour
1 teaspoon sugar
½ teaspoon salt
½ teaspoon pepper
1 large onion, grated
1 jalapeño pepper (optional), seeded and minced
2 cups buttermilk
1 large egg
Vegetable oil

1. Combine first 5 ingredients in a large bowl; stir in onion and, if desired, jalapeño.
2. Whisk together buttermilk and egg; add to flour mixture.
3. Pour oil to a depth of 3 inches in a Dutch oven; heat to 375°.
4. Drop batter by level tablespoonfuls into oil; fry in batches 5 to 7 minutes or until golden. Drain on paper towels.

Apple-Cheddar Cornbread

Cornbread gets interesting in this recipe with the interplay of chopped apple and Cheddar cheese.

MAKES 9 SERVINGS
PREP: 10 MIN., BAKE: 30 MIN.

1 cup yellow cornmeal
1 cup all-purpose flour
1 tablespoon baking powder
½ cup sugar
1 large egg, beaten
1 cup milk
¼ cup butter or margarine, melted
2 small tart red apples, chopped
½ cup (2 ounces) shredded sharp Cheddar cheese

1. Combine first 4 ingredients; make a well in center of mixture. Combine egg, milk, and butter; add to dry ingredients, stirring just until moistened. Stir in apple and cheese.
2. Place a well-greased 9-inch cast-iron skillet or 9-inch square pan in a 425° oven for 5 minutes or until hot. Remove from oven; pour batter into hot skillet. Bake at 425° for 25 minutes or until golden.

Creamed-Corn Cornbread

MAKES 9 SERVINGS
PREP: 15 MIN., BAKE: 22 MIN.

1 cup yellow cornmeal
¾ cup all-purpose flour
1 tablespoon sugar
1 tablespoon baking powder
½ teaspoon salt
¾ cup milk
1 large egg
2 tablespoons vegetable oil
1 (8½-ounce) can cream-style corn
2 to 3 teaspoons vegetable oil or bacon drippings

1. Combine first 5 ingredients in a bowl; make a well in center of mixture. Stir together milk and next 3 ingredients; add to dry ingredients, stirring just until dry ingredients are moistened.
2. Coat bottom and sides of a 9-inch cast-iron skillet with vegetable oil or bacon drippings. Place skillet in a 450° oven for 5 minutes. Remove from oven, and immediately spoon cornbread batter into hot skillet.
3. Bake at 450° for 20 to 22 minutes or until a wooden pick inserted in center comes out clean.
To Lighten: To reduce fat and calories, substitute ¾ cup fat-free milk for whole milk and ¼ cup egg substitute for 1 large egg.

Easy Focaccia

Southern women have been turning out homemade bread for centuries. And so have Italians, evidenced by the popularity of focaccia, an Old World crusty flatbread laden with olive oil. A staple across Italy, focaccia has now made its way into the heart of the American South.

MAKES 2 LOAVES
PREP: 10 MIN., BAKE: 25 MIN.

2 (1-pound) loaves frozen bread dough, thawed
¼ cup olive oil
1 small white or purple onion, thinly sliced and separated into rings
¼ cup freshly grated Parmesan cheese
2 tablespoons fresh or dried rosemary
½ teaspoon garlic powder
1 teaspoon coarse salt
½ teaspoon freshly ground pepper

1. Place each portion of dough on a lightly greased baking sheet; slightly flatten each portion of dough into a 12- x 8- x ½-inch rectangle. Press your finger or knuckle into dough at 2-inch intervals to create "dimples." Brush with olive oil. Top with onion rings; sprinkle evenly with cheese, rosemary, garlic powder, salt, and pepper.

2. Bake at 375° for 25 minutes or until lightly browned. Serve warm, or cool completely on wire racks.

Easy Focaccia

Cream Cheese
Coffee Cake

Cream Cheese Coffee Cake

This old-fashioned coffee cake is easy to make. A bumpy streusel top adds a rustic look and yummy flavor.

MAKES 12 SERVINGS
PREP: 10 MIN., BAKE: 40 MIN.

½ cup butter, softened
1 (8-ounce) package cream cheese, softened
1½ cups sugar
2 large eggs
2 cups all-purpose flour
2 teaspoons baking powder
½ teaspoon baking soda
½ teaspoon salt
½ cup milk
1 teaspoon vanilla extract
Topping

1. Beat butter and cream cheese at medium speed with an electric mixer until creamy; gradually add sugar, beating well. Add eggs, 1 at a time, beating after each addition.

2. Combine flour, baking powder, soda, and salt; add to butter mixture alternately with milk, beginning and ending with flour mixture. Mix at low speed just until blended after each addition. Stir in vanilla.

3. Pour batter into a greased 13- x 9-inch pan. Sprinkle with Topping. Bake at 350° for 40 minutes or until a wooden pick inserted in center comes out clean.

Topping:

MAKES 1½ CUPS
PREP: 5 MIN.

½ cup all-purpose flour
½ cup firmly packed brown sugar
½ cup chopped pecans
¼ cup butter, melted

1. Stir together all ingredients.

Apricot-Almond Coffee Cake

MAKES 15 SERVINGS
PREP: 25 MIN., BAKE: 28 MIN., COOL: 20 MIN.

4 ounces cream cheese, softened
½ cup apricot preserves
1 (16-ounce) package pound cake mix, divided
Pinch of orange food coloring powder (optional)
1 (8-ounce) container sour cream
½ cup milk
2 large eggs
½ teaspoon almond extract
½ cup sliced almonds
Glaze

1. Beat cream cheese, apricot preserves, 1 tablespoon pound cake mix, and, if desired, orange food coloring powder just until blended; set mixture aside.
2. Beat sour cream, milk, eggs, ½ teaspoon almond extract, and remaining pound cake mix at low speed with an electric mixer 30 seconds or until blended. Increase speed to medium, and beat 3 more minutes.
3. Pour sour cream mixture into a lightly greased 13- x 9-inch pan. Drop cream cheese mixture by rounded teaspoonfuls evenly over batter. Swirl batter gently with a knife. Sprinkle almonds evenly over top.
4. Bake at 350° for 25 to 28 minutes or until golden.
5. Cool on a wire rack 20 minutes. Drizzle Glaze over slightly warm cake or individual pieces.
Note: For testing purposes only, we used Candy-n-Cake Powdered Food Color #5531 Orange.

Glaze:

MAKES ⅓ CUP
PREP: 5 MIN.

1 cup powdered sugar
½ teaspoon vanilla extract
1 to 2 tablespoons milk

1. Stir together all ingredients until smooth. Add additional milk, if needed.

Cinnamon-Apple Breakfast Buns

MAKES 8 SERVINGS
PREP: 15 MIN., BAKE: 34 MIN.

1 (12.4-ounce) can refrigerated cinnamon rolls
1 small Granny Smith apple, peeled, cored, and cut into 8 rings
1 (1.62-ounce) package instant cinnamon and spice oatmeal
¼ cup firmly packed brown sugar
¼ cup chopped pecans
¼ teaspoon ground cinnamon
¼ teaspoon ground nutmeg
1 tablespoon butter or margarine, melted

1. Separate cinnamon rolls, and place in a lightly greased 8-inch round pan; set icing aside. Bake rolls according to package directions.
2. Place 1 apple ring on top of each roll. Combine oatmeal and remaining 5 ingredients in a small bowl. Sprinkle mixture evenly over apple layer.
3. Bake at 400° for 20 minutes or until apples are tender. Drizzle warm rolls with reserved icing.
Note: For testing purposes only, we used Pillsbury Cinnamon Rolls with Icing.

Sweet Potato-Pecan
Pancakes

The Best of Southern Living

Appetizers & Beverages → Appetizers

Sweet Potato-Pecan Pancakes

MAKES 21 (4-INCH) PANCAKES
PREP: 10 MIN., COOK: 24 MIN.

1¼ cups mashed cooked sweet potato
2 large eggs
¼ cup sugar
¼ cup butter, melted
1 teaspoon vanilla extract
1½ cups milk
2½ cups all-purpose baking mix
½ cup chopped pecans, toasted
Toppings: softened butter, orange marmalade,
    chopped pecans, maple syrup

1. Whisk together first 5 ingredients in a large bowl until blended. Gradually whisk in milk. Stir in baking mix and pecans just until blended.

2. Pour about ¼ cup batter for each pancake onto a hot, lightly greased griddle or large skillet. Cook pancakes 3 to 4 minutes or until tops are covered with bubbles and edges look dry and cooked; turn and cook other side. Serve with desired toppings.

PANCAKE POINTERS

We look forward to pancakes in the Test Kitchens, especially when someone brings fresh berries or peaches to adorn them. The secret to fluffy pancakes is in the batter—stir just enough to moisten the dry ingredients.

Having the griddle at the right temperature before adding the batter is also important. Preheat the griddle or skillet, and then sprinkle with water. If the water bounces across the surface, start spooning on the batter. (Water that sits and simmers indicates the temperature is too low; if the water vanishes, the temperature is too high.) When adding fruit, do so as soon as the batter is spooned onto the griddle.

Turn pancakes when bubbles appear on the surface and the edges begin to look cooked (about 2 to 3 minutes). The second side will take about half as long to cook. Keep pancakes warm in a 200° oven.

Maple-Bacon Oven Pancake

This oven pancake is really a breakfast casserole. Maple syrup, Cheddar cheese, and bacon make a surprising combination.

MAKES 8 SERVINGS
PREP: 3 MIN., BAKE: 17 MIN.

2 large eggs, lightly beaten
1½ cups all-purpose baking mix
1 tablespoon sugar
¾ cup milk
¼ cup maple syrup
1½ cups (6 ounces) shredded Cheddar cheese,
    divided
12 bacon slices, cooked and crumbled

1. Combine first 5 ingredients in a large bowl; beat at medium speed with an electric mixer until smooth. Stir in ½ cup cheese. Pour into a greased and floured 13- x 9-inch baking dish.

2. Bake at 425° for 12 minutes. Sprinkle pancake with remaining 1 cup cheese and bacon; bake 3 to 5 more minutes or until a wooden pick inserted in center comes out clean. Cut into squares, and serve with maple syrup.

Note: For testing purposes only, we used Bisquick All-Purpose Baking Mix.

Lemon Pancakes With Strawberry Butter

The lemon and strawberry flavors complement each other well in these upscale pancakes. Surprise your guests with this deliciously unique version at your next brunch. Or make it a new breakfast favorite at home.

MAKES 9 PANCAKES
PREP: 12 MIN., COOK: 12 MIN.

3 large eggs, separated
¼ teaspoon cream of tartar
¾ cup ricotta cheese
⅓ cup all-purpose flour
¼ cup butter or margarine, melted
2 tablespoons sugar
1 tablespoon grated lemon rind
⅛ teaspoon salt
Strawberry Butter

1. Beat egg whites and cream of tartar at high speed with an electric mixer until stiff peaks form.
2. Beat egg yolks, ricotta cheese, and next 5 ingredients at medium speed with an electric mixer until smooth. Fold in egg whites.
3. Pour about ¼ cup batter for each pancake onto a hot, lightly greased griddle. Cook until tops are covered with bubbles and edges look dry and cooked; turn and cook other side. Serve pancakes with Strawberry Butter.
To Lighten: ¾ cup egg substitute may be substituted for 3 eggs. Whisk together egg substitute, cream of tartar, and next 6 ingredients. Cook as directed.

Strawberry Butter:

MAKES ¾ CUP
PREP: 5 MIN.

½ cup butter or margarine, softened
¼ cup strawberry preserves

1. Stir together butter and preserves until blended.

Toasted Pecan Pancakes

Try these yummy pancakes with honey, apple butter, fresh berries, or traditional syrup. They'll be scrumptious with almost any topping you choose.

MAKES 8 PANCAKES
PREP: 10 MIN., COOK: 8 MIN.

½ cup all-purpose flour
⅓ cup whole wheat flour
¼ cup uncooked quick-cooking oats
2 tablespoons yellow cornmeal
1 tablespoon sugar
1 teaspoon baking powder
½ teaspoon baking soda
½ teaspoon salt
¼ cup chopped pecans, toasted
1 large egg, lightly beaten
1 cup buttermilk
2 tablespoons vegetable oil
Syrup (optional)
Toasted pecan halves (optional)

1. Stir together first 9 ingredients; make a well in center of mixture.
2. Stir together egg, buttermilk, and oil; add to dry ingredients, stirring just until moistened.
3. Pour about ¼ cup batter for each pancake onto a hot, lightly greased griddle. Cook until tops are covered with bubbles and edges look dry and cooked; turn and cook other side. Serve with syrup and pecan halves, if desired.
Note: To toast pecans, spread on a baking sheet. Bake at 350° for 6 minutes or until nuts are lightly toasted.

Corn Waffles With
Cilantro-Lime Butter

Corn Waffles With Cilantro-Lime Butter

These golden waffles are also great served with syrup or honey. Because there are various shapes and sizes of waffle irons, yields may vary.

MAKES 10 (4-INCH) WAFFLES
PREP: 20 MIN., COOK: 15 MIN.

1³/₄ cups self-rising flour
¹/₃ cup sugar
¹/₂ teaspoon salt
3 large eggs, separated
³/₄ cup buttermilk
¹/₃ cup vegetable oil
1 cup frozen whole kernel corn, thawed
Cilantro-Lime Butter

1. Stir together first 3 ingredients in a large bowl; make a well in center of mixture.
2. Stir together egg yolks, buttermilk, vegetable oil, and corn; add to dry ingredients, stirring just until dry ingredients are moistened.

3. Beat egg whites at high speed with an electric mixer until stiff peaks form; fold into batter.
4. Cook, according to manufacturer's instructions, in a preheated, oiled waffle iron until golden. Serve with Cilantro-Lime Butter.

Cilantro-Lime Butter:

MAKES ¹/₂ CUP
PREP: 5 MIN.

¹/₂ cup butter, softened
1 tablespoon chopped fresh cilantro
1 teaspoon grated lime rind
1 teaspoon fresh lime juice

1. Stir together butter and remaining ingredients until blended.

Belgian Waffles

MAKES 8 (4-INCH) WAFFLES
PREP: 10 MIN., COOK: 15 MIN.

4 large eggs, separated
3 tablespoons butter, melted
½ teaspoon vanilla extract
1 cup all-purpose flour
½ teaspoon salt
1 cup milk
Sweetened whipped cream
Sliced fresh strawberries

1. Beat egg yolks at medium speed with an electric mixer until thick and pale. Add butter and vanilla, beating until blended. Set aside.
2. Combine flour and salt. Add flour mixture and milk to egg mixture, beating until smooth. Set aside.
3. Beat egg whites until stiff peaks form, and fold into batter.
4. Bake in a preheated, oiled waffle iron until golden. Serve with sweetened whipped cream and strawberries.

Cinnamon Toast Rollups

MAKES 16 ROLLUPS
PREP: 7 MIN., BAKE: 12 MIN.

¼ cup firmly packed light brown sugar
½ cup granulated sugar
½ teaspoon ground cinnamon
2 (8-ounce) cans refrigerated crescent rolls
¼ cup butter or margarine, melted

1. Stir together first 3 ingredients.
2. Unroll crescent rolls; brush with melted butter; sprinkle evenly with sugar mixture. Separate dough into triangles. Roll up each triangle, starting with shortest side, and place on lightly greased baking sheets.
3. Bake at 350° for 10 to 12 minutes or until golden, and remove from pan immediately. Place on a wire rack to cool.

Peanut Butter and Jelly French Toast

Get creative with this not-so-ordinary French toast by trying different kinds of jelly or flavored syrups. Serve with fresh fruit and your favorite juice.

MAKES 4 SERVINGS
PREP: 8 MIN., COOK: 8 MIN.

8 white sandwich bread slices
4 teaspoons creamy peanut butter
4 teaspoons grape jelly
2 large eggs
¼ cup milk
1 tablespoon granulated sugar
Dash of ground cinnamon
1 tablespoon butter or margarine
Powdered sugar

1. Spread each of 4 bread slices with 1 teaspoon peanut butter. Spread each of remaining bread slices with 1 teaspoon grape jelly; place on top of slices with peanut butter.
2. Stir together eggs and next 3 ingredients in a shallow dish.
3. Melt butter on a griddle over medium heat. Dip sandwiches into egg mixture, evenly coating both sides. Cook sandwiches 4 minutes on each side or until golden.
4. To serve, cut sandwiches in half diagonally, and sprinkle with powdered sugar. Serve immediately.
Note: If using a large nonstick skillet instead of a griddle, melt butter and cook sandwiches in batches.

Make-Ahead French Toast
With Strawberry Sauce

Make-Ahead French Toast With Strawberry Sauce

Our Test Kitchens staff found the light version of this recipe just as delicious as the original.
Challah bread is a rich egg bread with a light, airy texture.

MAKES 10 SERVINGS
PREP: 25 MIN., CHILL: 8 HRS., BAKE: 45 MIN.

1 (16-ounce) challah bread loaf, cubed*
1 (8-ounce) package cream cheese, cut into pieces
6 large eggs
4 cups half-and-half
½ cup butter or margarine, melted
¼ cup maple syrup
2 cups fresh strawberries, sliced
1 (10-ounce) jar strawberry preserves

1. Arrange half of challah bread in a lightly greased
13- x 9-inch pan. Sprinkle with cheese pieces, and top
with remaining bread.

2. Whisk together eggs and next 3 ingredients; pour
over bread mixture, pressing bread cubes to absorb egg
mixture. Cover and chill 8 hours.
3. Bake, covered, at 350° for 25 minutes. Uncover and
bake 20 more minutes.
4. Heat sliced strawberries and strawberry preserves in
a saucepan over low heat, and serve over toast.
*Substitute French bread for challah.
To Lighten: Substitute 1 (8-ounce) package Neufchâtel
cheese for cream cheese, 1½ cups egg substitute for
eggs, and 4 cups fat-free half-and-half for regular
half-and-half.

Homemade Butter Rolls

Homemade Butter Rolls

MAKES 4 DOZEN
PREP: 15 MIN., STAND: 5 MIN., CHILL: 8 HRS., RISE: 2 HRS.,
BAKE: 10 MIN. PER BATCH

2 (¼-ounce) envelopes active dry yeast
1 cup sugar, divided
2 cups warm water (100° to 110°)
1 cup butter or margarine, melted
6 large eggs, lightly beaten
1½ teaspoons salt
8½ to 9½ cups all-purpose flour

1. Stir together yeast, 2 tablespoons sugar, and 2 cups warm water in a 4-cup liquid measuring cup; let stand 5 minutes.
2. Stir together yeast mixture, remaining sugar, and butter in a large bowl; stir in eggs and salt. Gradually stir in enough flour to make a soft dough. Cover and chill 8 hours.
3. Divide dough into 4 equal portions. Turn each portion out onto a lightly floured surface, and roll to a 12-inch circle. Cut each circle into 12 wedges. Roll up each wedge, starting at wide end; place on greased baking sheets. (Rolls may be frozen at this point.) Cover and let rise in a warm place (85°), free from drafts, 1½ to 2 hours or until doubled in bulk.
4. Bake rolls at 400° for 10 minutes or until golden.
Note: Unbaked rolls may be frozen for later use. To thaw, place frozen rolls on ungreased baking sheets. Cover and let rise in a warm place (85°), free from drafts, 2 hours or until doubled in bulk. Bake rolls as directed.

Two-Seed Bread Knots

Most yeast rolls require 2 risings of the dough, but this recipe needs only 1.

MAKES 20 ROLLS
PREP: 30 MIN., STAND: 5 MIN., RISE: 20 MIN., BAKE: 17 MIN.

1 (¼-ounce) envelope rapid-rise yeast
1 cup warm water (100° to 110°)
3½ cups bread flour
2 tablespoons sugar
1½ teaspoons salt
3 tablespoons olive oil
1 egg yolk
1 tablespoon water
1 tablespoon sesame seeds
1 teaspoon poppy seeds

1. Preheat oven to 200°. Combine yeast and 1 cup warm water in a 1-cup liquid measuring cup; let stand 5 minutes.
2. Combine flour, sugar, and salt in a heavy-duty mixing bowl. Add yeast mixture and oil. Beat at low speed with electric mixer 1 minute; beat at medium speed 5 minutes.
3. Divide dough into 20 equal balls. Roll each ball into a 7-inch rope, and twist into a knot. Combine egg yolk and 1 tablespoon water; brush over rolls. Sprinkle with seeds; place on parchment paper-lined baking sheets. Turn off oven, and cover rolls loosely with plastic wrap; place in oven, and let rise 15 to 20 minutes or until doubled in bulk. Remove from oven, and preheat oven to 400°. Discard plastic wrap.
4. Bake at 400° for 15 to 17 minutes or until golden.

yeast breads **67**

Caramel Sticky Buns

Caramel Sticky Buns

Our Test Kitchens staff couldn't resist these buns. Use any remaining sauce over pound cake or fresh fruit.

MAKES 1 DOZEN
PREP: 27 MIN., RISE: 30 MIN., BAKE: 20 MIN., STAND: 10 MIN.

Caramel Sauce
1 (16-ounce) package hot roll mix
1 cup chopped pecans, toasted
3 tablespoons butter, softened
¼ cup sugar
2 teaspoons ground cinnamon

1. Prepare Caramel Sauce; set aside.
2. Prepare roll mix according to package directions. Let stand 5 minutes.
3. Pour Caramel Sauce into a lightly greased 13- x 9-inch pan; sprinkle with pecans. Roll dough into a 15- x 10-inch rectangle. Spread with butter, and sprinkle with sugar and cinnamon. Roll up, jelly-roll fashion, starting at long edge. Cut into 12 slices. Arrange, cut sides down, over Caramel Sauce.
4. Cover and let rise in a warm place (85°), free from drafts, 30 minutes or until doubled in bulk.
5. Bake at 375° for 20 minutes. Let buns stand on a wire rack 10 minutes. Invert onto a serving platter. Serve buns warm.
Note: Buns may be frozen before rising. Remove from freezer, and let thaw at room temperature; continue as directed above.

Caramel Sauce:

Try this sweet sauce over ice cream, too.

MAKES 2½ CUPS
PREP: 3 MIN., COOK: 35 MIN., STAND: 1 MIN.

2 cups whipping cream
¼ cup butter
½ teaspoon baking soda
2 cups sugar
½ cup water
2 teaspoons lemon juice

1. Combine first 3 ingredients in a medium saucepan over medium heat until butter melts, stirring occasionally; remove from heat.
2. Bring sugar, water, and lemon juice to a boil in a Dutch oven over high heat, stirring occasionally. Reduce heat to medium-high, and boil, stirring occasionally, 8 minutes or until mixture begins to brown. Reduce heat to medium; cook 5 minutes or until caramel-colored, stirring occasionally.
3. Gradually whisk cream mixture into sugar mixture, whisking constantly. Remove from heat; let stand 1 minute. Whisk until smooth. Cook over medium-low heat until a candy thermometer reaches 230° (thread stage); cool.

Cheese Snack Bread

MAKES 12 TO 15 SERVINGS
PREP: 30 MIN.; STAND: 5 MIN.; RISE: 1 HR., 25 MIN.; BAKE: 15 MIN.

¾ cup milk
2 tablespoons shortening
1 tablespoon sugar
1 (¼-ounce) envelope active dry yeast
¼ cup warm water (100° to 110°)
2¼ cups all-purpose flour
1 teaspoon salt
1 large egg, lightly beaten
2 cups (8 ounces) shredded sharp Cheddar cheese
⅓ cup milk
¾ teaspoon grated onion
¼ teaspoon salt
1½ teaspoons caraway seeds or poppy seeds

1. Heat milk to 130°. Remove from heat; add shortening and sugar, stirring until shortening melts. Cool to 100° to 110°.
2. Combine yeast and warm water in a 1-cup liquid measuring cup; let stand 5 minutes.
3. Combine milk mixture, yeast mixture, flour, and 1 teaspoon salt in a large bowl; stir well. Turn dough out onto a heavily floured surface; knead until smooth and elastic (about 3 minutes). Place dough in a well-greased bowl, turning to grease top. Cover and let rise in a warm place (85°), free from drafts, 45 minutes or until doubled in bulk.
4. Punch dough down, and place in a greased 13- x 9-inch pan; gently press dough evenly in the pan. Cover and let rise in a warm place, free from drafts, 40 minutes or until doubled in bulk.
5. Combine egg and next 4 ingredients; spread over top of dough. Sprinkle with caraway seeds. Bake at 425° for 15 minutes. Serve warm.

Sage Bread

Sage Bread

This savory herb bread can be mixed with a regular mixer. Use a heavy-duty mixer to double the recipe and make 3 slightly larger loaves in 9- x 5-inch loaf pans. Give them more time to rise; bake at 375° for 30 minutes or until golden.

MAKES 2 LOAVES
PREP: 21 MIN., BAKE: 35 MIN., COOK: 8 MIN., RISE: 50 MIN., OTHER: 10 MIN.

2¼ to 2½ cups all-purpose flour, divided
2 cups whole wheat flour
2 (¼-ounce) envelopes active dry yeast
1 tablespoon minced fresh sage
1¾ cups milk
¼ cup firmly packed light brown sugar
2½ tablespoons butter or margarine
1 teaspoon salt
¼ cup plus 2 tablespoons yellow cornmeal, divided
1 large egg, lightly beaten
1 tablespoon water
Fresh sage leaves

1. Combine 1 cup all-purpose flour, whole wheat flour, yeast, and minced sage in a large bowl; stir well. Place milk and next 3 ingredients in a saucepan; cook over low heat until butter melts, stirring often. Cool to 120° to 130°.
2. Gradually add milk mixture to flour mixture, beating 30 seconds at low speed with an electric mixer. Beat 3 more minutes at medium-high speed. Gradually stir in ¼ cup cornmeal and remaining 1¼ to 1½ cups all-purpose flour to make a soft dough.
3. Turn dough out onto a floured surface, and knead until smooth and elastic (about 6 to 8 minutes). Shape into a ball. Place in a well-greased bowl, turning to grease top. Cover and let rise in a warm place (85°), free from drafts, 30 minutes or until doubled in bulk.
4. Punch dough down. Turn out onto a lightly floured surface; knead lightly 4 or 5 times. Divide in half. Cover; let rest 10 minutes.
5. Lightly grease a baking sheet; sprinkle with remaining 2 tablespoons cornmeal. Shape each half of dough into an 8½- x 4½-inch loaf. Place on prepared baking sheet.
6. Combine egg and water, stirring well. Brush loaves with egg mixture. Place sage leaves on top of loaves. Cover and let rise in a warm place, free from drafts, 20 minutes or until doubled in bulk. Brush again with egg mixture. (Do not brush sage leaves.)
7. Bake at 375° for 25 to 35 minutes or until golden; cover with aluminum foil last 15 minutes, if necessary, to prevent excessive browning. Cool on a wire rack.

Raisin-Nut Cocoa Bread

If you're going to make the effort for homemade bread, you might as well make 2 loaves. Keep one and give the other away, or freeze it for down the road.

MAKES 2 LOAVES
PREP: 27 MIN.; BAKE: 40 MIN.; COOK: 10 MIN.; RISE: 1 HR., 15 MIN.; STAND: 5 MIN.

2 cups water
1 cup uncooked regular oats
1 teaspoon salt, divided
6 cups all-purpose flour, divided
½ cup cocoa
2 (¼-ounce) envelopes active dry yeast
½ cup warm water (100° to 110°)
1 cup firmly packed light brown sugar
2 tablespoons butter, softened
1 cup chopped walnuts
1 cup raisins
Melted butter

1. Combine 2 cups water, oats, and ½ teaspoon salt in a medium saucepan. Bring to a boil; reduce heat, and simmer, uncovered, 5 minutes, stirring occasionally. Pour oat mixture into a large mixing bowl, and cool to lukewarm.
2. Combine 2 cups flour, cocoa, and remaining ½ teaspoon salt. Combine yeast and warm water in a 1-cup liquid measuring cup; let stand 5 minutes. Add flour mixture, yeast mixture, sugar, and softened butter to oat mixture. Beat at low speed with an electric mixer until dry ingredients are moistened. Beat at medium speed 2 minutes. Stir in walnuts and raisins.
3. Gradually stir in enough remaining flour to make a soft dough. Turn dough out onto a floured surface, and knead until smooth and elastic (6 to 8 minutes). Place dough in a well-greased bowl, turning to grease top. Cover and let rise in a warm place (85°), free from drafts, 45 minutes or until doubled in bulk. Punch dough down, and divide in half.
4. Roll half of dough into a 15- x 7-inch rectangle on a lightly floured surface. Roll up dough, starting at short side, pressing firmly to eliminate air pockets; pinch seams and ends to seal. Place loaf, seam side down, in a greased 9- x 5-inch loaf pan. Repeat procedure with remaining dough. Cover and let rise in a warm place, free from drafts, 30 minutes or until doubled.
5. Bake at 375° for 35 to 40 minutes or until loaves sound hollow when tapped. Remove bread from pans; immediately brush with melted butter. Cool completely on wire racks.

fish &
shellfish

Garlic-and-Rosemary
Shrimp, page 86

Catfish Classique

MAKES 4 SERVINGS

PREP: 30 MIN., FRY: 6 MIN. PER BATCH, COOK: 21 MIN.

1 large egg
½ cup milk
1½ cups all-purpose flour
1¼ teaspoons salt, divided
2½ teaspoons ground red pepper, divided
4 (6-ounce) catfish fillets (½ inch thick)
Vegetable oil
1 tablespoon butter or margarine
12 unpeeled, large fresh shrimp
2 teaspoons minced garlic (about 2 cloves)
¼ cup dry vermouth
2 cups whipping cream
¼ cup chopped green onions, divided
2 teaspoons fresh lemon juice
Garnish: lemon wedges

1. Combine egg and milk, stirring until blended. Combine flour, 1 teaspoon salt, and 1 teaspoon red pepper in a shallow dish. Dredge catfish fillets in flour mixture, dip in milk mixture, and dredge again in flour mixture.

2. Pour oil to depth of 2 inches into a Dutch oven; heat to 375°. Fry fillets, 2 at a time, 6 minutes or until golden; drain on paper towels. Set aside, and keep warm.

3. Peel and devein shrimp, if desired. Melt butter in a large skillet over medium heat. Add shrimp and garlic; sauté 4 minutes or until shrimp turn pink. Remove shrimp from skillet, reserving drippings in pan. Set shrimp aside; keep warm.

4. Add vermouth to skillet; bring to a boil, and cook 1 minute, stirring constantly. Add whipping cream, half of green onions, lemon juice, remaining ¼ teaspoon salt, and remaining 1½ teaspoons red pepper; cook sauce 15 minutes or until thickened, stirring often.

5. To serve, place catfish on a serving platter, and drizzle with sauce. Top with shrimp, and sprinkle with remaining green onions. Garnish, if desired.

Potato-Crusted Catfish and Chips

MAKES 4 SERVINGS

PREP: 15 MIN., FRY: 18 MIN.

Vegetable oil
3 large baking potatoes, peeled and cut into thin strips
1¼ teaspoons salt, divided
4 (6-ounce) catfish fillets
¼ teaspoon pepper
1 cup yellow cornmeal
1 cup instant potato flakes
¼ cup butter or margarine, melted

1. Pour oil to a depth of 4 inches into a large Dutch oven, and heat to 375°. Fry potato strips, in 4 batches, 2 to 3 minutes or until golden. Drain on paper towels, and sprinkle with 1 teaspoon salt. Keep warm.

2. Sprinkle catfish fillets evenly with remaining ¼ teaspoon salt and pepper. Combine cornmeal and instant potato flakes. Dip fish in melted butter, and then dredge in cornmeal mixture.

3. Heat oil in Dutch oven to 400°; add fish, and fry, 2 fillets at a time, 2 to 3 minutes or until fillets float. Drain on paper towels; serve with chips.

Catfish Classique

Jack's Fried Catfish

Catfish is done when most of the bubbling stops and the fillets begin to float.

MAKES 4 TO 8 SERVINGS
PREP: 10 MIN., CHILL: 1 HR., STAND: 10 MIN.,
FRY: 4 MIN. PER BATCH

8 (4- to 6-ounce) catfish fillets
2 cups milk
2 cups yellow cornmeal
1 tablespoon seasoned salt
2 teaspoons pepper
1/2 teaspoon onion powder
1/2 teaspoon garlic powder
1 teaspoon salt
Vegetable oil
Lemon wedges

Jack's Fried Catfish

1. Place catfish fillets in a single layer in a shallow dish; cover with milk. Cover and chill 1 hour.
2. Combine cornmeal and next 4 ingredients in a shallow dish. Set aside.
3. Remove catfish fillets from refrigerator, and let stand at room temperature 10 minutes. Remove from milk, allowing excess to drip off. Sprinkle evenly with 1 teaspoon salt.

4. Dredge catfish fillets in cornmeal mixture, shaking off excess.
5. Pour oil to depth of 1¾ inches into a large cast-iron skillet or heavy-duty Dutch oven; heat to 350°. Fry fillets, in batches, about 3 to 4 minutes (do not turn) or until golden brown. Drain on wire racks over paper towels. Serve with lemon wedges.

SUCCESSFUL FRYING

■ The secret to frying is using the right oil. Smoke point is the temperature at which fats and oils begin to smoke, indicating they've begun to break down. The higher the smoke point an oil has, the better it is for frying. Lard and some vegetable oils, such as corn, canola, safflower, and peanut, are good choices. Shortening is not suitable for high-temperature frying.

■ Moisture and food particles break down oil, so we recommend using it no more than twice. Between first and second uses, store oil in the refrigerator up to 1 week; let oil stand until it reaches room temperature before using. If you see smoke, discard the oil, and start over.

■ Achieving and maintaining proper oil temperature is a must. If the oil doesn't get hot enough (often caused by overcrowding), the food soaks up oil, leaving it greasy. Too hot, and the outside burns before the inside cooks, creating food that's soggy.

■ Food soaks up only a small amount of oil when fried at the proper temperature.

■ Use heavy-duty aluminum, cast-iron, or stainless steel cookware for even heat distribution and retention of high temperatures. Iron speeds up the breakdown of oil, so when using cast-iron cookware, it's best to use the oil only once.

■ Choose cookware that's large enough to leave at least 3 inches between the surface of the oil and the top of the skillet or Dutch oven.

■ Always allow the oil to return to its proper temperature between batches. We like to use a candy thermometer, which can handle high temperatures and can be attached to the side of a large skillet or Dutch oven for instant readings.

■ Make sure food is dry. Adding moist food to hot oil will cause spattering and popping.

Grilled Snapper With Orange-Almond Sauce

MAKES 6 SERVINGS
PREP: 20 MIN., GRILL: 12 MIN., COOK: 5 MIN.

6 (8-ounce) snapper or grouper fillets
2 tablespoons olive oil
1 teaspoon coarse-grain sea salt
1 teaspoon freshly ground pepper
4 fresh thyme sprigs
Vegetable cooking spray
½ cup butter
½ cup sliced almonds
½ to 1 tablespoon grated orange rind
Garnishes: orange wedges, thyme sprigs

1. Rub fish fillets with oil. Sprinkle evenly with salt and pepper.
2. Arrange thyme sprigs on hot charcoal or hot lava rocks on grill. Coat food rack with cooking spray; place on grill over high heat (400° to 500°). Place fish on rack, and grill 5 to 6 minutes on each side or until fish flakes with a fork.
3. Melt butter in a saucepan over medium-high heat; add almonds, and sauté 5 minutes or until butter is brown. Remove from heat. Stir in orange rind. Pour sauce over fish. Garnish, if desired.

Greek Snapper

The oregano, olives, and feta cheese help give a Mediterranean twist to this snapper. Serve with a fresh green salad for a satisfying meal.

MAKES 6 SERVINGS
PREP: 22 MIN., COOK: 25 MIN., BAKE: 20 MIN.

1 tablespoon olive oil
1 onion, chopped
1 garlic clove, minced
3 medium tomatoes, peeled, seeded, and chopped
¼ cup sliced ripe olives or pitted, sliced kalamata
    olives
¼ cup dry white wine
1 teaspoon dried oregano
½ teaspoon salt
¼ teaspoon pepper
1½ pounds red snapper fillets
2 ounces feta cheese, crumbled
2 tablespoons chopped fresh parsley

1. Pour oil into a large skillet. Place over medium heat until hot. Add onion and garlic; cook 3 minutes or until tender, stirring constantly. Stir in tomato and next 5 ingredients. Bring to a boil; reduce heat, and simmer, uncovered, 20 minutes.
2. Place snapper fillets in a greased 13- x 9-inch baking dish. Spoon tomato mixture over fillets. Bake, uncovered, at 350° for 20 minutes or until fish flakes with a fork. Sprinkle with cheese and parsley. Serve fish immediately.

Heavenly Broiled Grouper

MAKES 6 TO 8 SERVINGS
PREP: 10 MIN., BROIL: 10 MIN.

2 pounds grouper fillets
½ cup grated Parmesan cheese
3 tablespoons chopped green onions
3 tablespoons reduced-fat mayonnaise
1 tablespoon butter or margarine, softened
1 garlic clove, pressed
¼ teaspoon salt
Dash of hot sauce

1. Place fillets in a single layer in a lightly greased 13- x 9-inch pan.
2. Stir together Parmesan cheese and remaining ingredients, and spread over fillets.

3. Broil 6 inches from heat 10 minutes or until lightly browned and fish flakes with a fork.
Note: Do not broil closer than 6 inches to heat or topping may burn before fish is done.

Grouper Mediterranean

MAKES 6 SERVINGS
PREP: 15 MIN., COOK: 12 MIN., BAKE: 23 MIN.

3 tablespoons olive oil, divided
½ cup chopped onion
3 garlic cloves, minced
1 (28-ounce) can crushed tomatoes, undrained
½ cup dry white wine
½ cup chopped fresh parsley
¼ cup capers, drained
1 teaspoon chopped fresh rosemary
1 teaspoon chopped fresh oregano
¼ teaspoon dried crushed red pepper
6 (8-ounce) grouper fillets (about ¾ inch thick)
2 tablespoons dry white wine
2 (4-ounce) packages crumbled feta cheese

1. Heat 2 tablespoons oil in a large skillet over medium-high heat. Add onion and garlic, and sauté 2 minutes. Add tomatoes and next 6 ingredients to skillet. Bring to a boil; reduce heat, and simmer, uncovered, 10 minutes.
2. Pour remaining oil into a 15- x 10-inch jelly-roll pan, and tilt to coat bottom. Place fish fillets in a single layer on pan. Pour tomato mixture over fish. Bake, uncovered, at 450° for 15 minutes. Drizzle with white wine. Sprinkle with cheese, and cook 8 more minutes or until cheese begins to melt.

Swordfish Steaks With
Basil Butter

Swordfish Steaks With Basil Butter

Basil gives an accented herb punch to this mild-flavored fish. Team leftover butter with any fish, shellfish, or veggies within three days.

MAKES 8 SERVINGS
PREP: 5 MIN., COOK: 16 MIN., OTHER: 8 TO 24 HRS.

½ cup butter, softened
¼ cup loosely packed fresh basil leaves
¼ cup Dijon mustard
1½ teaspoons capers
8 (8-ounce) swordfish steaks (about 1 inch thick)
½ teaspoon salt
¼ teaspoon freshly ground pepper
Garnishes: basil sprigs and lemon wedges

1. Combine first 4 ingredients in a blender or food processor, and process until blended, stopping once to scrape down sides. Cover and chill 8 to 24 hours.
2. Sprinkle steaks with salt and pepper. Grill steaks, covered with grill lid, over medium-high heat (350° to 400°) about 8 minutes on each side or until fish flakes easily when tested with a fork.
3. Serve with basil butter. Garnish, if desired.

Grilled Fresh Tuna

Citrus juices and soy sauce give extra zip to these tuna steaks. Serve them with sugar snap peas and rice for a meal.

MAKES 4 SERVINGS
PREP: 10 MIN., CHILL: 1 HR., COOK: 3 MIN., GRILL: 6 MIN.

4 (5-ounce) tuna steaks (about ¾ inch thick)
¼ cup orange juice
¼ cup soy sauce
2 tablespoons ketchup
2 tablespoons chopped fresh parsley
1 tablespoon lemon juice
½ teaspoon dried oregano
⅛ teaspoon ground white pepper
1 garlic clove, minced

1. Place tuna in a large zip-top freezer bag. Combine orange juice and next 7 ingredients, and pour over tuna steaks. Seal bag, and chill 1 hour.
2. Remove tuna from marinade, reserving marinade. Pour marinade into a small saucepan. Bring to a boil; remove from heat.

3. Place a lightly greased food grate on grill over medium heat (300° to 350°). Place steaks on grate; brush with marinade. Grill, covered, 2 to 3 minutes. Brush with marinade; turn steaks, and brush with marinade. Grill, covered, 2 to 3 minutes or to desired degree of doneness.

Fabulous Tuna-Noodle Casserole

The mixture of fresh vegetables and seasonings turns ordinary tuna into something exceptionally good. You're sure to get rave reviews for this dish.

MAKES 6 TO 8 SERVINGS
PREP: 15 MIN., COOK: 10 MIN., BAKE: 30 MIN.

¼ cup butter or margarine
1 small red or green bell pepper, chopped
1 small onion, chopped
1 cup sliced fresh mushrooms
¼ cup all-purpose flour
2½ cups milk
2 cups (8 ounces) shredded Cheddar cheese
2 (9-ounce) cans solid white tuna in spring water, drained and flaked
1 (12-ounce) package egg noodles, cooked
2 teaspoons dried parsley flakes
½ teaspoon salt
½ teaspoon pepper
½ cup fine, dry breadcrumbs
2 tablespoons butter or margarine, melted

1. Melt ¼ cup butter in a large skillet over medium heat; add chopped bell pepper, onion, and sliced mushrooms, and sauté 5 minutes or until tender.
2. Whisk together flour and milk until smooth; stir into vegetable mixture, and cook, stirring constantly, 5 minutes or until thickened. Remove from heat; add cheese, stirring until melted.
3. Stir in tuna and next 4 ingredients; spoon into a lightly greased 13- x 9-inch baking dish.
4. Bake, covered, at 350° for 25 minutes. Stir together breadcrumbs and 2 tablespoons melted butter; sprinkle over casserole, and bake 5 more minutes.

Orange Roughy Dijon

MAKES 4 SERVINGS
PREP: 10 MIN., BAKE: 10 MIN.

4 (6- to 8-ounce) orange roughy fillets
½ teaspoon salt
¼ teaspoon pepper
¼ cup butter or margarine, softened
2 tablespoons Dijon mustard
1 tablespoon lemon juice
2 teaspoons Worcestershire sauce
1 garlic clove, minced
½ cup fine, dry breadcrumbs

1. Sprinkle fish with salt and pepper, and place in a lightly greased 13- x 9-inch baking dish. Combine softened butter and next 4 ingredients; spread on fish. Top with breadcrumbs.
2. Bake at 450° for 10 minutes or until fish flakes with a fork.

Crab-Stuffed Flounder

MAKES 6 SERVINGS
PREP: 30 MIN., COOK: 3 MIN., BAKE: 30 MIN.

1 celery rib, chopped
3 green onions, chopped
2 garlic cloves, minced
¼ cup olive oil
½ pound fresh lump crabmeat, drained
1 cup soft breadcrumbs (homemade)
½ cup grated Parmesan cheese
1 plum tomato, chopped
1 large egg, lightly beaten
2 tablespoons fresh lemon juice
1 tablespoon chopped fresh parsley
¼ teaspoon salt
¼ teaspoon pepper
6 (4-ounce) flounder fillets
½ cup butter or margarine, melted
Garnish: lemon wedges

1. Cook celery, green onions, and garlic in hot oil in a large skillet over medium-high heat, stirring constantly, 3 minutes or until tender. Remove skillet from heat; add crabmeat and next 8 ingredients, stirring well.
2. Brush fillets evenly with melted butter. Spoon 1 heaping tablespoon crabmeat mixture on top of each fillet. Roll up fillets; secure each with a wooden pick.

Place fillets in a lightly greased 13- x 9- inch baking dish. Spoon remaining crabmeat mixture over each stuffed fillet, and drizzle with any remaining butter.
3. Cover and bake at 375° for 20 minutes. Uncover and bake for 10 more minutes or until fish flakes with a fork. Garnish, if desired.

Creole Flounder With Lemon Couscous

MAKES 6 SERVINGS
PREP: 15 MIN., BAKE: 10 MIN.

2 pounds flounder fillets
1 large tomato, seeded and chopped
1 medium-size green bell pepper, chopped
2 tablespoons chopped fresh basil
1 tablespoon dried minced onion
1 teaspoon Creole seasoning
⅓ cup fresh lemon juice
1 tablespoon olive oil
¼ teaspoon hot sauce
Lemon Couscous

1. Cut fish into 6 pieces. Place fish in a lightly greased 13- x 9-inch pan.
2. Stir together tomato, bell pepper, basil, and next 5 ingredients; spoon over fish.
3. Bake at 500° for 7 to 10 minutes or until fish begins to flake and is opaque throughout. Serve with Lemon Couscous.

Lemon Couscous:

MAKES 6 SERVINGS
PREP: 5 MIN.

10 ounces couscous, cooked
2 tablespoons fresh lemon juice

1. Stir together couscous and 2 tablespoons lemon juice.

Orange Roughy With
Strawberry–Star Fruit Salsa

Orange Roughy With Strawberry–Star Fruit Salsa

Orange roughy is a tender, mild white fish that's easy to cook. Here, it's ready in just 5 minutes under the broiler.
And you can make the citrusy salsa ahead; it gives a kiss of beautiful color to the white fish.

MAKES 6 SERVINGS

PREP: 10 MIN., BROIL: 5 MIN., CHILL: 2 HRS.

1 cup sliced fresh strawberries
2 medium star fruit (carambola), thinly sliced
½ cup minced onion
1 tablespoon chopped jalapeño pepper
1 tablespoon minced fresh cilantro
1 teaspoon grated lime rind
1 tablespoon fresh lime juice
¼ teaspoon ground coriander
⅛ teaspoon ground red pepper
2 tablespoons fresh lime juice
2 teaspoons butter or margarine, melted
6 orange roughy fillets
Garnish: jalapeño peppers

1. Combine first 9 ingredients in a medium bowl to make salsa. Cover and chill 2 hours.
2. Combine 2 tablespoons lime juice and butter in a small bowl. Place orange roughy fillets on a lightly greased rack in a broiler pan. Brush with butter mixture. Broil 5½ inches from heat 5 minutes or until fish flakes with a fork. Serve with salsa. Garnish, if desired.

Pan-Grilled Salmon

Pan-Grilled Salmon

This dish pairs well with the Orange-Ginger Couscous on page 285.

MAKES 4 SERVINGS
PREP: 5 MIN., CHILL: 2 HRS., COOK: 8 MIN.

¼ cup firmly packed brown sugar
¼ cup soy sauce
4 (6-ounce) salmon steaks
Garnish: orange rind strips
Orange-Ginger Couscous (optional)

1. Combine brown sugar and soy sauce in a shallow dish or large zip-top freezer bag, and add salmon. Cover or seal, and chill 2 hours. Remove salmon from marinade, discarding marinade.
2. Cook salmon in a lightly greased skillet over medium-high heat 4 minutes on each side or until fish flakes with a fork. Garnish, if desired. Serve salmon with Orange-Ginger Couscous, if desired.

Sidecar Salmon

Big flavor comes from this short ingredients list.

MAKES 4 SERVINGS
PREP: 10 MIN., COOK: 20 MIN.

1 large red onion, chopped
2 tablespoons olive oil
4 (8-ounce) salmon fillets (about 1½ inches thick)
½ cup reduced-sodium soy sauce

1. Cook onion in hot oil in a large skillet over medium-high heat, stirring constantly, 5 minutes. Arrange salmon on top of onion. Pour soy sauce over salmon fillets. Bring to a boil; cover, reduce heat, and simmer 10 minutes or until fish flakes with a fork. Transfer fish to a serving platter, and keep warm.
2. Cook onion mixture over medium-high heat 5 minutes or until liquid evaporates. Spoon onion mixture over salmon.

Salmon With Basil, Tomato, and Capers

Coat salmon fillets with a little olive oil, run them under the broiler, and top them with tangy tomatoes and capers for a fine Mediterranean supper.

MAKES 4 SERVINGS
PREP: 10 MIN., BROIL: 10 MIN.

1 pound plum tomatoes, seeded and chopped
¾ cup lightly packed fresh basil leaves, chopped
½ cup olive oil
1 shallot, chopped (2 tablespoons)
1½ tablespoons lemon juice
1 tablespoon drained capers
⅛ teaspoon salt
⅛ teaspoon pepper
4 (6-ounce) salmon fillets
1 tablespoon olive oil
Garnish: lemon wedges (1 small lemon)

1. Combine first 8 ingredients in a small bowl, stirring well; set aside.
2. Brush both sides of salmon with 1 tablespoon olive oil. Place salmon on a rack in a broiler pan coated with cooking spray. Broil 3 inches from heat 10 minutes or until fish flakes with a fork.
3. To serve, transfer salmon to a serving plate; top with tomato mixture, and garnish, if desired.

Garlic-and-Rosemary Shrimp

Use this recipe as an appetizer or served over pasta as a main dish.

MAKES 4 SERVINGS
PREP: 20 MIN., COOK: 10 MIN.

1 pound unpeeled, medium-size fresh shrimp
2 tablespoons butter or margarine
¼ cup extra-virgin olive oil
1 large garlic bulb
½ cup dry white wine
2 tablespoons white wine vinegar
1 tablespoon lemon juice
2 tablespoons chopped fresh rosemary
1 teaspoon dried oregano
1 teaspoon salt
½ teaspoon dried crushed red pepper
3 dried red chile peppers
3 bay leaves
Garnishes: lemon slices, red chile peppers, fresh
    rosemary sprigs

1. Peel shrimp, leaving tails on; devein, if desired, and set aside.
2. Melt butter with oil in a large skillet over medium-high heat. Cut garlic bulb in half crosswise; separate and peel cloves. Add to butter mixture, and sauté 2 minutes.
3. Stir in wine and next 8 ingredients; cook, stirring constantly, 1 minute or until thoroughly heated.
4. Add shrimp; cook 3 to 5 minutes or just until shrimp turn pink. Garnish, if desired.
Note: If serving over pasta, remove and discard bay leaves.

Garlic-and-Rosemary
Shrimp

Nannie's Shrimp Croquettes

MAKES 8 SERVINGS
PREP: 10 MIN., COOK: 10 MIN., CHILL: 1 HR., FRY: 4 MIN.

3 tablespoons butter or margarine
¼ cup all-purpose flour
1 cup milk
1 tablespoon minced onion
1 teaspoon Worcestershire sauce
½ teaspoon salt
½ teaspoon ground black pepper
⅛ teaspoon ground red pepper
1 large egg, lightly beaten
2 cups chopped cooked shrimp
1¾ cups saltine crumbs
2 large eggs, lightly beaten
Vegetable oil

1. Melt butter in a large heavy saucepan over low heat, and whisk in flour. Cook, whisking constantly, 1 minute. Gradually whisk in milk, and cook over medium heat, whisking constantly, until thickened and bubbly.

2. Stir in onion and next 4 ingredients. Remove from heat, and stir in 1 egg and cooked shrimp. Cover and chill 1 hour.

3. Shape shrimp mixture into 16 balls. Roll mixture in saltine crumbs, dip in 2 beaten eggs, and roll mixture again in saltine crumbs.

4. Pour vegetable oil to a depth of 3 inches into a Dutch oven, and heat to 375°. Fry croquettes 3 to 4 minutes or until golden. Drain on paper towels.

Hickory-Smoked Shrimp

MAKES 8 TO 10 SERVINGS
PREP: 40 MIN., COOK: 20 MIN.

2 cups hickory chips
3 pounds unpeeled, large fresh shrimp
3 lemons, sliced
½ to ⅔ cup hickory-flavored barbecue sauce
½ cup dry shrimp-and-crab boil seasoning
1 teaspoon pepper
1 teaspoon hot sauce
¾ cup butter or margarine, cut up
¾ cup dry white wine

1. Soak wood chips in water at least 30 minutes.

2. Prepare charcoal fire in grill; let burn 15 to 20 minutes.

3. Drain chips, and place on coals.

4. Place layers of shrimp and lemon slices alternately in a baking dish; brush with barbecue sauce. Sprinkle with shrimp-and-crab boil seasoning, pepper, and hot sauce; dot with butter. Add wine to dish.

5. Place dish on grill rack, and cook, covered with grill lid, 15 to 20 minutes or just until shrimp turn pink, stirring once.

Note: For testing purposes only, we used Kraft Thick 'n' Spicy Hickory Smoked Barbecue Sauce and McCormick Shrimp-and-Crab Boil Seasoning.

Hot Red Curry Shrimp

The unusual ingredients in this dish offer a refreshing change of pace. It tastes great made with chicken, too.

MAKES 4 SERVINGS
PREP: 10 MIN., STAND: 45 MIN., COOK: 15 MIN.

1 dried whole red chile pepper
¼ cup boiling water
1 pound unpeeled, medium-size fresh shrimp
2¼ cups chicken broth
1 (14-ounce) can coconut milk
1 tablespoon hot curry paste
1 tablespoon fish sauce
2 (4.9-ounce) packages toasted Israeli couscous
1 tablespoon lime juice
3 tablespoons chopped fresh cilantro

1. Place chile pepper in ¼ cup boiling water; let stand 30 minutes. Drain, cool, and chop.

2. Peel shrimp, and devein, if desired.

3. Cook chile pepper, chicken broth, coconut milk, hot curry paste, and fish sauce in a saucepan over low heat, stirring often, 8 minutes. Add shrimp, and cook, stirring often, 2 to 3 minutes or until shrimp turn pink.

4. Remove seasoning packets from couscous, and reserve for another use. Stir couscous into broth mixture; remove from heat, cover, and let stand 15 minutes. Stir in juice; sprinkle with cilantro.

Note: For testing purposes only, we used Patak's Original Hot Curry Paste and Marrakesh Express CousCous Grande Toasted Onion, available at Asian markets or in the ethnic-food sections of larger supermarkets.

Shrimp Fettucine With
Dried Tomato Pesto

Shrimp Fettuccine With Dried Tomato Pesto

MAKES 4 SERVINGS
PREP: 30 MIN., COOK: 8 MIN.

1 pound unpeeled, medium-size fresh shrimp
Vegetable cooking spray
1 teaspoon olive oil
2 garlic cloves, minced
¼ cup dry white wine
Dried Tomato Pesto
8 ounces fettucine, cooked
¼ cup freshly grated Parmesan cheese

1. Peel shrimp, and devein, if desired.
2. Coat a large nonstick skillet with vegetable cooking spray, and add olive oil. Place over medium heat until hot. Add minced garlic, and cook, stirring constantly, until tender. Add shrimp; cook, stirring constantly, 1 minute.
3. Add wine; cook, stirring constantly, 3 to 4 minutes or until shrimp turn pink. Stir in Dried Tomato Pesto; cook until mixture is thoroughly heated, stirring often.
4. To serve, place 1 cup pasta on each individual serving plate; top evenly with shrimp mixture. Sprinkle each serving with 1 tablespoon Parmesan cheese.

Dried Tomato Pesto:

MAKES 1½ CUPS
PREP: 10 MIN., COOK: 5 MIN., STAND: 10 MIN.

½ cup (1 ounce) dried tomatoes (packed without oil)
1 cup vegetable broth, divided
½ cup fresh basil leaves
¼ cup freshly grated Parmesan cheese
1½ tablespoons pine nuts
1 tablespoon olive oil
¼ teaspoon salt
¼ teaspoon ground white pepper
1 garlic clove
1 teaspoon cornstarch

1. Combine tomatoes and ½ cup broth in a small saucepan; bring to a boil. Remove from heat; let stand 10 minutes.
2. Process tomato mixture, basil, and next 6 ingredients in a food processor or blender until smooth, stopping once to scrape down sides. Set tomato mixture aside.

3. Combine remaining ½ cup vegetable broth and cornstarch in a small saucepan. Bring to a boil over medium heat, stirring constantly; boil 1 minute. Remove from heat; stir in tomato mixture.

Shrimp-Herb Fettuccine

MAKES 4 TO 6 SERVINGS
PREP: 15 MIN., COOK: 20 MIN.

2 pounds unpeeled, medium-size fresh shrimp
½ cup butter or margarine, divided
3 garlic cloves, minced
½ cup dry white wine
1 cup whipping cream
1 cup finely shredded Parmesan cheese
¼ cup chopped fresh parsley
¼ cup chopped fresh basil
¼ cup chopped fresh chives
8 ounces fettuccine, cooked

1. Peel shrimp, and devein, if desired.
2. Melt 3 tablespoons butter in a large skillet over medium-high heat; add shrimp, and sauté 3 to 4 minutes. Remove shrimp with a slotted spoon.
3. Melt remaining 5 tablespoons butter in skillet over medium-high heat; add garlic, and sauté 1 minute. Add wine, and cook 4 minutes or until mixture is reduced by half. Stir in whipping cream, and cook, stirring occasionally, 4 to 5 minutes or until slightly thickened. Add shrimp, cheese, and herbs; cook, stirring occasionally, just until cheese melts. Serve over fettuccine.

Ragin' Cajun
Casserole

Ragin' Cajun Casserole

MAKES 4 SERVINGS
PREP: 15 MIN., COOK: 32 MIN.

8 ounces low-fat smoked sausage, cut into ¼-inch
   slices
1 small onion, diced
1 celery rib, diced
1 large green bell pepper, cut into thin strips
2 garlic cloves, minced
1 (14½-ounce) can diced tomatoes with garlic, basil,
   and oregano
1 (14-ounce) can fat-free chicken broth
1¾ teaspoons Creole seasoning
⅛ to ½ teaspoon ground red pepper
¾ cup uncooked long-grain rice
1 pound cooked medium shrimp, peeled and
   deveined

1. Sauté smoked sausage in a large nonstick skillet over medium-high heat 3 to 4 minutes or until browned. Add onion and next 3 ingredients; sauté 2 to 3 minutes.
2. Add tomatoes and next 3 ingredients. Bring to a boil, and stir in rice; cover, reduce heat to low, and simmer 15 to 20 minutes or until liquid is absorbed. Stir in shrimp, and cook 3 to 5 minutes or just until shrimp turn pink.

Grilled Shrimp With Citrus Salsa

Impress your guests with this zesty recipe.

MAKES 4 SERVINGS
PREP: 20 MIN., CHILL: 30 MIN., GRILL: 10 MIN.

2 oranges
2 peaches
1 jalapeño pepper, minced
2 tablespoons minced red onion
1 teaspoon chopped fresh rosemary
1 tablespoon olive oil
1 garlic clove, minced
1½ pounds unpeeled, medium-size fresh shrimp
1 cup fresh orange juice
1 tablespoon olive oil
¼ teaspoon freshly ground black pepper
1 bunch fresh rosemary, stemmed
5 garlic cloves, pressed
Vegetable cooking spray

1. Grate rind from oranges, reserving rind; peel, section, and coarsely chop oranges. Peel and chop peaches.
2. Stir together 2 tablespoons orange rind, chopped orange, peach, jalapeño pepper, and next 4 ingredients; cover and chill.
3. Peel shrimp, and devein, if desired.
4. Combine remaining orange rind, orange juice, and next 4 ingredients in a shallow dish or large zip-top freezer bag; add shrimp. Cover or seal; chill, turning occasionally, 30 minutes.
5. Remove shrimp from marinade, reserving marinade. Pour marinade into a small saucepan. Bring marinade to a boil; boil 1 minute.
6. Grill shrimp in a grill basket coated with cooking spray, covered with grill lid, over medium-high heat (350° to 400°) 5 minutes on each side, basting with reserved marinade. Serve with citrus salsa.

Poblano-Shrimp Enchiladas

MAKES 4 SERVINGS
PREP: 35 MIN., COOK: 5 MIN., COOL: 5 MIN., BAKE: 25 MIN.

¾ pound unpeeled, medium-size fresh shrimp
5 tablespoons olive oil, divided
1 large poblano pepper, halved and seeded
1 large onion, chopped
1 tomato, chopped
¼ teaspoon salt
½ teaspoon dried oregano
¼ teaspoon ground cumin
¼ teaspoon black pepper
½ cup sour cream
8 corn tortillas
1 (10-ounce) can green enchilada sauce
1½ cups (6 ounces) shredded Monterey Jack cheese

1. Peel shrimp, and devein, if desired. Coarsely chop shrimp, and set aside.
2. Brush an 11- x 7-inch baking dish with 2 tablespoons olive oil. Set aside.
3. Sauté pepper in remaining oil in a skillet over medium-high heat until skin looks blistered. Remove from skillet, and chop.
4. Return chopped pepper to skillet. Add onion and next 5 ingredients; sauté 4 minutes. Add chopped shrimp, and sauté 1 minute; remove from heat, and cool 5 minutes. Stir in sour cream.
5. Heat tortillas according to package directions. Spoon shrimp mixture evenly down center of each tortilla, and roll up. Arrange, seam sides down, in prepared pan. Top with sauce; sprinkle with cheese. Cover and chill up to 1 day ahead.
6. Bake at 350° for 25 minutes or until thoroughly heated.

Orange-Pecan
Shrimp Stir-fry

Orange-Pecan Shrimp Stir-fry

MAKES 6 SERVINGS
PREP: 30 MIN., COOK: 9 MIN.

2 pounds unpeeled, medium-size fresh shrimp
4 green onions
1 cup water
¼ cup soy sauce
4 teaspoons cornstarch
2 tablespoons orange marmalade
1 tablespoon grated orange rind
½ teaspoon ground ginger
1 tablespoon vegetable oil
1 large red bell pepper, cut into thin strips
1 cup chopped pecans, toasted
2 teaspoons sesame oil
Hot cooked rice

1. Peel shrimp, and devein, if desired. Set aside.
2. Cut white ends from green onions; cut into 1-inch pieces, and set aside. Cut green onion tops into 1-inch pieces, and set aside.
3. Stir together 1 cup water and next 5 ingredients; set aside.
4. Heat oil in a large skillet or wok over medium-high heat 2 minutes. Add shrimp, and stir-fry 3 minutes. Remove shrimp.
5. Add bell pepper and white ends of onions; stir-fry 2 minutes. Add green onion tops; stir-fry 1 minute. Add shrimp and soy sauce mixture; bring to a boil, and cook, stirring constantly, 1 minute or until thickened. Stir in pecans and sesame oil. Serve over hot cooked rice.

Creamy Shrimp-and-Scallops Casserole

MAKES 8 SERVINGS
PREP: 25 MIN., BAKE: 19 MIN., COOK: 15 MIN., STAND: 10 MIN.

16 frozen phyllo pastry sheets, thawed
Vegetable cooking spray
2½ pounds unpeeled, medium-size fresh shrimp
2 (10-ounce) packages frozen chopped spinach, thawed
5 tablespoons butter, divided
2 garlic cloves, minced
1 pound fresh bay scallops
1 (8-ounce) package cream cheese, softened
1 (8-ounce) container sour cream
⅓ cup shredded Parmesan cheese
1 teaspoon salt
½ teaspoon ground red pepper
¼ cup all-purpose flour
2 cups half-and-half

1. Cut phyllo sheets into 13- x 9-inch rectangles; reserve half, keeping covered with a damp towel to prevent drying out. Stack remaining 8 sheets in a lightly greased 13- x 9-inch baking dish, lightly coating each sheet with cooking spray.
2. Bake on lowest oven rack at 400° for 5 minutes or until lightly browned, and set aside.
3. Peel shrimp, and devein, if desired.
4. Drain spinach well, pressing between paper towels.
5. Melt 1 tablespoon butter in a large skillet over medium heat; add garlic, and sauté 2 minutes. Add shrimp and scallops; cook 5 minutes or just until shrimp turn pink. Stir in cream cheese and next 4 ingredients until blended; remove from heat. Stir in spinach.
6. Melt remaining ¼ cup butter in a large saucepan over medium heat. Add flour, whisking constantly; cook, whisking constantly, 1 minute. Gradually add 2 cups half-and-half; cook, whisking constantly, 3 minutes or until mixture is thickened. Stir flour mixture into shrimp mixture. Spoon into prepared baking dish.
7. Stack reserved phyllo sheets, coating each with cooking spray. Roll up, jelly-roll fashion, starting at long end, and cut into ¼-inch slices. Unroll each piece, and twist; arrange twists in a diamond pattern over casserole.
8. Bake casserole at 400° for 14 minutes or until golden. Let stand 10 minutes.

Crab Cakes With Sweet White
Corn-and-Tomato Relish

Crab Cakes With Sweet White Corn-and-Tomato Relish

These crab cakes caught our attention with the colorful relish. Seasonal fresh corn and tomatoes make this accompaniment irresistible.

MAKES 8 SERVINGS

PREP: 20 MIN., COOK: 8 MIN. PER BATCH

6 tablespoons butter, divided
1 small sweet onion, chopped
2 garlic cloves, minced
1 pound fresh lump crabmeat, drained
3 cups soft breadcrumbs, divided
¼ cup mayonnaise
1 large egg, lightly beaten
2 tablespoons chopped fresh parsley
1 tablespoon Dijon mustard
1 tablespoon Worcestershire sauce
¼ teaspoon salt
¼ teaspoon pepper
¼ teaspoon hot sauce
1 teaspoon lemon juice
Sweet White Corn-and-Tomato Relish

1. Melt 2 tablespoons butter in a large skillet over medium heat; add onion and garlic, and sauté until tender. Remove from heat; stir in crabmeat, 2 cups breadcrumbs, and next 9 ingredients. Shape mixture into 8 patties; dredge in remaining 1 cup breadcrumbs.
2. Melt 2 tablespoons butter in a large skillet over medium-high heat; cook 4 crab cakes 3 to 4 minutes on each side or until golden. Drain on paper towels. Repeat procedure with remaining 2 tablespoons butter and crab cakes. Serve immediately with Sweet White Corn-and-Tomato Relish, or cover and chill up to 4 hours.

Sweet White Corn-and-Tomato Relish:

MAKES 3 CUPS

PREP: 15 MIN., COOK: 1 MIN., CHILL: 3 HRS.

4 ears fresh sweet white corn
2 large tomatoes, peeled and chopped
3 green onions, sliced
2 tablespoons lemon juice
1 tablespoon olive oil
½ teaspoon salt
½ teaspoon pepper
¼ teaspoon garlic salt
⅛ teaspoon hot sauce

1. Cook corn in boiling water to cover 1 minute; drain and cool. Cut kernels from cobs.
2. Stir together corn, tomatoes, and remaining ingredients; cover and chill 3 hours.
Note: For sweet white corn, we used Silver Queen.

The Best of Southern Living p2

Breads

p68 Refrigerator Yeast Rolls
p71 Caramel Sticky Buns
p71 Cheese Snack Bread

Fish & Shellfish
   Fish
p76 Potato Crusted Catfish & Chips
p78 Grilled Snapper
p79 Greek Snapper
p79 Heavenly Broiled Grouper
p79 Grouper Mediterranean
p81 Swordfish Steaks with Basil Butter
p81 Grilled Fresh Tuna
p81 Tuna Noodle Casserole

Crab-Stuffed Potatoes

MAKES 4 SERVINGS
PREP: 1 HR., 15 MIN.; BAKE: 15 MIN.

4 large baking potatoes, baked
½ cup butter or margarine
½ cup whipping cream
2 cups fresh crabmeat, drained and flaked
1 cup (4 ounces) shredded Cheddar cheese
1 tablespoon grated onion
1½ teaspoons salt
Paprika

1. Cut a 1-inch-wide strip lengthwise from the top of each baked potato. Carefully scoop out the pulp, leaving shells intact.
2. Mash pulp with butter and whipping cream; stir in crabmeat and next 3 ingredients. Spoon evenly into shells, and place on a baking sheet. Sprinkle with paprika.
3. Bake stuffed potatoes at 425° for 15 minutes.

Mussels Steamed in White Wine

You'll need about a half bottle of wine for this dish. Chill and serve remaining wine with the mussels and some crusty French bread.

MAKES 2 TO 3 SERVINGS
PREP: 8 MIN., COOK: 12 MIN.

2 pounds raw mussels in shell
2 garlic cloves, minced
1 large shallot, minced
6 fresh thyme sprigs
2 bay leaves
½ teaspoon freshly ground pepper
2 tablespoons olive oil
1½ cups dry white wine
1 tablespoon chopped fresh Italian parsley
½ teaspoon salt
2 tablespoons butter

1. Scrub mussels with a brush; remove beards. Discard cracked or heavy mussels (they're filled with sand), or opened mussels that won't close when tapped.
2. Sauté garlic and next 4 ingredients in hot oil in a Dutch oven over medium heat 2 minutes. Add mussels; increase heat to high. Cover and cook 1 minute, shaking Dutch oven several times. Add wine; cover and cook 1 to 2 minutes or until mussels open, shaking pan several times. Transfer mussels to a serving dish with a slotted spoon, discarding any unopened mussels. Cover and keep warm.
3. Pour remaining liquid in Dutch oven through a strainer into a skillet, discarding solids. Bring to a boil. Add parsley and salt; cook 2 minutes. Remove from heat, and whisk in butter. Pour over mussels. Serve immediately.

Oyster Fritters

A rémoulade or cocktail sauce complements these tasty fritters.

MAKES 4 SERVINGS
PREP: 8 MIN., FRY: 3 MIN. PER BATCH

1 cup all-purpose flour
1 teaspoon salt
⅛ teaspoon ground red pepper
⅔ cup water
2 tablespoons butter or margarine, melted
1 large egg, separated
Vegetable oil
3 (8-ounce) containers Select oysters, rinsed and
   drained

1. Combine flour, salt, and pepper in a medium bowl. Combine water, butter, and egg yolk in a small bowl, beating well with a fork. Gradually add egg mixture to dry ingredients, stirring until blended. Beat egg white until soft peaks form; fold into batter.
2. Pour oil to a depth of 2 to 3 inches into a Dutch oven; heat to 375°. Dip oysters in batter; fry in batches in hot oil 2 to 3 minutes or until golden, turning once. Drain on paper towels. Serve immediately.

Crawfish Pasta
Casserole

Crawfish Pasta Casserole

The heat level of the jalapeño peppers will vary according to the season.

MAKES 6 SERVINGS
PREP: 15 MIN., COOK: 30 MIN., BAKE: 20 MIN.

7 ounces medium egg noodles, uncooked
2 tablespoons butter or margarine
1 large green bell pepper, chopped
1 large onion, chopped
1 celery rib, chopped
2 jalapeño peppers, seeded and minced
4 garlic cloves, minced
2 tablespoons all-purpose flour
1 cup half-and-half
1 (16-ounce) loaf pasteurized prepared cheese
    product, cubed
1 pound frozen, peeled, cooked crawfish tails,
    thawed and drained
2 tablespoons chopped fresh parsley
¼ cup freshly shredded Parmesan cheese
1 cup round buttery cracker crumbs
2 tablespoons butter or margarine, melted

1. Cook pasta according to package directions. Drain pasta, and set aside.
2. Melt 2 tablespoons butter in a Dutch oven over medium heat. Add bell pepper and next 4 ingredients; cook 10 minutes or until tender. Gradually add flour, stirring until well blended, and cook 1 minute. Gradually add half-and-half, stirring until smooth. Add cheese cubes, crawfish, and parsley; reduce heat to medium-low, and cook 3 minutes or until cheese melts, stirring constantly. Stir together pasta and crawfish mixture in a lightly greased 11- x 7-inch baking dish.
3. Combine Parmesan cheese, cracker crumbs, and 2 tablespoons melted butter in a small bowl. Sprinkle over casserole.
4. Bake at 350°, uncovered, for 20 minutes or until casserole is thoroughly heated.

Crawfish Étouffée

People in the South love their crawfish. Other parts of the country may refer to crawfish as "crayfish" or "crawdads."

MAKES 4 TO 6 SERVINGS
PREP: 35 MIN., COOK: 30 MIN.

¼ cup butter or margarine
1 medium onion, chopped
2 celery ribs, chopped
1 medium-size green bell pepper, chopped
4 garlic cloves, minced
1 large shallot, chopped
¼ cup all-purpose flour
1 teaspoon salt
½ to 1 teaspoon ground red pepper
1 (14-ounce) can chicken broth
¼ cup chopped fresh parsley
¼ cup chopped fresh chives
2 pounds cooked, peeled crawfish tails*
Hot cooked rice
Garnishes: chopped fresh chives, ground red pepper

1. Melt butter in a large Dutch oven over medium-high heat. Add onion and next 4 ingredients; sauté 5 minutes or until tender. Add flour, salt, and red pepper; cook, stirring constantly, until caramel colored (about 10 minutes). Add broth, parsley, and chives; cook, stirring constantly, 5 minutes or until thick and bubbly. Stir in crawfish; cook 5 minutes or until thoroughly heated. Serve with rice. Garnish, if desired.
*You can substitute 2 pounds frozen cooked crawfish tails, thawed and drained, for the fresh crawfish, if desired.

meats

Pork Fillets With Dark Cherry
Sauce, page 102

Prime Rib With Spicy Horseradish Sauce

During cooking, rock salt's protective covering makes for a juicy and perfectly seasoned beef dish. The salt is brushed off after baking.

MAKES 6 TO 8 SERVINGS
PREP: 15 MIN.; BAKE: 1 HR., 12 MIN.; STAND: 30 MIN.

1 (6-pound) boneless beef rib roast
3 garlic cloves, minced
2 tablespoons coarsely ground pepper
1 tablespoon Worcestershire sauce
2 (4-pound) packages rock salt
½ cup water
Spicy Horseradish Sauce

1. Rub roast on all sides with minced garlic, coarsely ground pepper, and Worcestershire sauce.
2. Pour salt to a depth of ½ inch into a disposable aluminum roasting pan; place roast in center of pan. Add remaining salt; sprinkle with ½ cup water.
3. Bake at 500° for 12 minutes per pound or until a meat thermometer inserted into thickest portion registers 145° (medium-rare) or to desired degree of doneness. (Use a meat thermometer for best results.) Let stand 10 minutes. Crack salt with a hammer; remove roast, and brush away salt. Let roast stand 20 minutes. Serve roast with Spicy Horseradish Sauce.

Spicy Horseradish Sauce:

MAKES ABOUT 1 CUP
PREP: 5 MIN., CHILL: 1 HR.

⅔ cup reduced-fat sour cream
3 tablespoons prepared horseradish
2 tablespoons light mayonnaise
1 tablespoon white wine vinegar
1 teaspoon dry mustard
¼ teaspoon salt
¼ teaspoon ground red pepper

1. Stir together all ingredients in a small bowl. Chill 1 hour.
Note: This sauce is also delicious served with pork or steamed shrimp, as a sandwich spread, on baked potatoes, or as a dip for chips or raw vegetables.

Beef Tenderloin With Henry Bain Sauce

Henry Bain Sauce originated with the maître d' at the Pendennis Club in Louisville. The sauce yields a lot, and it freezes well.

MAKES 10 TO 12 SERVINGS
PREP: 10 MIN., CHILL: 2 HRS., BAKE: 35 MIN., STAND: 15 MIN.

1 (8-ounce) jar chutney
1 (14-ounce) bottle ketchup
1 (12-ounce) bottle chili sauce
1 (11-ounce) bottle steak sauce
1 (10-ounce) bottle Worcestershire sauce
1 teaspoon hot sauce
¼ cup butter or margarine, softened
2 teaspoons salt
1 teaspoon freshly ground pepper
1 (4½- to 5-pound) beef tenderloin, trimmed

1. Process chutney in a blender or food processor until smooth. Add ketchup, chili sauce, steak sauce, Worcestershire sauce, and hot sauce; process until blended. Chill sauce at least 2 hours.
2. Stir together butter, salt, and pepper; rub over tenderloin. Place on a lightly greased rack in a jellyroll pan. Fold under 4 to 6 inches of narrow end of tenderloin to fit onto rack.
3. Bake at 500° for 30 to 35 minutes or to desired degree of doneness. Let stand 15 minutes before serving. Serve tenderloin with chilled sauce.
Note: For testing purposes only, we used Major Grey's Chutney and A.1. Steak Sauce.

Cajun Grilled Tenderloin With Mustard-Horseradish Cream

We chose to turn this luxurious entrée into an appetizer by thinly slicing the tenderloin and serving it on cocktail buns.

MAKES 24 APPETIZER SERVINGS OR 8 ENTRÉE SERVINGS
PREP: 15 MIN., GRILL: 35 MIN., OTHER: 2 HRS.

1 (3½-pound) beef tenderloin
¼ cup hot sauce
¼ cup teriyaki sauce
2 tablespoons Worcestershire sauce
1 tablespoon Creole seasoning
Vegetable cooking spray
Cocktail buns
Mustard-Horseradish Cream
Arugula (optional)

1. Place tenderloin in a large heavy-duty zip-top plastic bag. Combine hot sauce and next 3 ingredients. Pour over tenderloin. Seal bag; marinate in refrigerator 1½ hours, turning occasionally.
2. Remove tenderloin from marinade, discarding marinade.
3. Prepare a hot fire by piling charcoal on 1 side of grill, leaving other side empty. Coat food rack with cooking spray; place rack on grill. Place tenderloin on rack over

unlit side. Grill, covered with grill lid, 30 to 40 minutes or until meat thermometer inserted into thickest part of tenderloin registers 145° (medium-rare) or 160° (medium). Let stand at least 10 minutes before slicing. Serve on buns with Mustard-Horseradish Cream and, if desired, arugula.

Mustard-Horseradish Cream:

MAKES 2½ CUPS
PREP: 10 MIN., CHILL: 30 MIN.

¼ cup prepared horseradish
1 cup whipping cream
¼ cup Dijon mustard
1 tablespoon fresh lemon juice

1. Place horseradish in a fine wire-mesh strainer; press with back of a spoon against sides of strainer to squeeze out juice. Discard juice. Set horseradish aside.
2. Beat whipping cream at high speed with an electric mixer until soft peaks form. Fold in horseradish, mustard, and lemon juice. Cover and chill thoroughly.

Beef Fillets With Green
Peppercorn Sauce

Beef Fillets With
Green Peppercorn Sauce

MAKES 4 SERVINGS
PREP: 15 MIN., COOK: 40 MIN.

4 (8-ounce) beef tenderloin fillets
1/2 teaspoon salt
1/2 teaspoon pepper
1 teaspoon butter or margarine
1 teaspoon olive oil
2 cups Marsala wine
1 cup fat-free, low-sodium chicken broth
20 green peppercorns
1 (5-ounce) can fat-free evaporated milk
1/4 teaspoon Dijon mustard
Garnish: Italian parsley sprigs

1. Sprinkle beef fillets evenly with salt and pepper.
2. Melt butter and olive oil in a large nonstick skillet over medium-high heat. Add fillets, and cook 6 minutes on each side or to desired degree of doneness. Remove fillets from skillet, and keep warm.
3. Add wine, broth, and peppercorns to skillet; cook 20 minutes or until liquid is reduced by half. Stir in evaporated milk and mustard; cook over low heat 5 to 7 minutes or until slightly thickened. Return fillets to skillet, and serve warm. Garnish, if desired.

TENDERLOIN TIDBITS

There are many reasons to appreciate tenderloin. Carved from an area where there's little fat surrounding or running through the meat, this succulent selection is leaner than many other choices. It's pricey, but the nutritional bonus and great flavor make it worth the cost. Remember to keep an eye on cooking time—you don't want to dry out this delicacy.

Spicy Beef Fillets

MAKES 6 SERVINGS
PREP: 10 MIN., COOK: 20 MIN.

6 (6-ounce) beef tenderloin fillets (1 1/2 inches thick)
1/4 teaspoon salt
1/4 teaspoon pepper
1/4 cup butter or margarine
2 garlic cloves, pressed
2 tablespoons all-purpose flour
1 cup beef broth
1 cup dry red wine*
1/4 cup bourbon*
2 tablespoons Dijon mustard
1 teaspoon Worcestershire sauce

1. Sprinkle steaks with salt and pepper.
2. Melt butter in a large skillet over medium heat. Add steaks; cook 5 to 7 minutes on each side or to desired degree of doneness. Remove steaks from skillet, and keep warm.
3. Add garlic and flour to pan drippings; cook over medium heat, stirring constantly, 1 minute.
4. Gradually add beef broth, red wine, and bourbon, stirring to loosen particles from bottom; bring to a boil. Stir in Dijon mustard and Worcestershire sauce; reduce heat, and simmer 5 minutes. Top steaks with sauce.
*1 1/4 cups cranberry juice may be substituted for wine and bourbon.

Beef Fillets With Stilton-Portobello Sauce

If you like blue cheese, you'll love this simple entrée.

MAKES 6 SERVINGS
PREP: 10 MIN., COOK: 20 MIN.

6 (6-ounce) beef tenderloin fillets
2 teaspoons chopped fresh tarragon
1/2 teaspoon freshly ground pepper
5 tablespoons butter or margarine, divided
8 ounces portobello mushroom caps, sliced
1/3 cup dry red wine*
1/2 cup sour cream
3 ounces Stilton or blue cheese, crumbled and
    divided

1. Rub fillets with tarragon and pepper. Melt 2 table-spoons butter in a large skillet over medium-high heat. Cook fillets 4 to 5 minutes on each side or to desired degree of doneness. Remove fillets from skillet, and keep warm.
2. Melt remaining 3 tablespoons butter in skillet. Add mushrooms, and sauté 3 to 4 minutes or until tender. Add wine, and cook 1 to 2 minutes, stirring to loosen particles from bottom of skillet. Stir in sour cream. Sprinkle 1/4 cup cheese into sauce, stirring until melted.
3. Arrange fillets on a serving platter, and drizzle with sauce. Sprinkle with remaining cheese.
*Beef broth may be substituted for dry red wine.

Stuffed Beef Tenderloin

Succulent lobster tail meat nestles in the center of each tenderloin slice. A red wine and shallot sauce caps the steak and lobster duo nicely.

MAKES 6 TO 8 SERVINGS
PREP: 30 MIN., BAKE: 45 MIN., CHILL: 2 HRS., COOK: 25 MIN.

2 tablespoons juniper berries
1/4 cup chopped fresh rosemary
1/4 cup chopped fresh thyme
2 garlic cloves
10 black peppercorns
1 (4 1/2-pound) beef tenderloin, trimmed
3 (4-ounce) fresh or frozen lobster tails, thawed
1/4 cup butter or margarine, melted
2 tablespoons lemon juice
2 teaspoons chopped fresh thyme
1/2 teaspoon ground red pepper
6 thick bacon slices
1/2 cup butter or margarine
3 large shallots, chopped
1 cup dry red wine or beef broth

1. Bake berries in a shallow pan at 400° for 5 minutes.
2. Pulse berries, rosemary, and next 3 ingredients in a food processor 6 to 7 times. Spread mixture over beef. Cover and chill 1 to 2 hours.
3. Cut shell of lobster tail segments lengthwise on the top and underside. Pry open tail segments, and remove meat.
4. Make a lengthwise cut down center of tenderloin, cutting to, but not through, bottom; press to flatten. Arrange lobster tails down center of tenderloin. Drizzle lobster with 1/4 cup melted butter; sprinkle with lemon juice, 2 teaspoons thyme, and red pepper. Fold beef over lobster; tie with string at 1-inch intervals. Place in a roasting pan.
5. Bake at 425° for 30 minutes. Arrange bacon slices over beef, and bake 10 more minutes or until a meat thermometer inserted into thickest portion of beef registers 145° (medium-rare).
6. Melt 1/2 cup butter in a skillet over medium heat; add chopped shallots, and sauté until tender. Stir in wine; bring to a boil. Reduce heat, and simmer 20 minutes or until reduced to 1/2 cup. Slice beef; serve with wine sauce.
Note: Juniper berries can be found in the spice section of most supermarkets.

Peppery-Garlic Grilled Steaks

MAKES 4 SERVINGS
PREP: 15 MIN., CHILL: 2 HRS., GRILL: 12 MIN.

4 garlic cloves
2 tablespoons fresh lemon juice
2 tablespoons olive oil
1 tablespoon dried thyme
2 1/2 teaspoons freshly ground black pepper
1 1/2 teaspoons salt
1 1/2 teaspoons ground red pepper
4 (6- to 8-ounce) boneless beef chuck-eye steaks

1. Process garlic cloves, lemon juice, and next 5 ingredients in a food processor or blender until smooth, stopping to scrape down sides. Rub garlic mixture evenly over steaks, and place in a shallow dish or a large zip-top plastic freezer bag. Cover or seal, and chill at least 2 hours.
2. Grill steaks, covered with grill lid, over high heat (400° to 500°) 6 minutes on each side or to desired degree of doneness.

Peppered Rib-eye Steaks

A robust herb rub cloaks these steaks before grilling. The rub tastes great on pork and lamb, too.

MAKES 6 SERVINGS
PREP: 15 MIN., CHILL: 1 HR., GRILL: 20 MIN.

2 1/2 teaspoons freshly ground black pepper
1 tablespoon dried thyme
1 1/2 teaspoons salt
4 1/2 teaspoons garlic powder
1 1/2 teaspoons lemon pepper
1 1/2 teaspoons ground red pepper
1 1/2 teaspoons dried parsley flakes
6 (1 1/2-inch-thick) rib-eye steaks
3 tablespoons olive oil

1. Combine first 7 ingredients. Brush steaks with olive oil; rub with pepper mixture. Cover and chill 1 hour.
2. Grill, covered with grill lid, over medium-high heat (350° to 400°) 8 to 10 minutes on each side or to desired degree of doneness.

Peppery-Garlic
Grilled Steaks

Grilled Chile-Rubbed Steaks With Tex-Mex Sauce

This Southwestern combo is fancy enough for company and quick enough for a weeknight.

MAKES 4 SERVINGS
PREP: 5 MIN., GRILL: 10 MIN.

1 teaspoon chili powder
½ teaspoon ground cumin
½ teaspoon salt
¼ teaspoon pepper
4 (1-inch-thick) rib-eye steaks
Tex-Mex Sauce

1. Combine first 4 ingredients; rub seasoning mixture on both sides of steaks.
2. Grill steaks, covered with grill lid, over high heat (400° to 500°) 5 minutes on each side or to desired degree of doneness. Serve steaks with Tex-Mex Sauce.

Tex-Mex Sauce:

This sauce also dresses up grilled pork tenderloin or chicken.

MAKES ABOUT 1 CUP
PREP: 10 MIN., COOK: 11 MIN.

1 small onion, chopped
1 teaspoon vegetable oil
3 garlic cloves, minced
¾ teaspoon chili powder
¼ teaspoon ground cumin
1 (14.5-ounce) can petite diced tomatoes, undrained
½ teaspoon sugar
¼ teaspoon salt
1½ tablespoons fresh lime juice
3 tablespoons vegetable oil
2 tablespoons chopped fresh cilantro

1. Sauté chopped onion in 1 teaspoon hot oil 5 minutes or until tender. Add minced garlic, chili powder, and ground cumin; sauté 1 minute. Add petite diced tomatoes, sugar, and salt; simmer 5 minutes or until warm.
2. Process tomato mixture in a blender or food processor 20 seconds or until smooth, stopping to scrape down sides. Stir in fresh lime juice, 3 tablespoons oil, and chopped fresh cilantro.

Pot Roast With Mushroom Gravy

Substitute less expensive chuck roast for rump roast, if desired.

MAKES 8 TO 10 SERVINGS
PREP: 25 MIN., COOK: 4 HRS.

1 (3½-pound) boneless beef rump roast, trimmed
2 large garlic cloves, thinly sliced
1 teaspoon salt
1 teaspoon garlic salt
1 teaspoon pepper
¼ cup all-purpose flour
3 tablespoons vegetable oil
2 cups brewed coffee
1 (10¾-ounce) can cream of mushroom soup
1 tablespoon Worcestershire sauce
1 large onion, sliced
3 tablespoons cornstarch
3 tablespoons cold water

1. Cut slits in roast, using a sharp knife; push a garlic slice into each slit. Sprinkle roast with salts and pepper; lightly dredge in flour, patting off excess.
2. Brown roast on all sides in hot oil over medium-high heat in a large Dutch oven. Stir together coffee, soup, and Worcestershire sauce; pour over roast. Top with onion slices. Reduce heat, cover, and simmer 3 hours and 40 minutes or until tender. Transfer roast to a serving platter, reserving drippings in Dutch oven; keep roast warm.
3. Combine cornstarch and 3 tablespoons cold water; stir into drippings. Bring mixture to a boil, and cook, stirring constantly, 1 minute or until thickened. Pour gravy over roast.

Cowboy Pot Roast

Cowboy Pot Roast

Browning the meat before slow-cooking it enhances both the appearance and flavor.

MAKES 6 SERVINGS
PREP: 15 MIN.; COOK: 6 HRS., 30 MIN.

1 ½ teaspoons salt, divided
1 ½ teaspoons black pepper, divided
1 (14.5-ounce) can petite-cut diced tomatoes, drained
1 (10-ounce) can diced tomatoes and green chiles, undrained
1 onion, cut into 8 wedges
1 tablespoon chili powder
1 (2 ½- to 3-pound) eye-of-round roast, trimmed
2 tablespoons vegetable oil
2 (16-ounce) cans pinto beans, drained
1 (15-ounce) can black beans, drained
Pickled jalapeño pepper slices (optional)

1. Combine 1 teaspoon salt, 1 teaspoon pepper, and next 4 ingredients in a medium bowl.

2. Sprinkle roast evenly with remaining ½ teaspoon salt and ½ teaspoon pepper. Brown roast on all sides in hot oil in a large Dutch oven over medium-high heat. Transfer roast to a 5½-quart slow cooker. Pour tomato mixture over roast.

3. Cover and cook on HIGH 5 to 6 hours or until meat shreds easily with a fork.

4. Remove roast from slow cooker, and cut into large chunks; keep meat warm.

5. Skim fat from juices in slow cooker. Mash 1½ cans (about 2¾ cups) pinto beans; add to slow cooker, and stir until combined. Stir in black beans and remaining ½ can pinto beans. Add meat back to slow cooker; cover and cook on HIGH an additional 20 to 25 minutes. Serve with jalapeño pepper slices, if desired.

Eye-of-Round Roast
WIth Garlic Potatoes

Eye-of-Round Roast With Garlic Potatoes

Dress up this succulent roast with garnishes for a fancy dinner. Or serve it at your next family feast.

MAKES 4 SERVINGS
PREP: 15 MIN., CHILL: 8 HRS., BAKE: 45 MIN., STAND: 15 MIN.

1 (4½-pound) eye-of-round roast
1 (4-ounce) jar Chinese sweet-hot mustard
3 tablespoons olive oil
2 garlic cloves, pressed
2 teaspoons lite soy sauce
1 teaspoon Worcestershire sauce
Garlic Potatoes, uncooked
Garnishes: fresh rosemary sprigs, fresh sage sprigs

1. Place eye-of-round roast on an 18- x 11-inch piece of heavy-duty aluminum foil.
2. Stir together mustard and next 4 ingredients; spread over roast. Fold foil over roast to seal. Place in a shallow roasting pan, and chill for at least 8 hours.
3. Remove roast from foil; place in roasting pan.
4. Bake, covered, at 450° for 20 minutes. Arrange uncooked Garlic Potatoes around roast, and bake, uncovered, 25 more minutes or until potatoes are tender and roast is done. Remove from oven; cover and let stand 15 minutes before slicing. Garnish with fresh rosemary and sage, if desired.

Garlic Potatoes:

MAKES 4 SERVINGS
PREP: 10 MIN.

4 medium potatoes, cut into 8 wedges
2 tablespoons olive oil
2 garlic cloves, pressed
1 teaspoon salt
½ teaspoon pepper

1. Toss together all ingredients. Bake with roast as directed above.

Italian Pot Roast

Chuck roast is one of the most economical cuts of beef for pot roast, but it's a high-fat choice. Substitute eye-of-round (which is more expensive) or English shoulder roast for a low-fat option. The slow cooker simmers any of these roasts to be nice and tender.

MAKES 6 SERVINGS
PREP: 15 MIN.; COOK: 6 HRS., 40 MIN.

1 (8-ounce) package sliced fresh mushrooms
1 large onion, halved and sliced
1 (2½- to 3-pound) boneless chuck roast, trimmed
1 teaspoon pepper
2 tablespoons olive oil
1 (1-ounce) envelope dry onion soup mix
1 (14-ounce) can beef broth
1 (8-ounce) can tomato sauce
1 teaspoon dried Italian seasoning
3 tablespoons tomato paste
2 tablespoons cornstarch
2 tablespoons water
Hot cooked egg noodles

1. Place mushrooms and onion in the bottom of a 5½-quart slow cooker.
2. Sprinkle roast evenly with pepper. Brown roast on all sides in hot oil in a large Dutch oven over medium-high heat. Place roast on top of mushrooms and onion in slow cooker. Sprinkle onion soup mix evenly over roast. Pour beef broth and tomato sauce over roast.
3. Cover and cook on HIGH 5 to 6 hours or until meat shreds easily with a fork.
4. Remove roast from slow cooker, and cut into large chunks; keep warm.
5. Skim fat from juices in slow cooker; stir in dried Italian seasoning and tomato paste. Stir together cornstarch and 2 tablespoons water in a small bowl until smooth; add to juices in slow cooker, stirring until blended. Cover and cook on HIGH 20 to 30 more minutes or until mixture is thickened. Add roast pieces back to slow cooker. Cover and cook until thoroughly heated. Serve over hot cooked egg noodles.

Texas Grilled Sirloin
With Serrano Chile Salsa
MAKES 8 SERVINGS
PREP: 10 MIN., CHILL: 8 HRS., GRILL: 12 MIN.

2 pounds lean boneless top sirloin steak, trimmed
½ cup fresh lime juice
¼ cup chopped fresh oregano
2 tablespoons chopped fresh rosemary
2 teaspoons pepper
2 garlic cloves, pressed
Serrano Chile Salsa
Flour tortillas

1. Combine steak and next 5 ingredients in a large zip-top freezer bag; seal and shake well. Chill at least 8 hours, turning occasionally.
2. Remove steak from marinade, discarding marinade. Grill steak, covered with grill lid, over medium-high heat (350° to 400°) 5 to 6 minutes on each side or to desired degree of doneness. Cut diagonally across the grain into thin slices. Serve with Serrano Chile Salsa and flour tortillas.

Serrano Chile Salsa:
To make a milder salsa, use 2 or 3 serrano chile peppers. This salsa is also great served as a dip with tortilla chips.

MAKES 2 CUPS
PREP: 15 MIN., CHILL: 1 HR.

6 serrano chile peppers, diced
1 pound plum tomatoes, diced
2 tablespoons diced red onion
¼ cup orange juice
2 tablespoons diced yellow or red bell pepper
2 tablespoons minced fresh cilantro
1 tablespoon rice vinegar
½ teaspoon salt
½ teaspoon sugar

1. Combine all ingredients; cover and chill 1 hour.

Peppery Grilled Sirloin
MAKES 4 SERVINGS
PREP: 15 MIN.; CHILL: 2 HRS., 30 MIN.; GRILL: 14 MIN.

¼ cup olive oil
4½ tablespoons fresh lime juice (about 1 to 2 limes)
3 tablespoons soy sauce
1 teaspoon sugar
1 teaspoon garlic powder
1 teaspoon ground ginger
½ teaspoon crushed red pepper flakes
4 (¾-inch-thick) top sirloin steaks
½ teaspoon salt

1. Combine first 7 ingredients in a large shallow dish or zip-top freezer bag; add steaks. Cover or seal, and chill at least 2½ hours, turning occasionally.
2. Remove steaks, reserving marinade. Bring marinade to a boil in a small saucepan; boil 1 minute. Sprinkle steaks with salt.
3. Grill, covered with grill lid, over medium-high heat (350° to 400°), basting often with reserved marinade, 7 minutes on each side or to desired degree of doneness. Discard any excess marinade.

SHOPPING FOR BEEF

Beef should have a cherry red or—if it's vacuum-packed—a dark purplish-red color; avoid meat with gray or brown blotches. The visible fat should be very white. Seek a moist surface and a fresh aroma. Avoid packaged meat with a lot of liquid in the tray-that's a sign that the meat has been frozen and has thawed.

Chicken-fried Steak

Chicken-fried Steak

MAKES 4 SERVINGS
PREP: 10 MIN., COOK: 30 MIN.

¼ teaspoon salt
¼ teaspoon ground black pepper
4 (4-ounce) cube steaks
38 saltine crackers (1 sleeve), crushed
1¼ cups all-purpose flour, divided
½ teaspoon baking powder
2 teaspoons salt, divided
1½ teaspoons ground black pepper, divided
½ teaspoon ground red pepper
4¾ cups milk, divided
2 large eggs
3½ cups peanut oil
Mashed Potatoes (optional), see page 265

1. Sprinkle salt and pepper evenly over steaks. Set aside.
2. Combine cracker crumbs, 1 cup flour, baking powder, 1 teaspoon salt, ½ teaspoon black pepper, and red pepper.
3. Whisk together ¾ cup milk and eggs. Dredge steaks in cracker crumb mixture; dip in milk mixture, and dredge in cracker mixture again.
4. Pour oil into a 12-inch skillet; heat to 360°. (Do not use a nonstick skillet.) Fry steaks 10 minutes. Turn and fry 4 to 5 more minutes or until golden brown. Remove to a wire rack on a jellyroll pan. Keep steaks warm in a 225° oven. Carefully drain hot oil, reserving cooked bits and 1 tablespoon drippings in skillet.
5. Whisk together remaining ¼ cup flour, 1 teaspoon salt, 1 teaspoon black pepper, and 4 cups milk. Pour mixture into reserved drippings in skillet; cook over medium-high heat, whisking constantly, 10 to 12 minutes or until thickened. Serve gravy with steaks and mashed potatoes on page 265, if desired.

Orange-Kissed
Steak-and-Shrimp Kabobs

Orange-Kissed Steak-and-Shrimp Kabobs

MAKES 4 SERVINGS

PREP: 30 MIN., CHILL: 1 HR., GRILL: 20 MIN., COOK: 2 MIN.

16 unpeeled, jumbo fresh shrimp (about 9 ounces)
1½ pounds beef tenderloin fillets, cut into 1½-inch cubes
½ cup dry sherry
½ cup olive oil
1 tablespoon grated orange rind
½ cup fresh orange juice
¼ cup soy sauce
4 garlic cloves, minced
2 tablespoons grated fresh ginger
½ teaspoon dried crushed red pepper
1 (10-ounce) package gourmet mixed salad greens

1. Peel shrimp, leaving tails on, and devein, if desired. Place shrimp and beef in a large zip-top freezer bag.
2. Whisk together sherry and next 7 ingredients. Add to shrimp mixture; seal and chill 1 hour, turning occasionally.
3. Remove meat and shrimp from marinade, reserving marinade. Thread 4 shrimp onto 4 (6-inch) skewers. Repeat procedure with beef and additional skewers.
4. Grill beef, covered with grill lid, over medium-high heat (350° to 400°) 8 minutes on each side or to desired degree of doneness. Grill shrimp, covered with grill lid, over medium-high heat (350° to 400°) 4 minutes or until shrimp turn pink.
5. Pour marinade mixture through a wire-mesh strainer into a small saucepan, discarding solids. Bring to a boil over medium-high heat, and boil for 1 minute. Serve kabobs over salad greens. Drizzle marinade on top of kabobs.
Note: Soak wooden skewers in some water for 30 minutes to keep them from burning while grilling.

Peppery Grilled Flank Steak

This recipe makes enough flank steak for two meals. On the first night, serve with steamed zucchini and grilled corn on the cob. Serve the remaining beef on Beef Salad Niçoise, page 207.

MAKES 6 SERVINGS

PREP: 10 MIN., CHILL: 8 HRS., GRILL: 16 MIN.

⅔ cup dry white wine
¼ cup olive oil
2½ tablespoons cracked black pepper
4 teaspoons sugar
2 garlic cloves, pressed
2 red bell peppers, cut into thin strips
2 yellow bell peppers, cut into thin strips
2 (1½-pound) flank steaks, trimmed
Tomato-Cheese Bread

1. Combine first 7 ingredients in a shallow dish or large zip-top freezer bag; add steaks. Cover or seal, and chill 8 hours, turning occasionally.
2. Remove steaks and pepper strips from marinade, discarding marinade. Place pepper strips in a grill basket.
3. Grill steaks and pepper strips, covered with grill lid, over high heat (400° to 500°) 8 minutes on each side or to desired degree of doneness. Cut 1 flank steak diagonally across the grain into thin strips (reserve remaining steak for Beef Salad Niçoise, page 207.) Serve sliced steak and pepper strips with Tomato-Cheese Bread.

Tomato-Cheese Bread:

MAKES 6 SERVINGS

PREP: 8 MIN., BROIL: 5 MIN.

1 (8-ounce) container soft cream cheese
¼ cup shredded Parmesan cheese
1 garlic clove, pressed
2 tablespoons chopped fresh basil
¼ teaspoon salt
⅛ teaspoon pepper
1 (16-ounce) French bread loaf
2 plum tomatoes, sliced

1. Microwave cream cheese in a 1-quart microwave-safe bowl at HIGH 20 seconds. Stir in Parmesan cheese and next 4 ingredients.
2. Cut bread in half lengthwise; spread cream cheese mixture over cut sides of bread. Top with tomato slices. Place on a baking sheet, cut sides up. Broil 5½ inches from heat 4 to 5 minutes. Cut into slices.

Honey-Mustard Grilled Flank Steak

Just brush on the marinade and grill—there's no waiting for this flavorful mixture to soak into the flank steak. Serve the steak with veggies, or turn it into fajitas as directed below.

MAKES 6 SERVINGS
PREP: 5 MIN., GRILL: 20 MIN., STAND: 5 MIN.

¼ cup Creole mustard
1 tablespoon olive oil
1 tablespoon honey
1 (1½-pound) flank steak
¾ teaspoon kosher salt
¼ teaspoon freshly ground pepper

1. Whisk together first 3 ingredients.
2. Brush mustard mixture evenly on both sides of steak; sprinkle with salt and pepper.
3. Grill steak, covered with grill lid, over medium-high heat (350° to 400°) 8 to 10 minutes on each side or to desired degree of doneness. Let stand 5 minutes; cut steak diagonally across the grain into thin strips.

Easy Beef Fajitas: Prepare and grill flank steak as directed, cutting steak diagonally across the grain into very thin strips. Divide steak strips, and serve with 6 (8-inch) flour tortillas, warmed; 1 cup shredded lettuce; 1 large tomato, chopped; 1 cup (4 ounces) shredded Cheddar cheese; and ½ cup sour cream.

Flank Steak

Try this Asian-inspired steak with sautéed mushrooms. You can either grill it outdoors or broil it indoors.

MAKES 6 SERVINGS
PREP: 10 MIN., CHILL: 8 HRS., GRILL: 20 MIN.

¼ cup firmly packed light brown sugar
¼ teaspoon freshly ground pepper
1 cup lite soy sauce
2 tablespoons sesame oil
1 tablespoon minced fresh ginger or ¼ teaspoon ground ginger
2 garlic cloves, minced
2 (1-pound) flank steaks

1. Combine first 6 ingredients in a large zip-top freezer bag, and add steak. Seal and chill at least 8 hours, turning bag occasionally.
2. Remove steaks from marinade, discarding marinade.
3. Grill, covered with grill lid, over medium-high heat (350° to 400°) 10 minutes on each side or to desired degree of doneness.
4. Cut steaks diagonally across the grain into thin strips.
Note: To broil steaks, place on a lightly greased rack in a broiler pan. Broil 5½ inches from heat 10 minutes on each side or to desired degree of doneness.

Molasses Flank Steak

MAKES 6 SERVINGS
PREP: 5 MIN., CHILL: 2 HRS., GRILL: 12 MIN.

½ cup molasses
¼ cup coarse-grained mustard
1 tablespoon olive oil
1 (1½-pound) flank steak
1 teaspoon salt
6 (8-inch) flour tortillas
1 cup shredded lettuce
1 large tomato, chopped
¾ cup (3 ounces) reduced-fat shredded Cheddar
   cheese
½ cup light sour cream

1. Whisk together molasses, mustard, and olive oil.
2. Place steak in a shallow dish or large zip-top freezer bag. Pour molasses mixture over steak, reserving ¼ cup for basting. Cover or seal, and chill 2 hours, turning occasionally. Remove meat from marinade, discarding marinade. Sprinkle evenly with salt.
3. Grill, covered with grill lid, over medium-high heat (350° to 400°) 6 minutes on each side or to desired degree of doneness, brushing often with reserved marinade. Cut steak diagonally across the grain into very thin strips.
4. Serve steak in tortillas with lettuce, tomato, Cheddar cheese, and sour cream.

Molasses Flank Steak

Italian Beef Stir-fry With Linguine

Italian Beef Stir-fry With Linguine

MAKES 4 SERVINGS
PREP: 15 MIN., CHILL: 30 MIN., COOK: 11 MIN.

1 pound flank steak
½ cup Italian dressing, divided
½ teaspoon salt
¾ teaspoon pepper
2 small zucchini, thinly sliced (about 2 cups)
2 garlic cloves, pressed
1 cup cherry tomato halves
1 (9-ounce) package refrigerated linguine, cooked
½ cup shredded Parmesan cheese

1. Place steak in a zip-top freezer bag; pour ¼ cup Italian dressing over steak. Seal bag; chill 30 minutes.
2. Remove steak from marinade; discard marinade. Place a large nonstick skillet coated with cooking spray over medium-high heat. Add steak, and cook 2 minutes on each side. Remove steak from skillet; sprinkle with salt and pepper, and set aside. Add zucchini and garlic to the skillet. Stir-fry 2 to 3 minutes or until crisp-tender.
3. Cut steak diagonally across the grain into thin slices. Add steak, tomatoes, and remaining ¼ cup Italian dressing to zucchini mixture; stir-fry 4 minutes or until thoroughly heated. Serve over pasta; sprinkle with cheese.

Taco Casserole

Measure chips after coarsely crushing.

MAKES 6 SERVINGS
PREP: 10 MIN., COOK: 10 MIN., BAKE: 25 MIN.

1 pound ground chuck
½ cup chopped onion
1 (1.25-ounce) package taco seasoning mix
1 (16-ounce) can chili beans, undrained
1 (8-ounce) can tomato sauce
2 cups (8 ounces) shredded colby cheese
5 cups coarsely crushed nacho cheese–flavored
    tortilla chips (about 9 ounces)

1. Brown ground beef and onion in a large skillet over medium heat. Stir until beef crumbles and onion is tender; drain.
2. Return meat mixture to skillet; stir in taco seasoning, beans, and tomato sauce. Layer half each of meat mixture, shredded cheese, and tortilla chips in a lightly greased 13- x 9-inch baking dish. Repeat procedure with remaining meat mixture, shredded cheese, and tortilla ships.
3. Bake, uncovered, at 350° for 25 minutes or until casserole is thoroughly heated.
Note: For testing purposes only, we used Bush's Best Chili Beans.

Pizza Casserole

Kids will love to dig into this noodle-filled casserole.

MAKES 6 SERVINGS
PREP: 20 MIN., COOK: 10 MIN., BAKE: 28 MIN.

8 ounces uncooked elbow macaroni
1 pound lean ground beef
1 large onion, chopped (1¾ cups)
1 green bell pepper, chopped (1 cup)
1 (14-ounce) jar pizza sauce
¾ teaspoon garlic salt
¼ teaspoon black pepper
½ teaspoon dried Italian seasoning
½ (3.5-ounce) package sliced hot and spicy
    pepperoni, chopped
1 cup (4 ounces) shredded mozzarella
    cheese

1. Cook pasta according to package directions. Drain pasta, and set aside.

2. Cook ground beef, chopped onion, and bell pepper, stirring constantly, in a Dutch oven over medium heat 10 minutes or until vegetables are tender.
3. Stir in macaroni, pizza sauce, and next 4 ingredients. Spoon mixture into a lightly greased 11- x 7-inch baking dish.
4. Bake, covered, at 350° for 20 minutes. Uncover; top with cheese, and bake 8 more minutes or until cheese melts.
Note: For testing purposes only, we used Ragu Pizza Quick Sauce and Hormel Hot and Spicy Pepperoni.

Beef, Bean, and Cornbread Casserole

Fix this fiery casserole when you're looking for something hearty.

MAKES 6 SERVINGS
PREP: 25 MIN., COOK: 20 MIN., BAKE: 30 MIN.

1 pound lean ground beef
1 cup chopped onion
2 garlic cloves, pressed
Vegetable cooking spray
2 (8-ounce) cans no-salt-added tomato sauce
2 (16-ounce) cans pinto beans, rinsed and drained
1 (4.5-ounce) can chopped green chiles, undrained
1 tablespoon chili powder
1½ teaspoons ground cumin
½ teaspoon dried oregano
1 (6-ounce) package cornbread mix

1. Cook first 3 ingredients in a large skillet coated with vegetable cooking spray over medium-high heat, stirring until beef crumbles and is no longer pink. Drain and pat with paper towels. Wipe drippings from skillet with a paper towel.
2. Return beef mixture to skillet. Stir in tomato sauce and next 5 ingredients. Cover and cook over medium-low heat 10 minutes. Pour mixture into a lightly greased 2-quart baking dish.
3. Prepare cornbread batter according to package directions using fat-free milk. Pour batter over beef mixture.
4. Bake, uncovered, at 400° for 30 minutes or until lightly browned.

Easy Skillet Beef 'n' Pasta

Easy Skillet Beef 'n' Pasta

MAKES 6 TO 8 SERVINGS
PREP: 10 MIN., COOK: 35 MIN.

2 pounds lean ground beef
3 cups water
8 ounces uncooked elbow macaroni
1 (26-ounce) jar pasta sauce
2 cups (8 ounces) shredded mozzarella
    cheese
1 cup (4 ounces) shredded Parmesan cheese
3 large green onions, chopped
1 (4½-ounce) can sliced ripe olives, drained

1. Cook ground beef in a large skillet over medium heat 8 minutes, stirring until it crumbles and is no longer pink; drain well, and return to skillet.
2. Stir in 3 cups water, and bring to a boil; stir in pasta. Reduce heat, cover, and simmer, stirring often, 15 to 18 minutes or until pasta is tender.
3. Stir in pasta sauce; sprinkle with half each of mozzarella cheese and Parmesan cheese. Sprinkle evenly with chopped green onions and olives; sprinkle with remaining mozzarella cheese and remaining Parmesan cheese. Cover and cook 4 to 5 minutes or until cheeses are melted.

Individual Meat Loaves

MAKES 6 SERVINGS
PREP: 20 MIN., BAKE: 1 HR.

2 pounds lean ground beef
1 tablespoon reduced-sodium Worcestershire sauce
½ teaspoon seasoned salt
½ teaspoon seasoned pepper
1 medium onion, minced
5 white bread slices, crusts removed
½ cup fat-free milk
¼ cup egg substitute
1½ cups soft breadcrumbs
Vegetable cooking spray
1 (12-ounce) bottle chili sauce
½ cup boiling water

1. Combine first 5 ingredients.
2. Cut bread into small pieces. Place bread, milk, and egg substitute in a large bowl. Beat at medium speed with an electric mixer until blended. Stir in meat mixture.
3. Shape mixture into 6 loaves; roll in breadcrumbs.
4. Arrange loaves on a foil-lined broiler rack or in a 13- x 9-inch pan coated with cooking spray. Spread chili sauce over loaves. Pour ½ cup boiling water into bottom of pan. Bake at 350° for 1 hour.

Meatball Lasagna

MAKES 8 SERVINGS
PREP: 15 MIN., BAKE: 1 HR., STAND: 15 MIN.

1 (15-ounce) container ricotta cheese
1 (8-ounce) container onion-and-chive flavored cream cheese, softened
¼ cup chopped fresh basil
½ teaspoon garlic salt
½ teaspoon seasoned pepper
1 large egg, lightly beaten
2 cups (8 ounces) shredded mozzarella cheese, divided
1 (3-ounce) package shredded Parmesan cheese, divided
2 (26-ounce) jars tomato-basil pasta sauce, divided
1 (16-ounce) package egg roll wrappers
60 to 64 frozen cooked Italian-style meatballs

1. Stir together first 6 ingredients until blended. Stir in ½ cup mozzarella cheese and ½ cup Parmesan cheese; set aside.
2. Spread 1 cup pasta sauce in bottom of a lightly greased 13- x 9-inch baking dish.
3. Cut egg roll wrappers in half lengthwise; arrange 10 halves over pasta sauce. (Wrappers will overlap.) Top with meatballs. Spoon 3 cups pasta sauce over meatballs, and sprinkle with ¾ cup mozzarella cheese. Arrange 10 wrappers over mozzarella. Spread ricotta cheese mixture over wrappers, and top with remaining wrappers and pasta sauce.
4. Bake at 350° for 50 minutes. Top with remaining ¾ cup mozzarella cheese and remaining ¼ cup Parmesan cheese. Bake 10 more minutes. Let stand 15 minutes.
Note: For testing purposes only, we used Classico Tomato & Basil pasta sauce.

Marmalade-Glazed Beef Patties

MAKES 4 SERVINGS
PREP: 10 MIN., COOK: 22 MIN.

1 pound ground beef
1 large egg
½ cup fine, dry breadcrumbs
2 tablespoons prepared horseradish
½ teaspoon salt
1 (8-ounce) can water chestnuts, drained and diced
⅔ cup orange marmalade
½ cup water
⅓ cup soy sauce
2 tablespoons lemon juice
1 garlic clove, pressed
Hot cooked rice

1. Combine ground beef, egg, and next 4 ingredients; shape mixture into 4 patties.
2. Cook patties in a large nonstick skillet over medium-high heat 2 minutes on each side or until browned; remove from skillet.
3. Add orange marmalade, ½ cup water, soy sauce, lemon juice, and garlic to skillet. Bring to a boil over medium heat; cook, stirring constantly, 6 minutes. Add patties; reduce heat to low, and simmer 10 minutes. Serve over rice.

Marmalade-Glazed Meatballs: Shape beef mixture into 1-inch balls; place on a rack in a broiler pan, and broil 5½ inches from heat 5 minutes or until no longer pink. Place in a chafing dish. Bring orange marmalade and next 4 ingredients to a boil in a saucepan over medium heat; cook, stirring constantly, 6 minutes. Pour over meatballs.

Barbecued Beef Burgers With Creamy Coleslaw

MAKES 8 SERVINGS
PREP: 20 MIN., GRILL: 20 MIN.

3 pounds ground round
½ cup Spicy Barbecue Sauce
1 tablespoon chili powder
1 teaspoon ground cumin
1½ teaspoons salt
½ teaspoon pepper
½ teaspoon garlic powder
8 hamburger buns
Spicy Barbecue Sauce
Creamy Coleslaw

Barbecued Beef Burgers With Creamy Coleslaw

1. Combine first 7 ingredients in a large bowl. Shape mixture into 8 patties.
2. Grill, covered with grill lid, over medium-high heat (350° to 400°) 8 to 10 minutes on each side or until beef is no longer pink.
3. Serve hamburgers on buns, and top with additional Spicy Barbecue Sauce and Creamy Coleslaw.

Spicy Barbecue Sauce:

MAKES ABOUT 1½ CUPS
PREP: 5 MIN.

1 cup bottled barbecue sauce
¼ cup spicy brown mustard
¼ cup Worcestershire sauce

1. Stir together all ingredients. Cover and chill until ready to serve.

Creamy Coleslaw:

Country shredded cabbage mix has red, green, and traditional cabbage.

MAKES ABOUT 4 CUPS
PREP: 10 MIN.

½ cup mayonnaise
2¼ teaspoons cider vinegar
¼ teaspoon sugar
¼ teaspoon salt
⅛ teaspoon pepper
Hot sauce to taste
1 (10-ounce) bag country shredded cabbage mix

1. Whisk together first 6 ingredients in a large bowl.
2. Add cabbage just before serving, tossing to coat. Serve immediately, or chill up to 1 hour, if desired.

Italian Burgers

Italian Burgers

Fennel seeds offer delicately sweet Mediterranean flair to these flavorful burger patties. Look for the seeds on the spice aisle.

MAKES 4 SERVINGS
PREP: 15 MIN., GRILL: 20 MIN.

1 pound lean ground beef
1 small onion, minced
¾ cup grated Parmesan cheese
¼ cup minced fresh parsley
1 large egg, lightly beaten
2 tablespoons dried Italian seasoning
¾ teaspoon pepper
½ teaspoon garlic salt
¼ teaspoon fennel seeds
4 (1-ounce) provolone cheese slices
4 English muffins, split
½ cup pasta sauce
Garnish: fresh basil sprigs

1. Combine first 9 ingredients; shape into 4 patties.
2. Grill, covered with grill lid, over medium-high heat (350° to 400°) 7 to 8 minutes on each side or until beef is no longer pink. Top patties with cheese, and grill 1 more minute or until cheese melts.
3. Place muffins on grill, cut sides down, and grill 1 minute or until lightly toasted. Top each muffin bottom with 2 tablespoons pasta sauce, a hamburger patty, and muffin tops. Garnish, if desired.

Marinated Lamb Kabobs

Marinated Lamb Kabobs

You often can find cubes of lamb in the supermarket; if not, cut them from a leg rather than from expensive chops.

MAKES 8 SERVINGS
PREP: 20 MIN., CHILL: 3 HRS., GRILL: 10 MIN.

2½ pounds lamb, cut into 1½-inch cubes
¼ cup olive oil
4 fresh rosemary sprigs
8 (12-inch) wooden skewers
2 red onions, quartered
1 green bell pepper, cut into 1-inch pieces
½ pound fresh mushrooms
1 lemon, quartered and cut into 1-inch pieces
1 cup drained pineapple chunks
1 teaspoon salt
Vegetable cooking spray

1. Combine first 3 ingredients in a large shallow dish or heavy-duty zip-top bag; cover or seal, and chill 3 hours. Soak wooden skewers in water during last 30 minutes of chilling lamb.
2. Remove lamb from dish, discarding marinade. Thread lamb cubes, onions, and next 4 ingredients alternately onto skewers. Sprinkle kabobs evenly with salt.
3. Coat cold cooking grate with cooking spray; place grate on grill over medium-high heat (350° to 400°). Place kabobs on rack; grill, covered with grill lid, 5 minutes on each side or to desired degree of doneness.

Grilled Lamb Patties

Open up your spice drawer. The herbs used in this recipe give these patties a superb taste.

MAKES 8 SERVINGS
PREP: 25 MIN., CHILL: 30 MIN., GRILL: 14 MIN.

2 pounds lean ground lamb
1 large onion, chopped
½ cup chopped fresh cilantro
⅓ cup chopped fresh parsley
¼ cup chopped fresh mint
2 teaspoons salt
1½ teaspoons ground cumin
1 teaspoon pepper
1 teaspoon ground allspice

1. Combine all ingredients in a bowl. Process lamb mixture, in batches, in a food processor until well combined, stopping to scrape down sides. Cover lamb mixture, and chill at least 30 minutes. Shape lamb mixture into 16 (4- to 5-inch) patties.
2. Grill, covered with grill lid, over medium-high heat (350° to 400°) 5 to 7 minutes on each side or until meat is no longer pink.
Note: If ground lamb is unavailable, purchase either a 2⅓-pound boneless leg of lamb or a 4-pound bone-in leg of lamb, and ask the butcher to grind it for you.

Lamb Chops With Mint Aïoli

MAKES 6 TO 8 SERVINGS
PREP: 15 MIN., BAKE: 40 MIN.

6 garlic cloves, minced
2 teaspoons dried summer savory
1 teaspoon salt
1 teaspoon pepper
16 (2-inch-thick) lamb chops
1 tablespoon olive oil
Mint Aïoli
Garnish: fresh mint sprigs

1. Combine first 4 ingredients; rub evenly onto both sides of lamb chops.
2. Brown chops in hot oil in a large nonstick skillet over medium-high heat 2 to 3 minutes on each side. Arrange chops on a lightly greased rack in a broiler pan.
3. Bake chops at 350° for 35 to 40 minutes or until a meat thermometer inserted into thickest portion registers 145° (medium rare). Serve lamb with Mint Aïoli. Garnish, if desired.

Mint Aïoli:
MAKES 1¼ CUPS
PREP: 5 MIN.

1 cup mayonnaise
¼ cup coarsely chopped fresh mint
4 garlic cloves, minced
1 teaspoon grated lemon rind
2 tablespoons fresh lemon juice
½ teaspoon salt
½ teaspoon pepper

1. Process all ingredients in a blender or food processor until smooth, stopping to scrape down sides.

Maple-Glazed Lamb Chops With Zesty Horseradish Sauce

MAKES 4 MAIN-DISH OR 8 APPETIZER SERVINGS
PREP: 10 MIN., CHILL: 8 HRS., BROIL: 14 MIN., STAND: 5 MIN.

⅓ cup maple syrup
¼ cup Dijon mustard
2 tablespoons balsamic vinegar
2 tablespoons olive oil
1 shallot, minced
¼ teaspoon crushed red pepper
8 (½-inch-thick) lamb loin chops
½ teaspoon salt
½ teaspoon ground black
    pepper
Zesty Horseradish Sauce

1. Combine first 6 ingredients in a shallow dish or large zip-top freezer bag; add lamb chops. Cover or seal, and chill up to 8 hours, turning lamb chops occasionally.

2. Remove lamb chops from marinade, discarding marinade. Sprinkle chops evenly with salt and pepper; place chops on a lightly greased rack in a broiler pan.
3. Broil lamb chops 3 inches from heat 5 to 7 minutes on each side or to desired degree of doneness. Cover lamb chops with aluminum foil, and let stand 5 minutes. Serve with Zesty Horseradish Sauce.

Zesty Horseradish Sauce:

MAKES ABOUT ½ CUP
PREP: 5 MIN.

½ cup sour cream
2 tablespoons prepared horseradish
2 tablespoons coarsely chopped fresh mint

1. Stir together all ingredients. Cover and chill until ready to serve.

Maple-Glazed Lamb Chops
With Zesty Horseradish Sauce

Pork Chops With Warm Pineapple Salsa

MAKES 6 SERVINGS
PREP: 5 MIN., BROIL: 10 MIN.

6 (6-ounce) lean boneless pork chops
Caribbean Spice Rub
Warm Pineapple Salsa

1. Rub pork chops evenly with Caribbean Spice Rub. Place on a lightly greased broiler rack, and place rack in a broiler pan.
2. Broil 5 inches from heat 5 minutes on each side or until done. Serve with Warm Pineapple Salsa.

Caribbean Spice Rub:

MAKES ⅓ CUP
PREP: 5 MIN.

2 tablespoons ground allspice
1 tablespoon ground ginger
1 tablespoon crushed dried thyme
1 tablespoon garlic powder
1 tablespoon onion powder
2 teaspoons salt
½ teaspoon freshly ground black pepper
⅛ teaspoon ground red pepper

1. Combine all ingredients. Store in an airtight container.

Warm Pineapple Salsa:

MAKES 6 TO 8 SERVINGS
PREP: 10 MIN., COOK: 10 MIN.

2 shallots, finely chopped
1 jalapeño pepper, minced
1½ teaspoons grated fresh ginger
Vegetable cooking spray
1¼ cups fresh orange juice
1 pineapple, peeled and chopped
1 tablespoon chopped fresh mint
1 tablespoon chopped fresh basil
½ teaspoon curry powder

1. Sauté first 3 ingredients in a skillet coated with cooking spray over high heat 2 minutes. Add juice; cook 5 minutes or until mixture is reduced by half. Stir in pineapple and remaining ingredients; reduce heat to low, and cook until thoroughly heated.

Pork Chops With Warm
Pineapple Salsa

Grilled Pork Chops With Garlic Mashed Potatoes

MAKES 8 SERVINGS
PREP: 10 MIN., GRILL: 12 MIN.

¼ cup olive oil
1 tablespoon salt
1 tablespoon coarsely ground pepper
2 tablespoons chopped fresh oregano
1 tablespoon chopped fresh or dried rosemary
1 tablespoon chopped fresh thyme
8 (12-ounce) bone-in pork loin chops*
Garlic Mashed Potatoes

1. Stir together first 6 ingredients. Rub evenly over both sides of pork chops.
2. Grill, covered with grill lid, over medium-high heat (350° to 400°) 12 minutes or until a meat thermometer inserted into thickest portion registers 160°, turning once. Serve with Garlic Mashed Potatoes.
*8 (12-ounce) bone-in veal chops may be substituted.

Garlic Mashed Potatoes:

MAKES 8 SERVINGS
PREP: 20 MIN., COOK: 35 MIN.

8 baking potatoes, peeled and quartered
     (about 4 pounds)
1¾ teaspoons salt, divided
½ cup butter, softened
¾ cup half-and-half
3 large garlic cloves, pressed
½ teaspoon ground white pepper
¼ cup chopped fresh parsley

1. Bring potatoes, 1 teaspoon salt, and water to cover to a boil in a Dutch oven or stockpot; cover, reduce heat, and simmer 30 minutes or until tender. Drain.
2. Beat potatoes, remaining ¾ teaspoon salt, butter, half-and-half, garlic cloves, and ground white pepper at medium speed with an electric mixer until smooth. Stir in fresh parsley.

Grilled Pork Chops

Turn your traditional staple pork chops into a special dish. The fresh herbs in this recipe bring new life to an old favorite.

MAKES 8 SERVINGS
PREP: 10 MIN., GRILL: 12 MIN.

¼ cup olive oil
1 tablespoon salt
1 tablespoon chopped fresh or dried rosemary
1 tablespoon chopped fresh thyme
2 tablespoons chopped fresh oregano
1 tablespoon coarsely ground pepper
8 (12-ounce) bone-in pork loin chops*
Garnish: fresh thyme sprigs

1. Stir together first 6 ingredients. Rub evenly over both sides of pork chops.
2. Grill, covered with grill lid, over medium-high heat (350° to 400°) 12 minutes or until meat thermometer inserted into the thickest portion registers 160°, turning once. Garnish, if desired.
*Substitute 8 (12-ounce) bone-in veal chops for bone-in pork loin chops, if desired.

Oven-Fried Pork Chops

Now here's an easy dish. Just dip the pork chops in an egg white mixture, dredge them in seasoned breadcrumbs, and relax while they bake.

MAKES 4 SERVINGS
PREP: 7 MIN., BAKE: 50 MIN.

4 (6-ounce) lean center-cut pork loin chops
1 egg white
2 tablespoons unsweetened pineapple juice
1 tablespoon lite soy sauce
¼ teaspoon ground ginger
¼ teaspoon paprika
⅛ teaspoon garlic powder
⅓ cup Italian-seasoned breadcrumbs
Vegetable cooking spray

1. Trim fat from pork chops. Combine egg white and next 5 ingredients in a shallow bowl, and whisk gently. Dip pork chops in egg mixture, and dredge in breadcrumbs.
2. Place chops on a rack in a roasting pan coated with cooking spray. Bake at 350° for 25 minutes; turn and bake 25 more minutes or until pork chops are done.

Tuscan Pork Chops

Tuscan Pork Chops

*Serve crusty bread and a robust red wine to turn this quick
entrée into an elegant meal.*

Easy Scalloped Potatoes and Chops

*Five simple ingredients cook into a great one-dish meal. Serve a
salad on the side, if you'd like.*

pork loin or rib chops

potatoes
iento, drained

h ½ teaspoon salt and ¼ tea-

ghtly greased large nonstick
heat 3 minutes on each side
pork chops from skillet.
bes (do not cook) in skillet
ctions for the stove top. Stir
ng mixture to a boil, stirring
k chops. Cover, reduce heat,
ncover and cook 5 more
are tender.
only, we used Betty Crocker

The Best of Southern Living p.3
Meats - Beef
p.105 Peppery Rib Eye Steak
p.106 Pot Roast with Mushroom Gravy
p.109 Eye of Round Roast with Garlic Potatoes
p.109 Italian Pot Roast
p.111 Chicken Fried Steak
p.113 Peppery Grilled Flank Steak
p.113 Tomato Cheese Bread
p.114 Honey Mustard Grilled Flank Steak
p.114 Flank Steak
p.115 Molasses Flank Steak

Margarita Pork Kabobs

Margarita Pork Kabobs

These kabobs taste great with couscous.

MAKES 4 SERVINGS
PREP: 25 MIN., CHILL: 30 MIN., GRILL: 10 MIN.

1 cup frozen margarita mix concentrate, thawed
1 teaspoon ground coriander
2 teaspoons grated lime rind
3 garlic cloves, minced
2 pounds pork tenderloin, cut into 1-inch cubes
3 ears fresh corn
1 tablespoon water
1 large onion, quartered
1 large green bell pepper, cut into 1-inch pieces
1 large red bell pepper, cut into 1-inch pieces

1. Combine first 4 ingredients in a large shallow dish or zip-top freezer bag, and add pork. Cover or seal, and chill 30 minutes, turning occasionally.
2. Cut each ear of corn into 4 pieces. Place corn and 1 tablespoon water in an 8-inch square microwave-safe dish. Cover with plastic wrap, folding back 1 corner to allow steam to escape. Microwave at HIGH 4 minutes, giving dish a half turn after 2 minutes.
3. Remove pork from marinade, discarding marinade. Thread pork, corn, onion, and bell pepper onto skewers.
4. Coat food grate with vegetable cooking spray; place on grill over medium-high heat (350° to 400°). Place kabobs on food grate; grill, covered with grill lid, 5 minutes on each side or until done.

Adobo Grilled Pork Tacos With Cucumber-Radish Salsa

MAKES 24 TACOS
PREP: 15 MIN., STAND: 30 MIN., CHILL: 30 MIN., GRILL: 20 MIN.

1 (2-ounce) package dried mild New Mexico
    chiles
2 teaspoons cumin seeds
1 tablespoon dried oregano
3 garlic cloves
2 tablespoons cider vinegar
1 teaspoon sugar
¼ teaspoon salt
¼ teaspoon ground red pepper
2 (¾-pound) pork tenderloins
1 (8-ounce) container sour cream
Cucumber-Radish Salsa
24 corn or flour tortillas, warmed
Garnishes: lime wedges, fresh cilantro

1. Slice dried chiles in half lengthwise. Remove and discard stems and seeds. Place chiles in a bowl, and add boiling water to cover. Let stand 20 minutes or until chiles are softened. Drain chiles, reserving liquid.
2. Cook cumin seeds in a skillet over medium heat 30 seconds. Add oregano, and cook, stirring constantly, 30 seconds or until cumin is toasted.
3. Process cumin mixture, soaked chiles, 1 cup reserved liquid, garlic, and next 4 ingredients in a blender or food processor until smooth, adding more reserved liquid if needed.

4. Place pork in a shallow dish. Pour half of chile mixture over meat. Cover and chill 30 minutes. Remove pork from marinade, discarding marinade.
5. Stir together sour cream and ½ cup Cucumber-Radish Salsa; cover and chill until ready to serve.
6. Grill pork, covered with grill lid, over medium-high heat (350° to 400°), turning occasionally and basting with reserved chile mixture, 20 minutes or until a meat thermometer inserted into thickest portion registers 155°.
7. Remove from grill; let stand 10 minutes until pork reaches 160°. Coarsely chop pork. Serve in warm tortillas with remaining Cucumber-Radish Salsa and sour cream mixture. Garnish, if desired.

Cucumber-Radish Salsa:

MAKES 3 CUPS
PREP: 10 MIN.

2 cucumbers, peeled, seeded, and chopped
1 (6-ounce) package radishes, grated
1 small onion, minced
2 tablespoons chopped fresh cilantro
¼ cup lime juice
½ teaspoon salt
¼ teaspoon ground red pepper
Garnish: whole radish

1. Stir together first 7 ingredients. Cover and chill, if desired. Garnish, if desired.

Adobo Grilled Pork Tacos With
Cucumber-Radish Salsa

Pork Fillets With Dark
Cherry Sauce

Pork Fillets With Dark Cherry Sauce

MAKES 4 SERVINGS
PREP: 10 MIN., COOK: 25 MIN.

2 pounds pork loin
1/2 teaspoon salt
1/2 teaspoon freshly ground pepper
Kitchen string (optional)
2 tablespoons olive oil
1/2 cup beef broth
1/4 cup bourbon
1 (17-ounce) can pitted dark sweet cherries
1 tablespoon cornstarch
2 teaspoons grated lemon rind
2 tablespoons fresh lemon juice
1 1/2 teaspoons chopped fresh rosemary
1/2 teaspoon whole cloves
1/2 cup chopped pecans, toasted
Garnish: fresh watercress

1. Cut pork loin into 4 (1 1/2-inch-thick) fillets; sprinkle evenly with salt and pepper. Securely tie a 12-inch piece of kitchen string around each fillet, if desired.
2. Cook pork fillets in hot oil in a skillet over medium-high heat 2 to 3 minutes on each side or until golden brown. Stir together beef broth and bourbon; add to skillet, stirring to loosen particles from bottom of skillet. Reduce heat to low; cover and simmer for 10 to 15 minutes or until pork is done. Remove fillets to a serving platter, reserving pan juices, and keep warm. Remove and discard kitchen string.
3. Drain cherries, reserving syrup in a small bowl.
4. Whisk together cherry syrup, cornstarch, and next 4 ingredients; add to skillet with reserved pan juices. Bring to a boil over medium heat, and cook, stirring constantly, 1 minute or until thickened. Remove from heat; remove cloves, and stir in cherries and chopped toasted pecans. Spoon mixture evenly over warm pork fillets. Garnish, if desired, and serve immediately.

Caribbean Pork Tenderloin With Rum Jezebel Sauce

Looking for a fabulous sandwich for a party? This recipe is delicious served on dinner rolls.

MAKES 6 SERVINGS
PREP: 5 MIN., BAKE: 30 MIN., STAND: 5 MIN.

2 (³/₄- to 1-pound) pork tenderloins
3 tablespoons orange juice
2 tablespoons light brown sugar
1 tablespoon Caribbean jerk seasoning
¹/₂ tablespoon salt
Rum Jezebel Sauce

1. Brush pork tenderloins with orange juice. Stir together brown sugar, Caribbean jerk seasoning, and salt. Rub mixture evenly over pork tenderloins. Place on a lightly greased rack in a roasting pan.
2. Bake at 425° for 25 to 30 minutes or until a meat thermometer inserted into thickest portion registers 155°. Remove pork from oven, and loosely cover with aluminum foil. Let stand until thermometer registers 160° (about 5 minutes). Serve with Rum Jezebel Sauce.

Rum Jezebel Sauce:

Jerk seasoning is typically a blend of chiles, thyme, spices, onions, and garlic.

MAKES ABOUT 1¹/₄ CUPS
PREP: 5 MIN.

¹/₂ cup pineapple preserves
¹/₂ cup apple jelly
¹/₂ (5.25-ounce) jar Creole mustard
¹/₄ teaspoon Caribbean jerk seasoning
1¹/₂ teaspoons dark rum or orange juice

1. Whisk together all ingredients.
2. Cover and chill until ready to serve.

Asian Pork Tenderloin

MAKES 6 SERVINGS
PREP: 20 MIN., CHILL: 8 HRS., BAKE: 25 MIN., STAND: 5 MIN.

¹/₃ cup lite soy sauce
¹/₄ cup sesame oil
¹/₃ cup firmly packed light brown sugar
2 tablespoons Worcestershire sauce
2 tablespoons lemon juice
1 tablespoon dry mustard
1¹/₂ teaspoons pepper
4 garlic cloves, crushed
1¹/₂ to 2 pounds pork tenderloin

1. Whisk together first 8 ingredients in a large shallow dish; add pork, turning pork to coat. Cover and chill 8 hours. Remove pork from marinade, discarding marinade. Place in an aluminum foil-lined roasting pan.
2. Bake, uncovered, at 450° for 25 minutes or until a meat thermometer inserted into thickest portion registers 160°. Let pork stand 5 minutes.

Chinese-Style Spareribs

MAKES 6 SERVINGS
PREP: 20 MIN.; COOK: 1 HR., 10 MIN.; BAKE: 1 HR.

2 pounds pork spareribs, cut into small pieces
2 garlic cloves, minced
1 teaspoon grated fresh ginger
1 tablespoon vegetable oil
1 (8-ounce) jar black bean sauce
¹/₄ cup teriyaki sauce
2 tablespoons chile-garlic sauce

1. Rub pork spareribs with garlic and ginger.
2. Brown ribs in hot oil in a Dutch oven over medium-high heat 4 to 5 minutes on each side.
3. Stir together sauces. Pour over ribs; reduce heat, and simmer, stirring occasionally, 1 hour. Arrange ribs in a 13- x 9-inch pan. Pour sauce mixture from Dutch oven over ribs.
4. Bake pork spareribs at 350° for 1 hour.
Note: For testing purposes only, we used Ka-Me Black Bean Sauce.

Baby Back Ribs

Baby Back Ribs

Plug one of our flavorful rub-and-sauce combinations (Sweet-and-Sour or Smoky Chipotle) into these simple directions for grilling ribs.

MAKES 6 SERVINGS
PREP: 15 MIN.; CHILL: 8 HRS.;, STAND: 30 MIN.;
GRILL: 2 HRS., 30 MIN.

3 slabs baby back pork ribs (about 5½ pounds)
2 citrus fruits, halved
1 recipe Ginger Rub or Chipotle Rub
Vegetable cooking spray
1 recipe Sweet-and-Sour 'Cue Sauce or
    Smoky Chipotle 'Cue Sauce

1. Rinse and pat ribs dry. If desired, remove thin membrane from back of ribs by slicing into it with a knife, and then pulling it off. (This will make ribs more tender.)

2. Rub meat with cut sides of citrus fruit, squeezing as you rub. Massage desired rub into meat, covering all sides. Wrap tightly with plastic wrap, and place in a zip-top freezer bag or 13- x 9-inch baking dish; chill 8 hours. Let ribs stand at room temperature 30 minutcs before grilling. Remove plastic wrap.

Sweet-and-Sour Baby Back Ribs: Prepare ribs as directed using 4 lime halves, Ginger Rub, and Sweet-and-Sour 'Cue Sauce. Garnish with sesame seeds and green onions, if desired.

Ginger Rub:

Look for ground ginger on the spice aisle in the grocery store.

MAKES ABOUT 3 TABLESPOONS
PREP: 5 MIN.

2 tablespoons ground ginger
1/2 teaspoon dried crushed red pepper
1 teaspoon salt
1 teaspoon black pepper

1. Combine all ingredients.

Sweet-and-Sour 'Cue Sauce:

MAKES 3 1/2 CUPS
PREP: 5 MIN., COOK: 35 MIN.

2 (10-ounce) bottles sweet-and-sour sauce
2 cups ketchup
1/2 cup cider vinegar
1/2 teaspoon ground ginger
2 teaspoons hot sauce

1. Stir together all ingredients in a saucepan over medium-high heat. Bring to a boil; reduce heat, and simmer 30 minutes.
Note: For testing purposes only, we used Ty Ling Sweet & Sour Sauce.

Smoky Chipotle Baby Back Ribs: Prepare ribs as directed using 4 orange halves, Chipotle Rub, and Smoky Chipotle 'Cue Sauce.

Chipotle Rub:

MAKES 1/3 CUP
PREP: 5 MIN.

2 to 3 canned chipotle chile peppers
1/4 cup firmly packed brown sugar
1 tablespoon chili powder
1 teaspoon salt

1. Chop chipotle chile peppers.
2. Stir together chopped peppers, brown sugar, chili powder, and salt to form a paste.

Smoky Chipotle 'Cue Sauce:

MAKES ABOUT 2 1/2 CUPS
PREP: 5 MIN., COOK: 35 MIN.

2 (18-ounce) bottles barbecue sauce
2 canned chipotle chile peppers
2 tablespoons brown sugar
1 teaspoon chili powder

1. Process all ingredients in blender until smooth. Pour into a saucepan, and bring to a boil over medium-high heat. Reduce heat, and simmer 30 minutes.
Note: For testing purposes only, we used Stubb's Original Bar-B-Q Sauce.

TO GRILL ON A CHARCOAL GRILL:

Coat cold food grate with cooking spray. Prepare hot fire by piling charcoal on one side of grill, leaving the other side empty. Place grate on grill; position rib rack on grate over unlit side. Place slabs in rack. Grill, covered with grill lid, over medium-high heat (350° to 400°) 1 hour. Reposition slabs, placing the one closest to the heat source away from heat, and moving other slabs closer. Grill 1 more hour or until meat is tender. Grill 30 more minutes over medium heat (325° to 350°), basting with half of desired 'Cue Sauce. Remove ribs from grill; let stand 10 minutes. Cut ribs, slicing between bones. Serve with remaining sauce.

TO GRILL ON A GAS GRILL:

Coat cold food grate with cooking spray, and place on grill. Light only one side, and position rib rack on grate over unlit side. Place rib slabs in rack. Grill, covered with grill lid, over medium-high heat (350° to 400°) 1 hour. Reposition slabs, placing the one closest to the heat source away from heat, and moving other slabs closer. Grill 1 more hour or until meat is tender. Lower temperature to medium heat (325° to 350°), and cook ribs 30 more minutes, basting with half of 'Cue Sauce. Remove ribs from grill; let stand 10 minutes. Cut ribs, slicing between bones. Serve ribs with remaining sauce.

Harvest Ham

Harvest Ham

This salty ham is full of flavor. Serve it with your favorite biscuits.

MAKES 26 SERVINGS
PREP: 1 HR.; SOAK: 24 HRS.; BAKE: 3 HRS., 30 MIN.

1 (15-pound) uncooked country ham
2 tablespoons whole cloves
½ cup firmly packed dark brown sugar
½ cup honey mustard
½ cup honey
1 teaspoon ground ginger
2 cups apple juice
1 cup pineapple juice
1 cup Madeira
2 cups dried apricot halves
1 cup golden raisins

1. Place ham in a very large container; cover with water, and soak at least 24 hours. Pour off water. Scrub ham with cold water, using a stiff brush, and rinse well.
2. Remove skin, leaving a ¼-inch layer of fat. Score fat in a diamond design using a sharp knife. Stud with whole cloves. Place ham in a large roasting pan.
3. Combine brown sugar, mustard, honey, and ginger. Coat exposed portion of ham evenly with mustard mixture. Pour apple juice and pineapple juice into roasting pan. Cover and bake at 350° for 2 hours. Add Madeira, apricot halves, and raisins to pan. Cover and bake 1½ more hours or until a meat thermometer inserted into thickest portion of ham registers 142°. To serve, slice ham across the grain into thin slices.

Country Ham

MAKES 35 TO 40 SERVINGS
PREP: 1 HR., SOAK: 24 HRS., BAKE: 4 HRS.

1 (12- to 14-pound) uncooked country ham
2 quarts cider vinegar
1 tablespoon whole cloves
Hot biscuits

1. Place ham in a large container. Cover with water, and soak 24 hours. Drain. Scrub ham 3 to 4 times in cold water with a stiff brush, and rinse well.
2. Place ham, fat side up, in a large roasting pan. Pour vinegar over ham; sprinkle with cloves. Cover with lid or aluminum foil.
3. Bake, covered, at 325° for 4 hours or until a meat thermometer inserted into thickest portion registers 140°. Remove from oven, and cool slightly. Slice ham across the grain into thin slices, and serve with hot biscuits.

Praline-Mustard Glazed Ham

MAKES 12 SERVINGS
PREP: 10 MIN.; BAKE: 2 HRS., 30 MIN.; STAND: 10 MIN.;
COOK: 5 MIN.

1 (7- to 8-pound) bone-in smoked spiral-cut ham half
1 cup maple syrup
¾ cup firmly packed light brown sugar
¾ cup Dijon mustard
⅓ cup apple juice
¼ cup raisins
1 cooking apple, thinly sliced

1. Remove skin and excess fat from smoked ham; place ham in a lightly greased 13- x 9-inch pan.
2. Stir together maple syrup and next 3 ingredients. Pour mixture over ham.
3. Bake at 350° on lower oven rack 2½ hours or until a meat thermometer inserted into thickest portion registers 140°, basting every 20 minutes with glaze. Let ham stand 10 minutes. Remove from pan, reserving drippings. If desired, cool, cover, and chill ham.
4. Remove fat from drippings with a fat separator, and discard. Cover and chill drippings, if desired. Cook drippings, raisins, and apple slices in a saucepan over low heat 5 minutes. Serve warm sauce with ham.

Cheesy Bacon-and-Ham Casserole

Use reduced-sodium bacon, if desired.

MAKES 8 SERVINGS
PREP: 10 MIN., COOK: 25 MIN., BAKE: 35 MIN., STAND: 5 MIN.

1 (8-ounce) package bacon slices, cut into 1-inch pieces
1 (8-ounce) package diced cooked ham
¾ cup uncooked quick-cooking grits
1 (16-ounce) loaf pasteurized cheese product, cubed
¼ cup butter or margarine
6 large eggs
½ cup milk
½ teaspoon freshly ground black pepper

1. Cook bacon and ham in a large nonstick skillet over medium-high heat 12 minutes or until bacon is crisp; remove bacon and ham, and drain on paper towels.
2. Cook grits according to package directions. Add cheese and butter; beat at medium speed with an electric mixer until blended and cheese melts. Beat in eggs, milk, and pepper. Stir in bacon mixture. Pour into a lightly greased 13- x 9-inch baking dish.
3. Bake at 350° for 30 to 35 minutes or until set. Let stand 5 minutes before serving.

Country Ham
Eggs Benedict

Country Ham Eggs Benedict

MAKES 10 SERVINGS
PREP: 35 MIN., COOK: 20 MIN.

1 (12-ounce) package thinly sliced country ham
1 cup yellow cornmeal
½ cup all-purpose flour
2 teaspoons baking powder
1 teaspoon sugar
¼ teaspoon salt
2 large eggs, lightly beaten
¾ cup buttermilk
1 (8.75-ounce) can cream-style corn
2 tablespoons vegetable oil
10 large eggs, poached
Swiss Cheese Sauce
Garnishes: shredded Swiss cheese, paprika

1. Brown country ham in a large skillet coated with cooking spray over medium-high heat. Remove browned ham from skillet, and keep warm.
2. Stir together cornmeal and next 4 ingredients in a large bowl; make a well in center of mixture. Stir together 2 eggs, buttermilk, cream-style corn, and vegetable oil; add to cornmeal mixture, stirring just until dry ingredients are moistened.
3. Pour about ¼ cup batter for each pancake onto a hot, lightly greased griddle or into a nonstick skillet. Cook pancakes until tops are covered with bubbles and edges look cooked; turn and cook other side.
4. Top each pancake with browned country ham, 1 poached egg, and warm Swiss Cheese Sauce. Garnish, if desired, and serve immediately.

Swiss Cheese Sauce:

MAKES 2 CUPS
PREP: 10 MIN., COOK: 10 MIN.

2 tablespoons butter
2 tablespoons all-purpose flour
2 cups milk
1 cup (4 ounces) shredded Swiss cheese
½ teaspoon salt
¼ teaspoon pepper

1. Melt butter in a heavy saucepan over low heat; whisk in flour until smooth. Cook, whisking constantly, 1 minute. Gradually whisk in milk; cook over medium heat, whisking constantly until thickened and bubbly. Add cheese, salt, and pepper, stirring until melted.

Sausage-Filled Crêpes

MAKES 6 TO 8 SERVINGS
PREP: 15 MIN., COOK: 15 MIN., BAKE: 20 MIN.

1 pound ground pork sausage
1 small onion, diced
2 cups (8 ounces) shredded Cheddar cheese, divided
1 (3-ounce) package cream cheese
½ teaspoon dried marjoram
Crêpes
½ cup sour cream
¼ cup butter or margarine, softened
¼ cup chopped fresh parsley

1. Cook sausage and onion in a large skillet over medium heat, stirring until sausage crumbles and is no longer pink; drain well. Return mixture to skillet; add 1 cup Cheddar cheese, cream cheese, and marjoram, stirring until cheeses melt. Spoon 3 tablespoons filling down center of each crêpe. Roll up and place, seam sides down, in a lightly greased 13- x 9-inch baking dish.
2. Bake, covered, at 350° for 15 minutes. Stir together sour cream and butter; spoon over crêpes. Bake 5 more minutes. Sprinkle with remaining 1 cup Cheddar cheese and parsley.
To Make Ahead: Make Sausage-Filled Crêpes ahead, if desired, and freeze. To reheat, let stand for 30 minutes at room temperature. Bake, covered, at 350° for 40 minutes. Proceed as directed, adding sour cream and remaining ingredients.

Crêpes:

MAKES 12 (7-INCH) CRÊPES
PREP: 5 MIN., CHILL: 1 HR., COOK: 18 MIN.

3 large eggs
1 cup milk
1 tablespoon vegetable oil
1 cup all-purpose flour
½ teaspoon salt

1. Beat first 3 ingredients at medium speed with an electric mixer until blended. Gradually add flour and salt, beating until smooth. Cover mixture, and chill 1 hour.
2. Place a lightly greased 7-inch nonstick skillet over medium heat until hot.
3. Pour 3 tablespoons batter into skillet, and quickly tilt in all directions so batter covers bottom of skillet.
4. Cook 1 minute or until crêpe can be shaken loose from skillet. Turn crêpe over, and cook about 30 seconds. Place on a dish towel to cool. Repeat procedure with remaining batter. Stack crêpes between sheets of wax paper.

poultry

Peppery Chicken-fried Chicken,
page 147

Greek Roasted Chicken With Rosemary Potatoes

MAKES 6 SERVINGS
PREP: 20 MIN.; BAKE: 1 HR., 15 MIN.; STAND: 10 MIN.

2 tablespoons Greek seasoning
2 tablespoons fresh lemon juice
3 tablespoons olive oil, divided
1 (5-pound) whole chicken
2 lemons, thinly sliced
1 celery rib, cut into thirds
1 carrot, cut into thirds
1 small onion, halved
1¼ teaspoons salt, divided
½ teaspoon pepper, divided
2 pounds small new potatoes, halved
¾ teaspoon dried rosemary
2 cups chicken broth
Fresh spinach leaves (optional)

1. Whisk together Greek seasoning, lemon juice, and 2 tablespoons olive oil in a small bowl.
2. Loosen skin from chicken breasts and drumsticks without totally detaching skin. Rub Greek seasoning mixture evenly under skin. Arrange 3 lemon slices on each side of breast under skin; carefully replace skin.

Place remaining lemon slices and next 3 ingredients into chicken cavity. Tie ends of legs together with string; tuck wing tips under.
3. Place chicken, breast side up, on a lightly greased rack in a lightly greased shallow roasting pan. Lightly coat chicken with cooking spray; sprinkle evenly with 1 teaspoon salt and ¼ teaspoon pepper.
4. Bake at 450° for 30 minutes.
5. Stir together new potatoes, rosemary, and remaining 1 tablespoon oil, ¼ teaspoon salt, and ¼ teaspoon pepper in a bowl.
6. Remove chicken from oven; pour 2 cups chicken broth over chicken. Arrange potato mixture in a single layer on wire rack around chicken; return to oven. Reduce oven temperature to 400°.
7. Bake at 400° for 40 minutes or until meat thermometer inserted into thigh registers 175°, basting every 15 minutes with pan juices. Cover loosely with aluminum foil to prevent excessive browning, if necessary. Remove from oven, and let stand 10 minutes before carving. Serve chicken and potatoes on fresh spinach leaves drizzled with pan juices, if desired. (The hot pan juices will wilt the spinach.)

Greek Roasted Chicken
With Rosemary Potatoes

Our Best Fried Chicken

Substitute 2 cups buttermilk for the saltwater solution used to soak the chicken pieces, if desired.

MAKES 4 SERVINGS
PREP: 10 MIN., CHILL: 8 HRS., FRY: 30 MIN.

3 quarts water
1 tablespoon salt
1 (2- to 2½-pound) whole chicken, cut up
1 teaspoon salt, divided
1 teaspoon pepper, divided
1 cup all-purpose flour
2 cups vegetable oil
¼ cup bacon drippings

1. Combine 3 quarts water and 1 tablespoon salt in a large bowl; add chicken. Cover and chill 8 hours.
2. Drain chicken; rinse with cold water, and pat dry.
3. Sprinkle ½ teaspoon salt and ½ teaspoon pepper over chicken.
4. Combine flour, remaining ½ teaspoon salt, and remaining ½ teaspoon pepper in a large freezer bag. Place 2 pieces of chicken in bag; seal and shake to coat. Remove chicken, and repeat procedure with remaining pieces.
5. Combine vegetable oil and bacon drippings in an electric skillet; heat to 360°.
6. Add chicken, a few pieces at a time, skin side down. Cover and cook 6 minutes; uncover and cook 9 more minutes. Turn chicken pieces; cover and cook 6 minutes. Uncover and cook 5 to 9 more minutes, turning pieces during the last 3 minutes for even browning, if necessary. Drain on paper towels.

Chicken With White Barbecue Sauce

MAKES 8 SERVINGS
PREP: 30 MIN., CHILL: 8 HRS., SOAK: 30 MIN., COOK: 2 HRS.

1 cup mayonnaise
½ cup white vinegar
1 tablespoon lemon juice
1 teaspoon salt
1 teaspoon pepper
Hickory wood chips
2 (2½-pound) whole chickens
1 teaspoon salt
1 teaspoon pepper
2 lemons, cut in half

1. Stir together first 5 ingredients; cover sauce, and chill 8 hours.
2. Soak wood chips in water at least 30 minutes.
3. Prepare charcoal fire in smoker; let burn 15 to 20 minutes.
4. Rinse chickens, and pat dry. Sprinkle each chicken with ½ teaspoon salt and ½ teaspoon pepper. Place 2 lemon halves into cavity of each chicken.
5. Drain chips, and place on coals. Place water pan in smoker; add water to depth of fill line. Place chickens on lower food rack; cover with smoker lid.
6. Cook 1 hour and 30 minutes or until a meat thermometer inserted into thigh registers 175°. Serve chicken with sauce.

Pineapple-Glazed
Chicken Thighs

Pineapple-Glazed Chicken Thighs

MAKES 8 SERVINGS
PREP: 15 MIN., COOK: 17 MIN.

1 cup pineapple juice
2 tablespoons brown sugar
1 tablespoon lite soy sauce
1 teaspoon cornstarch
¾ teaspoon salt
½ teaspoon pepper
2 pounds skinned and boned chicken thighs
¼ cup all-purpose flour
1 tablespoon butter or margarine

1. Whisk together first 4 ingredients until smooth; set aside.
2. Sprinkle salt and pepper evenly over chicken. Dust evenly with flour.
3. Melt butter in a large nonstick skillet coated with cooking spray over medium-high heat. Cook chicken 6 to 8 minutes on each side or until done. Remove chicken from pan, and keep warm. Add pineapple juice mixture to skillet, and cook, whisking constantly, 1 minute or until thickened and bubbly. Pour over chicken.

Tandoori Chicken

This spicy chicken dish calls for quite a few ingredients, but it's well worth it. High-heat roasting makes for a short cooking time.

MAKES 8 SERVINGS

PREP: 20 MIN., CHILL: 8 HRS., BAKE: 35 MIN.

6 tablespoons fresh lime juice (about 3 limes)
3 tablespoons plain yogurt
1 to 2 small jalapeño or serrano chile peppers,
    seeded and minced
1½ teaspoons salt
1 teaspoon ground turmeric
1 teaspoon ground coriander
1 teaspoon ground cumin
½ teaspoon ground ginger
½ teaspoon garlic powder
½ teaspoon ground red pepper
¼ teaspoon ground cinnamon
¼ teaspoon ground cloves
2 tablespoons vegetable oil, divided
3 pounds chicken pieces

1. Stir together first 12 ingredients and 1 tablespoon vegetable oil in a large bowl until blended.
2. Skin chicken breasts. Remove breastbones by inserting a sharp knife tip between bone and meat, cutting gently to remove as much meat as possible. Cut breast halves into thirds. Cut deep slits, 1 inch apart, into remaining chicken pieces. (Do not skin pieces.) Add to chicken spice mixture. Thoroughly rub spice mixture into slits. Cover and chill 8 hours.
3. Drizzle remaining 1 tablespoon oil into a large aluminum foil-lined roasting pan. Arrange chicken in a single layer in pan.
4. Bake chicken at 450° for 35 minutes or until done.
Note: We used a cut-up mix of chicken breasts, thighs, legs, and wings.

Beer-Smothered Chicken

MAKES 4 SERVINGS

PREP: 15 MIN.; COOK: 1 HR., 30 MIN.; STAND: 5 MIN.

4 chicken leg-thigh quarters (about 2 pounds),
    separated
½ cup all-purpose flour
2 garlic cloves, minced
¼ cup vegetable oil
1 small onion, diced
½ medium-size green bell pepper, diced
2 (12-ounce) bottles nonalcoholic beer
1 (6-ounce) jar sliced mushrooms, drained
¼ cup lite soy sauce
1 (10¾-ounce) can cream of celery soup, undiluted
1 cup whipping cream
Hot cooked rice

1. Place chicken pieces in a large freezer bag; add flour, and seal. Shake to coat.
2. Sauté garlic in hot oil in a large skillet. Add chicken, and fry, in batches, 5 minutes on each side or until golden brown. Remove chicken, reserving drippings in skillet. Sauté onion and bell pepper in drippings 5 minutes or until tender; add chicken, beer, mushrooms, and soy sauce.
3. Cook over medium heat for 30 minutes. Stir in soup; cook, stirring occasionally, 30 more minutes. Add whipping cream; cook until thoroughly heated. Let stand 5 minutes. Serve over hot cooked rice.

Chicken in Lemon Marinade

Chicken in Lemon Marinade

MAKES 6 SERVINGS
PREP: 10 MIN., CHILL: 2 HRS., GRILL: 10 MIN.

⅔ cup vegetable oil
½ cup lemon juice
1 tablespoon Worcestershire sauce
⅛ teaspoon hot sauce
1 small onion, grated
1 teaspoon salt
1 teaspoon pepper
1 teaspoon celery salt
6 skinned and boned chicken breasts
Garnishes: lemon rind curls, parsley sprigs

1. Process first 8 ingredients in a blender until smooth, stopping to scrape down sides. Reserve ¼ cup lemon mixture, and chill.
2. Place chicken in a shallow dish or zip-top freezer bag; pour remaining lemon mixture over chicken. Cover or seal, and chill 2 hours, turning chicken occasionally.
3. Remove chicken from marinade, discarding marinade.
4. Grill chicken, covered with grill lid, over medium-high heat (350° to 400°) for 3 to 5 minutes on each side or until done, basting chicken frequently with reserved ¼ cup lemon mixture. Garnish, if desired.

Peppery Chicken-fried Chicken

Cut leftover chicken into strips, and serve over salad greens. Drizzle with creamy Ranch or blue cheese dressing. (Pictured on page 141.)

MAKES 8 TO 10 SERVINGS
PREP: 30 MIN., FRY: 15 MIN. PER BATCH, COOK: 12 MIN.

8 (6-ounce) skinned and boned chicken breasts
4½ teaspoons salt, divided
2½ teaspoons freshly ground black pepper, divided
76 saltine crackers (2 sleeves), crushed
2½ cups all-purpose flour, divided
1 teaspoon baking powder
1 teaspoon ground red pepper
8 cups milk, divided
4 large eggs
Peanut oil

1. Place chicken breasts between 2 sheets of heavy-duty plastic wrap, and flatten to a ¼-inch thickness, using the flat side of a meat mallet or rolling pin.
2. Sprinkle ½ teaspoon salt and ½ teaspoon black pepper evenly over chicken. Set aside.
3. Combine cracker crumbs, 2 cups flour, baking powder, 1½ teaspoons salt, 1 teaspoon black pepper, and ground red pepper.
4. Whisk together 1½ cups milk and eggs. Dredge chicken in cracker crumb mixture; dip in milk mixture, and dredge in cracker mixture again.
5. Pour oil to a depth of ½ inch in a 12-inch skillet. (Do not use a nonstick skillet.) Heat to 360°. Fry chicken, in batches, 10 minutes, adding oil as needed. Turn and fry 4 to 5 more minutes or until golden brown. Remove to a wire rack in a jelly-roll pan. Keep chicken warm in a 225° oven. Carefully drain hot oil, reserving cooked bits and 2 tablespoons drippings in skillet.
6. Whisk together remaining ½ cup flour, 2½ teaspoons salt, remaining 1 teaspoon black pepper, and 6½ cups milk. Pour mixture into reserved drippings in skillet; cook over medium-high heat, whisking constantly, 10 to 12 minutes or until thickened. Serve gravy with chicken.

Buttermilk Baked Chicken

MAKES 4 SERVINGS
PREP: 10 MIN., BAKE: 45 MIN.

¼ cup butter or margarine
4 bone-in chicken breasts*
½ teaspoon salt
½ teaspoon pepper
1½ cups buttermilk, divided
¾ cup all-purpose flour
1 (10¾-ounce) can cream of mushroom soup, undiluted

1. Melt butter in a lightly greased 13- x 9-inch baking dish in a 425° oven.
2. Sprinkle chicken with salt and pepper. Dip chicken in ½ cup buttermilk, and dredge in flour. Arrange chicken, breast side down, in baking dish.
3. Bake at 425° for 25 minutes. Turn chicken, and bake 10 more minutes.
4. Stir together remaining 1 cup buttermilk and soup; pour over chicken, and bake 10 more minutes, shielding chicken with aluminum foil to prevent excessive browning, if necessary. Drizzle gravy in dish over chicken when serving.
*4 skinned and boned chicken breast halves may be substituted for 4 bone-in chicken breast halves, if desired. Bake chicken at 425° for 15 minutes. Turn and bake 10 more minutes.

Arroz Con Pollo

Arroz Con Pollo

The recipe name is Spanish for "rice with chicken." This dish includes all the traditional flavors, but convenience products reduce hands-on time in the kitchen.

MAKES 8 SERVINGS
PREP: 10 MIN., COOK: 1 HR., STAND: 5 MIN.

8 skinned and boned chicken breasts
3 tablespoons olive oil, divided
1 teaspoon salt
1 large onion, diced
1 large green bell pepper, chopped
1 (14½-ounce) can diced tomatoes with basil, garlic, and oregano
1 (10-ounce) package yellow rice with seasoning mix
2 (14½-ounce) cans chicken broth
½ teaspoon ground black pepper

1. Brush chicken evenly with 2 tablespoons oil; sprinkle with salt.
2. Heat a large nonstick skillet over medium heat. Add chicken, and brown, in two batches, 4 to 5 minutes on each side. Remove chicken, and set aside.
3. Sauté diced onion and chopped bell pepper in remaining 1 tablespoon hot oil in skillet over medium heat 8 to 10 minutes or until tender.
4. Return chicken to skillet; stir in diced tomatoes and remaining ingredients. Cover, reduce heat to low, and cook 40 minutes or until liquid is absorbed and rice is tender. Remove skillet from heat, and let stand, covered, 5 minutes before serving.
Note: For testing purposes only, we used Vigo Yellow Rice. It can found with rice mixes at your local grocery.

Chicken With Onions

Crushed red pepper packs a punch in these chicken breasts smothered with onions and served over rice. You pick the amount of red pepper based on your taste preferences.

MAKES 8 SERVINGS
PREP: 15 MIN., COOK: 24 MIN.

3 cups uncooked long-grain rice
8 skinned and boned chicken breasts
2 teaspoons salt
2 to 3 teaspoons dried crushed red pepper
2 tablespoons bacon drippings
4 large onions, thinly sliced (6 cups)

1. Cook rice according to package directions. Set aside, and keep warm.
2. Sprinkle chicken breasts with salt and crushed red pepper.
3. Brown chicken breasts, 4 at a time, in hot bacon drippings in a large skillet over high heat 2 minutes. Remove chicken from skillet.
4. Add onion slices to skillet, and sauté 10 minutes. Return chicken breasts to skillet, and cook 10 more minutes. Serve with hot cooked rice.

Rosemary Grilled Chicken

Rosemary Grilled Chicken

Be careful when basting over an open flame, especially if your sauce contains oil or butter because any drippings can cause your grill to flare.

MAKES 6 TO 8 SERVINGS
PREP: 20 MIN., CHILL: 4 HRS., GRILL: 28 MIN.

1 cup dry white wine
½ cup olive oil
1 teaspoon Worcestershire sauce
2 tablespoons chopped fresh parsley
2 bay leaves
2 green onions, chopped
3 garlic cloves, minced
1 teaspoon dried oregano
2 teaspoons salt, divided
1 teaspoon pepper, divided
3 pounds bone-in and skin-on chicken thighs
Fresh rosemary sprigs
Juice of 1 lemon
Garnishes: fresh rosemary sprigs, lemon wedges

1. Stir together first 8 ingredients, 1 teaspoon salt, and ½ teaspoon pepper. Reserve ⅓ cup wine mixture.
2. Place chicken in a large shallow dish or large zip-top freezer bag. Pour remaining wine mixture over chicken. Cover or seal, and chill 2 to 4 hours, turning occasionally.
3. Remove chicken from marinade, discarding marinade. Sprinkle chicken with remaining 1 teaspoon salt and ½ teaspoon pepper.
4. Grill chicken, covered with grill lid, over medium-low heat (300° to 325°) for 14 minutes on each side or until done, brushing occasionally with reserved ⅓ cup wine mixture using rosemary sprigs. Place chicken on a serving platter; drizzle with lemon juice. Garnish, if desired.

Grilled Chicken With Spicy Soba Noodles

Find soba noodles in the Asian section of a supermarket or in an Asian market.

MAKES 4 SERVINGS
PREP: 25 MIN., CHILL: 3 HRS., GRILL: 12 MIN., COOK: 4 MIN.

3 tablespoons soy sauce
2 teaspoons grated fresh ginger
2 garlic cloves, minced
4 skinned and boned chicken breasts
8½ ounces soba noodles, uncooked (about 4 cups
    cooked noodles)
1 red bell pepper, cut into thin strips
1 cup snow peas, cut diagonally into thin strips
5 green onions, sliced
Asian Dressing
2 tablespoons sesame seeds, toasted

1. Combine first 3 ingredients in a zip-top freezer bag, and add chicken. Seal bag, and chill 3 hours, turning occasionally. Remove chicken from marinade, discarding marinade.
2. Grill, covered with grill lid, over medium heat (300° to 350°) for 6 minutes on each side or until chicken is done. Cool; slice thinly, and set aside.
3. Cook noodles in boiling water according to package directions (do not overcook); drain. Rinse in cold running water until chilled; drain well.
4. Combine chicken, noodles, bell pepper, snow peas, and green onions. Drizzle with Asian Dressing, tossing to coat. Sprinkle with sesame seeds. Serve immediately, or cover and chill up to 2 days.

Asian Dressing:

MAKES ¾ CUP
PREP: 5 MIN.

2 tablespoons light brown sugar
2 tablespoons chili garlic sauce
2½ tablespoons rice vinegar
2½ tablespoons soy sauce
2 tablespoons vegetable oil
2 tablespoons dark sesame oil

1. Whisk together all ingredients. Cover and chill until ready to use.

Garlicky-Lime Grilled Chicken Breasts

MAKES 4 SERVINGS
PREP: 10 MIN., CHILL: 1 HR., GRILL: 16 MIN.

1 teaspoon grated lime rind
⅓ cup fresh lime juice
1 tablespoon sesame oil*
1 teaspoon salt
2 garlic cloves, minced
4 skinned and boned chicken breasts

1. Stir together first 5 ingredients in a shallow dish or zip-top freezer bag; add chicken. Cover or seal, and chill 1 hour.
2. Remove chicken from marinade, discarding marinade.
3. Grill, covered with grill lid, over medium-high heat (350° to 400°) 6 to 8 minutes on each side or until done.

Garlicky-Lime Grilled Chicken Thighs: Substitute 4 skinned and boned chicken thighs for breasts.

*1 tablespoon olive oil may be substituted for 1 tablespoon sesame oil.

Quick Chicken Tostadas

Accompany these tostadas with orange wedges and salsa-spiked refried beans.

MAKES 6 SERVINGS
PREP: 15 MIN., BAKE: 9 MIN.

6 (6-inch) flour tortillas
2 tablespoons butter, melted
4 grilled chicken breasts, chopped (from Chicken Fajitas recipe at right)
2 tomatoes, chopped
1 (4.5-ounce) can chopped green chiles
½ cup (2 ounces) shredded Monterey Jack cheese
½ cup (2 ounces) shredded Cheddar cheese
3 green onions, chopped
Paprika (optional)
Sour cream

1. Place tortillas in a single layer on baking sheets; brush with butter.
2. Bake at 400° for 4 to 5 minutes or until lightly browned.
3. Combine chicken, tomato, and chiles; spoon evenly onto tortillas. Top evenly with cheeses and green onions; sprinkle with paprika, if desired. Bake 3 to 4 more minutes or until cheeses melt. Serve tostadas with sour cream.

Chicken Fajitas

Serve these fajitas when company's coming. Complete the meal with spicy salsa, tortilla chips, drinks on ice, and chocolate cookies. Save 4 of the chicken breasts to prepare the recipe at left for another meal.

MAKES 6 SERVINGS
PREP: 10 MIN., CHILL: 2 HRS., GRILL: 25 MIN.

1 cup vegetable oil
½ cup lime juice
½ cup chopped fresh cilantro
4 garlic cloves, pressed
2 teaspoons salt
1½ tablespoons black pepper
8 large skinned and boned chicken breasts
12 (6-inch) flour tortillas
1 avocado, peeled and sliced
2 cups (8 ounces) shredded Monterey Jack cheese
1 red bell pepper, cut into strips
1 yellow bell pepper, cut into strips
12 romaine lettuce leaves
Sour cream
Salsa

1. Whisk together first 6 ingredients in a shallow dish or large zip-top freezer bag; add chicken. Cover or seal, and chill 1 to 2 hours, turning occasionally.
2. Remove chicken from marinade, discarding marinade.
3. Grill, covered with grill lid, over medium-high heat (350° to 400°) 20 to 25 minutes or until done. Chop 4 chicken breasts (reserve remaining chicken for Quick Chicken Tostadas at left). Top tortillas evenly with chicken, avocado, and next 4 ingredients; roll up, and serve with sour cream and salsa.

Grilled Chicken and Vegetables

MAKES 6 SERVINGS
PREP: 10 MIN., CHILL: 8 HRS., GRILL: 18 MIN.

6 skinned and boned chicken breasts 2 small
   zucchini, cut into ¼-inch-thick slices
2 yellow squash, cut into ¼-inch-thick slices
2 medium-size red bell peppers, seeded and cut into
   2-inch pieces
2 large onions, cut into 8 wedges
1 (8-ounce) bottle sweet and sour dressing
1 (8-ounce) bottle Italian dressing
½ cup dry white wine or chicken broth
¼ cup soy sauce

1. Place chicken breasts in a large zip-top freezer bag. Place zucchini and next 3 ingredients in a zip-top freezer bag. Whisk together dressings, white wine, and soy sauce, reserving ½ cup of marinade mixture for other uses. Pour remaining marinade evenly over both chicken and vegetables; seal bags, and chill 8 hours, turning occasionally.
2. Remove chicken and vegetables from marinade; discard marinade. Arrange vegetables evenly in a lightly greased grill basket. Coat chicken with cooking spray. Place chicken and grill basket on grill rack.
3. Grill, covered with grill lid, over medium-high heat (350° to 400°) 18 minutes or until vegetables are crisp-tender and chicken is done, turning once.
Note: The unused marinade mixture can be used in coleslaw.

Chicken and Grits

A classic Southern dish, grits pair well with a variety of main dishes such as shrimp, pork, and sausage. Grits taste delicious here mixed with chopped cooked chicken.

MAKES 4 TO 6 SERVINGS
PREP: 10 MIN., COOK: 15 MIN., BAKE: 30 MIN.

2 (14-ounce) cans chicken broth
1 cup uncooked quick-cooking grits
1 (8-ounce) jar process cheese spread
3 large eggs, lightly beaten
2 cups chopped cooked chicken
1/2 teaspoon poultry seasoning

1. Bring broth to a boil in a large saucepan over medium-high heat; stir in grits. Cover, reduce heat, and simmer 5 minutes; stir occasionally.
2. Add cheese and remaining ingredients, stirring well. Pour into a greased 11- x 7-inch baking dish.
3. Bake, uncovered, at 375° for 30 minutes.

Grilled Chicken Tortas

MAKES 8 SERVINGS
PREP: 35 MIN., CHILL: 1 HR., STAND: 10 MIN., GRILL: 17 MIN.

4 large skinned and boned chicken breasts
1 (16-ounce) container refrigerated hot chile salsa
1/4 cup tequila
2 tablespoons chopped fresh cilantro
2 tablespoons lime juice
3 poblano chile peppers
1/4 teaspoon salt
1 (16-ounce) can refried beans or black beans
1 tablespoon olive oil
8 (6-inch) crusty sandwich rolls, split
3 avocados, peeled and mashed
2 cups (8 ounces) shredded Monterey Jack cheese

1. Place chicken breasts between 2 sheets of heavy-duty plastic wrap, and flatten to a 1/4-inch thickness, using a meat mallet or rolling pin.
2. Stir together salsa and next 3 ingredients. Remove 1 cup mixture, and reserve; set aside remaining mixture.
3. Place chicken in a shallow dish or zip-top freezer bag; pour 1 cup reserved salsa mixture over chicken. Cover or seal; chill 1 hour, turning occasionally. Remove chicken from marinade; discard marinade.
4. Grill peppers, covered with grill lid, over medium-high heat (350° to 400°) 5 to 7 minutes, turning often, until peppers look blistered.
5. Place peppers in a zip-top freezer bag; seal and let stand 10 minutes to loosen skins. Peel peppers; remove and discard seeds. Cut peppers into thin strips; set aside.
6. Grill chicken, covered with grill lid, over medium-high heat (350° to 400°) about 5 minutes on each side or until done. Cool slightly. Cut chicken into thin slices, and sprinkle evenly with salt.
7. Stir together beans and olive oil in a 1-quart glass bowl, and microwave at HIGH 2 minutes or until thoroughly heated, stirring once.
8. Spread beans evenly over bottom halves of rolls. Spread avocado over top halves of rolls. Top bottom halves evenly with chicken, pepper strips, cheese, and top halves of rolls. Serve with remaining salsa mixture.

Chicken Cakes With Rémoulade Sauce

These cakes also make terrific appetizers. Just halve the amount of mixture, and form into 18 patties.

MAKES 4 SERVINGS
PREP: 15 MIN., COOK: 16 MIN.

2 tablespoons butter or margarine
½ medium-size red bell pepper, diced
4 green onions, thinly sliced
1 garlic clove, pressed
3 cups chopped cooked chicken
1 cup soft breadcrumbs
1 large egg, lightly beaten
2 tablespoons mayonnaise
1 tablespoon Creole mustard
1 teaspoon Creole seasoning
¼ cup vegetable oil
Rémoulade Sauce
Garnish: mixed baby greens

1. Melt butter in a large skillet over medium heat.
2. Add bell pepper, green onions, and garlic, and sauté 3 to 4 minutes or until vegetables are tender.
3. Stir together bell pepper mixture, chicken, and next 5 ingredients in a bowl. Shape chicken mixture into 8 (3½-inch) patties.

4. Fry 4 patties in 2 tablespoons hot oil in a large skillet over medium heat 3 minutes on each side or until golden brown. Drain on paper towels.
5. Repeat procedure with remaining 2 tablespoons oil and patties. Serve chicken cakes immediately with Rémoulade Sauce. Garnish, if desired.

Rémoulade Sauce:

MAKES ABOUT 1¼ CUPS
PREP: 5 MIN.

1 cup mayonnaise
3 green onions, sliced
2 tablespoons Creole mustard
2 garlic cloves, pressed
1 tablespoon chopped fresh parsley
¼ teaspoon ground red pepper

1. Stir together all ingredients until sauce is well blended.

Chicken Cakes With
Rémoulade Sauce

Chicken Tetrazzini

Chicken Tetrazzini

This casserole is perfect for a ladies luncheon. Serve with steamed asparagus, broiled tomatoes, and dinner rolls or sweet rolls.

MAKES 8 SERVINGS
PREP: 30 MIN., COOK: 15 MIN., BAKE: 35 MIN.

½ cup butter or margarine
½ medium-size sweet onion, diced
½ cup all-purpose flour
4 cups milk
½ cup dry white wine
2 tablespoons chicken bouillon granules
1 teaspoon seasoned pepper
1½ cups freshly grated Parmesan cheese, divided
4 cups diced cooked chicken
12 ounces vermicelli, cooked
1 (6-ounce) jar sliced mushrooms, drained
1 cup soft breadcrumbs
2 tablespoons butter or margarine, melted

1. Melt ½ cup butter in a Dutch oven over medium-high heat; add diced onion, and sauté 5 minutes or until tender.
2. Whisk in flour until smooth, and cook, whisking constantly, 1 minute. Gradually add milk and wine; cook, whisking constantly, 5 to 6 minutes or until mixture is thickened.
3. Add bouillon granules, pepper, and 1 cup cheese. Cook, whisking constantly, 1 minute or until granules dissolve and cheese melts; remove from heat. Stir in chicken, pasta, and mushrooms. Spoon into a lightly greased 13- x 9-inch baking dish.
4. Bake chicken mixture, covered, at 350° for 20 minutes.
5. Stir together remaining ½ cup cheese, breadcrumbs, and 2 tablespoons melted butter, and sprinkle evenly over casserole. Bake casserole 10 to 15 more minutes.

Leslie's Favorite Chicken-and-Wild Rice Casserole

MAKES 6 TO 8 SERVINGS
PREP: 20 MIN., COOK: 10 MIN., BAKE: 35 MIN.

2 (6.2-ounce) packages fast-cooking long-grain and wild rice mix
¼ cup butter or margarine
2 medium onions, chopped
4 celery ribs, chopped
2 (8-ounce) cans sliced water chestnuts, drained
5 cups chopped cooked chicken
4 cups (1 pound) shredded Cheddar cheese, divided
2 (10¾-ounce) cans cream of mushroom soup, undiluted
2 (8-ounce) containers sour cream
1 cup milk
½ teaspoon salt
½ teaspoon pepper
½ cup soft breadcrumbs (optional)

1. Prepare rice according to package directions; set aside.
2. Melt butter in a large skillet over medium heat; add onions, celery, and water chestnuts. Sauté 10 minutes or until vegetables are tender.
3. Stir in rice, chicken, 3 cups Cheddar cheese, and next 5 ingredients; spoon mixture into a lightly greased 15- x 10-inch baking dish or a 4-quart casserole. Top with breadcrumbs, if desired.
4. Bake casserole at 350° for 30 minutes. Sprinkle with remaining 1 cup Cheddar cheese, and bake 5 more minutes.
To Make Ahead: Casserole may be frozen up to 1 month. Let stand at room temperature 1 hour. Bake, covered, at 350° for 30 minutes. Uncover and bake 55 more minutes. Sprinkle with cheese, and bake 5 more minutes.

Individual Chicken Pot Pies

Individual Chicken Pot Pies

MAKES 4 SERVINGS
PREP: 25 MIN., BAKE: 20 MIN.

1 (14½-ounce) can chicken broth
1 (2.64-ounce) package country gravy mix
3 cups finely chopped cooked chicken
1 (16-ounce) package frozen cut vegetable medley,
    thawed
¼ to ½ teaspoon garlic powder
1 (15-ounce) package refrigerated piecrusts

1. Whisk together chicken broth and gravy mix in a medium saucepan; cook over medium heat, whisking constantly, until thickened. Remove from heat. Stir in chopped cooked chicken, vegetable medley, and garlic powder.

2. Cut each piecrust into fourths. Press 1 portion into the bottom and up the sides of each of 4 (10-ounce) ramekins or soufflé dishes. Trim pointed ends.

3. Spoon chicken mixture evenly into prepared cups. Top with remaining piecrust portions, pulling crust slightly to fit if necessary. Trim pointed ends; fold edges under, and crimp. Cut a small slit in center of each pie.

4. Heat a baking sheet at 400° for 5 minutes. Remove from oven, and place ramekins on baking sheet.

5. Bake at 400° on lower rack 15 to 20 minutes or until golden brown.

Note: To prepare 1 pot pie, place 1 piecrust in a 9-inch deep-dish pie plate; spoon in chicken mixture. Top with remaining piecrust, pinching edges to seal. Cut several small slits in crust. Bake at 400° for 35 to 40 minutes or until golden brown.

Quick Chicken and Dumplings

One whole roasted chicken or 6 skinned and boned cooked chicken breasts yield about 3 cups chopped meat.

MAKES 4 TO 6 SERVINGS
PREP: 10 MIN., COOK: 25 MIN.

4 cups water
3 cups chopped cooked chicken
2 (10¾-ounce) cans cream of chicken soup, undiluted
2 teaspoons chicken bouillon granules
1 teaspoon seasoned pepper
1 (7.5-ounce) can refrigerated buttermilk biscuits

1. Bring first 5 ingredients to a boil in a Dutch oven over medium-high heat, stirring often.
2. Separate biscuits in half, forming 2 rounds; cut each round in half. Drop biscuit pieces, 1 at a time, into boiling mixture; stir gently. Cover, reduce heat to low, and simmer, stirring occasionally, 15 to 20 minutes.
To Lighten: Use reduced-sodium, reduced-fat cream of chicken soup; reduced-fat biscuits; and chopped, cooked chicken breasts.

Old Fashioned Chicken and Dumplings

MAKES 8 SERVINGS
PREP: 30 MIN.; COOK: 1 HR., 30 MIN.

1 (2½-pound) whole chicken, cut up
2½ teaspoons salt, divided
¾ teaspoon black pepper, divided
½ teaspoon garlic powder
½ teaspoon dried thyme
¼ teaspoon ground red pepper
1 teaspoon chicken bouillon granules
3 cups self-rising flour
½ teaspoon poultry seasoning
⅓ cup shortening
2 teaspoons bacon drippings
1 cup milk

1. Cover chicken with water, and bring to a boil in a large Dutch oven. Add 1½ teaspoons salt, ½ teaspoon pepper, garlic powder, thyme, and red pepper. Cover, reduce heat, and simmer 1 hour.
2. Remove chicken, reserving broth in Dutch oven; cool chicken. Skim fat from broth, and bring broth to a simmer.

3. Skin, bone, and coarsely chop chicken. Add chicken, bouillon granules, and remaining salt and pepper to broth. Return to simmer.
4. Combine flour and poultry seasoning in a bowl. Cut in shortening and bacon drippings with a pastry blender until mixture is crumbly. Add milk, stirring until dry ingredients are moistened.
5. Turn dough out onto a lightly floured surface. Roll out to ⅛-inch thickness; cut into 1-inch pieces.
6. Bring broth mixture to a boil. Drop dumplings, a few at a time, into boiling broth, stirring gently. Reduce heat, cover, and simmer, stirring often, for 25 minutes.

Creamy Chicken Casserole

MAKES 6 SERVINGS
PREP: 9 MIN., COOK: 1 HR., BAKE: 35 MIN.

1 (3½-pound) whole chicken*
1 quart water
1 teaspoon salt
1 teaspoon pepper
1 bay leaf
1 (10¾-ounce) can cream of chicken soup with herbs, undiluted
1 (10¾-ounce) can cream of celery soup, undiluted
1 (8-ounce) container sour cream
½ teaspoon pepper
½ (16-ounce) package oval-shaped buttery crackers, crushed (2 stacks; 3 cups)
¼ cup butter or margarine, melted

1. Combine first 5 ingredients in a large Dutch oven; bring to a boil. Reduce heat, and simmer, uncovered, 1 hour or until tender. Remove chicken, and cool slightly. (Discard bay leaf, and reserve broth for another use.)
2. Skin and bone chicken; cut chicken into bite-size pieces. Combine chicken, chicken soup, and next 3 ingredients, stirring well.
3. Place half of crushed crackers in a lightly greased 11- x 7-inch baking dish; spoon chicken mixture over crackers. Top the chicken mixture with remaining crackers, and drizzle with butter.
4. Bake, uncovered, at 325° for 35 minutes or until casserole is lightly browned.
*3¼ cups leftover chopped chicken may be substituted for the whole chicken.

Deluxe Chicken Casserole

Deluxe Chicken Casserole

If this dish reminds you of similar casseroles you had growing up, then you'll enjoy it as much as we did.
The chopped nuts are an added pleasure.

MAKES 6 SERVINGS
PREP: 15 MIN., BAKE: 15 MIN.

1½ cups diced cooked chicken
1½ cups cooked rice
1 cup chopped celery
½ cup chopped walnuts or pecans
1 (10¾-ounce) can cream of chicken soup, undiluted
2 teaspoons finely chopped onion
½ teaspoon salt
½ teaspoon black pepper
¼ teaspoon ground red pepper
1 tablespoon lemon juice
¾ cup mayonnaise
¼ cup water
3 hard-cooked eggs, sliced
2 cups coarsely crumbled potato chips

1. Combine first 10 ingredients in a large bowl. Combine mayonnaise and water; stir with a wire whisk until smooth. Add mayonnaise mixture to chicken mixture. Gently fold in egg slices.
2. Spoon mixture into a greased 11- x 7-inch baking dish; top with potato chips. Bake, uncovered, at 400° for 15 minutes or until bubbly.

Chicken Cobbler With Caramelized Sweet Onions

MAKES 6 SERVINGS
PREP: 45 MIN., BAKE: 40 MIN.

⅓ cup butter
2 cups Caramelized Sweet Onions (see recipe on page 256)
¼ cup all-purpose flour
1 (12-ounce) can evaporated milk
1 cup chicken broth
½ cup dry white wine
1 tablespoon chicken bouillon granules
¼ teaspoon pepper
3 cups coarsely chopped cooked chicken
3 tablespoons chopped fresh parsley
1 (15-ounce) package refrigerated piecrusts
½ cup finely chopped pecans, toasted
½ cup grated Parmesan cheese

1. Melt butter in a large skillet over medium heat; add Caramelized Sweet Onions, and cook 1 to 2 minutes. Add flour; cook, stirring constantly, 1 minute. Gradually stir in evaporated milk, chicken broth, and wine; cook, stirring constantly, 5 minutes or until thickened. Add bouillon and pepper. Remove from heat; stir in chicken and parsley. Pour chicken mixture into a lightly greased 10-inch deep dish pieplate.
2. Unroll piecrusts. Sprinkle 1 piecrust with pecans and Parmesan cheese. Top with remaining piecrust. Roll into a 14-inch circle; press edges to seal. Cut into ¾-inch-wide strips. Arrange strips in a lattice design over filling, reserving any extra strips; fold edges under.
3. Bake at 425° for 35 to 40 minutes or until golden.
4. Place remaining strips on a lightly greased baking sheet. Bake at 425° for 10 to 12 minutes or until golden brown. Serve with cobbler.
Note: You can use an 11- x 7-inch lightly greased baking dish instead of a pieplate.

Heavenly Chicken Lasagna

MAKES 8 TO 10 SERVINGS
PREP: 30 MIN., COOK: 10 MIN., BAKE: 50 MIN., STAND: 10 MIN.

1 tablespoon butter or margarine
½ large onion, chopped
1 (10½-ounce) can reduced-fat cream of chicken soup, undiluted
1 (10-ounce) container refrigerated reduced-fat Alfredo sauce
1 (7-ounce) jar diced pimiento, undrained
1 (6-ounce) jar sliced mushrooms, drained
⅓ cup dry white wine
½ teaspoon dried basil
1 (10-ounce) package frozen chopped spinach, thawed
1 cup cottage cheese
1 cup ricotta cheese
½ cup grated Parmesan cheese
1 large egg, lightly beaten
9 lasagna noodles, cooked
2½ cups chopped cooked chicken
3 cups (12 ounces) shredded sharp Cheddar cheese, divided

1. Melt butter in a skillet over medium-high heat. Add onion, and sauté 5 minutes or until tender. Stir in soup and next 5 ingredients. Reserve 1 cup sauce.
2. Drain spinach well, pressing between layers of paper towels.
3. Stir together spinach, cottage cheese, ricotta cheese, grated Parmesan cheese, and egg.
4. Place 3 lasagna noodles in a lightly greased 13- x 9-inch baking dish. Layer with half each of sauce, spinach mixture, and chicken. Sprinkle with 1 cup Cheddar cheese. Repeat procedure. Top with remaining 3 noodles and reserved 1 cup sauce. Cover and chill up to 1 day ahead, if desired.
5. Bake at 350° for 45 minutes. Sprinkle with remaining 1 cup Cheddar cheese, and bake 5 more minutes or until cheese is melted. Let stand 10 minutes before serving.
Note: For testing purposes only, we used Buitoni Refrigerated Light Alfredo Sauce, found in the dairy section of the supermarket.

Chicken Enchilada Casserole

Chicken Enchilada Casserole

MAKES 8 SERVINGS
PREP: 40 MIN., COOK: 38 MIN., BAKE: 45 MIN.

2 tablespoons olive oil, divided
1½ pounds skinned and boned chicken breasts
1 large onion, chopped
4 garlic cloves, minced
2 (14.5-ounce) cans Mexican-style stewed tomatoes,
    undrained and chopped
¼ teaspoon ground red pepper
2 (4.5-ounce) cans chopped green chiles, drained
½ cup butter or margarine
⅓ cup all-purpose flour
2 tablespoons fajita seasoning
2 cups half-and-half
9 (6-inch) corn tortillas, cut in half
1 (8-ounce) package shredded Mexican cheese blend,
    divided
Garnishes: sour cream, salsa, avocado slices, cilantro
    sprigs

1. Heat 1 tablespoon oil in a large skillet over medium-high heat; add chicken breasts. Cook 6 to 7 minutes on each side or until done. Remove from pan; cool and shred chicken.

2. Heat remaining 1 tablespoon oil in skillet over medium-high heat. Add onion and garlic; cook 4 minutes or until tender. Add tomatoes and red pepper; cook for 15 minutes or until most of liquid evaporates. Remove from heat, and stir in shredded chicken and green chiles.

3. Melt butter in a heavy saucepan over low heat. Add flour and fajita seasoning; whisk until smooth. Cook 1 minute, whisking constantly. Gradually add half-and-half; cook over medium heat 4 minutes or until thick and bubbly, whisking constantly.

4. Spread one-fourth white sauce in a lightly greased 13- x 9-inch baking dish. Arrange 6 tortilla halves over sauce. Top with half of chicken mixture and ⅔ cup cheese. Repeat layers once, ending with cheese. Spoon one-fourth sauce over the cheese, and top with remaining tortilla halves. Spoon remaining sauce over tortillas. Reserve remaining ⅔ cup cheese. Bake, uncovered, at 350° for 40 minutes or until thoroughly heated. Sprinkle with reserved ⅔ cup cheese, and bake 5 more minutes. Garnish, if desired.

Chicken Cannelloni With Roasted Red Bell Pepper Sauce

MAKES 6 TO 8 SERVINGS

PREP: 30 MIN., COOK: 10 MIN., BAKE: 30 MIN.

1 (8-ounce) package cannelloni or manicotti shells
4 cups finely chopped cooked chicken
2 (8-ounce) containers chive-and-onion cream cheese
1 (10-ounce) package frozen chopped spinach,
    thawed and well drained
2 cups (8 ounces) shredded mozzarella cheese
1/2 cup Italian-seasoned breadcrumbs
3/4 teaspoon garlic salt
1 teaspoon seasoned pepper
Roasted Red Bell Pepper Sauce
Garnish: chopped fresh basil or parsley

1. Cook pasta according to package directions; drain.
2. Stir together chicken and next 6 ingredients.
3. Cut a slit down length of each pasta shell. Spoon about 1/2 cup chicken mixture into each shell, gently pressing cut sides back together. Place, cut sides down, in 2 lightly greased 11- x 7-inch baking dishes. Pour Roasted Red Bell Pepper Sauce evenly over shells.
4. Bake, covered, at 350° for 25 to 30 minutes or until thoroughly heated. Garnish, if desired.
To Make Ahead: For quick weeknight solutions, prepare and stuff cannelloni shells. Wrap tightly with wax paper; freeze until ready to serve. Let thaw in the refrigerator. Unwrap cannelloni, and place in a baking dish; top with your favorite supermarket pasta sauce, and bake as directed.

Roasted Red Bell Pepper Sauce:

This sauce is also great over your favorite noodles.

MAKES 3 1/2 CUPS

PREP: 5 MIN.

2 (7-ounce) jars roasted red bell peppers, drained
1 (16-ounce) jar creamy Alfredo sauce
1 (3-ounce) package shredded Parmesan cheese

1. Process all ingredients in a blender until smooth, stopping to scrape down sides.
Note: For testing purposes only, we used Bertolli Five Brothers Creamy Alfredo Sauce.

King Ranch Chicken Casserole

If you're watching your fat intake, just substitute low-fat soups for the full-fat version, and use baked tortilla chips.

MAKES 6 TO 8 SERVINGS

PREP: 35 MIN., COOK: 5 MIN., BAKE: 35 MIN.

1 large onion, chopped
1 large green bell pepper, chopped
2 tablespoons vegetable oil
2 cups chopped cooked chicken
1 (10 3/4-ounce) can cream of chicken soup, undiluted
1 (10 3/4-ounce) can cream of mushroom soup,
    undiluted
1 (10-ounce) can diced tomatoes and green chiles,
    undrained
1 teaspoon chili powder
1/4 teaspoon salt
1/4 teaspoon garlic powder
1/4 teaspoon black pepper
12 (6-inch) corn tortillas
2 cups (8 ounces) shredded Cheddar cheese, divided

1. Sauté onion and bell pepper in hot oil in a large skillet over medium-high heat 5 minutes or until tender. Stir in chicken and next 7 ingredients; remove from heat.
2. Tear tortillas into 1-inch pieces; layer one-third of tortilla pieces in bottom of a lightly greased 13- x 9-inch baking dish. Top with one-third of chicken mixture and 2/3 cup cheese. Repeat layers twice.
3. Bake casserole at 350° for 30 to 35 minutes.
To Make Ahead: Freeze casserole up to 1 month, if desired. Thaw in refrigerator overnight; let stand at room temperature 20 minutes, and bake as directed.

Chicken Basque

Chicken Basque

Chock-full of zucchini, roasted red peppers, Italian sausage, and chicken, this Mediterranean-inspired dish easily serves as a one-dish meal.

MAKES 6 TO 8 SERVINGS
PREP: 17 MIN., COOK: 27 MIN.

2 pounds zucchini, cut into ³/₄-inch-thick slices
2 tablespoons olive oil
1¹/₂ teaspoons salt
1 teaspoon pepper
³/₄ pound mild or hot Italian link sausage
1 tablespoon butter or margarine, melted
1 medium onion, chopped
8 ounces small fresh mushrooms
1 garlic clove, minced
¹/₄ cup olive oil
1¹/₂ pounds skinned and boned chicken breasts, left intact or cut into 1-inch pieces
1 cup all-purpose flour
1 cup dry vermouth
1 (15-ounce) jar roasted red peppers, coarsely chopped
1 tablespoon chopped fresh parsley
1 bay leaf
¹/₂ teaspoon dried basil
¹/₂ teaspoon dried thyme

1. Sauté zucchini in 2 tablespoons hot olive oil in a large skillet over high heat 3 minutes or until browned. Sprinkle with salt and pepper; stir well. Remove from skillet with a slotted spoon; set aside.
2. Reduce heat to medium-high. Add sausage to skillet; cook 8 minutes or until browned and no longer pink. Drain, reserving 1 tablespoon drippings in skillet. Cut sausage into ³/₄-inch-thick slices; set aside.
3. Add butter and next 3 ingredients to skillet; cook, stirring often, until onion is tender and mushroom liquid evaporates. Remove vegetables from skillet, using a slotted spoon.
4. Heat ¹/₄ cup olive oil in same skillet over medium-high heat. Dredge chicken in flour; cook chicken in hot oil 8 minutes or until done, turning once. Stir in vermouth, roasted red pepper, reserved sliced sausage, reserved vegetables, parsley, bay leaf, basil, and thyme; bring to a boil. Reduce heat, and simmer, uncovered, 5 minutes; discard bay leaf.

Thai Chicken Stir-fry

Try this flavorful stir-fry when you're preparing a special meal for two.

MAKES 2 TO 3 SERVINGS
PREP: 25 MIN., COOK: 20 MIN.

1 (14-ounce) can coconut milk, divided
1 cup water
¹/₂ teaspoon salt
1 cup uncooked long-grain rice
3 tablespoons creamy peanut butter
2 tablespoons soy sauce
2 teaspoons chili-garlic paste
2 tablespoons dark sesame oil
2 skinned and boned chicken breasts, cubed
3 green onions, diagonally sliced
1 medium-size red bell pepper, cut into thin strips

1. Bring 1 cup coconut milk, 1 cup water, and salt to a boil in a saucepan. Stir in rice; cover, reduce heat, and simmer 20 minutes.
2. Whisk together the remaining coconut milk, peanut butter, soy sauce, and chili-garlic paste until blended.
3. Heat sesame oil in a large skillet or wok over medium-high heat 2 minutes. Add chicken, and stir-fry 5 minutes or until browned. Add green onions and bell pepper.
4. Cook, covered, stirring occasionally, 10 minutes. Add peanut butter mixture, and bring to a boil. Cook, stirring constantly, 3 minutes. Serve over rice.

Easy Chicken Cassoulet

Put this recipe on your list of weeknight favorites. For a time-saver, use matchstick carrots cut in half.

MAKES 4 TO 6 SERVINGS
PREP: 25 MIN., COOK: 10 MIN., BAKE: 1 HR.

8 skinned and boned chicken thighs
3 tablespoons olive oil
1 (8-ounce) package sliced fresh mushrooms
¾ cup chopped carrots
2 to 3 teaspoons minced fresh rosemary
½ cup vermouth
2 (15-ounce) cans navy beans, drained and divided
1 cup shredded Parmesan cheese, divided
¾ cup fine, dry breadcrumbs*, divided
1 teaspoon salt
½ teaspoon pepper
1 cup jarred chicken gravy
2 tablespoons butter, cut into pieces

1. Brown chicken on both sides in hot oil in a 10-inch cast-iron skillet over medium-high heat.
2. Add mushrooms, carrots, and rosemary; sauté 3 minutes.
3. Stir in vermouth, and cook 5 minutes. Add 1 can navy beans, gently pressing into skillet. Sprinkle with ½ cup Parmesan cheese, ½ cup breadcrumbs, salt, and pepper. Drizzle with gravy. Add remaining can of navy beans. Sprinkle with remaining ½ cup Parmesan cheese and remaining ¼ cup breadcrumbs, and dot with butter.
4. Bake, covered with aluminum foil, 40 minutes. Remove foil, and bake for 20 more minutes or until golden.
*Soft breadcrumbs may be substituted for fine, dry breadcrumbs.
Note: For testing purposes only, we used Franco American Chicken Gravy.

Crispy Chicken-Broccoli Casserole

Treat a friend who has had a baby or a family illness to the comfort of a homecooked meal, and deliver this casserole for tonight's supper or to freeze for later. If you deliver it frozen, don't forget to attach thawing and baking instructions. Include a salad and French bread to complete this meal.

MAKES 8 SERVINGS
PREP: 20 MIN., COOK: 8 MIN., BAKE: 38 MIN.

2 (6-ounce) packages long-grain and wild rice mix
1 small onion, chopped
3 tablespoons melted butter, divided
2 cups chopped cooked chicken
1 (10-ounce) box frozen chopped broccoli, thawed
2 (10¾-ounce) cans cream of chicken soup, undiluted
1 (8-ounce) container sour cream
1 cup (4 ounces) shredded Cheddar cheese
¼ cup lemon juice
¾ teaspoon salt
2 cups crushed cornflakes cereal

1. Reserve seasoning packets from wild rice mix for another use. Prepare rice according to package directions.
2. Sauté chopped onion in a Dutch oven in 1 tablespoon melted butter over medium-high heat for 8 minutes or until onion is tender.
3. Add rice, chicken, and next 6 ingredients to Dutch oven; stir until blended. Spoon into a lightly greased 13- x 9-inch baking dish or disposable aluminum pan. Toss together cornflakes and remaining 2 tablespoons melted butter. Sprinkle cornflake mixture evenly over casserole.
4. Bake, covered with aluminum foil, at 350° for 30 minutes. Remove foil, and bake 8 more minutes or until golden and bubbly.
To Make Ahead: Unbaked casserole may be frozen up to 1 month. Thaw in refrigerator 24 hours. Bake, covered with foil, at 350° for 45 minutes. Remove foil; bake 15 more minutes or until thoroughly heated.

Southwestern Casserole

Try this as a lighter alternative to King Ranch Chicken Casserole (on page 163).

MAKES 8 SERVINGS
PREP: 25 MIN., BAKE: 33 MIN.

1 onion, chopped
1 green bell pepper, chopped
1 jalapeño pepper, seeded and chopped
2 garlic cloves, minced
2 to 3 teaspoons chili powder
1 teaspoon dried oregano
Vegetable cooking spray
1 (10¾-ounce) can reduced-sodium, reduced-fat
    cream of mushroom soup, undiluted
1 (10¾-ounce) can reduced-sodium, reduced-fat
    cream of chicken soup, undiluted
1 (10-ounce) can diced tomatoes and green chiles,
    undrained
2¼ cups chopped cooked chicken
2 cups crumbled baked tortilla chips
5 tablespoons chopped fresh cilantro, divided
1 cup (4 ounces) shredded reduced-fat Cheddar
    cheese

1. Sauté first 6 ingredients in a large nonstick skillet coated with vegetable cooking spray over medium heat 8 minutes. Stir in mushroom soup, next 4 ingredients, and 4 tablespoons cilantro; spoon into a lightly greased 13- x 9-inch baking dish.
2. Bake, covered, at 350° for 30 minutes or until bubbly.
3. Toss remaining 1 tablespoon cilantro with cheese. Uncover casserole; sprinkle with cheese mixture. Bake 3 minutes.

Blackened Chicken
Fettuccine

Blackened Chicken Fettuccine

Use a cast-iron skillet for best results.

MAKES 6 SERVINGS
PREP: 8 MIN., CHILL: 8 HRS., COOK: 35 MIN.

1 tablespoon garlic powder
1 tablespoon onion powder
1 tablespoon dried thyme
1 tablespoon dried oregano
1 tablespoon paprika
1 tablespoon dried tarragon
1 tablespoon ground nutmeg
1 teaspoon salt
1 teaspoon ground red pepper
1/2 teaspoon black pepper
2/3 cup olive oil
1/2 cup Worcestershire sauce
5 skinned and boned chicken breasts
1/4 cup butter, melted
1 (12-ounce) package fettuccine
1/2 red bell pepper, cut into thin strips
1/2 yellow bell pepper, cut into thin strips
1/2 green bell pepper, cut into thin strips
2 celery ribs, sliced
1 medium onion, chopped
2 carrots, diagonally sliced
1 cup dry white wine
3/4 cup whipping cream
3 medium tomatoes, chopped
2 tablespoons water
1 teaspoon cornstarch
Freshly shredded Parmesan cheese

1. Combine first 12 ingredients in a zip-top freezer bag; add chicken. Seal bag, and marinate in refrigerator 8 hours, turning occasionally. Remove chicken from bag, discarding marinade. Cook chicken in melted butter in a large skillet over medium-high heat 5 minutes on each side or until well browned. Remove chicken from skillet, reserving drippings in skillet. Slice chicken diagonally; set aside.
2. Cook pasta according to package directions; drain well. Set aside. Sauté peppers, celery, onion, and carrot in drippings in skillet 4 minutes or until vegetables are crisp-tender. Add wine, whipping cream, and tomato; simmer 5 minutes.
3. Combine water and cornstarch; stir well. Add to vegetable mixture in skillet. Bring to a boil; boil 1 minute or until thickened, stirring constantly. Remove from heat. Add chicken and pasta, tossing well; sprinkle with Parmesan cheese.

Thai Pasta With Chicken

MAKES 4 SERVINGS
PREP: 15 MIN., COOK: 14 MIN.

12 ounces linguine
1/2 cup chicken broth
3 tablespoons seasoned rice vinegar
2 tablespoons soy sauce
2 tablespoons creamy peanut butter
1 tablespoon minced fresh garlic
1/2 teaspoon ground ginger
1/2 teaspoon dried crushed red pepper
1 (10-ounce) package roasted chicken, coarsely
    chopped
1/3 cup minced fresh cilantro
1/4 cup chopped dry-roasted peanuts

1. Cook the pasta according to package directions. Drain and keep warm.
2. While pasta cooks, combine broth and next 6 ingredients in a small saucepan. Cook over medium heat until mixture comes to a simmer, stirring occasionally.
3. Add the broth mixture to warm pasta; stir well. Add chicken and cilantro; toss gently. Sprinkle with peanuts.
Note: For testing purposes only, we used Perdue Short Cuts Original Roasted Carved Chicken Breast.

Chicken Linguine

Our Test Kitchens staff agreed that this is a recipe that their children would enjoy. Serve it tonight, and watch your kids go back for seconds.

MAKES 8 SERVINGS
PREP: 30 MIN., COOK: 40 MIN., BAKE: 30 MIN.

8 ounces uncooked linguine
4 tablespoons butter or margarine, divided
4 skinned and boned chicken breasts (about
    1½ pounds)
½ cup dry sherry
½ cup water
1 small onion, diced
1 (8-ounce) package sliced fresh mushrooms
⅔ cup all-purpose flour
2 cups chicken broth, divided
1 (8-ounce) container sour cream
1 cup (4 ounces) shredded Monterey Jack cheese
½ cup freshly grated Parmesan cheese, divided
½ cup chopped fresh parsley, divided
½ teaspoon freshly ground black pepper
½ cup fine, dry breadcrumbs

1. Cook pasta according to package directions. Set aside.
2. Melt 1 tablespoon butter in a large skillet over medium-high heat. Add chicken, and cook 3 minutes on each side or until lightly browned. Stir in sherry and water. Cover, reduce heat to low, and simmer 20 minutes or until done. Drain chicken, reserving 1 cup liquid; set aside. Cut chicken into 1-inch pieces; set aside.
3. Melt 1 tablespoon butter in skillet. Sauté onion and mushrooms over medium-high heat 5 minutes or until tender.
4. Stir together flour and ½ cup broth. Add reserved liquid, flour mixture, and remaining 1½ cups broth to mushroom mixture in skillet. Cook, stirring often, over medium-high heat until thickened. Remove from heat. Stir in chicken, pasta, sour cream, Monterey Jack cheese, ¼ cup Parmesan cheese, ¼ cup parsley, and pepper.
5. Spoon mixture into a lightly greased 13- x 9-inch baking dish. Combine breadcrumbs, remaining 2 tablespoons butter, remaining ¼ cup Parmesan cheese, and remaining ¼ cup parsley in a small bowl. Sprinkle mixture evenly over the casserole. Bake at 350° for 30 minutes or until thoroughly heated.

Smoked Turkey Tetrazzini

The hot sauce in this casserole offers an extra kick.

MAKES 8 SERVINGS
PREP: 10 MIN., COOK: 15 MIN., BAKE: 25 MIN.

1 (12-ounce) package spinach-and-egg fettuccine
¼ cup butter or margarine
1 (8-ounce) package sliced fresh mushrooms
1 medium-size yellow onion, coarsely chopped
3 tablespoons all-purpose flour
1½ teaspoons salt
1 teaspoon freshly ground pepper
¼ teaspoon hot sauce
3 cups milk
3 cups chopped smoked turkey
1 cup white wine
½ cup shredded Parmesan cheese

1. Cook pasta according to package directions; drain.
2. Melt butter in a large skillet over medium-high heat; add mushrooms and onion, and sauté 7 to 10 minutes or until tender. Gradually stir in flour and next 3 ingredients until smooth; add milk, and cook, stirring constantly, 5 minutes or until thickened. Remove from heat, and stir in turkey and wine.
3. Layer a lightly greased 13- x 9-inch baking dish with half each of pasta, turkey mixture, and cheese. Repeat layers with remaining ingredients.
4. Bake at 400° for 20 to 25 minutes or until bubbly and golden.

Lattice-Topped Turkey Pie

Lattice-Topped Turkey Pie

MAKES 4 SERVINGS

PREP: 10 MIN., COOK: 7 MIN., BAKE: 20 MIN., STAND: 5 MIN.

¼ cup butter or margarine

1 tablespoon all-purpose flour

1 cup milk

1 teaspoon chicken-flavored bouillon granules

½ teaspoon salt

1 (10-ounce) package frozen mixed vegetables, thawed and drained

2 cups chopped cooked turkey

⅛ teaspoon pepper

1 (4-ounce) can refrigerated crescent rolls

1. Melt butter in a medium saucepan over medium heat; whisk in flour. Gradually add milk and bouillon granules, whisking constantly, over medium heat about 3 to 4 minutes, until thickened and bubbly. Add salt; remove from heat.

2. Stir in vegetables, turkey, and pepper; toss until thoroughly coated. Spoon mixture into an ungreased 9-inch pieplate.

3. Unroll crescent rolls, and place rectangular pieces side by side on a lightly floured surface. Press perforations together to seal. Roll dough to a 10-inch square; cut into 1-inch strips. Arrange strips in a lattice design over turkey mixture.

4. Bake at 375° for 15 to 20 minutes or until lightly browned and thoroughly heated. Let stand 5 minutes before serving.

Turkey Tenderloin Scaloppini

Sold whole or in medallions, turkey tenderloins are great for family meals as well as fancier occasions.

MAKES 4 SERVINGS
PREP: 15 MIN., COOK: 15 MIN.

2 turkey breast tenderloins (about 1½ pounds)
⅓ cup all-purpose flour
½ teaspoon salt
½ teaspoon pepper
3 tablespoons butter, divided
1 tablespoon olive oil
½ cup dry white wine
3 tablespoons lemon juice
2 tablespoons chopped fresh flat-leaf parsley
2 garlic cloves, minced
2 tablespoons capers
Hot cooked angel hair pasta (optional)
Garnishes: lemon wedges, fresh flat-leaf parsley

1. Cut tenderloins into ½-inch-thick slices. Place between 2 sheets of heavy-duty plastic wrap, and flatten to ⅛-inch thickness, using a rolling pin or the flat side of a meat mallet.

2. Combine flour, salt, and pepper; dredge turkey in mixture.

3. Melt 2 tablespoons butter with oil in a large skillet over medium-high heat. Add turkey; cook, in batches, 1½ minutes on each side or until golden. Remove from skillet, and keep warm.

4. Add remaining 1 tablespoon butter, wine, and juice to skillet, stirring to loosen bits from bottom of skillet. Cook 2 minutes or just until thoroughly heated.

5. Stir in 2 tablespoons parsley, garlic, and capers; spoon over turkey. Serve immediately over hot cooked pasta, if desired. Garnish, if desired.

Turkey Tenderloin
Scaloppini

Parmesan Turkey Cutlets

Turkey tenderloins are small strips of the breast. Look for them with fresh turkey products in the meat case.

MAKES 4 TO 6 SERVINGS
PREP: 25 MIN., COOK: 4 MIN.

$2/3$ cup Italian-seasoned breadcrumbs
$2/3$ cup grated Parmesan cheese
1 teaspoon paprika
$1/2$ teaspoon pepper
2 turkey breast tenderloins (about 1 $1/2$ pounds)
Olive oil

1. Combine first 4 ingredients; set aside.
2. Cut tenderloins into 1-inch-thick slices. Place between 2 sheets of heavy-duty plastic wrap, and flatten to $1/4$-inch thickness, using a meat mallet or rolling pin. Brush both sides of turkey with olive oil; dredge in breadcrumb mixture.
3. Cook half of turkey slices in 2 tablespoons hot olive oil in a large nonstick skillet over medium-high heat 1 minute on each side or until done. Repeat procedure with remaining turkey and oil.

Citrus-and-Herb Turkey

The delicate seasonings and flavorful fresh fruit make this a tasty main dish.

MAKES 18 SERVINGS
PREP: 20 MIN.; BAKE: 2 HRS., 15 MIN.

1 (7 $1/2$-pound) bone-in turkey breast
1 teaspoon salt
1 teaspoon freshly ground pepper
1 tablespoon butter or margarine, softened
3 tablespoons chopped fresh rosemary
3 tablespoons chopped fresh sage
2 oranges, thinly sliced and divided
2 lemons, thinly sliced and divided
Vegetable cooking spray
1 large onion, quartered
3 cups Riesling

1. Sprinkle turkey breast evenly with salt and pepper.
2. Stir together softened butter, rosemary, and sage. Loosen skin from turkey without detaching it; spread butter mixture under skin. Arrange one-fourth of orange and lemon slices over butter mixture. Gently pull skin over fruit. Coat skin with cooking spray.
3. Place turkey in an aluminum foil-lined pan coated with cooking spray. Place onion and remaining orange and lemon slices in pan. Drizzle with wine.
4. Bake at 325° for 2 hours and 15 minutes or until a meat thermometer inserted in thickest portion registers 165°, basting every 30 minutes. Cover loosely with aluminum foil coated with cooking spray to prevent excessive browning after 1 hour and 30 minutes, if necessary.

salads

Fresh Pear Salad With
Asian Sesame Dressing, page 187

Baby Blue Salad

Baby Blue Salad

Chef Franklin Biggs, of Franklin's Homewood Gourmet in Homewood, Alabama, shares his signature salad.

MAKES 6 SERVINGS
PREP: 10 MIN.

¾ pound mixed salad greens
4 ounces blue cheese, crumbled
Balsamic Vinaigrette
2 oranges, peeled and cut into thin slices
1 pint strawberries, quartered
Sweet-and-Spicy Pecans

1. Toss greens with crumbled blue cheese and Balsamic Vinaigrette. Place on 6 individual plates. Arrange orange slices over greens; sprinkle with strawberries, and top with Sweet-and-Spicy Pecans.

Balsamic Vinaigrette:

MAKES 1⅔ CUPS
PREP: 5 MIN.

½ cup balsamic vinegar
3 tablespoons Dijon mustard
3 tablespoons honey
2 garlic cloves, minced
2 small shallots, minced
¼ teaspoon salt
¼ teaspoon pepper
1 cup olive oil

1. Whisk together first 7 ingredients until blended. Gradually whisk in olive oil.

Sweet-and-Spicy Pecans:

MAKES 1 CUP
PREP: 5 MIN., SOAK: 10 MIN., BAKE: 10 MIN.

¼ cup sugar
1 cup warm water
1 cup pecan halves
2 tablespoons sugar
1 tablespoon chili powder
⅛ teaspoon ground red pepper

1. Stir together ¼ cup sugar and 1 cup warm water until sugar dissolves. Add pecan halves, and soak 10 minutes. Drain, discarding sugar mixture.
2. Combine 2 tablespoons sugar, chili powder, and red pepper. Add pecans, tossing to coat. Place on a lightly greased baking sheet.
3. Bake at 350° for 10 minutes or until pecans are golden, stirring once.

Warm Spinach-Orange Salad

MAKES 4 SERVINGS
PREP: 15 MIN.

1 (10-ounce) package fresh spinach, stems removed
2 oranges, peeled and sectioned
½ cup sliced almonds
¼ cup cider vinegar
3 tablespoons orange juice
3 tablespoons honey
3 tablespoons olive oil

1. Combine first 3 ingredients in a large bowl.
2. Bring vinegar, orange juice, and honey to a boil in a small saucepan over medium heat. Remove from heat, and stir in oil. Pour over spinach mixture, and toss. Serve immediately.

Spinach Salad With Apricot Vinaigrette

MAKES 6 SERVINGS
PREP: 10 MIN.

2 (6-ounce) packages fresh baby spinach
1 pint grape tomatoes, halved
1 small red onion, thinly sliced
½ cup chopped dried apricots
1 ripe avocado, peeled and diced
½ cup chopped pecans, toasted
Apricot Vinaigrette

1. Place first 6 ingredients in a large bowl, tossing gently. Drizzle with Apricot Vinaigrette, tossing gently to coat.

Apricot Vinaigrette:

MAKES ½ CUP
PREP: 5 MIN.

⅓ cup vegetable oil
2 tablespoons white wine vinegar
2 tablespoons orange juice
2 tablespoons apricot jam
½ teaspoon salt
½ teaspoon ground coriander
½ teaspoon freshly ground pepper

1. Whisk together all ingredients in a small bowl.

Harvest Salad With Cider Vinaigrette

MAKES 6 SERVINGS
PREP: 30 MIN., CHILL: 1 HR.

2 red pears, chopped
1 tablespoon lemon juice
¾ cup dried apricots, cut into thin strips
¾ cup dried figs, cut into thin strips
½ cup golden raisins
1 small red onion, thinly sliced
1 cup diced jícama
Cider Vinaigrette
1 (6-ounce) package fresh spinach leaves
½ cup coarsely chopped walnuts or pecans, toasted
1 (4-ounce) package crumbled Gorgonzola or blue cheese

1. Toss together chopped pears and lemon juice in a medium bowl. Add apricots and next 5 ingredients, tossing well. Chill 1 hour or overnight.
2. Arrange spinach leaves on 6 individual plates; top evenly with pear mixture, and sprinkle with walnuts and cheese.

Cider Vinaigrette:

MAKES ½ CUP
PREP: 5 MIN.

3 tablespoons cider vinegar
1 garlic clove, pressed
1 teaspoon Dijon mustard
½ teaspoon sugar
⅓ cup olive oil

1. Whisk together first 4 ingredients; gradually whisk in oil until mixture is blended.

Bacon-Mandarin Salad

Bacon-Mandarin Salad

Wash the lettuces the night before. Wrap the leaves in a damp paper towel, and chill in zip-top freezer bags.
Cook the bacon, and toast the almonds ahead, too. Assemble and dress the salad right before serving.

MAKES 12 SERVINGS
PREP: 15 MIN., COOK: 18 MIN.

½ cup olive oil
¼ cup red wine vinegar
¼ cup sugar
1 tablespoon chopped fresh basil
⅛ teaspoon hot sauce
2 (15-ounce) cans mandarin oranges, drained and
    chilled*
1 bunch red leaf lettuce, torn
1 head romaine lettuce, torn
1 (16-ounce) package bacon, cooked and crumbled
1 (4-ounce) package sliced almonds, toasted

1. Whisk together first 5 ingredients in a large bowl, blending well. Add oranges and lettuces, tossing gently to coat. Sprinkle with crumbled bacon and sliced almonds. Serve immediately.
*Fresh orange segments can be substituted for canned mandarin oranges, if desired.

Romaine Salad With Raspberry Salad Dressing

For more subtle onion flavor, soak the slices in water 30 minutes, drain, and pat dry with paper towels. Toast a small amount of pecans in a skillet over medium-high heat 2 to 3 minutes, or just until the nuts are warm to the touch. (Be sure not to let nuts overbrown.) As pecans cool, they'll continue to develop the toasted flavor.

MAKES 6 SERVINGS
PREP: 20 MIN.

1 head romaine lettuce, torn
1 small red onion, sliced
4 ounces crumbled feta cheese
½ cup chopped toasted pecans
4 bacon slices, cooked and crumbled
Raspberry Salad Dressing

1. Place first 5 ingredients in a large bowl, and toss. Drizzle with Raspberry Salad Dressing just before serving.

Raspberry Salad Dressing:

MAKES ABOUT 2 CUPS
PREP: 5 MIN.

1 (10-ounce) jar seedless raspberry fruit spread or preserves
½ cup seasoned rice wine vinegar
¼ cup olive oil

1. Microwave raspberry spread in a microwave-safe bowl at LOW (30%) power 1 minute or until melted. Whisk in vinegar and olive oil until blended; let cool. Serve at room temperature.

Romaine Salad With
Raspberry Salad Dressing

Warm Goat Cheese Salad

MAKES 6 SERVINGS

PREP: 20 MIN., CHILL: 2 HRS., COOK: 5 MIN.

½ cup olive oil

⅓ cup lemon juice

1 tablespoon diced green onions

1½ teaspoons Dijon mustard

½ cup Italian-seasoned breadcrumbs

1½ tablespoons grated Parmesan cheese

1½ tablespoons sesame seeds

3 (4-ounce) goat cheese logs

1 large egg, lightly beaten

3 tablespoons butter or margarine

6 cups torn mixed salad greens

12 pitted ripe olives, sliced

1. Combine first 4 ingredients, and set aside.

2. Combine breadcrumbs, Parmesan cheese, and sesame seeds.

3. Cut each goat cheese log into 4 slices. Dip in egg, and dredge in breadcrumb mixture. Cover and chill for 2 hours.

4. Melt butter in a large skillet over medium-high heat. Add goat cheese slices, and fry 1 to 2 minutes on each side or until browned; drain cheese slices on paper towels.

5. Toss mixed greens with dressing; add olives, and top with warm goat cheese. Serve immediately.

Warm Goat Cheese Salad

With
d Basil Dressing
ing, you can store it in the
se in other salads.

The Best of Southern Living p 4

Poultry - Chicken

p159 Old Fashioned Chicken&Dumplings

p159 Creamy Chicken Casserole

p160 Deluxe Chicken Casserole

p161 Chicken Cobbler with Caramelized Onions

p161 Heavenly Chicken Lasagna

p163 Chicken Cannelloni with Roasted Red Pepper Sauce

p165 Chicken Basque

p166 Ecasy Chicken Cassoulet

p166 Crispy Chicken Broccoli Casserole

p170 Chicken Linguine

esh basil

baby spinach
d cubed
ese
ives, sliced

ents in a jar; cover tightly,
12 hours.
emaining 4 ingredients in a
nount of dressing, tossing to
over and chill remaining

of pine nuts if you would
ecipe.

Garden Salad

Garden Salad

MAKES 24 SERVINGS
PREP: 20 MIN.

6 (5-ounce) packages gourmet mixed salad greens
1 large red onion, halved and thinly sliced
2 red bell peppers, cut into thin strips
4 small yellow squash, thinly sliced
Vinaigrette Salad Dressing

1. Toss together first 4 ingredients, and serve with
Vinaigrette Salad Dressing.

Vinaigrette Salad Dressing:

MAKES 3 CUPS
PREP: 10 MIN.

1 cup apple cider vinegar
6 tablespoons chopped onion
5 tablespoons sugar
2 large garlic cloves
2 teaspoons salt
2 teaspoons dry mustard
1 teaspoon pepper
2 cups vegetable oil

1. Process first 7 ingredients in a blender until smooth.
With blender running, add oil in a slow, steady stream;
process until smooth. Cover and chill dressing until
ready to serve.

Peppered-Ham Tossed Salad

This salad complements most Italian dishes well.

MAKES 4 TO 6 SERVINGS
PREP: 20 MIN.

½ cup vegetable oil
½ cup red wine vinegar
¼ cup water
½ pound thinly sliced black-peppered ham, cut into
    thin strips
½ medium-size red onion, thinly sliced
1 medium-size green bell pepper, seeded and cut into
    thin strips
2 celery ribs, sliced
4 pickled cherry peppers, seeded and chopped
1 tablespoon chopped fresh oregano
2 heads Boston lettuce, torn into bite-size pieces
Garnish: pickled cherry peppers

1. Combine first 3 ingredients in a jar; cover tightly. Set
aside.
2. Toss together ham and next 6 ingredients in a large
bowl. Shake dressing vigorously, and drizzle ¾ cup
over salad; toss gently. Reserve remaining dressing for
another use. Garnish salad, if desired.

Winter Green Salad With Cranberry Vinaigrette

MAKES 8 SERVINGS
PREP: 40 MIN., BAKE: 15 MIN.

¾ cup pecan halves
⅓ cup honey
¼ cup butter or margarine, melted
½ cup sugar
4 heads Belgian endive
2 large watercress bunches
4 cups finely shredded radicchio
4 tangerines, peeled and sectioned
1 cup packed fresh mint leaves, chopped
Cranberry Vinaigrette
Garnish: fresh mint sprigs

1. Stir together first 3 ingredients; spread in a shallow roasting pan.
2. Bake at 350° for 15 minutes, stirring once. Remove pecans with a slotted spoon, and toss with sugar. Cool.
3. Separate endive leaves, and cut larger leaves in half. Discard coarse watercress stems. Toss together endive, watercress, and next 4 ingredients. Sprinkle with pecans, and garnish, if desired.

Cranberry Vinaigrette:

MAKES 1⅓ CUPS
PREP: 15 MIN., COOK: 11 MIN.

½ cup fresh or frozen cranberries, thawed
⅔ cup fresh tangerine juice (about 3 tangerines)
⅓ cup tarragon vinegar
2 tablespoons Dijon mustard
2 shallots, quartered
½ teaspoon salt
½ teaspoon pepper
½ cup olive oil

1. Bring cranberries and tangerine juice to a boil in a medium saucepan over medium-high heat; reduce heat to medium, and simmer 5 minutes. Drain cranberries, reserving juice and cranberries; set aside. Return juice to saucepan, and simmer 5 minutes.
2. Process juice, vinegar, and next 4 ingredients in a blender until blended. With blender running, add oil in a slow, steady stream. Stir in reserved cranberries.

Winter Green Salad With
Cranberry Vinaigrette

Layered Southwestern Salad

Layered Southwestern Salad

MAKES 8 TO 10 SERVINGS
PREP: 15 MIN.

1/3 cup chopped fresh cilantro
1/2 cup lime juice
1/2 cup olive oil
1/2 cup sour cream
1 teaspoon sugar
1/2 teaspoon salt
1/2 teaspoon pepper
1 (16-ounce) package romaine lettuce, shredded
5 plum tomatoes, chopped
1 (15-ounce) can black beans, rinsed and drained
1 small red onion, chopped
1 (8-ounce) package shredded Mexican four-cheese
      blend
1 (15-ounce) can whole kernel corn with red and
      green peppers, drained
1 (6-ounce) can sliced ripe olives, drained
2 cups crushed tortilla chips
Garnish: fresh cilantro leaves

1. Process first 7 ingredients in a blender or food processor until smooth, stopping to scrape down sides.
2. Layer lettuce and next 7 ingredients in a 3-quart glass bowl. Garnish, if desired, and serve immediately with vinaigrette.

Mesclun Salad With Cranberries and Avocado

MAKES 6 SERVINGS
PREP: 7 MIN.

2 (5-ounce) bags gourmet mixed salad greens with
      herbs
2 ripe avocados, coarsely chopped
1 cup walnut halves, toasted
3/4 cup dried cranberries
1/2 cup blush wine vinaigrette
1/4 teaspoon freshly ground pepper

1. Toss first 4 ingredients in a serving bowl. Lightly dress salad with desired amount of vinaigrette; toss gently to coat. Sprinkle with pepper; toss again before serving.
Note: For testing purposes only, we used Dole Gourmet Mixed Salad Greens with Herbs and Briannas Blush Wine Vinaigrette.

Caesar Salad

The creamy goodness of this classic salad is too tasty to resist. Add grilled chicken or shrimp if you'd like to serve it for dinner.

MAKES 8 SERVINGS
PREP: 15 MIN.

1 head romaine lettuce, torn
1/2 head iceberg lettuce, torn
1/4 cup egg substitute
3 tablespoons olive oil
1 garlic clove, minced
1 tablespoon lemon juice
1/2 to 1 teaspoon salt
1/2 teaspoon coarsely ground pepper
1/2 teaspoon Dijon mustard
1 (2-ounce) can anchovy fillets, drained (optional)
1 cup croutons
1/4 cup shredded Parmesan cheese

1. Place lettuces in a large bowl.
2. Process egg substitute, next 6 ingredients, and, if desired, anchovy fillets in a blender. Drizzle dressing over lettuce, tossing well. Sprinkle with croutons and Parmesan cheese.

Fresh Pear Salad With
Asian Sesame Dressing

Fresh Pear Salad With Asian Sesame Dressing

MAKES 6 SERVINGS

PREP: 15 MIN.

2 cups shredded red cabbage
2 cups shredded romaine lettuce
3 red Bartlett pears, sliced
2 medium carrots, shredded (about 1 cup)
1 green onion, chopped
Asian Sesame Dressing
2 teaspoons sesame seeds, toasted (optional)

1. Toss together first 5 ingredients in a large bowl, and drizzle with Asian Sesame Dressing, tossing gently to coat. Sprinkle salad with sesame seeds, if desired. Serve immediately.

Asian Sesame Dressing:

MAKES ½ CUP

PREP: 5 MIN.

¼ cup vegetable oil
2 tablespoons white wine vinegar
1 tablespoon soy sauce
2 teaspoons sugar
½ teaspoon sesame oil
¼ teaspoon dried crushed red pepper

1. Whisk together all ingredients.

Apple-Spinach Salad

MAKES 4 SERVINGS

PREP: 5 MIN.

1 (6-ounce) package fresh baby spinach
2 small Granny Smith apples, chopped
½ cup cashews
¼ cup golden raisins
½ cup sweet and sour dressing (we used Old Dutch)

1. Combine first 4 ingredients in a bowl. Add dressing, tossing gently to coat.

Pear Salad With Raspberry Cream

MAKES 4 SERVINGS

PREP: 20 MIN.

¾ cup sour cream
¼ cup raspberry preserves
3 tablespoons red wine vinegar
⅛ teaspoon Dijon mustard
4 ripe pears
2 tablespoons lemon juice
1 head Bibb lettuce, torn
1 small head romaine lettuce, torn
½ cup freshly shredded Parmesan cheese
4 to 6 bacon slices, cooked and crumbled
½ cup fresh raspberries

1. Whisk together first 4 ingredients. Set dressing aside.
2. Peel pears, if desired; quarter pears. Brush with lemon juice.
3. Arrange Bibb and romaine lettuces on 4 plates. Arrange pear quarters over lettuce. Drizzle with dressing; sprinkle salad with Parmesan cheese, crumbled bacon, and raspberries.

Italian Bread Salad

With meat, cheese, and bread, this salad makes a filling meal.

MAKES 4 SERVINGS
PREP: 30 MIN., BAKE: 15 MIN., STAND: 15 MIN.

4 cups (1-inch) cubed French bread
6 tablespoons olive oil
3 tablespoons red wine vinegar
2 garlic cloves, minced
1 teaspoon dried oregano
1 teaspoon salt
¾ teaspoon freshly ground black pepper
⅛ to ¼ teaspoon dried crushed red pepper
1 large head romaine lettuce, chopped
4 to 5 large plum tomatoes, chopped
2 cups chopped smoked ham
1 (8-ounce) package fresh mozzarella cheese, cubed
3 green onions, chopped

1. Place bread cubes on a baking sheet.
2. Bake at 325° for 15 minutes or until lightly browned.
3. Whisk together oil, vinegar, and next 5 ingredients.
4. Place 3 cups toasted bread cubes in a large bowl or on a large serving platter. Top with lettuce and next 3 ingredients. Drizzle with dressing. Let stand 15 minutes; toss. Sprinkle evenly with remaining bread cubes and green onions.

Panzanella

Every ingredient in this Italian bread salad adds its own unique flavor to the recipe.

MAKES 6 TO 8 SERVINGS
PREP: 20 MIN., BAKE: 15 MIN., CHILL: 1 HR.

1 (16-ounce) stale French or Italian bread loaf
10 plum tomatoes, halved and sliced
½ teaspoon salt, divided
½ teaspoon pepper, divided
2 red onions, halved and thinly sliced
1 cup firmly packed basil leaves, shredded
1 cup kalamata olives, pitted
1 cup walnuts, toasted
1 cucumber, seeded and sliced
1 red bell pepper, quartered and thinly sliced
1 green bell pepper, quartered and thinly sliced
1 cup (4 ounces) crumbled Gorgonzola cheese
4 garlic cloves, minced
1 cup red wine vinegar, divided
1 cup extra-virgin olive oil, divided

1. Cut bread into 1-inch cubes, and place on a baking sheet.
2. Bake bread cubes at 350° for 10 to 15 minutes or until bread is toasted.
3. Place bread cubes in a large bowl. Top with tomato; sprinkle with ¼ teaspoon salt and ¼ teaspoon pepper. Layer with onions and next 4 ingredients, and sprinkle with remaining ¼ teaspoon salt and ¼ teaspoon pepper. Layer with red bell pepper and next 3 ingredients. Drizzle with ½ cup red wine vinegar and ½ cup oil. Cover and chill 1 hour.
4. Drizzle with remaining ½ cup vinegar and ½ cup oil; serve immediately.

FESTIVE SALAD BAR

For easy entertaining, tender lettuces tossed with crisp garden vegetables turn a lined terra-cotta planter into a festive salad bowl. Fill your salad bar with ingredients like mixed lettuces and spinach, sugar snap peas, cherry tomatoes, hard-cooked eggs, and homemade croutons. Add colorful containers filled with both light and hearty toppings, and let guests have fun assembling their own salads.

Festive Salad Bar

Dianne's Southwestern Cornbread Salad

MAKES 10 TO 12 SERVINGS
PREP: 30 MIN., BAKE: 15 MIN., CHILL: 2 HRS.

1 (6-ounce) package Mexican cornbread mix
1 (1-ounce) envelope buttermilk-Ranch dressing mix
1 small head romaine lettuce, shredded
2 large tomatoes, chopped
1 (15-ounce) can black beans, rinsed and drained
1 (15-ounce) can whole kernel corn with red and
    green peppers, drained
1 (8-ounce) package shredded Mexican four-cheese
    blend
6 bacon slices, cooked and crumbled
5 green onions, chopped

1. Prepare cornbread according to package directions; cool and crumble. Set aside.
2. Prepare dressing mix according to package directions.
3. Layer a large serving bowl with half each of cornbread, lettuce, and next 6 ingredients; spoon half of dressing evenly over top. Repeat layers with remaining ingredients and dressing. Cover salad, and chill at least 2 hours.

Arugula, Melon, and Prosciutto Salad With Fig Vinaigrette

MAKES 4 SERVINGS
PREP: 25 MIN.

4 ounces arugula leaves, trimmed
3 ounces thin prosciutto or country ham slices, cut
    into strips
4 cups seedless watermelon balls or cubes (about
    5-pound watermelon)
2 ounces Parmesan cheese, shaved
Fig Vinaigrette

1. Place arugula evenly on 4 salad plates. Top evenly with prosciutto strips and watermelon; sprinkle with Parmesan cheese. Serve with Fig Vinaigrette.

Fig Vinaigrette:

MAKES ABOUT ¾ CUP
PREP: 5 MIN.

¼ cup fig preserves
3 tablespoons fresh lime juice
1 tablespoon balsamic vinegar
½ teaspoon dry mustard
½ teaspoon salt
½ cup olive oil

1. Whisk together first 5 ingredients until smooth. Add oil in a slow, steady stream, whisking until smooth. Chill until ready to serve. Store in refrigerator for up to 1 week; bring to room temperature, and whisk before serving.

Raspberry Vinaigrette: Substitute seedless raspberry preserves for fig preserves. Proceed as directed.

Arugula, Melon, and Prosciutto
Salad With Fig Vinaigrette

Crisp Plum Salad

Crisp Plum Salad

*Jícama, available in most supermarkets year-round, is a root vegetable with a sweet,
crunchy texture, similar to a water chestnut.*

MAKES 4 SERVINGS
PREP: 25 MIN., CHILL: 2 HRS.

1 teaspoon grated lime rind
6 tablespoons fresh lime juice
2 tablespoons olive oil
1 teaspoon salt
1 teaspoon sugar
¼ teaspoon ground red pepper
1 pound jícama, peeled and chopped
4 green onions, chopped
2 tablespoons chopped fresh cilantro
6 plums, chopped
Garnishes: plum slices, fresh cilantro leaves

1. Whisk together first 6 ingredients in a large bowl; add chopped jícama, green onions, and cilantro; toss. Add plums, tossing gently to coat. Cover and chill 2 hours. Garnish, if desired.

Ambrosia

Five fresh fruits mingle in a sweet blend of peach nectar and honey balanced with pungent
balsamic vinegar and lemon juice. This blissful salad is special enough to serve as a light dessert.

MAKES 8 SERVINGS
PREP: 10 MIN., CHILL: 1 HR.

1 medium cantaloupe, peeled, seeded, and cut into
    chunks
2 navel oranges, sectioned
2 cups fresh pineapple chunks
2 fresh plums, sliced
1 cup seedless green or red grapes or ½ cup of each
¾ cup peach nectar
¼ cup honey
2 tablespoons balsamic vinegar
2 tablespoons lemon juice

1. Combine first 5 ingredients in a large bowl. Combine peach nectar and remaining 3 ingredients, stirring with a wire whisk until blended. Pour dressing over fruit mixture, stirring gently to coat fruit. Cover and chill at least 1 hour, stirring occasionally.

Ambrosia

Roasted New Potato Salad

Roasted New Potato Salad

If you like your potatoes crispier, bake the potatoes about 10 minutes longer, stirring once.

MAKES 4 TO 6 SERVINGS
PREP: 20 MIN., BAKE: 35 MIN.

2 tablespoons olive oil
2 pounds small red potatoes, chopped
½ medium-size sweet onion, chopped
2 teaspoons minced garlic
1 teaspoon coarse salt
½ teaspoon freshly ground pepper
8 to 10 cooked crisp bacon slices, crumbled
1 bunch green onions, chopped
¾ cup Ranch dressing
Salt and pepper to taste

1. Place oil in a 15- x 10-inch jelly-roll pan; add potatoes and next 4 ingredients, tossing to coat. Arrange potato mixture in a single layer.
2. Bake at 425° for 30 to 35 minutes or until potatoes are tender, stirring occasionally. Transfer potatoes to a large bowl.
3. Toss together potatoes, bacon, green onions, and dressing. Add salt and pepper to taste. Serve immediately, or cover and chill.

German Potato Salad

German potato salad can be served warm or cold. You're sure to enjoy it both ways.

MAKES 6 SERVINGS
PREP: 15 MIN., COOK: 30 MIN.

16 new potatoes (1½ pounds)
6 bacon slices
½ cup chopped celery
1 tablespoon all-purpose flour
1 tablespoon sugar
2 teaspoons Dijon mustard
½ teaspoon salt
½ teaspoon celery seeds
Dash of ground white pepper
⅓ cup water
¼ cup white vinegar
½ cup chopped green onions
1 (2-ounce) jar sliced pimiento, drained

1. Cook potatoes in boiling, salted water to cover 15 minutes or until potatoes are tender. Drain, cool, and quarter potatoes.
2. Cook bacon in a large skillet over medium heat until crisp. Drain bacon, reserving 3 tablespoons drippings in skillet. Discard remaining drippings. Crumble bacon, and set aside.
3. Cook celery in bacon drippings over medium-high heat, stirring constantly, until tender. Add flour and next 5 ingredients, stirring until smooth. Cook 1 minute, stirring constantly. Gradually add water and vinegar; cook over medium heat, stirring constantly, until mixture is slightly thickened. Stir in potato, green onions, and pimiento. Cook just until thoroughly heated, stirring gently to coat. Transfer to a serving bowl. Sprinkle with bacon.

Fipps Family Potato Salad

Try grating the eggs on the largest holes of a cheese grater.

MAKES 8 TO 10 SERVINGS
PREP: 20 MIN., COOK: 40 MIN.

4 pounds baking potatoes (8 large)
3 hard-cooked eggs, grated
1 cup low-fat mayonnaise
1 tablespoon spicy brown mustard
1½ teaspoons salt
¾ teaspoon pepper

1. Cook potatoes in boiling water to cover 40 minutes or until tender; drain and cool. Peel potatoes, and cut into 1-inch cubes.
2. Stir together potato and egg.
3. Stir together mayonnaise and next 3 ingredients; gently stir into potato mixture. Serve immediately, or cover and chill, if desired.

Red Potato Salad: Substitute 8 large red potatoes (4 pounds) for baking potatoes.

Potato Salad With Sweet Pickle: Add ⅓ cup sweet salad cube pickles to potato mixture.

Potato Salad With Onion and Celery: Add 2 celery ribs, diced, and ½ small sweet onion, diced, to potato mixture.

Lemon-Basil Potato Salad

Lemon-Basil Potato Salad

MAKES 6 SERVINGS
PREP: 20 MIN., BAKE: 25 MIN.

2 1/2 pounds small Yukon gold potatoes, cut into
    eighths*
Vegetable cooking spray
1/2 teaspoon salt
1/4 cup lemon juice
4 garlic cloves, minced
3/4 cup chopped fresh basil
1 tablespoon Dijon mustard
1 teaspoon salt
1/2 teaspoon freshly ground pepper
2/3 cup olive oil
1/2 medium-size red onion, chopped
1 (10-ounce) package fresh spinach, cut into thin
    strips
10 thick bacon slices, cooked and crumbled

1. Arrange potatoes evenly on a lightly greased 15- x 10-inch jelly-roll pan, and coat potatoes with cooking spray. Sprinkle with 1/2 teaspoon salt.
2. Bake at 475°, stirring occasionally, 20 to 25 minutes or until tender and golden.
3. Whisk together lemon juice and next 5 ingredients; whisk in oil in a slow, steady stream. Gently toss potatoes and onion with 1/2 cup of vinaigrette.
4. Arrange spinach evenly in 6 bowls, and drizzle with remaining vinaigrette. Top with potato mixture; sprinkle with bacon.
*2 1/2 pounds small new potatoes may be substituted.

Rice Primavera Salad

MAKES 8 SERVINGS
PREP: 15 MIN., CHILL: 8 HRS.

2 zucchini
2 yellow squash
1 large red bell pepper, chopped
1 medium-size red onion, chopped
5 cups cooked long-grain rice
3/4 cup mayonnaise
1/3 cup buttermilk
2 tablespoons Dijon mustard
2 tablespoons white vinegar
1 1/2 teaspoons salt
1/2 teaspoon black pepper

1. Cut zucchini and yellow squash in half lengthwise; cut into slices. Stir together vegetables, rice, and remaining ingredients; cover and chill 8 hours.

Mediterranean Pasta Salad

MAKES 8 SERVINGS
PREP: 40 MIN., COOK: 14 MIN.

12 ounces uncooked orzo
2 tablespoons olive oil
1 large yellow bell pepper, seeded and diced
1 medium tomato, seeded and diced
1 small cucumber, seeded and diced
1 medium carrot, shredded
1 (8-ounce) package crumbled feta cheese
3 tablespoons pine nuts, toasted
2 to 3 tablespoons chopped fresh basil
2 tablespoons drained capers
1/2 cup olive oil
1/3 cup lemon juice
1 shallot, minced
6 garlic cloves, minced
2 teaspoons chopped fresh or 1 teaspoon dried mint
1 teaspoon ground cumin
1 teaspoon Dijon mustard
1/8 teaspoon salt
1/8 teaspoon black pepper

1. Cook orzo according to package directions. Drain and rinse with cold water; drain again thoroughly.
2. Stir together orzo and 2 tablespoons olive oil in a large bowl. Stir in bell pepper and next 7 ingredients.
3. Whisk together 1/2 cup olive oil and next 8 ingredients. Pour over orzo mixture, and toss to coat.

Basil-Fettuccine Salad

Wonderful peppery-scented basil abounds in this pasta salad and vinaigrette. This is a great recipe to try if you grow basil in your garden.

MAKES 8 SERVINGS
PREP: 10 MIN., COOK: 16 MIN.

1 pound fresh green beans
1 (8-ounce) package fettuccine
Red Wine-Basil Vinaigrette
6 plum tomatoes
2 cups pitted ripe olives
1 1/2 cups loosely packed, julienne-sliced fresh basil leaves
2 tablespoons chopped fresh parsley
4 ounces Parmesan cheese, shaved

1. Wash beans and remove strings. Arrange beans in a steamer basket over boiling water. Cover and steam 4 minutes or until tender. Rinse beans with cold water; drain and set aside.
2. Cook pasta according to package directions. Drain and place in a large bowl. Toss with 1/2 cup Red Wine-Basil Vinaigrette; set aside.
3. Cut each tomato into 8 wedges. Add tomato, green beans, olives, basil, and parsley to pasta; toss gently. Pour remaining Red Wine-Basil Vinaigrette over pasta; toss gently. Sprinkle with cheese.

Red Wine-Basil Vinaigrette:

MAKES 2 CUPS
PREP: 10 MIN.

1/2 cup red wine vinegar
2 garlic cloves, crushed
2 tablespoons Dijon mustard
1 teaspoon freshly ground pepper
1 cup light olive oil
1/2 cup loosely packed, julienne-sliced fresh basil leaves
1/2 cup chopped fresh parsley

1. Combine first 4 ingredients in a small bowl. Add oil in a slow, steady stream, whisking until blended. Stir in basil and parsley.

Bean-and-Fennel Salad

Bean-and-Fennel Salad

Fresh fennel lends a celery-like crunch and licorice flavor to this salad. To cut a fennel bulb, cut the stalks from the top of the bulb, and then remove the tough outer layers.

MAKES 6 TO 8 SERVINGS
PREP: 20 MIN., CHILL: 1 HR.

6 tablespoons olive oil
3 tablespoons white wine vinegar
¾ teaspoon coarsely ground black pepper
½ teaspoon salt
½ teaspoon fresh thyme
½ teaspoon dried crushed red pepper
2 (15.5-ounce) cans chickpeas, rinsed and drained*
2 medium fennel bulbs, thinly sliced
3 garlic cloves, minced
½ cup crumbled Gorgonzola cheese*
¼ cup minced fresh flat-leaf parsley
Garnish: fresh fennel fronds

1. Whisk together first 6 ingredients in a bowl; add chickpeas, fennel, and garlic, tossing gently to coat. Sprinkle with cheese and parsley. Cover and chill at least 1 hour. Garnish, if desired.
*Two (15-ounce) cans navy beans and ½ cup crumbled blue cheese may be substituted for chickpeas and Gorgonzola.

Hoppin' John Salad

The fresh mint added to this classic Southern black-eyed pea-and-rice salad not only makes it exceptionally original, but it also helps the salad taste extra good.

MAKES 6 SERVINGS
PREP: 15 MIN.

2 cups cooked black-eyed peas
3 cups cooked long-grain rice
½ cup chopped red onion
¼ cup chopped celery
1 jalapeño pepper, seeded and minced
¼ cup loosely packed fresh chervil or parsley
¼ cup loosely packed fresh mint
1 garlic clove
½ teaspoon salt
3 tablespoons fresh lemon juice
¼ cup olive oil
¼ teaspoon freshly ground black pepper

1. Combine first 5 ingredients in a large bowl.
2. Place herbs and garlic on a cutting board, and sprinkle evenly with salt; finely chop herbs and garlic. Sprinkle over rice mixture, and stir gently.
3. Combine lemon juice, olive oil, and pepper, and stir into rice mixture.

Tomato Napoleons With Fresh Tomato Dressing

MAKES 4 SERVINGS
PREP: 30 MIN., CHILL: 1 HR.

8 ounces fresh mozzarella cheese, cut into 8 slices
¾ cup Fresh Tomato Dressing
3 large tomatoes, each cut into 4 slices
1 teaspoon salt
1 teaspoon pepper
24 fresh basil leaves, shredded

1. Place fresh mozzarella cheese in a shallow dish. Pour Fresh Tomato Dressing over cheese, and cover and chill 1 hour. Remove cheese slices, reserving Tomato Dressing marinade.
2. Sprinkle tomato slices evenly with salt and pepper.
3. Place 1 tomato slice on each of 4 salad plates; top each with 1 cheese slice and 2 shredded basil leaves. Repeat with tomato slice, cheese slice, and basil. Top with remaining tomato slice and basil. Drizzle evenly with reserved Tomato Dressing marinade.

Fresh Tomato Dressing:

MAKES 4 CUPS
PREP: 20 MIN., STAND: 1 HR., CHILL: 8 HRS.

1 cup olive oil
½ cup balsamic vinegar
3 garlic cloves, sliced
1 tablespoon sugar
1 tablespoon salt
1 teaspoon pepper
4 large tomatoes, peeled and chopped
2 tablespoons fresh thyme leaves or 4 thyme sprigs

1. Whisk together first 6 ingredients in a large glass bowl. Stir in chopped tomatoes and fresh thyme. Cover and let stand at room temperature 1 hour, stirring occasionally. Cover and chill 8 hours.
Note: Dressing may be stored in refrigerator up to 1 month. Stir additional fresh chopped tomato into dressing after each use.

Tomato Napoleons With Fresh
Tomato Dressing

Cherry Tomato Salad

MAKES 8 SERVINGS

PREP: 15 MIN., CHILL: 1 HR.

4 pints cherry tomatoes (about 3 pounds), halved
2 tablespoons white wine vinegar
2 tablespoons olive oil
1 teaspoon salt
½ teaspoon pepper
1 garlic clove, finely chopped
¼ cup chopped fresh mint

1. Stir together first 6 ingredients in a large bowl. Add mint, tossing gently to coat. Cover and chill 1 hour.

Cherry Tomato-Caper Salad

Reduce the sodium in this recipe by rinsing the capers well and omitting the salt.

MAKES 2 SERVINGS

PREP: 15 MIN., STAND: 15 MIN.

1 tablespoon drained small capers
1 tablespoon balsamic vinegar
2 teaspoons olive oil
¼ teaspoon salt
¼ teaspoon pepper
8 large cherry tomatoes, halved
3 fresh basil leaves, shredded
Bibb lettuce leaves (optional)

1. Stir together first 5 ingredients. Drizzle over tomatoes, tossing to coat. Let stand at least 15 minutes or up to 1 hour. Sprinkle with basil. Serve over lettuce, if desired.

Roasted Tomato-and-Pepper Salad

MAKES 6 SERVINGS

PREP: 15 MIN., BROIL: 30 MIN., STAND: 10 MIN.

6 large plum tomatoes
Vegetable cooking spray
1 yellow bell pepper
1 green bell pepper
1 red bell pepper
1 medium-size red onion, cut into eighths
1 tablespoon olive oil
1 tablespoon balsamic vinegar
1 garlic clove, minced
½ teaspoon salt
½ teaspoon dried oregano
½ teaspoon freshly ground black pepper
¼ cup sliced fresh basil

1. Cut tomatoes into ¼-inch-thick slices.
2. Arrange tomato slices on an aluminum foil-lined baking sheet coated with cooking spray.
3. Broil 5 inches from heat 5 minutes on each side; set tomato aside.
4. Cut bell peppers in half lengthwise; remove and discard seeds.
5. Arrange peppers, cut sides down, and onion on a foil-lined baking sheet coated with cooking spray.
6. Broil 5 inches from heat 8 to 10 minutes on each side or until peppers look blistered. Remove peppers, and broil onion pieces 3 more minutes, if necessary.
7. Place peppers in a zip-top plastic bag; seal and let stand 10 minutes to loosen skins. Peel peppers; cut into thin strips.
8. Whisk together oil and next 5 ingredients in a large bowl; add vegetables, tossing to coat. Sprinkle with sliced basil.

Chilled Vegetable Salad

Chilled Vegetable Salad

This colorful salad is sure to be a hit at cookouts and other gatherings.

MAKES 8 TO 10 SERVINGS
PREP: 15 MIN., COOK: 5 MIN., COOL: 30 MIN., CHILL: 8 HRS.

1 cup sugar
3/4 cup cider vinegar
1/2 cup vegetable oil
1 medium-size green bell pepper, chopped
1 medium onion, chopped
3 celery ribs, sliced
1 (7-ounce) jar diced pimiento, undrained
1 (15 1/4-ounce) can small sweet peas, drained
1 (14 1/2-ounce) can French-cut green beans, drained
1 (11-ounce) can white shoepeg corn, drained
1/2 teaspoon salt
1/4 teaspoon black pepper

1. Bring first 3 ingredients to a boil in small saucepan over medium heat; cook, stirring often, 5 minutes or until sugar dissolves. Remove dressing from heat, and cool 30 minutes.
2. Stir together chopped bell pepper and next 8 ingredients in a large bowl; gently stir in dressing. Cover and chill for 8 hours. Serve with a slotted spoon.
Note: Salad may be stored in an airtight container in the refrigerator for several days.

Layered Vegetable Salad With Parmesan Dressing

MAKES 8 TO 10 SERVINGS
PREP: 10 MIN., CHILL: 8 HRS.

1 (8-ounce) package sliced fresh mushrooms
2 cups broccoli florets, chopped
1 (10-ounce) package shredded carrot
5 small yellow squash, sliced
2 large red bell peppers, cut into 1-inch pieces
2 green onions, sliced (optional)
Parmesan Dressing

1. Layer half each of first 5 ingredients and, if desired, green onions in a 3-quart glass bowl. Spread half of Parmesan Dressing over top; repeat layers. Cover and chill 8 hours.

Parmesan Dressing:

MAKES ABOUT 2 CUPS
PREP: 5 MIN.

3/4 cup grated Parmesan cheese
1/2 cup sour cream
1/2 cup mayonnaise
1/4 cup Italian dressing with balsamic vinegar
1/4 teaspoon cracked pepper

1. Whisk together all ingredients until smooth.

Collard Greens Salad

MAKES 8 TO 10 SERVINGS
PREP: 35 MIN., CHILL: 1 HR.

12 pounds fresh collard greens, washed, trimmed, and shredded
3 small carrots, shredded
1 onion, minced
3 garlic cloves, minced
1/4 cup olive oil
3 tablespoons apple cider vinegar
1/2 teaspoon dried oregano

1. Toss together all ingredients in a large bowl. Chill 1 hour.

Grilled Marinated
Vegetable Salad

Grilled Marinated Vegetable Salad

MAKES 8 TO 10 SERVINGS
PREP: 35 MIN., GRILL: 14 MIN., CHILL: 8 HRS.

4 tablespoons olive oil, divided
3 tablespoons honey
2 tablespoons balsamic vinegar
1 teaspoon salt
½ teaspoon black pepper
3 large yellow squash
3 large zucchini
2 medium-size green bell peppers
2 medium-size red bell peppers
2 medium-size orange bell peppers
2 medium-size yellow bell peppers
1 pound fresh green beans

1. Stir together 1 tablespoon oil, honey, and next 3 ingredients until blended. Set aside.
2. Slice squash and zucchini; cut bell peppers into 1-inch pieces, and trim green beans. Toss squash, zucchini, and bell pepper with 2 tablespoons oil. Toss green beans with remaining 1 tablespoon oil.
3. Grill squash, zucchini, and bell pepper in a grill wok, covered with grill lid, over medium-high heat (350° to 400°), stirring occasionally, 5 to 7 minutes or until vegetables are tender. Remove from wok.
4. Grill green beans in grill wok, covered with grill lid, over medium-high heat, stirring occasionally, 5 to 7 minutes or until tender.
5. Toss vegetables with honey mixture; cover and chill 8 hours.

Marinated Green Bean-and-Okra Salad

MAKES 8 SERVINGS

PREP: 15 MIN., COOK: 3 MIN., CHILL: 3 HRS.

1½ pounds fresh green beans, trimmed
1½ pounds small fresh okra
¾ cup olive oil
6 tablespoons white wine vinegar
1 tablespoon chopped fresh basil
½ teaspoon salt
½ teaspoon pepper
¼ teaspoon dry mustard
¼ cup crumbled feta cheese

1. Cook beans and okra in boiling water to cover 3 minutes. Plunge beans and okra into ice water to stop the cooking process; drain.
2. Whisk together olive oil and next 5 ingredients; pour over beans and okra. Cover and chill 3 hours.
3. Drain beans and okra; sprinkle with cheese before serving.

Broccoli and Orange Salad

This creamy broccoli salad isn't a new concept, but the orange segments and almonds update it.

MAKES 10 SERVINGS

PREP: 12 MIN.

¾ cup mayonnaise
¼ cup sugar
2 tablespoons white vinegar
1 large bunch broccoli, cut into florets, or
      1 (16-ounce) package broccoli florets
½ cup golden raisins
½ small red onion, thinly sliced and separated into
      rings
4 bacon slices, cooked and crumbled
1 (11-ounce) can mandarin oranges, drained
⅓ cup sliced almonds, toasted

1. Stir together mayonnaise, sugar, and vinegar in a large bowl. Add broccoli and raisins; toss well. Cover and chill thoroughly. Top with onion, crumbled bacon, mandarin oranges, and toasted almonds.

Grilled Corn Salad

Not much else says summer like a pile of golden ears of corn wrapped in their crisp, green husks. This grilled salad brings out the natural sweetness of fresh corn.

MAKES 8 SERVINGS

PREP: 25 MIN., GRILL: 20 MIN., SOAK: 15 MIN., COOL: 10 MIN.

18 ears fresh corn in husks
1 large red bell pepper
5 green onions, chopped
½ cup plus 1 tablespoon cider vinegar
1½ tablespoons honey
¾ teaspoon ground cumin
½ teaspoon salt
¼ teaspoon black pepper
⅓ cup vegetable oil

1. Soak corn in husks in water 15 minutes.
2. Cut bell pepper in half lengthwise; remove and discard seeds and membrane, and flatten pepper with palm of hand. Set aside.
3. Coat grill rack with cooking spray, and place on grill over medium-high heat (350° to 400°). Place bell pepper, skin side down, on rack; remove corn from water and add corn in husks to grill. Grill, covered with grill lid, 15 to 20 minutes or until corn is tender and slightly charred, turning occasionally, and pepper is charred. Cool corn. Place pepper in ice water until cool; peel and discard skin.
4. Remove husks, and cut kernels from cob; place kernels in a large bowl. Chop pepper; add pepper and green onions to corn.
5. Combine vinegar and next 4 ingredients. Gradually add oil, stirring constantly with a wire whisk. Pour dressing over corn salad; toss gently. Serve immediately, or chill thoroughly.

Asparagus, Roasted Beet, and Goat Cheese Salad

MAKES 6 SERVINGS
PREP: 15 MIN., BAKE: 45 MIN., COOK: 2 MIN.

18 small red beets (about 6 pounds)
1 cup olive oil
1/3 cup red wine vinegar
1/2 teaspoon salt, divided
1/2 teaspoon freshly ground pepper, divided
60 small fresh asparagus spears
1 (11-ounce) goat cheese log
1 tablespoon chopped fresh chives
Cracked pepper
Chopped fresh chives
Gourmet salad greens (optional)

1. Arrange beets in a single layer on a lightly greased baking sheet.
2. Bake at 425° for 40 to 45 minutes or until tender, stirring every 15 minutes. Cool beets completely.
3. Whisk together oil, vinegar, 1/4 teaspoon salt, and 1/4 teaspoon ground pepper in a small bowl.
4. Peel beets, and cut into wedges. Toss together beets, 1/2 cup vinaigrette, remaining 1/4 teaspoon salt, and remaining 1/4 teaspoon ground pepper; set aside.
5. Snap off tough ends of asparagus, discarding ends; cook asparagus in boiling water to cover 1 to 2 minutes or until crisp-tender. Plunge into ice water to stop the cooking process, and drain. Combine asparagus and 1/2 cup vinaigrette; set aside.
6. Cut cheese into 6 equal slices. Place 1 cheese slice in a 3-inch round cutter or ring mold; sprinkle with 1/2 teaspoon chives. Press chives into cheese; remove cutter. Repeat procedure with remaining cheese and 2 1/2 teaspoons chives.
7. Arrange asparagus over cheese. Surround with beets, and drizzle with remaining vinaigrette. Sprinkle with cracked pepper and chives; serve with salad greens, if desired.

Party Taco Salad

To serve this taco salad neatly and easily, just layer it in a big bowl, and provide salad tongs. Serve it right away so the warm cheese sauce doesn't wilt the other ingredients.

MAKES 6 TO 8 SERVINGS
PREP: 8 MIN., COOK: 12 MIN.

1 pound lean ground beef
1/2 cup chopped green bell pepper
1 cup chopped onion
1 tablespoon chili powder
1 1/2 pounds iceberg lettuce, shredded
2 large tomatoes, chopped
1 (10.5-ounce) package corn chips
1 (16-ounce) loaf process cheese spread, cut into
    pieces
1 (10-ounce) can diced tomatoes and green chiles

1. Cook first 4 ingredients in a large nonstick skillet over medium heat until beef is done, stirring to crumble beef; drain.
2. Place shredded lettuce in a large bowl; top with chopped tomato, corn chips, and beef mixture.
3. Combine cheese spread and diced tomatoes in a saucepan; cook over low heat, stirring often, until cheese melts. Pour cheese sauce over salad, and serve immediately.

Beef Salad Niçoise

Beef Salad Niçoise

Serve this hearty salad with crusty baguettes and red wine or sparkling water. Look for niçoise olives at specialty stores and kalamata olives in the ethnic foods section of the supermarket. We used the Peppery Grilled Flank Steak on page 113 for this salad.

MAKES 6 TO 8 SERVINGS
PREP: 25 MIN.

1 pound fresh green beans, trimmed
6 small new potatoes, cut in half
1 grilled flank steak (recipe, page 113)
9 to 12 cups gourmet mixed greens
2 red onions, halved and sliced
12 plum tomatoes, quartered
¾ cup niçoise or kalamata olives
1 (8-ounce) bottle balsamic vinaigrette or Ranch dressing

1. Cook green beans in boiling water in a saucepan 5 minutes or until crisp-tender; drain. Plunge into ice water to stop the cooking process; drain and set aside.
2. Cook potatoes in boiling water to cover in saucepan 15 minutes or until tender; drain and cool slightly. Cut into quarters.
3. Cut grilled flank steak diagonally across the grain into thin strips.
4. Mound steak strips in center of a lettuce-lined platter. Arrange green beans, potato, onion, tomato, and olives around flank steak. Serve with balsamic vinaigrette or Ranch dressing.

Apricot-Chicken Salad

Apricot-Chicken Salad

Apricot-Chicken Salad becomes an elegant entrée when served in stemmed dessert bowls and stacked on a glass cake stand. Fresh apricot slices and herb sprigs make up the garnish.

MAKES 6 SERVINGS

PREP: 25 MIN.

½ cup plain yogurt
¼ cup mayonnaise
3 tablespoons apricot preserves
2 teaspoons grated fresh ginger
½ teaspoon salt
½ teaspoon freshly ground pepper
3 cups chopped cooked chicken
1 cup sliced almonds, toasted
¾ cup sliced celery
1 (6-ounce) package dried apricots, chopped
Garnishes: fresh apricot slices, fresh thyme sprigs

1. Whisk together first 6 ingredients in a large bowl; add chicken and next 3 ingredients, tossing gently. Chill until ready to serve. Garnish, if desired.

Broccoli-Chicken Salad

MAKES 6 SERVINGS
PREP: 20 MIN., COOK: 15 MIN., CHILL: 1 HR.

4 skinned and boned chicken breasts
4 cups water
1/4 cup soy sauce
2 garlic cloves, minced
1 (16-ounce) package fresh broccoli florets
4 green onions, chopped
1 medium-size red bell pepper, chopped
1 cup sweetened dried cranberries
Chutney Dressing
1/4 cup chopped peanuts

1. Bring first 4 ingredients to a boil in a medium saucepan. Boil 15 minutes or until chicken is done; drain. Cool chicken, and cut into bite-size pieces.
2. Toss together chicken, broccoli, and next 4 ingredients. Chill 1 hour. Sprinkle with chopped peanuts before serving.

Chutney Dressing:

MAKES 1 3/4 CUPS
PREP: 5 MIN.

1 (9-ounce) jar mango chutney
1/2 cup mayonnaise
2 garlic cloves, minced
1/4 teaspoon dried crushed red pepper

1. Stir together all ingredients.
Note: For testing purposes only, we used Major Grey Chutney.

Strawberry-Chicken Salad

Replace the chicken with a sprinkling of blue cheese, and serve as a dinner salad with grilled steaks.

MAKES 4 SERVINGS
PREP: 30 MIN., CHILL: 1 HR., GRILL: 8 MIN., STAND: 10 MIN.

4 skinned and boned chicken breasts
Raspberry Vinaigrette, divided
8 cups mixed salad greens
1 quart strawberries, sliced
2 pears, sliced
2 avocados, peeled and sliced
1/2 small sweet onion, diced
1/2 cup pecan halves, toasted

1. Combine chicken and 1/2 cup Raspberry Vinaigrette in a large zip-top freezer bag; seal. Chill 1 hour.
2. Remove chicken from marinade, discarding marinade.
3. Grill chicken, covered with grill lid, over medium-high heat (350° to 400°) 4 minutes on each side or until done. Let stand 10 minutes; cut into slices.
4. Place salad greens and next 5 ingredients in a large bowl; toss gently. Divide salad greens mixture evenly among 4 serving plates; top with chicken slices. Serve with remaining Raspberry Vinaigrette.

Raspberry Vinaigrette:

MAKES 1 1/2 CUPS
PREP: 5 MIN.

3/4 cup pear nectar
1/3 cup vegetable oil
1/3 cup raspberry vinegar
3 tablespoons chopped fresh basil
1 tablespoon Dijon mustard
1 tablespoon sesame oil
1/2 teaspoon freshly ground pepper
1/4 teaspoon salt

1. Whisk together all ingredients. Store vinaigrette in an airtight container in refrigerator up to 2 weeks; whisk before serving.

Wild Rice-Chicken Salad

MAKES 8 SERVINGS
PREP: 40 MIN., CHILL: 8 HRS.

2 (6.2-ounce) packages long-grain and wild rice mix
2 (6-ounce) jars marinated quartered artichoke
    hearts, undrained
4 cups chopped cooked chicken
1 medium-size red bell pepper, chopped
2 celery ribs, thinly sliced
5 green onions, chopped
1 (2.25-ounce) can sliced ripe olives, drained
1 cup mayonnaise
1 1/2 teaspoons curry powder
Green leaf lettuce

1. Cook rice mix according to package directions.
2. Drain artichoke heart quarters, reserving 1/2 cup liquid. Stir together rice, artichokes, chicken, and next 4 ingredients.
3. Stir together reserved 1/2 cup artichoke heart liquid, mayonnaise, and curry powder; toss with rice and chicken mixture. Cover and chill mixture 8 hours. Serve on leaf lettuce.

Greek-Style Tuna Salad

Tuna salad goes Greek with the addition of feta cheese, olives, and oregano.

MAKES 6 SERVINGS
PREP: 10 MIN., COOK: 12 MIN., CHILL: 30 MIN.

1 cup orzo, uncooked
1 (6-ounce) can solid white tuna, drained and flaked
2 cups chopped tomato
1/2 cup crumbled feta cheese
1/4 cup chopped red onion
3 tablespoons sliced ripe olives
1/2 cup red wine vinegar
2 tablespoons water
2 tablespoons olive oil
1 garlic clove, minced
1/2 teaspoon dried basil
1/2 teaspoon dried oregano
Green leaf lettuce (optional)

1. Cook orzo according to package directions; drain, rinse with cold water, and drain again. Combine orzo, tuna, and next 4 ingredients in a large bowl; toss gently.
2. Process vinegar and next 5 ingredients in a blender until smooth, stopping to scrape down sides. Pour vinegar mixture over pasta mixture, and toss gently. Cover and chill thoroughly. Serve on lettuce leaves, if desired.

Tropical Spinach Salad With Grilled Shrimp

Omit the shrimp, and serve this as a side salad, or try one of the variations on the opposite page with grilled sliced chicken or pork tenderloin.

MAKES 6 SERVINGS
PREP: 30 MIN., CHILL: 1 HR., SOAK: 30 MIN., GRILL: 4 MIN.

2 pounds unpeeled, large fresh shrimp
Citrus Marinade
8 (12-inch) wooden skewers
2 (6-ounce) bags fresh baby spinach
2 mangoes, peeled and sliced
1 medium-size red onion, sliced
1 (3-ounce) package goat cheese, crumbled
1 cup fresh raspberries
1/2 cup chopped pistachios
Fresh Basil Vinaigrette

1. Peel shrimp; devein, if desired.
2. Place shrimp in a large zip-top freezer bag; add Citrus Marinade, seal, and shake to coat. Chill shrimp 1 hour.
3. Soak skewers in water to cover for 30 minutes.
4. Remove shrimp from marinade, discarding marinade. Thread shrimp onto skewers.
5. Grill, covered with grill lid, over medium-high heat (350° to 400°) 2 minutes on each side or just until shrimp turn pink. Remove shrimp from skewers.
6. Divide spinach evenly among 6 serving plates; top with mango slices, onion slices, and grilled shrimp. Sprinkle with crumbled goat cheese, raspberries, and pistachios. Serve with Fresh Basil Vinaigrette.

Citus Marinade:

MAKES 1 CUP

PREP: 5 MIN.

¾ cup fresh orange juice
1 garlic clove, crushed
2 tablespoons chopped fresh basil
2 tablespoons fresh lime juice
2 tablespoons extra-virgin olive oil
½ teaspoon dried crushed red pepper
¼ teaspoon salt

1. Whisk together all ingredients.

Fresh Basil Vinaigrette:

MAKES 1 CUP

PREP: 5 MIN.

¼ cup chopped fresh basil
¼ cup raspberry vinegar
1 teaspoon Dijon mustard
1 garlic clove, chopped
¼ teaspoon salt
¼ teaspoon pepper
¾ cup extra-virgin olive oil

1. Process first 6 ingredients in a blender or food processor until smooth. With blender running, gradually add oil in a slow, steady stream; process until smooth.

Tropical Spinach Salad With Grilled Chicken: Substitute 6 skinned and boned chicken breasts for shrimp; omit skewers. Grill chicken, covered with grill lid, over medium-high heat (350° to 400°) 4 minutes on each side or until done. Let stand 10 minutes. Cut chicken into slices, and serve as directed.

Tropical Spinach Salad With Grilled Pork Tenderloin: Substitute 2 (1-pound) pork tenderloins for shrimp; omit skewers. Grill pork, covered with grill lid, over medium-high heat (350° to 400°) 10 to 12 minutes on each side or until a meat thermometer inserted into thickest portion registers 155°. Remove from grill, and let stand 10 minutes until meat thermometer reaches 160°. Cut pork tenderloin into slices, and serve as directed.

**Tropical Spinach Salad
With Grilled Shrimp**

sandwiches

Caribbean Seafood Wraps, page 236

Grilled Four-Cheese Sandwiches With Tomato, Avocado, and Bacon

Grilled Four-Cheese Sandwiches With Tomato, Avocado, and Bacon

MAKES 4 SERVINGS
PREP: 30 MIN., COOK: 6 MIN. PER BATCH

8 microwave bacon slices
2 large tomatoes, each cut into 4 slices
¼ teaspoon salt
¼ teaspoon pepper
1 large avocado, cut into 8 slices*
1 tablespoon rice vinegar*
¼ cup butter, softened
1 teaspoon grated Parmesan cheese
2 tablespoons mayonnaise
8 sourdough bread slices
4 ounces sharp Cheddar cheese, sliced
4 ounces Monterey Jack cheese with peppers, sliced
4 ounces white Cheddar cheese, sliced
¼ cup Thousand Island dressing

1. Cook bacon according to package directions; drain, and set aside.

2. Sprinkle tomatoes evenly with salt and pepper; sprinkle avocado with vinegar. Stir together butter and Parmesan cheese. Set aside.

3. Spread mayonnaise on 1 side of 4 bread slices; layer each with 1 sharp Cheddar cheese slice, 1 tomato slice, 2 avocado slices, 2 bacon slices, 1 Monterey Jack cheese slice, 1 tomato slice, and 1 white Cheddar cheese slice. Spread remaining 4 bread slices with dressing; place on top of sandwich with dressing side down.

4. Spread half of butter mixture evenly on 1 side of sandwiches. Cook 2 sandwiches, buttered side down, in a hot nonstick skillet or griddle over medium heat 2 to 3 minutes. Spread remaining butter mixture evenly on ungrilled sides of sandwiches; turn and cook sandwiches 2 to 3 minutes. Repeat procedure with remaining sandwiches.

*½ cup guacamole may be substituted for avocado and rice vinegar.

Caramelized Onion BLT

MAKES 4 SERVINGS
PREP: 15 MIN.

2 medium tomatoes
⅓ cup mayonnaise
2 tablespoons chopped fresh basil
8 sourdough bread slices, toasted
12 bacon slices, cooked
8 Swiss cheese slices
1 cup Caramelized Sweet Onions (see recipe on
    page 256)
Salt and pepper to taste
4 lettuce leaves

1. Cut each tomato into 4 slices.
2. Stir together mayonnaise and basil; spread on 1 side of each bread slice. Top 4 bread slices each with 3 bacon slices, 2 tomato slices, and 2 cheese slices. Top evenly with onions; sprinkle with salt and pepper. Top with lettuce and remaining bread slices.

BLTs With a Twist

BLT goes gourmet! This sandwich is fit for a queen with its unique blend of goat cheese, basil, garlic, and dried tomatoes.

MAKES 4 SERVINGS
PREP: 13 MIN.

1 (4-ounce) package goat cheese, softened
1 tablespoon mayonnaise
¼ cup chopped fresh basil
2 garlic cloves, minced
¼ teaspoon salt
¼ teaspoon pepper
8 (1-ounce) sourdough bread slices, toasted
½ cup dried tomatoes in oil, drained and chopped
4 green leaf lettuce leaves
½ small red onion, thinly sliced
8 fully cooked bacon slices

1. Combine first 6 ingredients.
2. Spread cheese mixture evenly on 1 side of 4 bread slices. Sprinkle tomato evenly over coated side of 4 bread slices. Top evenly with lettuce, onion, bacon, and remaining bread slices, coated side down.
Note: For testing purposes only, we used Oscar Mayer Ready to Serve bacon.

French Onion Sandwiches

MAKES 8 SANDWICHES
PREP: 5 MIN., BAKE: 8 MIN., COOK: 10 MIN., BROIL: 2 MIN.

8 (1-ounce) French bread slices
2 teaspoons butter
1 large onion, very thinly sliced
1½ tablespoons brown sugar
1 cup (4 ounces) shredded Swiss cheese

1. Arrange bread slices on a baking sheet. Bake at 375° for 8 minutes or until lightly toasted. Remove from oven, and leave bread slices on baking sheet.
2. While bread toasts, coat a large heavy saucepan with cooking spray; add butter, and place over high heat until butter melts. Add onion, and cook, stirring constantly, 3 minutes or until onion is tender. Add brown sugar, and cook 5 more minutes or until onion is tender and browned, stirring often.
3. Spoon onion mixture evenly onto bread slices; top with cheese. Broil 5½ inches from heat 2 minutes. Serve immediately.

Grilled Pesto Sandwiches

Grilled Pesto Sandwiches

MAKES 4 SERVINGS
PREP: 15 MIN., COOK: 6 MIN.

1 (6-ounce) package sliced mozzarella cheese, cut
    into thirds
8 (½-inch-thick) Italian bread slices
¼ cup pizza sauce
¼ cup pesto
28 slices pepperoni
2 tablespoons butter or margarine, softened
Garnish: pepperoni slices

1. Arrange one-third of cheese slices on each of 4 slices
of bread; spread evenly with pizza sauce. Top each with
another one-third of cheese slices, and spread evenly
with pesto. Arrange pepperoni slices evenly over pesto;
top with remaining one-third of cheese slices and remaining bread slices.
2. Spread half of butter on tops of sandwiches. Invert
sandwiches onto a hot nonstick skillet or griddle, and
cook over medium heat 3 minutes or until browned.
Spread remaining butter on ungrilled sides of sandwiches; turn and cook 3 more minutes or until
browned. Garnish, if desired.

Good-Start Sandwiches

Bacon, eggs, and cheese are sandwiched inside these turnovers for a morning meal handy to enjoy at home or easy to eat on the road.

MAKES 8 SERVINGS
PREP: 30 MIN., COOK: 10 MIN., BAKE: 12 MIN.

2 tablespoons butter or margarine
9 large eggs
½ teaspoon salt
¼ teaspoon pepper
½ (8-ounce) package cream cheese, cut into
    ¼-inch cubes and softened
1 (16.3-ounce) can refrigerated jumbo flaky biscuits
8 bacon slices, cooked and crumbled
1 cup (4 ounces) shredded sharp Cheddar cheese

1. Melt butter in a large nonstick skillet over medium heat. Whisk together eggs, salt, and pepper; pour into skillet, and sprinkle with cream cheese cubes. Cook, without stirring, until eggs begin to set on bottom. Draw a spatula across bottom of skillet to form large curds; continue cooking until eggs are thickened but still moist. (Do not stir constantly.) Remove from heat, and let cool.
2. Pat or roll each biscuit on a lightly floured surface into a 6-inch circle. Spoon egg mixture evenly over tops of biscuit dough circles, leaving a small border around edge. Sprinkle evenly with crumbled bacon and Cheddar cheese. Brush edges with water; fold biscuit dough circles in half over filling, gently pressing edges with tines of a fork to seal. Place on a lightly greased baking sheet.
3. Bake sandwiches at 375° for 10 to 12 minutes or until golden.
Note: For testing purposes only, we used Pillsbury (8-count) Grands! Original Flaky Biscuits.

Egg Salad Club Sandwiches

MAKES 4 SERVINGS
PREP: 25 MIN.

⅔ cup mayonnaise, divided
4 large hard-cooked eggs, chopped
1 celery rib, diced
4 bacon slices, cooked and crumbled
¼ cup chopped fresh chives
1 tablespoon minced sweet onion
¼ teaspoon seasoned salt
½ teaspoon freshly ground pepper
12 very thin white or wheat sandwich bread slices,
    lightly toasted
1 cup firmly packed fresh spinach

1. Stir together ⅓ cup mayonnaise and next 7 ingredients.
2. Spread remaining ⅓ cup mayonnaise evenly over 1 side of each bread slice. Spread 4 bread slices, mayonnaise side up, evenly with half of egg salad. Top evenly with half of spinach and 4 bread slices.
3. Repeat procedure with remaining egg salad, spinach, and bread slices. Cut each sandwich into quarters.

Sweet Pickle-Egg Salad Club: Omit bacon and chives. Add 2 tablespoons instant potato flakes and 1 tablespoon sweet pickle relish; proceed with recipe as directed.

Shrimp-Egg Salad Club: Omit bacon. Add ⅔ cup finely chopped boiled shrimp, ½ teaspoon grated lemon rind, and ¼ teaspoon ground red pepper. Proceed with recipe as directed.

Savory Petits Fours Sandwiches

Use a combination of white and whole wheat bread slices to add visual interest to these sandwiches.

MAKES 4 DOZEN
PREP: 1 HR.

Curried Chicken Salad Spread
36 very thin white or whole wheat bread slices
Ham-and-Olive Salad Spread
Garnish: Decorative Cream Cheese Topping (see box
    on opposite page)

1. Spread about ¼ cup Curried Chicken Salad Spread on 1 side of each of 6 bread slices. Top each with 1 bread slice; spread slices with an additional ¼ cup Curried Chicken Salad Spread, and top each with 1 bread slice. Trim crusts from sandwiches; cut each into fourths. Repeat procedure with remaining 18 bread slices, using Ham-and-Olive Salad Spread. Garnish, if desired.

Curried Chicken Salad Spread:

MAKES ABOUT 3 CUPS
PREP: 20 MIN.

2 cups diced cooked chicken
2 celery ribs, diced
½ cup golden raisins, chopped
4 green onions, minced
1 (8-ounce) package cream cheese, softened
3 tablespoons mayonnaise
1 teaspoon curry powder
½ teaspoon seasoned salt

1. Stir together all ingredients. Cover and chill until ready to serve.

Savory Petits Fours Sandwiches

Ham-and-Olive Salad Spread:

MAKES ABOUT 3 CUPS
PREP: 20 MIN.

2½ cups minced cooked ham
⅔ cup finely chopped pimiento-stuffed Spanish olives
2 green onions, minced
1 (8-ounce) package cream cheese, softened
3 tablespoons mayonnaise
1 tablespoon sweet hot mustard
½ teaspoon seasoned pepper

1. Stir together all ingredients. Cover and chill until ready to serve.

PETITS FOURS SANDWICH POINTERS

Decorative Cream Cheese Topping: Stir together 1 container cream cheese, softened, and desired amount of liquid food coloring. Pipe tinted cream cheese on tops of sandwiches. We tinted our cream cheese with a mixture of green and yellow liquid food coloring to resemble spring leaves, and then we used red and yellow liquid food coloring to make rosebuds. We used a decorating bag with different metal tips to pipe the tinted cream cheese. You can also snip a tiny hole in one corner of a zip-top freezer bag to pipe.

Make ahead: Place sandwiches, covered with damp paper towels, in an airtight container, and chill up to 24 hours. To freeze, do not trim crusts or cut into fourths after assembling sandwiches. Place whole sandwiches into small zip-top freezer bags. Freeze sandwiches for up to 2 weeks. Thaw in the refrigerator overnight, and proceed as directed.

Cucumber Sandwiches

These petite sandwiches are a classic for showers and teas.

MAKES 16 SANDWICHES
PREP: 10 MIN.

1 large cucumber, peeled, seeded, and grated
1 (8-ounce) package cream cheese, softened
1 tablespoon mayonnaise
1 small shallot, minced
¼ teaspoon seasoned salt
1 (16-ounce) loaf sandwich bread, crusts removed
Garnish: cucumber slices

1. Drain cucumber well, pressing between layers of paper towels.
2. Stir together cucumber, cream cheese, and next 3 ingredients. Spread mixture evenly over half of bread slices. Top with remaining bread slices.
3. Cut sandwiches in half diagonally. Garnish, if desired. Store sandwiches in an airtight container.

Miniature Tomato Sandwiches

MAKES 16 APPETIZER SERVINGS
PREP: 10 MIN.

1 French baguette
¼ cup mayonnaise
1 (3-ounce) package cream cheese, softened
2 teaspoons chopped fresh basil
¼ teaspoon salt, divided
¼ teaspoon pepper, divided
4 plum tomatoes, sliced

1. Cut baguette into 16 slices.
2. Stir together mayonnaise, cream cheese, basil, ⅛ teaspoon salt, and ⅛ teaspoon pepper; cover and chill 8 hours, if desired.
3. Spread cheese mixture on 1 side of each baguette slice. Top evenly with tomatoes, and sprinkle with remaining salt and pepper.

Green Chile-Pimiento Cheese

*A poblano pepper and green chiles enliven this favorite sandwich spread that will keep in your refrigerator
up to a week. Slather it on sandwiches or celery sticks per your cravings. For the creamiest blend possible,
we recommend grating the cheese yourself rather than using preshredded.*

MAKES ABOUT 6 CUPS
PREP: 15 MIN.

2 (8-ounce) blocks extra-sharp Cheddar cheese,
    grated
1 (8-ounce) block Monterey Jack cheese with
    peppers, shredded
1 cup mayonnaise
1 (4.5-ounce) can chopped green chiles
1 (4-ounce) jar diced pimiento, drained
1 medium poblano chile pepper, seeded and minced
¼ small sweet onion, minced
2 teaspoons Worcestershire sauce

1. Stir together all ingredients in a large bowl. Store in
refrigerator up to a week.

Green Chile-Pimiento Cheese Sandwiches: Spread
½ cup cheese mixture on 6 to 8 white bread slices; top
with bread slices.

220 sandwiches

Bat Sandwiches

A bat-shaped cookie cutter turns these delicious little sandwiches into Halloween Party fare. You can also adapt this recipe for other festive occasions by using cookie cutters shaped as a Christmas tree, heart, or Easter egg.

MAKES 24 SANDWICHES
PREP: 30 MIN.

3 cups (12 ounces) shredded sharp Cheddar cheese
1 (8-ounce) container chive-and-onion cream cheese, softened
1 (4-ounce) jar diced pimiento, drained
$\frac{1}{2}$ cup chopped pecans, toasted
24 whole wheat or pumpernickel bread slices

1. Stir together first 4 ingredients. Using a 3- to 4-inch bat-shaped cutter, cut 2 bats from each bread slice. Spread about 2 tablespoons filling over each of 24 bats. Top each with remaining 24 bats.

Turkey-Cranberry Croissants

MAKES 6 SERVINGS
PREP: 20 MIN.

1 (8-ounce) package cream cheese, softened
$\frac{1}{4}$ cup orange marmalade
$\frac{1}{2}$ cup chopped pecans
6 large croissants, split
Lettuce leaves
1 pound thinly sliced cooked turkey
$\frac{3}{4}$ cup whole-berry cranberry sauce

1. Stir together first 3 ingredients until blended. Spread evenly on cut sides of croissants. Place lettuce and turkey on croissant bottoms; spread with cranberry sauce, and cover with croissant tops.

Turkey Wraps

MAKES 4 SERVINGS
PREP: 25 MIN.

4 (10-inch) flour tortillas
$\frac{3}{4}$ cup whole-berry cranberry sauce
2 tablespoons spicy brown mustard
2 cups chopped cooked turkey
$\frac{1}{4}$ cup chopped pecans, toasted
2 green onions, diced
2 tablespoons minced crystallized ginger
2 cups shredded lettuce

1. Heat tortillas according to package directions.
2. Stir together cranberry sauce and mustard, and spoon mixture evenly down center of each tortilla.
3. Combine turkey and next 3 ingredients; spoon evenly over cranberry mixture. Top each evenly with lettuce, and roll up.

Avocado Sandwiches Deluxe

Avocado Sandwiches Deluxe

Stir up a pitcher of iced tea, and take these sandwiches out to the patio on a pretty day.

MAKES 2 SERVINGS
PREP: 20 MIN.

1 avocado, cut into 8 wedges
¼ cup Italian dressing
1 tablespoon mayonnaise
4 oatmeal or whole wheat bread slices, toasted
2 (1-ounce) processed American cheese slices
4 thin tomato slices
½ cup alfalfa sprouts

1. Toss avocado wedges gently with Italian dressing; drain well, reserving dressing.

2. Spread mayonnaise evenly over 1 side of each bread slice. Top 2 bread slices evenly with American cheese slices, tomato, avocado, and alfalfa sprouts.

3. Drizzle sandwiches evenly with reserved Italian dressing, and top with remaining 2 bread slices. Serve immediately.

Cobb Sandwiches

Similar to the famous Cobb Salad, this sandwich boasts the same stack of great ingredients: chicken, bacon, tomato, avocado, and blue cheese.

MAKES 4 SERVINGS
PREP: 15 MIN., GRILL: 10 MIN., CHILL: 30 MIN.

4 skinned and boned chicken breasts
½ teaspoon salt
½ teaspoon pepper
¼ cup olive oil
¼ cup balsamic vinegar
1 tablespoon Dijon mustard
1 ripe avocado
1 teaspoon fresh lemon juice
⅓ cup mayonnaise
8 slices challah or other egg bread, toasted
4 Boston lettuce leaves
1 tomato, thinly sliced
8 ounces blue cheese, thinly sliced
8 bacon slices, cooked and crumbled

1. Sprinkle chicken with salt and pepper; place in a shallow dish.
2. Combine oil, vinegar, and mustard; pour over chicken. Cover chicken, and marinate in refrigerator at least 30 minutes, turning occasionally. Drain chicken, discarding marinade.
3. Coat grill rack with cooking spray; place on grill over medium-high heat (350° to 400°). Grill chicken, covered with grill lid, 5 minutes on each side or until done. Let chicken stand until cool to touch; cut chicken diagonally into thin slices.
4. Slice avocado, and sprinkle with lemon juice. Spread mayonnaise evenly on 1 side of each bread slice. Layer 4 slices of bread with lettuce, tomato, avocado, cheese, bacon, and chicken; top with remaining bread slices.

Italian Club Sandwiches

Mortadella is most frequently produced in Bologna, Italy. Similar to bologna, this smoked sausage can be found in the supermarket with the deli meats.

MAKES 4 SERVINGS
PREP: 25 MIN., BAKE: 6 MIN.

½ (16-ounce) Italian bread loaf
¼ cup Italian dressing
⅓ cup shredded Parmesan cheese
½ cup mayonnaise
½ cup mustard
½ pound thinly sliced Genoa salami
½ pound thinly sliced mortadella or bologna
4 (1-ounce) provolone cheese slices
Romaine lettuce leaves
3 plum tomatoes, sliced
8 bacon slices, cooked and cut in half

1. Cut bread diagonally into 12 (¼-inch-thick) slices; arrange on a baking sheet. Brush slices evenly with Italian dressing, and sprinkle with Parmesan cheese.
2. Bake at 375° for 5 to 6 minutes or until lightly toasted.
3. Spread untoasted sides of bread slices evenly with mayonnaise and mustard. Layer 4 bread slices, mayonnaise side up, with salami, mortadella, and provolone. Top with 4 bread slices, mayonnaise side up; layer with lettuce, tomatoes, and bacon. Top with remaining 4 bread slices, mayonnaise side down. Cut in half, and secure with wooden picks.

Grilled Avocado-Cheese
Sandwiches

Grilled Avocado-Cheese Sandwiches

Portobello Mushroom Burgers
MAKES 6 SERVINGS

GRILL: 10 MIN.

lic
, cut into 6 slices
oom caps

sil
:ard

ces each

er at least 30 minutes; drain.
on grill, and scatter wood

garlic; brush on both sides of

ooms, covered with grill lid,
350° to 400°) 4 minutes on
Grill bun halves, cut sides
ightly browned.
se and next 5 ingredients.
evenly with mayonnaise mix-
room, and 2 tomato slices;
alves.

Spicy Bean Burgers

There's no meat but plenty of protein in this vegetarian burger. Slather a little mayo laced with a little sauce from chipotle peppers for an eye-opening entrée.

MAKES 10 SERVINGS
PREP: 10 MIN., COOK: 12 MIN.

2 (15-ounce) cans pinto beans with jalapeño peppers, rinsed and drained
1 (16-ounce) can black beans, rinsed and drained
1 cup uncooked quick-cooking oats
4 green onions, chopped
1 large egg, lightly beaten
½ cup ketchup
1 teaspoon garlic salt
1 teaspoon Worcestershire sauce
½ teaspoon liquid smoke
¼ cup vegetable oil
Hamburger buns
Toppings: lettuce leaves, tomato slices

1. Mash beans in a large bowl. Stir in oats, green onions, and next 5 ingredients.
2. Shape mixture into 10 (4-inch) patties. Cook half of patties in 2 tablespoons hot oil in a large skillet over medium-high heat 2 to 3 minutes on each side or until lightly browned.
3. Repeat with remaining patties and oil. Serve on warm buns with desired toppings.

Easy Spanish Pork Dip Sandwiches

This family-pleasing recipe was an Easy Entrée finalist in one of our $100,000 Southern Living *Cook-Off contests.*

MAKES 8 SERVINGS
PREP: 20 MIN., COOK: 6 HRS.

1 (4- to 5-pound) boneless pork butt roast
3 tablespoons garlic pepper
2 teaspoons salt
¼ cup vegetable oil
12 ounces mojo criollo Spanish marinating sauce
2 (0.75-ounce) envelopes pork gravy mix
2 cups water
¼ cup white vinegar
2 bay leaves
1 medium-size sweet onion, thinly sliced
1 fresh Cuban bread loaf

1. Rinse roast, and pat dry with paper towels. Cut in half. Sprinkle garlic pepper and salt evenly on halves of roast.
2. Cook roast in hot vegetable oil in a large skillet 2 minutes on each side or until lightly browned. Place roast halves in a 6-quart slow cooker, fat sides up.
3. Combine Spanish marinating sauce, gravy mix, 2 cups water, and ¼ cup vinegar; pour over roast in slow cooker. Add bay leaves; top with onion slices.
4. Cover and cook on HIGH 1 hour. Reduce heat to LOW, and cook 4 to 5 hours or until meat is tender and shreds easily. Remove and discard bay leaves.
5. Remove pork and onion slices to a large bowl, reserving liquid; shred meat. Add 1 cup reserved liquid to shredded pork to moisten.
6. Slice bread into 8 equal portions; slice each portion in half lengthwise. Place shredded pork on bottom bread slices; top with remaining bread slices.
7. Spoon remaining liquid into individual bowls for dipping.
Note: For testing purposes only, we used La Lechonera Mojo Criollo Spanish Marinating Sauce.

Mango Chutney Chicken Pitas

MAKES 4 SERVINGS

PREP: 11 MIN.

1 (10-ounce) package finely shredded cabbage
1 Granny Smith apple, diced
1 (6-ounce) container plain fat-free yogurt
1 teaspoon grated lemon rind
½ teaspoon dry mustard
2 (6-ounce) packages grilled chicken strips
1 cup warm mango chutney
4 pita bread rounds, halved crosswise

1. Combine first 5 ingredients. Layer chicken, mango chutney, and slaw mixture evenly inside pita halves.

Mango Chutney
Chicken Pitas

Open-Faced Southwestern
Chicken Sandwiches

Open-Faced Southwestern Chicken Sandwiches

*Want a showy presentation when having guests over for lunch? This sandwich
topped with colorful black bean salsa will do the trick.*

MAKES 4 SERVINGS
PREP: 15 MIN., GRILL: 20 MIN., BROIL: 2 MIN.

4 skinned and boned chicken breasts
2 tablespoons chopped fresh cilantro
2 tablespoons vegetable oil
2 teaspoons chili powder
1/4 teaspoon ground red pepper
1 garlic clove, minced
1 cup (4 ounces) shredded Mexican four-cheese blend
1/3 cup mayonnaise
4 (1-inch-thick) French bread slices, lightly toasted
Black bean salsa

1. Place chicken between 2 sheets of heavy-duty plastic
wrap, and flatten to 1/2-inch thickness using a meat
mallet or rolling pin.
2. Stir together cilantro and next 4 ingredients. Spread
on chicken.
3. Grill, covered with grill lid, over medium-high heat
(350° to 400°) 8 to 10 minutes on each side or until
chicken is done.
4. Meanwhile, stir together cheese and mayonnaise.
Spread on bread slices. Place bread, cheese mixture side
up, on a baking sheet.
5. Broil 6 inches from heat 1 to 2 minutes or until
cheese melts. Place chicken on bread, and serve with
black bean salsa.

London Broil Sandwiches With Yogurt-Cucumber Sauce

MAKES 6 SERVINGS

PREP: 15 MIN., CHILL: 8 HRS., GRILL: 14 MIN., STAND: 5 MIN.

1½ pounds London broil (about ¾ inch thick)
2 garlic cloves, minced
⅓ cup fresh lemon juice
1 tablespoon Greek seasoning
1 tablespoon olive oil
1 (8-ounce) container plain fat-free yogurt
1 large cucumber, peeled, seeded, and chopped
1 tablespoon fresh lemon juice
½ teaspoon dried dillweed
6 pita bread rounds, warmed
Shredded lettuce
1 large tomato, diced

1. Place beef between 2 sheets of heavy-duty plastic wrap, and flatten to ½-inch thickness using a meat mallet or a rolling pin.
2. Combine garlic and next 3 ingredients in a shallow dish or large zip-top freezer bag; add beef. Cover or seal, and chill 8 hours. Remove beef from marinade, discarding marinade.
3. Stir together yogurt and next 3 ingredients. Set aside.
4. Grill beef, covered with grill lid, over medium-high heat (350° to 400°) 7 minutes on each side or to desired degree of doneness. Let stand 5 minutes. Cut into thin slices.
5. Place beef evenly down center of warm pita rounds. Top with yogurt mixture, lettuce, and tomato; roll up. Serve immediately.

Meat Loaf Sandwich

MAKES 4 SERVINGS

PREP: 20 MIN.; COOK: 10 MIN.; BAKE: 1 HR., 15 MIN.

1 (16-ounce) Italian or sourdough bread loaf
2½ tablespoons butter or margarine, divided
1 small onion, chopped
½ (8-ounce) package sliced fresh mushrooms
1 large egg
6 to 7 tablespoons ketchup, divided
1½ cups (6 ounces) shredded Cheddar cheese, divided
1 pound lean ground beef
½ cup dry red wine or beef broth
1 teaspoon garlic salt
¼ teaspoon dried thyme
2 to 3 tablespoons mayonnaise

1. Cut bread loaf in half lengthwise. Scoop out bread, leaving ¼-inch-thick shells. Tear reserved bread into pieces, and measure 1½ cups, reserving remaining bread pieces for another use. Set bread shells and 1½ cups breadcrumbs aside.
2. Melt 1½ tablespoons butter in a large skillet over medium heat; add chopped onion and mushrooms, and sauté 8 minutes or until tender.
3. Stir together egg and 2 tablespoons ketchup in a large bowl. Add onion mixture, 1½ cups breadcrumbs, ½ cup cheese, ground beef, and next 3 ingredients, blending well. Shape mixture into a 6- to 7-inch loaf. Place on a lightly greased rack in a roasting pan. Bake at 350° for 1 hour or until done.
4. Spread bottom of bread shell with mayonnaise; top with meat loaf. Top with remaining 4 to 5 tablespoons ketchup; sprinkle with remaining 1 cup cheese. Top with remaining bread half. Melt remaining 1 tablespoon butter; brush over bread top. Wrap in aluminum foil. Bake at 350° for 10 to 15 minutes or until heated.

Golden-Baked Mini Reubens

Golden-Baked Mini Reubens

These tangy little sandwiches are full of kraut and corned beef—perfect pickups for game-day fun!

MAKES 20 SANDWICHES
PREP: 20 MIN., BAKE: 10 MIN.

½ cup Thousand Island dressing
1 (16-ounce) loaf party rye bread
1 (6-ounce) package Swiss cheese slices, halved
12 ounces thinly sliced corned beef
1 (14.5-ounce) can shredded sauerkraut, well drained
Butter-flavored cooking spray

1. Spread dressing evenly on 1 side of each bread slice; top half of slices evenly with half of cheese, corned beef, sauerkraut, and remaining cheese. Top with remaining bread slices.
2. Coat a baking sheet with butter-flavored cooking spray; arrange sandwiches on baking sheet. Coat the bottom of a second baking sheet with cooking spray; place, coated side down, on sandwiches to provide pressure while cooking.
3. Bake at 375° for 8 to 10 minutes or until bread is golden and cheese melts.

Muffulettas

Olive Salad can also be served on mixed greens or as a salsa for grilled chicken. Store it in the refrigerator in a nonmetal container up to 2 weeks.

MAKES 6 SERVINGS
PREP: 20 MIN.

2 cups Olive Salad
1 (16-ounce) French bread loaf, split horizontally
½ pound sliced hard salami
½ pound sliced cooked ham
6 (1-ounce) Swiss cheese slices
6 (1-ounce) provolone cheese slices

1. Spread 1 cup Olive Salad evenly on cut side of bread half; layer evenly with salami, ham, and cheeses, and spread remaining Olive Salad over cheeses. Cover with bread half. Cut crosswise into 6 sandwiches.

Olive Salad:

MAKES 6 CUPS
PREP: 10 MIN., CHILL: 8 HRS.

1 (1-quart) jar mixed pickled vegetables
1 (16-ounce) jar pitted green olives, drained
2 (2¼-ounce) cans chopped ripe olives, drained
½ cup olive oil
¼ cup chopped pepperoncini peppers
2 tablespoons capers
1 tablespoon minced garlic
1½ teaspoons dried parsley flakes
1 teaspoon dried oregano
1 teaspoon dried basil
½ teaspoon pepper
1 red onion, quartered (optional)
1 (7.25-ounce) jar roasted red peppers, drained and
      coarsely chopped (optional)

1. Drain pickled vegetables, reserving ¼ cup liquid.
2. Pulse pickled vegetables, next 10 ingredients, and, if desired, onion, in a food processor until coarsely chopped.
3. Stir in reserved ¼ cup vegetable liquid and, if desired, roasted red peppers; cover and chill 8 hours. Chill leftover mixture up to 2 weeks.
Note: For testing purposes, we used mixed pickled vegetables that contained cauliflower, onion, carrot, pepper, and celery.

Beef, Bacon, and Blue Cheese Sandwiches

MAKES 6 SERVINGS

PREP: 25 MIN., COOK: 5 MIN.

½ (4-ounce) package crumbled blue cheese
¼ cup butter or margarine, softened
½ (8-ounce) package cream cheese
½ cup sour cream
1 tablespoon finely chopped onion
⅛ teaspoon ground white pepper
⅛ teaspoon garlic salt
1 (12-ounce) package bacon, cooked and crumbled
12 pumpernickel or sourdough bread slices, toasted
1 tablespoon chopped fresh chives
12 ounces thinly sliced cooked roast beef
2 tomatoes, thinly sliced
1 head curly endive, separated

1. Combine blue cheese and butter; set aside.
2. Combine cream cheese and next 4 ingredients in a small saucepan; cook, stirring constantly, over low heat until blended. Let cool, and stir in bacon.
3. Spread cream cheese mixture evenly on 1 side of 6 bread slices, and sprinkle with chives.
4. Spread blue cheese mixture evenly on 1 side of remaining bread slices; top evenly with roast beef, tomato slices, and curly endive leaves. Top with other bread slices, cream cheese sides down.

Roast Beef Wraps

Mealtime's a wrap with these easy-to-prepare and easy-to-eat sandwiches.

MAKES 8 SERVINGS

PREP: 20 MIN., CHILL: 8 HRS.

½ cup sour cream*
½ cup mayonnaise*
1 green onion, chopped
2 tablespoons prepared horseradish
½ teaspoon salt
½ teaspoon pepper
8 (12-inch) flour tortillas
1 pound roast beef, cut into 24 thin slices
2 (6-ounce) packages deli-style sharp Cheddar cheese slices (optional)
2 cups shredded iceberg lettuce

1. Stir together first 6 ingredients until blended. Spread evenly on 1 side of each tortilla; top with 3 beef slices and, if desired, 2 cheese slices. Sprinkle each evenly with shredded lettuce.
2. Roll up tortillas tightly; wrap in parchment paper or plastic wrap. Chill 8 hours.
Note: For testing purposes only, we used Sargento Deli Style Sharp Cheddar Cheese slices.
To Lighten: Substitute ½ cup light sour cream and ½ cup light mayonnaise.

Baja-Style Fried
Catfish Tacos

Baja-Style Fried Catfish Tacos

MAKES 12 TACOS
PREP: 20 MIN., FRY: 6 MIN PER BATCH

¾ cup all-purpose flour
½ teaspoon salt
¼ teaspoon pepper
¼ teaspoon garlic powder
1½ pounds catfish fillets, cut into 4- x ½-inch strips
Canola oil
12 super-size corn tortillas, warmed
¼ head red cabbage, thinly sliced
Pico de Gallo
3 limes, cut into wedges
Creamy Jalapeño-Cilantro Dressing

1. Combine flour, salt, pepper, and garlic powder;
dredge catfish strips in flour mixture.
2. Pour oil to a depth of ½ inch into a large skillet, and
heat to 375°. Fry catfish in hot oil, in batches, 2 to 3
minutes on each side or until lightly browned. Drain
catfish on a wire rack over paper towels.
3. Place catfish on warmed tortillas; top with cabbage
and Pico de Gallo. Squeeze lime juice over tacos, and
drizzle with Creamy Jalapeño-Cilantro Dressing. Serve
immediately

Pico de Gallo:

MAKES 2½ CUPS
PREP: 20 MIN.

1 large tomato, coarsely chopped
½ large red onion, coarsely chopped
1 cup loosely packed fresh cilantro leaves, coarsely
    chopped
1 jalapeño pepper, finely chopped
¼ teaspoon salt
¼ teaspoon pepper

1. Stir together all ingredients.

Creamy Jalapeño-Cilantro Dressing:

MAKES 1¼ CUPS
PREP: 10 MIN.

1 cup loosely packed fresh cilantro leaves
1 cup sour cream
1 large jalapeño pepper, seeded and cut into large
    pieces
2 tablespoons fresh lime juice
4 teaspoons powdered Ranch dressing mix
⅛ teaspoon salt

1. Place all ingredients in a blender; blend just until
combined. (Dressing should be slightly chunky.) Cover
and chill until ready to serve.

Shrimp Po'boys

Shrimp Po'boys

MAKES 4 SANDWICHES
PREP: 35 MIN., FRY: 2 MIN. PER BATCH, BAKE: 8 MIN.

2 pounds unpeeled, large fresh shrimp
1¼ cups all-purpose flour
½ teaspoon salt
½ teaspoon pepper
½ cup milk
1 large egg
Peanut oil
⅓ cup butter
1 teaspoon minced garlic
4 French bread rolls, split
Rémoulade Sauce
1 cup shredded lettuce

1. Peel shrimp, and devein, if desired.
2. Combine flour, salt, and pepper. Stir together milk and egg until smooth. Toss shrimp in milk mixture; dredge in flour mixture.
3. Pour oil to a depth of 2 inches into a Dutch oven; heat to 375°. Fry shrimp, in batches, 1 to 2 minutes or until golden; drain on wire racks.
4. Melt butter; add garlic. Spread cut sides of rolls evenly with butter mixture, and place on a large baking sheet.
5. Bake at 450° for 8 minutes. Spread cut sides of rolls evenly with Rémoulade Sauce. Place lettuce and shrimp evenly on bottom halves of rolls; cover with roll tops. Serve immediately.

Rémoulade Sauce:

MAKES 1½ CUPS
PREP: 5 MIN.

1 cup mayonnaise
3 green onions, sliced
2 tablespoons Creole mustard
1 tablespoon chopped fresh parsley
1 teaspoon minced garlic
1 teaspoon prepared horseradish

1. Stir together all ingredients; cover and chill until ready to serve.

Dressed Mini Oyster Po'boys

To save time, purchase premade coleslaw.

MAKES 4 TO 6 SERVINGS
PREP: 30 MIN., FRY: 4 MIN. PER BATCH

1¼ cups self-rising cornmeal
2 tablespoons Creole seasoning
2 (8-ounce) containers fresh oysters, drained
Peanut or vegetable oil
1 cup mayonnaise, divided
2 tablespoons white vinegar
2 tablespoons Dijon mustard
1 (10-ounce) package shredded cabbage
2 tablespoons ketchup
1 tablespoon prepared horseradish
1 teaspoon Creole seasoning
¾ teaspoon paprika
12 French bread rolls, split and toasted

1. Combine cornmeal and 2 tablespoons Creole seasoning. Dredge oysters in cornmeal mixture.
2. Pour oil to a depth of 1 inch into a Dutch oven; heat to 375°.
3. Fry oysters, in 3 batches, 3 to 4 minutes or until golden. Drain oysters on paper towels.
4. Stir together ½ cup mayonnaise, vinegar, and mustard. Stir in cabbage; set slaw aside.
5. Stir together remaining ½ cup mayonnaise, ketchup, and next 3 ingredients in a small bowl.
6. Spread cut sides of French bread rolls with mayonnaise mixture; place oysters and slaw evenly on bottom halves of each roll. Cover with tops. Serve immediately.

side dishes

Fried Green Tomato Stacks, page 274

Asparagus With Garlic Cream

MAKES 8 TO 10 SERVINGS
PREP: 20 MIN., COOK: 3 MIN., CHILL: 8 HRS.

1 (8-ounce) container sour cream
2 tablespoons milk
1 tablespoon white wine vinegar
1 tablespoon olive oil
¼ teaspoon salt
¼ teaspoon freshly ground pepper
2 garlic cloves, minced
2 pounds fresh asparagus

1. Stir together first 7 ingredients. Cover and chill 8 hours.
2. Snap off tough ends of asparagus. Cook in boiling water to cover 3 minutes or until crisp-tender; drain.
3. Plunge asparagus into ice water to stop the cooking process; drain.
4. Serve with garlic cream.

Greek Asparagus

MAKES 4 SERVINGS
PREP: 6 MIN., BAKE: 15 MIN.

1 pound fresh asparagus
¼ cup Greek dressing, divided
¼ cup crumbled feta cheese

1. Snap off tough ends of asparagus. Toss asparagus and 2 tablespoons dressing together; arrange in a single layer on a baking sheet. Bake at 475° for 15 minutes or until crisp-tender. Toss with remaining 2 tablespoons dressing. Sprinkle with feta cheese.
Note: For testing purposes only, we used Ken's Steak House Greek Dressing.

Asian-Glazed Asparagus

Toast sesame seeds by spreading them out in a thin layer in a shallow pan. Bake at 350° for 4 to 6 minutes, stirring twice.

MAKES 4 TO 6 SERVINGS
PREP: 3 MIN., COOK: 9 MIN.

1 tablespoon cornstarch
¾ cup chicken broth
3 tablespoons soy sauce
1 garlic clove, minced
2 pounds fresh asparagus
2 tablespoons olive oil
⅛ teaspoon pepper
1 tablespoon sesame seeds, toasted

1. Combine first 4 ingredients in a small saucepan. Bring to a boil; cook 1 minute, stirring constantly. Remove from heat; set aside
2. Snap off tough ends of asparagus. Cook asparagus in hot olive oil in a large skillet over medium-high heat, stirring often, 6 minutes or until crisp-tender. Add chicken broth mixture to asparagus; cook, stirring constantly 1 minute or until thoroughly heated. Stir in pepper. Sprinkle with sesame seeds. Serve immediately.

Home-Cooked Pole Beans

Here's a classic, easy bean recipe flavored with bacon drippings and enhanced with a little sugar.

MAKES 6 TO 8 SERVINGS
PREP: 12 MIN., COOK: 22 MIN.

2 pounds fresh pole beans
3 bacon slices
1 cup water
1 teaspoon salt
¼ teaspoon sugar
¼ teaspoon pepper

1. Wash beans; trim stem ends. Snap beans in half, and set aside.

2. Cook bacon in a large saucepan until crisp; remove bacon, reserving drippings in pan. Crumble bacon, and set aside.

3. Add water and remaining 3 ingredients to saucepan; bring to a boil over high heat. Add beans; cover, reduce heat to medium, and cook 15 minutes or to desired doneness. Sprinkle with crumbled bacon. Serve with a slotted spoon.

Home-Cooked Pole Beans

Green Beans With Shallots and Parmesan

Green Beans With Shallots and Parmesan

Fresh ingredients topped with Parmesan cheese make a delicious side dish your guests will love.

MAKES 8 SERVINGS
PREP: 15 MIN., COOK: 24 MIN.

2 tablespoons butter or margarine
8 large shallots, sliced vertically
2 pounds fresh green beans, trimmed
¼ teaspoon salt
¼ teaspoon freshly ground pepper
⅓ cup shredded Parmesan cheese

1. Melt butter in a saucepan over medium-high heat; add sliced shallots, and sauté 12 minutes or until golden. Remove from heat.
2. Cook green beans in boiling water to cover 10 to 12 minutes or until tender, and drain. Stir in shallots, salt, and pepper. Sprinkle with Parmesan cheese.

Tangy Green Beans With Pimiento

MAKES 6 SERVINGS
PREP: 10 MIN., COOK: 20 MIN.

1 1/2 pounds green beans, trimmed
3 bacon slices
1 large onion, chopped
3 garlic cloves, minced
1 (2-ounce) jar diced pimiento, drained
1/4 cup red wine vinegar
1 teaspoon sugar
1/2 teaspoon salt
1/2 teaspoon pepper
1/2 teaspoon cumin seeds

1. Cook green beans in boiling water to cover 4 to 5 minutes. Drain and plunge beans into ice water to stop the cooking process; drain and set aside.
2. Cook bacon in a large skillet until crisp; remove bacon, and drain on paper towels, reserving 2 tablespoons drippings in skillet. Crumble bacon.
3. Sauté onion and garlic in hot bacon drippings over medium-high heat until tender. Stir in pimiento and next 5 ingredients. Stir in green beans; reduce heat, cover, and simmer 5 minutes. Sprinkle with bacon.

Baked Beans

Go for the full cup of brown sugar if you like sweet baked beans.

MAKES 8 TO 10 SERVINGS
PREP: 8 MIN.; COOK: 3 HRS., 30 MIN.

2 pounds ground chuck
1 large onion, chopped
3 (16-ounce) cans pork and beans
1 (12-ounce) jar chili sauce
1 (8-ounce) can crushed pineapple, drained
1/2 to 1 cup firmly packed light brown sugar
1 tablespoon dry mustard
1 tablespoon Worcestershire sauce

1. Brown meat and onion in a large skillet for about 8 minutes, stirring until meat crumbles and onion is tender; drain.
2. Combine meat mixture, pork and beans, and remaining ingredients in a 4-quart electric slow cooker, stirring well. Cover and cook on HIGH setting 3 1/2 hours.

Homestyle Baked Beans

This quick-and-easy dish makes the perfect side for a cookout.

MAKES 6 TO 8 SERVINGS
PREP: 10 MIN., BAKE: 46 MIN.

2 (28-ounce) cans baked beans with tangy sauce, bacon, and brown sugar
1 sweet onion, quartered
1 cup ketchup
1/2 to 3/4 cup prepared mustard
2 tablespoons light brown sugar
4 bacon slices

1. Stir together first 5 ingredients; pour into a lightly greased 11- x 7-inch baking dish. Top with bacon.
2. Bake, uncovered, at 400° for 45 minutes. Broil 5 inches from heat 1 minute or until bacon is browned.
Note: For testing purposes only, we used Bush's Original Baked Beans.

Root Beer Baked Beans

Root Beer Baked Beans

MAKES 4 SERVINGS
PREP: 5 MIN., COOK: 12 MIN., BAKE: 55 MIN.

3 bacon slices
1 small onion, diced
2 (16-ounce) cans pork and beans
½ cup root beer (not diet)
¼ cup hickory-smoked barbecue sauce
½ teaspoon dry mustard
⅛ teaspoon hot sauce

1. Cook bacon in a skillet over medium heat until crisp; remove and drain on paper towels, reserving drippings in skillet. Crumble bacon.

2. Sauté diced onion in hot bacon drippings in skillet over medium-high heat 5 minutes or until tender. Stir together onion, crumbled bacon, beans, and remaining ingredients in a lightly greased 2-quart baking dish.

3. Bake beans, uncovered, at 400° for 55 minutes or until sauce thickens.

John's Famous Beans

What makes these beans famous is perhaps the memorable blend of garlic, cilantro, cumin, and chili powder that simmers long and slow with the beans.

MAKES 7 SERVINGS
PREP: 10 MIN.; COOK: 3 HRS., 15 MIN.; OTHER: 8 HRS.

1 pound dried pinto beans
10 cups water
2 teaspoons vegetable oil
1 medium onion, diced
4 garlic cloves, crushed
1 (16-ounce) can stewed tomatoes, undrained and
    chopped
¼ cup Worcestershire sauce
2 tablespoons mild picante sauce
1 teaspoon chopped fresh cilantro
1 teaspoon salt
1 teaspoon ground cumin
¼ teaspoon chili powder
1 cup (4 ounces) shredded sharp Cheddar cheese

1. Sort and wash beans; place in a large Dutch oven. Cover with water 2 inches above beans; let soak at least 8 hours. Drain. Add 10 cups water and vegetable oil to beans; bring to a boil. Reduce heat, and simmer, uncovered, 1½ hours.
2. Add onion and next 8 ingredients; bring to a boil. Reduce heat, and simmer, uncovered, 1½ hours.
3. To serve, ladle beans into individual serving bowls. Top evenly with cheese.

Southwestern Black Bean-and-Rice Cakes

MAKES 5 SERVINGS (10 CAKES)
PREP: 10 MIN., COOK: 12 MIN.

2 cups cooked rice
1 (15-ounce) can black beans, rinsed and drained
1 cup all-purpose baking mix
1 (4.5-ounce) can chopped green chiles
3 green onions, sliced
1 tablespoon taco seasoning mix
1 large egg, lightly beaten
Toppings: salsa, sour cream, shredded Cheddar
    cheese, diced tomato, shredded lettuce

1. Stir together first 6 ingredients. Add egg to rice mixture, stirring just until moistened.
2. Drop mixture by ⅓ cupfuls, in 2 batches, into a hot nonstick skillet coated with cooking spray, and cook over medium heat 3 minutes on each side or until golden. (Coat skillet with cooking spray again before cooking second batch.) Serve with desired toppings.
Note: If you don't have leftover rice on hand, cook ½ (7-ounce) package quick-cooking rice according to package directions to yield about 2 cups cooked rice.

Black-eyed Pea Cakes

Canned black-eyed peas and packaged hush puppy mix make this recipe a snap to prepare.

MAKES 8 TO 10 SERVINGS (30 CAKES)
PREP: 20 MIN., CHILL: 1 HR., COOK: 30 MIN.

1 small onion, chopped
1 tablespoon olive oil
2 (15.5-ounce) cans black-eyed peas, rinsed, drained,
    and divided
1 (8-ounce) container chive-and-onion cream cheese,
    softened
1 large egg
½ teaspoon salt
1 teaspoon hot sauce
1 (8-ounce) package hush puppy mix with onion
Olive oil
Toppings: sour cream, green tomato relish

1. Sauté onion in 1 tablespoon hot oil in a large skillet over medium-high heat until tender.
2. Process onion, 1 can of peas, and next 4 ingredients in a blender or food processor until mixture is smooth, stopping to scrape down sides. Stir in hush puppy mix, and gently fold in remaining can of peas.
3. Shape mixture by 2 tablespoonfuls into 3-inch patties, and place on a wax paper-lined baking sheet. Cover and chill 1 hour.
4. Cook patties, in batches, in 3 tablespoons hot oil, adding oil as needed, in a large skillet over medium heat for 1½ minutes on each side or until patties are golden brown. Drain patties on paper towels, and keep them warm. Serve with desired toppings.

Lima Beans

Lima Beans

Crisp bits of bacon and melted Monterey Jack liven up these limas.

MAKES 6 SERVINGS
PREP: 8 MIN., COOK: 25 MIN., BAKE: 25 MIN.

1 1/2 cups water
1/2 teaspoon salt
2 (10-ounce) packages frozen lima beans
8 bacon slices, diced
1 cup chopped onion
1/2 cup chopped celery
1 1/2 cups (6 ounces) shredded Monterey Jack cheese
1/4 teaspoon pepper
Dash of Worcestershire sauce

1. Combine water and salt in a large saucepan; bring to a boil. Add lima beans; cover, reduce heat, and simmer 8 to 10 minutes or until tender. Drain beans, reserving 1/2 cup liquid; set aside.

2. Cook bacon in a large skillet until crisp; remove bacon, reserving 3 tablespoons drippings in skillet. Set bacon aside.

3. Sauté onion and celery in drippings in skillet until tender.

4. Combine reserved lima beans, reserved liquid, onion mixture, cheese, pepper, and Worcestershire sauce. Spoon into a lightly greased 2-quart baking dish. Sprinkle with bacon. Bake, uncovered, at 350° for 25 minutes or until heated.

Caramelized Onion-and-Pecan Brussels Sprouts

These Brussels sprouts are sliced into thin shreds so they cook quickly once the onions are caramelized.

MAKES 8 SERVINGS
PREP: 15 MIN., COOK: 25 MIN.

1 large onion
1 pound Brussels sprouts
1/4 cup butter or margarine
1 cup pecan pieces
1 teaspoon salt
1/2 teaspoon pepper

1. Cut onion in half, and thinly slice. Cut Brussels sprouts in half, and cut each half crosswise into thin slices.
2. Melt butter in a large heavy skillet over medium-high heat; add pecan pieces, and sauté 5 minutes or until pecans are toasted. Remove pecans from skillet with a slotted spoon. Add onion slices, and cook, stirring often, 15 minutes or until caramel colored. Add pecans and Brussels sprouts, and cook about 3 minutes or until heated. Sprinkle with salt and pepper.

Broccoli With Garlic Butter and Cashews

Soy sauce and fresh garlic add an Asian flair to this highly rated recipe.

MAKES 6 SERVINGS
PREP: 15 MIN., COOK: 7 MIN.

1 1/2 pounds fresh broccoli (about 1 bunch)
1/3 cup butter or margarine
1 tablespoon brown sugar
3 tablespoons soy sauce
2 teaspoons white vinegar
1/4 teaspoon pepper
2 garlic cloves, minced
1/3 cup salted roasted cashews

1. Remove and discard broccoli leaves and tough ends of stalks; cut broccoli into spears. Arrange broccoli in a steamer basket over boiling water. Cover and steam 5 to 6 minutes or until crisp-tender. Arrange broccoli on a serving platter. Set aside, and keep warm.
2. Place butter in a 1-cup glass measuring cup. Microwave at HIGH 15 seconds or until butter melts. Stir in brown sugar and next 4 ingredients. Microwave at HIGH 45 seconds or until mixture comes to a boil. Stir in cashews. Pour garlic sauce over broccoli, and serve immediately.

Roasted Broccoli With
Buttered Walnuts

Roasted Broccoli With Buttered Walnuts

MAKES 6 TO 8 SERVINGS
PREP: 10 MIN., COOK: 5 MIN., BAKE: 14 MIN.

3 pounds fresh broccoli (about 2 bunches)
$\frac{1}{3}$ cup olive oil
1 teaspoon salt
$\frac{1}{2}$ teaspoon pepper
1 cup walnut halves
3 tablespoons butter, melted
1 lemon, halved

1. Cut broccoli into 3-inch lengths; cut thick pieces in half lengthwise. Place in a roasting pan, and drizzle with olive oil; toss to coat well. Sprinkle with salt and pepper. Roast at 500° for 14 minutes, stirring once after 8 minutes.
2. Meanwhile, toast walnuts in melted butter in a skillet over medium-high heat 5 minutes or until fragrant.
3. Spoon broccoli into a serving bowl. Squeeze cut lemon over broccoli, tossing well. Stir in walnuts and butter.

Stir-fried Broccoli

MAKES 6 SERVINGS
PREP: 10 MIN., COOK: 7 MIN.

2 slices peeled fresh ginger
3 tablespoons vegetable oil
1 (16-ounce) package fresh broccoli florets
$\frac{1}{2}$ teaspoon salt
$\frac{1}{4}$ teaspoon sugar
$\frac{1}{2}$ cup water
$\frac{1}{2}$ teaspoon chicken bouillon granules
1 tablespoon sesame oil
1 tablespoon sesame seeds, toasted

1. Sauté ginger in hot oil in a large skillet over medium-high heat 1 minute. Add broccoli florets; stir-fry 2 minutes. Sprinkle with salt and sugar.
2. Stir together $\frac{1}{2}$ cup water and $\frac{1}{2}$ teaspoon bouillon granules until dissolved. Pour over broccoli mixture. Cover, reduce heat to medium, and cook 2 to 3 minutes. Drizzle with sesame oil; sprinkle with sesame seeds.

Sweet-and-Sour Red Cabbage and Apples

The flavors of this dish make a memorable combination, especially when served bubbly and hot. It pairs well with pork.

MAKES 6 SERVINGS
PREP: 20 MIN., COOK: 40 MIN.

2 tablespoons butter or margarine
2 tablespoons olive oil
1 large red cabbage, thinly sliced
3 Granny Smith apples, cut into $\frac{1}{2}$-inch wedges
1 cup sugar
1 cup red wine vinegar
$\frac{1}{4}$ teaspoon salt
$\frac{1}{4}$ teaspoon pepper

1. Melt butter with oil in a large skillet over medium-high heat; add cabbage, and sauté 10 minutes. Stir in apple, and set aside.
2. Melt sugar in a large heavy saucepan over medium heat, stirring constantly; stir in vinegar (mixture will bubble, and sugar will clump), and bring to a boil. Cook, stirring often, until sugar dissolves and mixture is caramel colored. Stir in cabbage mixture; cook over medium heat, stirring occasionally, 20 minutes. Stir in salt and pepper.

Scalloped Cabbage

MAKES 6 TO 8 SERVINGS
PREP: 10 MIN., BAKE: 1 HR.

2 cups crushed cornflakes cereal
1/4 cup butter or margarine, melted
1 (10-ounce) package shredded angel hair cabbage
1 large sweet onion, halved and thinly sliced
1/2 cup milk
1/2 cup mayonnaise
1 (10 1/2-ounce) can cream of celery soup, undiluted
1 cup (4 ounces) shredded sharp Cheddar cheese

1. Stir together cereal and butter; spoon half of cereal mixture into a lightly greased 11- x 7-inch baking dish. Top with cabbage and onion.
2. Stir together milk, mayonnaise, and soup; pour over cabbage. Sprinkle with cheese and remaining cereal mixture.
3. Bake cabbage, covered, at 350° for 1 hour.
To Lighten: Use light butter, fat-free milk, reduced-fat mayonnaise, reduced-fat soup, and 2% reduced-fat cheese.

Carrot-Sweet Potato Puree

MAKES 4 SERVINGS
PREP: 20 MIN., COOK: 17 MIN.

5 carrots, sliced
3/4 cup water
1/4 cup butter or margarine
1 (29-ounce) can sweet potatoes, drained
1 (16-ounce) can sweet potatoes, drained
1 (8-ounce) container sour cream
1 tablespoon sugar
1 teaspoon grated lemon rind
1/2 teaspoon ground nutmeg
1/4 teaspoon salt
1/4 teaspoon ground black pepper
1/8 teaspoon ground red pepper

1. Microwave carrots and 3/4 cup water in a glass bowl at HIGH 10 to 12 minutes or until tender. Drain.
2. Process carrots and butter in a food processor until mixture is smooth, stopping to scrape down sides. Transfer to a large bowl.
3. Process sweet potatoes until smooth, stopping to scrape down sides. Add to carrot mixture.

4. Stir together sweet potato mixture, sour cream, and remaining ingredients. Spoon into a 1 1/2-quart glass dish. (Cover and chill up to 2 days, if desired; let stand at room temperature 30 minutes.) Microwave at HIGH 4 to 5 minutes or until thoroughly heated.

Carrot-Pecan Casserole

This dish is a nice alternative to sweet potatoes. If you have a food processor, you can mash the cooked carrots in a snap.

MAKES 6 TO 8 SERVINGS
PREP: 15 MIN., COOK: 25 MIN., BAKE: 40 MIN.

3 pounds baby carrots, sliced
2/3 cup sugar
1/2 cup butter or margarine, softened
1/2 cup chopped pecans, toasted
1/4 cup milk
2 large eggs, lightly beaten
3 tablespoons all-purpose flour
1 tablespoon grated orange rind
1 teaspoon vanilla extract
1/4 teaspoon ground nutmeg

1. Cook sliced carrots in boiling water to cover in a saucepan 20 to 25 minutes or until tender; drain and let cool slightly. Mash carrots in a bowl until smooth.
2. Stir together mashed carrots, sugar, and remaining ingredients until blended. Spoon mixture into a lightly greased 11- x 7-inch baking dish.
3. Bake, uncovered, at 350° for 40 minutes.
To Make Ahead: Cover uncooked carrot mixture, and refrigerate overnight. Let stand at room temperature 20 minutes before baking; bake as directed.

Pepper Jelly-Glazed Carrots

Pepper Jelly-Glazed Carrots

MAKES 6 SERVINGS
PREP: 5 MIN., COOK: 14 MIN.

1 (2-pound) package baby carrots
1 (10½-ounce) can condensed chicken broth,
    undiluted
2 tablespoons butter or margarine
1 (10½-ounce) jar red pepper jelly

1. Combine carrots and chicken broth in a skillet over medium-high heat. Bring to a boil, and cook, stirring often, 6 to 8 minutes or until carrots are crisp-tender and broth is reduced to ¼ cup.
2. Stir in butter and red pepper jelly, and cook, stirring constantly, 5 minutes or until mixture is thickened and glazes carrots.

Creamy Fried
Confetti Corn

Creamy Fried Confetti Corn

MAKES 6 TO 8 SERVINGS
PREP: 15 MIN., COOK: 22 MIN.

8 bacon slices, chopped
4 cups fresh sweet corn kernels (about 8 ears)
1 medium-size white onion, chopped
1/3 cup chopped red bell pepper
1/3 cup chopped green bell pepper
1 (8-ounce) package cream cheese, cubed
1/2 cup half-and-half
1 teaspoon sugar
1 teaspoon salt
1 teaspoon pepper

1. Cook chopped bacon in a large skillet until crisp; remove bacon, and drain on paper towels, reserving 2 tablespoons drippings in skillet. Set bacon aside.
2. Sauté corn, onion, and bell peppers in hot drippings in skillet over medium-high heat 6 minutes or until tender. Add cream cheese and half-and-half, stirring until cream cheese melts. Stir in sugar, salt, and pepper. Top with reserved bacon.

Grilled Corn, Squash, and Poblanos

MAKES 6 TO 8 SERVINGS
PREP: 25 MIN., GRILL: 25 MIN.

4 medium-size yellow squash
1/2 medium-size sweet onion
4 ears fresh corn
3 poblano chile peppers
1 garlic clove, pressed
2 tablespoons chopped fresh basil
1 tablespoon chopped fresh
    oregano
1/2 teaspoon salt
1/2 teaspoon ground cumin

1. Cut squash in half lengthwise, and cut onion into 1/4-inch-thick slices. Coat corn, squash, and onion with cooking spray, and set aside.
2. Grill chile peppers, covered with grill lid, over medium-high heat (350° to 400°) 5 minutes on each side. Set aside.
3. Grill corn and onion, covered with grill lid, over medium-high heat 4 minutes on each side. Set aside.

4. Grill squash, cut sides down, covered with grill lid, over medium-high heat 5 minutes; turn and grill 2 more minutes.
5. Cut corn kernels from cobs. Chop squash, onion, and chile peppers, discarding chile pepper stems and seeds; place corn kernels and vegetables in a large bowl. Toss vegetable mixture with garlic, basil, and remaining ingredients.

Baked Jack Corn

Green chiles add a flavorful kick to this rich, cheesy, quiche-like side.

MAKES 6 SERVINGS
PREP: 20 MIN., BAKE: 40 MIN., STAND: 10 MIN.

2 large eggs
1 1/2 cups sour cream
2 cups fresh corn kernels
1 (8-ounce) package Monterey Jack cheese, cut into
    1/2-inch cubes
1/2 cup soft breadcrumbs
1 (4.5-ounce) can chopped green chiles, drained
1/2 teaspoon salt
1/4 teaspoon pepper
1/2 cup (2 ounces) shredded Cheddar cheese

1. Combine eggs and sour cream in a large bowl; stir in corn and next 5 ingredients. Pour into a greased 10-inch quiche dish or 2-quart baking dish.
2. Bake at 350° for 35 minutes or until a knife inserted in center comes out clean. Sprinkle with shredded Cheddar cheese, and bake 5 more minutes. Let stand 10 minutes before serving.

Grilled Corn With
Jalapeño-Lime Butter

Grilled Corn With Jalapeño-Lime Butter

Minced jalapeño mixed into butter adds a tinge of kick to this corn. Use any leftover butter for steamed vegetables within 5 days.

MAKES 6 SERVINGS
PREP: 7 MIN., GRILL: 20 MIN.

½ cup butter, softenened
2 jalapeño peppers, seeded and minced
2 tablespoons grated lime rind
1 teaspoon fresh lime juice
6 ears fresh corn
1 tablespoon olive oil
2 teaspoons kosher salt
1 teaspoon freshly ground black pepper

1. Combine first 4 ingredients, and shape into a 6-inch log; wrap in wax paper, and chill while grilling corn.
2. Rub corn with olive oil; sprinkle evenly with salt and black pepper.
3. Grill corn, covered with grill lid, over high heat (400° to 500°), turning often, 15 to 20 minutes or until tender. Serve with flavored butter.

Creamy Sweet Slaw

MAKES 8 SERVINGS
PREP: 20 MIN.

½ cup sugar
¼ cup white vinegar
¾ cup mayonnaise
⅓ cup evaporated milk
1 teaspoon salt
½ teaspoon black pepper
1 large cabbage, shredded*
4 celery ribs, chopped
1 small green bell pepper, finely chopped
1 (2-ounce) jar diced pimiento, drained

1. Stir together first 6 ingredients in a large bowl; add cabbage and remaining ingredients, tossing to coat.
*2 (10-ounce) bags angel hair cabbage may be substituted for shredded cabbage.

Creamy Dill Slaw

Dill adds just the right flavor to make this quick-and-easy coleslaw a standout favorite.

MAKES 8 SERVINGS
PREP: 10 MIN., CHILL: 8 HRS.

4 green onions, sliced
1 (8-ounce) container sour cream
1 cup mayonnaise
2 tablespoons sugar
2 tablespoons chopped fresh dill
2 tablespoons white vinegar
1 teaspoon salt
½ teaspoon pepper
1 (16-ounce) package coleslaw mix
1 (10-ounce) package finely shredded cabbage
Garnish: chopped fresh dill

1. Stir together first 8 ingredients in a large bowl until mixture is blended; stir in coleslaw mix and cabbage. Cover and chill 8 hours. Garnish, if desired.
To Lighten: Substitute 1 (8-ounce) container light sour cream and 1 cup light mayonnaise.

Best Barbecue Coleslaw

MAKES 8 TO 10 SERVINGS
PREP: 10 MIN., CHILL: 2 HRS.

½ cup sugar
½ cup mayonnaise
¼ cup milk
¼ cup buttermilk
2½ tablespoons lemon juice
1½ tablespoons white vinegar
½ teaspoon salt
⅛ teaspoon pepper
2 (10-ounce) packages finely shredded cabbage
1 carrot, shredded

1. Whisk together first 8 ingredients in a large bowl; add cabbage and carrot, tossing to coat. Cover and chill at least 2 hours.

Mushroom Matzo Kugel

Double this stuffinglike recipe, and freeze half before baking, if desired.

MAKES 6 SERVINGS
PREP: 20 MIN., BAKE: 30 MIN.

1 small onion, diced
3 celery ribs, diced
1 (8-ounce) package sliced fresh mushrooms
⅓ cup canola oil
3½ cups matzo farfel
2 large eggs, lightly beaten
1 (10½-ounce) can condensed chicken broth, undiluted
1¼ cups hot water
1 teaspoon salt
¼ teaspoon pepper

1. Sauté first 3 ingredients in hot oil in a large skillet until tender; remove from heat.
2. Stir in matzo farfel and remaining ingredients. Spoon into a lightly greased 1½-quart baking dish.
3. Bake at 375° for 30 minutes.

Grilled Portobello Mushrooms and Asparagus

MAKES 6 SERVINGS
PREP: 5 MIN., GRILL: 14 MIN.

4 portobello mushroom caps
2 tablespoons Rosemary Oil
1 pound fresh asparagus

1. Remove brown gills from undersides of mushroom caps using a spoon; discard gills. Brush caps with 1 tablespoon Rosemary Oil. Snap off tough ends of asparagus; brush with remaining 1 tablespoon Rosemary Oil.
2. Grill mushrooms, covered with grill lid, over high heat (400° to 500°) 5 minutes on each side. Cut mushrooms into strips. Grill asparagus, covered with grill lid, over high heat 2 minutes on each side. Serve together.

Rosemary Oil:

MAKES ⅓ CUP
PREP: 5 MIN., COOK: 3 MIN.

2 fresh rosemary sprigs
1 teaspoon pepper
⅓ cup olive oil

1. Add rosemary and pepper to hot oil in a skillet over high heat; cook, stirring occasionally, 3 minutes. Remove from heat; cool. Discard rosemary.
Note: Store remaining Rosemary Oil in an airtight container in the refrigerator up to 1 week. Or use the remaining oil to make a great vinaigrette (see below).

Rosemary Vinaigrette: Whisk together ¼ cup balsamic vinegar; 3 tablespoons Rosemary Oil; 1 garlic clove, pressed; 1 teaspoon chopped fresh rosemary; and ½ teaspoon salt.

Caramelized Sweet Onions

Serve these glistening onions alone as a side dish, stirred into the pudding and tart recipes that follow, on the Caramelized Onion BLT on page 215, or on the Chicken Cobbler With Caramelized Sweet Onions on page 161.

MAKES 2½ CUPS
PREP: 10 MIN., COOK: 40 MIN.

4 pounds sweet onions (about 6 medium)
2 tablespoons olive oil
½ teaspoon salt

1. Cut onions into ¼- to ½-inch-thick slices, and place in hot olive oil in a large deep skillet over medium heat.
2. Cook onion slices, stirring often. (After about 20 minutes, onions will begin turning from white to golden.)
3. Continue cooking onion slices, stirring often, for 15 to 20 more minutes or until onion slices are caramel colored (a deep golden brown). Remove from heat, stir in salt, and let cool completely.

Sweet Onion Pudding

MAKES 8 TO 10 SERVINGS
PREP: 10 MIN., BAKE: 30 MIN.

2 cups whipping cream
1 cup shredded Parmesan cheese
6 large eggs, lightly beaten
3 tablespoons all-purpose flour
2 tablespoons sugar
2 teaspoons baking powder
½ teaspoon salt
¼ teaspoon pepper
Caramelized Sweet Onions (recipe above)

1. Stir together first 3 ingredients in a large bowl.
2. Combine flour, sugar, and next 3 ingredients; gradually stir into egg mixture.
3. Stir Caramelized Sweet Onions into egg mixture; pour into a lightly greased 13- x 9-inch baking dish.
4. Bake at 350° for 30 minutes or until pudding is set.

Caramelized Onion Tart

Caramelized Onion Tart

Don't have a tart pan? We also baked this on a baking sheet with fantastic results. See instructions below.

MAKES 6 SERVINGS
PREP: 15 MIN., BAKE: 30 MIN.

Caramelized Sweet Onions (see recipe on opposite
page)
1 tablespoon Dijon mustard
1½ teaspoons chopped fresh rosemary
¼ teaspoon pepper
½ (17.3-ounce) package frozen puff pastry sheets,
thawed
½ cup shredded Parmesan cheese
Garnish: fresh rosemary sprigs

1. Stir together first 4 ingredients; set mixture aside.
2. Unfold pastry sheet; roll into a 10-inch square. Fit pastry sheet into a 9-inch square metal tart pan, gently pressing onto bottom and up sides.
3. Bake, on bottom oven rack, at 400° for 20 to 25 minutes or until browned. Remove from oven. Press pastry with back of a spoon to flatten. Spoon onion mixture onto pastry; sprinkle with Parmesan. Bake 5 more minutes. Garnish, if desired, and serve immediately.
Note: If you don't have a tart pan, unfold pastry sheet onto a lightly greased baking sheet. Bake, on bottom rack, at 400° for 16 to 18 minutes or until puffed and golden. Using a serrated knife, cut a slit around top of pastry, leaving a ½-inch border on all sides. (Do not cut through or to bottom.) Press cut square center to flatten. Spoon onion mixture onto pastry; sprinkle with Parmesan cheese, and bake 5 more minutes.

Slow Cooker Caramelized Onions

Use a slotted spoon for serving, if you'd like, and save the broth to make soup.

MAKES 2 CUPS
PREP: 5 MIN., COOK: 8 HRS.

2 extra-large sweet onions (about 3 pounds)
1 (10½-ounce) can condensed chicken or beef broth, undiluted
¼ cup butter or margarine

1. Cut onions in half; cut each half into ½-inch-thick slices.
2. Combine onions, broth, and butter in a 3½-quart slow cooker. Cook, covered, at HIGH 8 hours or until golden brown and very soft.
3. Store onions in an airtight container; refrigerate up to 1 week, or freeze up to 2 months, if desired.

Fried Okra

If bacon drippings aren't in your favorite fried okra recipe, try adding them like we did in this recipe. Bacon drippings make a great recipe even better.

MAKES 4 SERVINGS
PREP: 12 MIN., CHILL: 45 MIN., COOK: 4 MIN. PER BATCH

1 pound fresh okra
2 cups buttermilk
1 cup self-rising cornmeal
1 cup self-rising flour
1 teaspoon salt
¼ teaspoon ground red pepper
Vegetable oil
¼ cup bacon drippings

1. Cut off and discard tip and stem ends from okra; cut okra into ½-inch-thick slices. Stir into buttermilk; cover and chill 45 minutes.
2. Combine cornmeal and next 3 ingredients in a bowl.
3. Remove okra from buttermilk with a slotted spoon, and discard buttermilk. Dredge okra, in batches, in cornmeal mixture.
4. Pour oil to a depth of 2 inches into a Dutch oven or cast-iron skillet; add bacon drippings, and heat to 375°. Fry okra, in batches, 4 minutes or until golden; drain on paper towels.

Fried Okra Pods: Trim stem ends but do not trim tips or slice okra. Proceed as directed.

Fried Okra

Spicy Okra-Tomato-Corn Sauté

MAKES 6 SERVINGS
PREP: 5 MIN., COOK: 15 MIN.

½ small onion, chopped
½ tablespoon vegetable oil
1 (16-ounce) package frozen whole okra, thawed
1 cup frozen corn, thawed
1 (10-ounce) can diced tomatoes and green chiles
1 teaspoon sugar
¾ teaspoon salt
¼ teaspoon pepper

1. Sauté chopped onion in hot oil in a large nonstick skillet over medium-high heat 5 minutes or until tender. Add okra; cook, stirring occasionally, 5 minutes.
2. Stir in corn, tomatoes, and remaining ingredients, and cook 5 minutes or until thoroughly heated. Serve immediately.

Spicy Okra-Tomato-Corn Sauté

Okra Creole

Okra Creole

MAKES 4 SERVINGS
PREP: 15 MIN., COOK: 25 MIN.

3 bacon slices
1 (16-ounce) package frozen sliced okra
1 (14.5-ounce) can chopped tomatoes
1 cup frozen onion seasoning blend
1 cup frozen corn kernels
½ cup water
1 teaspoon Creole seasoning
¼ teaspoon pepper
Hot cooked rice (optional)

1. Cook bacon in a Dutch oven until crisp; remove bacon, and drain on paper towels, reserving drippings. Crumble bacon, and set aside.

2. Cook okra and next 6 ingredients in hot drippings in Dutch oven over medium-high heat, stirring occasionally, 5 minutes.

3. Reduce heat to low, cover, and simmer 15 minutes or until vegetables are tender. Top with crumbled bacon. Serve over rice, if desired.

Two-Cheese Squash
Casserole

Two-Cheese Squash Casserole

MAKES 8 TO 10 SERVINGS
PREP: 30 MIN., COOK: 20 MIN., BAKE: 40 MIN.

4 pounds yellow squash, sliced
4 tablespoons butter or margarine, divided
1 large sweet onion, finely chopped
2 garlic cloves, minced
2½ cups soft breadcrumbs, divided
1¼ cups shredded Parmesan cheese, divided
1 cup (4 ounces) shredded Cheddar cheese
½ cup chopped fresh chives
½ cup minced fresh parsley
1 (8-ounce) container sour cream
1 teaspoon salt
1 teaspoon freshly ground pepper
2 large eggs, lightly beaten
¼ teaspoon garlic salt

1. Cook squash in boiling water to cover in a large skillet 8 to 10 minutes or just until tender. Drain well; gently press between paper towels.
2. Melt 2 tablespoons butter in skillet over medium-high heat; add onion and garlic, and sauté 5 to 6 minutes or until tender. Remove skillet from heat; stir in squash, 1 cup breadcrumbs, ¾ cup Parmesan cheese, and next 7 ingredients. Spoon mixture into a lightly greased 13- x 9-inch baking dish.
3. Melt remaining 2 tablespoons butter. Stir together melted butter, remaining 1½ cups soft breadcrumbs, ½ cup Parmesan cheese, and garlic salt. Sprinkle mixture evenly over top of casserole.
4. Bake at 350° for 35 to 40 minutes or until set.

Sautéed Zucchini and Yellow Squash

This fresh and simple side dish goes well with just about any entrée.

MAKES 6 SERVINGS
PREP: 10 MIN., COOK: 6 MIN.

3 small zucchini, sliced
3 yellow squash, sliced
2 tablespoons olive oil
1 garlic clove, minced
1/2 teaspoon salt
1/2 teaspoon freshly ground pepper

1. Sauté zucchini and squash in hot olive oil in a skillet over medium-high heat 5 minutes or until crisp-tender.
2. Stir in garlic and remaining ingredients; cook, stirring constantly, 1 minute. Serve immediately.

Southern Summer Squash

MAKES 6 SERVINGS
PREP: 10 MIN., COOK: 15 MIN.

1/4 cup water
2 tablespoons butter or margarine
1 sweet onion, thinly sliced
1 pound small yellow squash, thinly sliced
1 pound small zucchini, thinly sliced
3 medium tomatoes, peeled, seeded, and chopped*
1 tablespoon chopped fresh basil
1/2 teaspoon salt
1/4 teaspoon pepper
1 cup (4 ounces) shredded Cheddar cheese

1. Bring 1/4 cup water and butter to a boil in a large skillet over medium-high heat.
2. Add onion, squash, and zucchini; return to a boil. Cover, reduce heat, and simmer 5 minutes. Stir in tomato and next 3 ingredients; cover and simmer 5 minutes or until thoroughly heated. Sprinkle with cheese, and serve immediately.
* 1 (14.5-ounce) can diced tomatoes, drained, may be substituted.

Roasted Zucchini

If you don't have sesame oil, olive oil will work just fine.

MAKES 12 SERVINGS
PREP: 10 MIN., BAKE: 30 MIN., COOK: 4 MIN.

4 pounds zucchini, sliced
1/4 cup sesame oil, divided
1 (12-ounce) jar roasted red bell peppers, drained and coarsely chopped
1/2 cup coarsely chopped walnuts
1/2 teaspoon ground ginger or 1 teaspoon minced fresh ginger
2 garlic cloves, minced
1/4 teaspoon dried crushed red pepper
1/4 cup chicken broth
1/4 cup soy sauce
1/2 to 1 teaspoon sugar

1. Arrange zucchini in an aluminum foil-lined jelly-roll pan; drizzle with 2 tablespoons sesame oil.
2. Bake at 475° for 30 minutes, turning once.
3. Sauté bell pepper and next 4 ingredients in remaining 2 tablespoons hot sesame oil in a large skillet over medium-high heat 2 minutes. Reduce heat to medium. Stir in chicken broth, soy sauce, and sugar; cook until thoroughly heated. Serve over zucchini.

Squash Puppies

Squash Puppies

This fun side can double as an appetizer.

MAKES 20 SQUASH PUPPIES
PREP: 10 MIN., FRY: 6 MIN. PER BATCH

¾ cup self-rising cornmeal
¼ cup all-purpose flour
½ teaspoon salt
¼ teaspoon black pepper
⅛ teaspoon ground red pepper
6 medium-size yellow squash, cooked and mashed
½ cup buttermilk
1 small onion, minced
1 large egg
Vegetable oil
½ teaspoon salt

1. Combine first 5 ingredients in a large bowl.
2. Stir together squash and next 3 ingredients; add to cornmeal mixture, stirring until blended.
3. Pour oil to a depth of ½ inch into a deep cast-iron skillet; heat to 350°. Drop batter by tablespoonfuls, in batches, into oil; fry 3 minutes on each side or until golden brown. Drain on paper towels; sprinkle evenly with ½ teaspoon salt.

Broiled Yellow Tomatoes

If you don't want to broil the tomatoes, just slice and season as directed.

MAKES 24 SERVINGS
PREP: 15 MIN., BROIL: 5 MIN.

12 large yellow or red tomatoes, cut in half
¼ cup olive oil
Salt and seasoned pepper to taste
½ cup chopped fresh chives
24 small fresh dill sprigs

1. Brush cut sides of tomatoes with olive oil, and sprinkle with a pinch of salt and seasoned pepper.
2. Broil 6 inches from heat 5 minutes or until thoroughly heated. Sprinkle evenly with chives; top each with a fresh dill sprig.

Grilled Summer Squash and Tomatoes

MAKES 6 SERVINGS
PREP: 5 MIN., CHILL: 30 MIN., GRILL: 10 MIN.

¼ cup olive oil
2 tablespoons balsamic vinegar
1 teaspoon salt
½ teaspoon pepper
4 garlic cloves, minced
4 medium-size green tomatoes, cut into ¼-inch-thick slices
1 pound yellow squash, cut diagonally into ½-inch-thick slices

1. Combine first 5 ingredients in a shallow dish or freezer bag; add tomatoes and squash. Cover or seal; chill 30 minutes.
2. Remove vegetables from marinade, reserving marinade.
3. Grill vegetables, covered with grill lid, over medium-high heat (350° to 400°) 10 minutes or until tender, turning occasionally. Toss with reserved marinade.

Fried Green Tomato Stacks

Fried Green Tomato Stacks

For bacon drippings, fry 3 or 4 bacon slices in a skillet until crisp; remove bacon from skillet.

MAKES 6 SERVINGS
PREP: 15 MIN., COOK: 10 MIN., FRY: 4 MIN. PER BATCH

3 fresh tomatillos, husks removed
2 tablespoons bacon drippings
1 garlic clove, pressed
1½ teaspoons salt, divided
1 teaspoon pepper, divided
½ teaspoon paprika
¼ cup thinly sliced fresh basil
1½ cups self-rising yellow cornmeal
4 large green tomatoes, cut into 18 (¼-inch) slices
1 cup buttermilk
Peanut oil
1 (8-ounce) package cream cheese, softened
1 (4-ounce) package goat cheese, softened
⅓ cup milk
1 teaspoon sugar
Garnishes: chopped fresh basil, fresh basil sprigs

1. Bring tomatillos and water to cover to a boil in a small saucepan; reduce heat, and simmer 10 minutes. Drain tomatillos, and cool.
2. Process tomatillos, drippings, garlic, ½ teaspoon salt, ½ teaspoon pepper, and paprika in a food processor or blender until smooth; stir in sliced basil. Cover mixture, and chill.
3. Stir together cornmeal, ¾ teaspoon salt, and remaining ½ teaspoon pepper. Dip tomato slices in buttermilk; dredge in cornmeal mixture.
4. Pour oil to a depth of ½ inch into a skillet; heat to 375°. Fry tomato slices, in batches, in hot oil 1 to 2 minutes on each side; drain on a wire rack over paper towels. Keep warm.
5. Combine cream cheese, next 3 ingredients, and remaining ¼ teaspoon salt. Place 1 fried tomato slice on each of 6 salad plates; top each evenly with half of cream cheese mixture. Top each with 1 fried tomato slice and remaining cream cheese mixture. Top with remaining 6 fried tomato slices; drizzle with tomatillo mixture. Garnish, if desired.

Cheesy Tomato Pie

Round out the meal with fresh sliced melon, a bowlful of berries, and tangy lemonade.

MAKES 8 SERVINGS
PREP: 20 MIN., BAKE: 1 HR., STAND: 5 MIN.

½ (15-ounce) package refrigerated piecrusts
1 small red bell pepper, chopped
½ red onion, chopped
2 garlic cloves, minced
2 tablespoons olive oil
2 tablespoons chopped fresh basil
4 large eggs
1 cup half-and-half
1 teaspoon salt
½ teaspoon black pepper
2 cups (8 ounces) shredded Monterey Jack cheese
⅓ cup shredded Parmesan cheese
3 plum tomatoes, cut into ¼-inch-thick slices

1. Fit piecrust into a 9-inch deep-dish tart pan; prick bottom and sides of piecrust with a fork.
2. Bake at 425° for 10 minutes. Remove from oven; set aside.
3. Sauté bell pepper, onion, and garlic in hot oil in a large skillet 5 minutes or until tender; stir in basil.
4. Whisk together eggs and next 3 ingredients in a large bowl; stir in sautéed vegetables and cheeses. Pour into crust; top with tomato slices.
5. Bake at 375° for 45 to 50 minutes or until set, shielding edges with strips of aluminum foil after 30 minutes to prevent excessive browning. Let stand 5 minutes before serving.

Honey-Baked Tomatoes

MAKES 8 SERVINGS
PREP: 10 MIN., BAKE: 30 MIN., BROIL: 5 MIN.

8 medium-size ripe tomatoes, cut into 1-inch slices
4 teaspoons honey
2 white bread slices
1 tablespoon dried tarragon
1½ teaspoons salt
2 teaspoons freshly ground pepper
4 teaspoons butter

1. Place ripe tomato slices in a single layer in a lightly greased aluminum foil-lined 15- x 10-inch jelly-roll pan. Drizzle with honey, spreading honey into hollows.
2. Process bread in a food processor or blender until finely chopped.
3. Stir together breadcrumbs, tarragon, salt, and pepper; sprinkle evenly over tomato slices. Dot with butter.
4. Bake at 350° for 30 minutes or until tomato skins begin to wrinkle.
5. Broil 5 inches from heat 5 minutes or until tops are golden. Serve warm.

Italian Vegetable
Medley

Italian Vegetable Medley

MAKES 6 SERVINGS
PREP: 25 MIN., STAND: 1 HR., GRILL: 19 MIN.

2 large eggplants
2 1/2 teaspoons salt, divided
2 small zucchini
2 yellow squash
1/2 cup olive oil
4 garlic cloves, minced (about 2 tablespoons)
1/4 cup chopped fresh basil
2 tablespoons chopped fresh mint
6 tablespoons balsamic vinegar
Garnish: fresh basil sprig

1. Cut eggplants crosswise into 1/2-inch-thick slices; sprinkle cut sides with 1 1/2 teaspoons salt. Place eggplant slices in a single layer on paper towels; let stand 1 hour.
2. Cut zucchini and squash lengthwise into 1/8- to 1/4-inch-thick slices; set slices aside.
3. Process 1/2 teaspoon salt, 1/2 cup olive oil, minced garlic, 1/4 cup chopped fresh basil, 2 tablespoons chopped mint, and 6 tablespoons balsamic vinegar in a food processor, stopping to scrape down sides.
4. Rinse eggplant slices with water, and pat dry. Lightly brush slices with olive oil mixture, and sprinkle with 1/4 teaspoon salt.
5. Coat cold grill grate with cooking spray; place on grill over medium-high heat (350° to 400°). Place eggplant on grate, and grill, covered with lid, 10 to 12 minutes or until lightly browned, turning occasionally and lightly brushing with olive oil mixture. Remove eggplant from grill.
6. Sprinkle zucchini and squash slices with remaining 1/4 teaspoon salt, and lightly brush with olive oil mixture. Place slices on lightly greased grill grate.
7. Grill zucchini and squash slices, covered with grill lid, over medium-high heat 5 minutes; turn, brush with olive oil mixture, and grill 2 more minutes.
8. Arrange grilled eggplant, zucchini, and squash on a serving platter. Drizzle with remaining olive oil mixture. Garnish, if desired.

Grilled Vegetables With Herbs

A grill wok or basket lets you cook these chunky vegetables on the grill without risk of the pieces falling through the grill grate.

MAKES 4 SERVINGS
PREP: 20 MIN., GRILL: 25 MIN.

1 tablespoon chopped fresh parsley
2 tablespoons olive oil
½ teaspoon salt
¼ teaspoon black pepper
8 new potatoes, quartered
3 medium-size yellow squash, cut into 1-inch pieces
1 large onion, cut into 8 pieces
1 large green bell pepper, cut into 8 pieces
2 tablespoons butter or margarine, softened
1 tablespoon chopped fresh oregano

1. Stir together first 4 ingredients. Toss 1 tablespoon olive oil mixture with potatoes. Toss remaining olive oil mixture with squash, onion, and bell pepper.
2. Place potatoes in a lightly greased grill wok or metal basket. Grill, covered with grill lid, over medium-high heat (350° to 400°) 10 minutes.
3. Add squash, onion, and bell pepper; grill, tossing occasionally, 15 more minutes or until potatoes are tender.
4. Stir together butter and oregano; add to vegetables, tossing to coat. Serve immediately.

Grilled Vegetable Skewers

These vegetables are tasty and versatile. Sprinkle leftovers with balsamic vinegar, and use them in sandwiches or on salads.

MAKES 6 SERVINGS
PREP: 25 MIN., MARINATE: 2 HRS., GRILL: 12 MIN.

¼ cup olive oil
2 tablespoons white wine vinegar
2 garlic cloves, minced
1 tablespoon minced fresh thyme
½ teaspoon salt
¼ teaspoon pepper
2 large yellow squash, cut into ¾-inch-thick slices
1 large zucchini, cut into ¾-inch-thick slices
1 large green bell pepper, cut into 1-inch squares
1 large red bell pepper, cut into 1-inch squares
1 large yellow bell pepper, cut into 1-inch squares
¾ pound medium-size fresh mushrooms

1. Combine first 6 ingredients in a large bowl; stir well. Add squash and remaining ingredients, and toss well. Cover and marinate in refrigerator for 2 hours, tossing occasionally.
2. Drain vegetables, and thread alternately on skewers. Grill, covered with grill lid, over medium heat (300° to 350°) 12 minutes or until tender, turning once.
Note: If you're using a grill basket, grill the vegetables in 2 batches in a single layer.

Grilled Marinated Vegetables

Grilled Marinated Vegetables

MAKES 10 SERVINGS
PREP: 30 MIN., MARINATE: 30 MIN., GRILL: 10 MIN.

8 large button mushrooms
4 yellow squash
4 zucchini
2 red bell peppers
2 yellow bell peppers
1 medium-size red onion
½ cup olive oil
¼ cup lite soy sauce
¼ cup lemon juice
2 garlic cloves, pressed
¼ teaspoon black pepper
Salt to taste

1. Remove mushroom stems, and discard; cut mushrooms in half. Diagonally slice squash and zucchini; cut bell peppers and onion into 1-inch strips. Place vegetables in a large zip-top freezer bag.
2. Whisk together olive oil and remaining ingredients until blended. Pour over vegetables in bag, and seal. Chill at least 30 minutes. Remove vegetables from marinade, reserving marinade.
3. Grill vegetables in a grill wok or metal basket, covered with grill lid, over medium-high heat (350° to 400°) 10 minutes, stirring occasionally and basting with reserved marinade.

Honey-Glazed Roasted Fall Vegetables

MAKES 8 SERVINGS
PREP: 30 MIN., BAKE: 40 MIN.

3 medium beets
3 medium Yukon Gold or other thin-skinned potatoes
3 red onions
¾ cup chicken broth
3 tablespoons olive oil
1 teaspoon salt
½ teaspoon pepper
3 medium turnips
2 tablespoons lemon juice
1½ tablespoons honey

1. Peel first 3 ingredients; cut each into 8 wedges. Toss together vegetable wedges, chicken broth, and next 3 ingredients in a large bowl.
2. Spread wedges evenly in a 15- x 10-inch jelly-roll pan; pour chicken broth mixture over vegetables in pan. Bake at 375° for 20 minutes.
3. Peel turnips, and cut each into 8 wedges. Add to baked vegetables, stirring to coat well; bake 20 more minutes or until liquid is absorbed.
4. Stir together lemon juice and honey; add to vegetables, tossing well.
To Make Ahead: Chill vegetables after baking 40 minutes. Remove from refrigerator; let stand 30 minutes. Bake, covered, at 375° for 15 minutes; toss with lemon juice mixture.

Vegetables With Arugula Broth

The arugula broth is slightly thickened and glossy with flecks of wilted arugula. Serve the vegetable medley in shallow bowls to enjoy all the juices.

MAKES 8 SERVINGS
PREP: 10 MIN., COOK: 20 MIN.

1 (1-pound) package baby carrots
1 pound turnips, peeled and cut into 1-inch cubes
6 cups chicken broth, divided
1 pound fresh broccoli, cut into florets
1 pound asparagus, trimmed and cut into 1-inch pieces
2 teaspoons cornstarch
¼ teaspoon freshly ground pepper
1 (0.75-ounce) package arugula*

1. Combine carrots and turnips in a Dutch oven. Add 4 cups broth. Bring to a boil; cook 10 minutes. Add broccoli and asparagus; cook 5 minutes. Drain.
2. Whisk together remaining 2 cups broth and cornstarch. Cook in a large skillet over medium-high heat 5 minutes or until slightly thickened. Stir in pepper. Add arugula; cook just until arugula wilts. Drizzle over cooked vegetables.
*2 cups chopped fresh spinach may be substituted for arugula.

Margaret's Creamy Grits

Cornbread Dressing

Margaret's Creamy Grits

MAKES 4 SERVINGS
PREP: 10 MIN., COOK: 10 MIN.

2 cups half-and-half or whipping cream
1/4 teaspoon salt
1/8 teaspoon granulated garlic
1/8 teaspoon pepper
1/2 cup uncooked quick-cooking grits
2 ounces cream cheese, cubed
3/4 cup (3 ounces) shredded sharp Cheddar cheese
1/4 teaspoon hot sauce

1. Bring first 4 ingredients to a boil in a Dutch oven; gradually stir in grits. Return to a boil; cover, reduce heat, and simmer, stirring occasionally, 5 to 7 minutes or until thickened.
2. Add cheeses and hot sauce, stirring until cheeses melt. Serve grits immediately.

Garlic-Cheese Grits

MAKES 8 TO 10 SERVINGS
PREP: 5 MIN., COOK: 20 MIN., STAND: 10 MIN., BAKE: 1 HR.

4 cups water
1 teaspoon salt
2 garlic cloves, pressed
1 cup uncooked regular grits
1 (12-ounce) block sharp Cheddar cheese, shredded
½ cup butter or margarine
1 teaspoon seasoned pepper
1 teaspoon Worcestershire sauce
¼ teaspoon hot sauce
3 large eggs, lightly beaten
Paprika

1. Bring first 3 ingredients to a boil in a large saucepan; gradually stir in grits. Return to a boil; reduce heat, and simmer, stirring occasionally, 15 minutes or until thickened.
2. Add Cheddar cheese and next 4 ingredients, stirring until cheese melts. Remove from heat; let stand 10 minutes.
3. Stir in eggs, and pour into a lightly greased 11- x 7-inch baking dish or 2-quart baking dish. Sprinkle with paprika.
4. Bake grits at 350° for 1 hour or until set.

Cornbread Dressing

MAKES 16 TO 18 SERVINGS
PREP: 30 MIN.; BAKE: 1 HR., 14 MIN.; COOK: 5 MIN.;
CHILL: 8 HRS.

1 cup butter or margarine, divided
3 cups white cornmeal
1 cup all-purpose flour
2 tablespoons sugar
2 teaspoons baking powder
1½ teaspoons salt
1 teaspoon baking soda
7 large eggs, divided
3 cups buttermilk
3 cups soft breadcrumbs
2 medium onions, diced (2 cups)
1 large bunch celery, diced (3 cups)
½ cup finely chopped fresh sage*
6 (10½-ounce) cans condensed chicken broth,
    undiluted
1 tablespoon pepper

1. Place ½ cup butter in a 13- x 9-inch pan; heat in oven at 425° for 4 minutes. Combine cornmeal and next 5 ingredients; whisk in 3 eggs and buttermilk.
2. Pour hot butter into cornbread batter, stirring until blended. Pour cornbread batter into pan.
3. Bake at 425° for 30 minutes or until golden brown. Cool.
4. Crumble cornbread into a large bowl; stir in breadcrumbs, and set aside.
5. Melt remaining ½ cup butter in a large skillet over medium heat; add onions and celery, and sauté until tender. Stir in chopped sage, and sauté 1 more minute.
6. Stir vegetables, remaining 4 eggs, chicken broth, and pepper into cornbread mixture; pour evenly into 1 lightly greased 13- x 9-inch baking dish and 1 lightly greased 8-inch square baking dish. Cover and chill 8 hours.
7. Bake, uncovered, at 375° for 35 to 40 minutes or until dressing is golden brown.
*1 tablespoon dried rubbed sage may be substituted for fresh sage.

Andouille Sausage, Apple, and Pecan Dressing:
Brown ¾ pound diced andouille sausage in a skillet over medium heat; drain. Add sausage; 2 Granny Smith apples, chopped; and 2 cups chopped toasted pecans to dressing. Proceed as directed, baking 40 to 45 minutes or until done.

Golden Macaroni
and Cheese

Golden Macaroni and Cheese

MAKES 8 SERVINGS
PREP: 10 MIN., BAKE: 45 MIN.

1 (8-ounce) package elbow macaroni (about 2 cups
    uncooked macaroni)
2 cups milk
¼ cup all-purpose flour
1 teaspoon onion salt
2 (10-ounce) blocks sharp Cheddar cheese, shredded
    (about 4½ cups) and divided
1 cup soft breadcrumbs (4 slices, crusts removed)
¼ cup butter or margarine, melted
Garnish: black pepper

1. Cook macaroni according to package directions;
drain well. Set aside.
2. Place milk, flour, and onion salt in a quart jar; cover
tightly, and shake vigorously 1 minute.
3. Stir together flour mixture, 3½ cups cheese, and
macaroni.
4. Pour macaroni mixture into a lightly greased
13- x 9-inch baking dish or 2 (11-inch) oval baking
dishes. Sprinkle evenly with breadcrumbs and remaining 1 cup cheese; drizzle evenly with melted butter.
5. Bake at 350° for 45 minutes or until golden brown.
Note: For testing purposes only, we used Kraft Cracker
Barrel Sharp Cheddar Cheese.

Penne With Spinach and Feta

This quick and flavorful pasta dish pairs well with steak.

MAKES 4 TO 6 SERVINGS
PREP: 10 MIN., COOK: 15 MIN.

½ (1-pound) box penne pasta
5 large plum tomatoes, seeded and chopped
3 cups fresh spinach
2 tablespoons olive oil
½ teaspoon Greek seasoning
¼ teaspoon salt
¼ teaspoon dried crushed red pepper
½ cup crumbled feta cheese

1. Cook penne pasta in a large Dutch oven according to package directions; drain. Return pasta to Dutch oven. Stir in chopped plum tomatoes and next 5 ingredients; cook over medium heat 2 minutes or until thoroughly heated. Sprinkle with cheese. Serve immediately.

Pasta With Creamy Alfredo Sauce

MAKES 4 SIDE-DISH OR 2 MAIN-DISH SERVINGS
PREP: 20 MIN., COOK: 10 MIN.

1 tablespoon olive oil
⅓ cup diced cooked ham
1 large red bell pepper, diced
1 garlic clove, minced
1 (10-ounce) container fresh Alfredo sauce
1 tablespoon chopped fresh sage
½ teaspoon freshly ground black pepper
2 cups bow tie pasta, uncooked
¼ cup freshly grated Parmesan cheese

1. Heat oil in a large skillet over medium-high heat. Add ham, bell pepper, and garlic; cook 3 minutes, stirring often. Reduce heat to medium-low; stir in Alfredo sauce, sage, and pepper. Cook, stirring constantly, until thoroughly heated.
2. While ham mixture cooks, cook pasta according to package directions; drain. Add pasta to skillet; toss well. Sprinkle with cheese.
Note: For testing purposes only, we used Contadina Alfredo Sauce.

Orzo Primavera

MAKES 6 TO 8 SERVINGS
PREP: 15 MIN., COOK: 12 MIN.

3 quarts water
1 teaspoon salt
2 cups orzo, uncooked
1 pound fresh asparagus, cut into 1-inch pieces
3 garlic cloves, minced
½ cup chopped red bell pepper
1 tablespoon olive oil
1 teaspoon butter or margarine, melted
1 cup frozen English peas, thawed
½ cup chicken broth
1 teaspoon grated lemon rind
¼ teaspoon ground white pepper
½ cup freshly grated Parmesan cheese

1. Combine water and salt in a large Dutch oven; bring to a boil. Add orzo, and cook 5 minutes. Add asparagus, and cook 4 minutes. Drain mixture, and set aside in a large serving bowl.
2. Cook garlic and red bell pepper in oil and butter in Dutch oven over medium heat, stirring constantly, 1 minute or until crisp-tender. Add peas; cook 1 minute, stirring constantly. Add chicken broth, lemon rind, and white pepper; bring to a boil, and cook 1 minute.
3. Add vegetable mixture to orzo mixture, tossing well. Sprinkle with Parmesan cheese. Serve immediately.

Orange-Ginger Couscous

MAKES 4 TO 6 SERVINGS
PREP: 20 MIN., STAND: 5 MIN.

1 teaspoon grated orange rind
2 cups orange juice
⅓ cup sweetened dried cranberries
½ tablespoon butter or margarine
½ teaspoon salt
¼ teaspoon ground cinnamon
1 teaspoon minced fresh ginger
1 (10-ounce) package couscous
¼ cup sliced almonds, toasted

1. Bring first 7 ingredients to a boil in a saucepan over medium heat; remove from heat.
2. Stir in couscous. Cover and let stand 5 minutes. Fluff with a fork; stir in almonds.
Note: For testing purposes only, we used Craisins Sweetened Dried Cranberries.

Company Rice

This savory rice will complement a variety of entrées. It's likely to be the most popular dish on the table!

MAKES 6 SERVINGS
PREP: 10 MIN.; COOK: 1 HR., 10 MIN.

¼ cup butter or margarine
1 (6-ounce) package wild rice*
1 (8-ounce) package sliced fresh mushrooms
3 green onions, chopped
1 (14-ounce) can chicken broth
2 tablespoons dry sherry
½ teaspoon salt
¼ cup chopped fresh parsley
½ cup sliced almonds, toasted

1. Melt butter in a medium saucepan over medium heat. Add rice and mushrooms; sauté 5 minutes. Add green onions and next 3 ingredients; bring to a boil. Cover, reduce heat, and simmer 1 hour and 5 minutes or until rice is done; drain excess liquid. Stir in parsley, and sprinkle with toasted almonds.
*1 (6.2-ounce) package fast-cooking long-grain and wild rice mix may be substituted for the wild rice; omit ½ teaspoon salt.

Fried Rice

If you have time, cook and chill the rice a day ahead. Chilled rice has a firmer texture that's easy to stir-fry.

MAKES 4 SERVINGS
PREP: 15 MIN., COOK: 15 MIN.

¼ cup vegetable oil, divided
2 large eggs
1 cup diced cooked ham
½ large red bell pepper, diced
½ large sweet onion, diced
½ cup frozen sweet peas, thawed
3 cups cooked rice
¼ cup soy sauce
1 teaspoon chili-garlic sauce
4 green onions, sliced

1. Heat 1 tablespoon oil in a skillet or wok at medium-high heat 2 minutes. Add eggs; cook 1 minute on each side. Remove from skillet; chop and set aside.
2. Heat remaining 3 tablespoons oil in skillet or wok; add ham, and stir-fry 1 to 2 minutes or until golden. Add bell pepper and onion; stir-fry 5 minutes. Add peas and next 3 ingredients; stir-fry 3 to 4 minutes or until thoroughly heated.
3. Stir in reserved egg, and sprinkle with green onions.

Lemon Rice Pilaf

Lemon Rice Pilaf

MAKES 6 SERVINGS
PREP: 15 MIN., COOK: 12 MIN.

2 tablespoons butter or margarine
4 celery ribs, sliced
6 green onions, chopped
3 cups hot cooked rice
2 tablespoons grated lemon rind
½ teaspoon salt
¼ teaspoon pepper

1. Melt butter in a large skillet over medium-high heat; add celery and green onions, and sauté until celery is tender. Stir in cooked rice, lemon rind, salt, and pepper; cook over low heat 2 minutes or until thoroughly heated.

soups

Bistro Onion Soup, page 291

Cream of Cilantro Soup

Cream of Cilantro Soup

MAKES 6 SERVINGS
PREP: 5 MIN., COOK: 20 MIN.

1 bunch fresh cilantro
1 (32-ounce) container low-sodium fat-free chicken broth, divided
2 tablespoons butter
2 tablespoons all-purpose flour
1 (8-ounce) package fat-free cream cheese
1 (8-ounce) container light sour cream
1 garlic clove, minced
¼ teaspoon salt
¼ teaspoon ground red pepper
¼ teaspoon ground cumin
Garnishes: fresh cilantro sprigs, light sour cream

1. Remove stems from cilantro, and coarsely chop leaves.
2. Process cilantro and 1 cup chicken broth in a blender or food processor until blended, stopping to scrape down sides.
3. Melt butter in a Dutch oven over medium heat; whisk in flour. Gradually add remaining 3 cups broth, whisking constantly until mixture is smooth. Boil 1 minute. Stir in cilantro mixture, cream cheese, and next 5 ingredients; simmer 15 minutes. Garnish, if desired.

Cream of Roasted Tomato Soup With Parsley Croutons

Roasting tomatoes brings out the sweet, intense flavor of the vine-ripened fruit. Thin, crispy croutons seasoned with garlic and topped with Muenster cheese grace each serving of this soup that's good hot or cold year-round.

MAKES 6 SERVINGS
PREP: 10 MIN., COOK: 44 MIN., BAKE: 45 MIN.

3 pounds tomatoes, cut in half crosswise and seeded
3 tablespoons olive oil
1 small head fennel
3 tablespoons unsalted butter
3 small shallots, coarsely chopped
1 small carrot, coarsely chopped
3 cups chicken broth, divided
5 fresh tarragon sprigs
5 fresh parsley sprigs
1 cup whipping cream
¼ teaspoon salt
¼ teaspoon pepper
Parsley Croutons
Garnish: chopped tomato

1. Brush tomato halves with olive oil; place tomato halves, cut sides down, in an aluminum foil-lined shallow baking dish. Bake, uncovered, at 400° for 45 minutes or until tomato is soft and skins are dark. Cool to touch; remove skins.
2. Rinse fennel thoroughly. Trim and discard bulb base. Trim stalks from bulb; discard stalks. Coarsely chop fennel bulb.
3. Melt butter in a large saucepan over medium heat; add fennel, shallot, and carrot, and cook 12 minutes or until vegetables are tender. Add 2 cups chicken broth, tarragon, and parsley. Reduce heat, and simmer, uncovered, 30 minutes. Remove from heat. Discard herb sprigs, and add tomato halves. Cool slightly.
4. Pour mixture into a blender; process until smooth, stopping to scrape down sides. Return puree to saucepan; stir in whipping cream. Bring just to a simmer; stir in remaining 1 cup chicken broth, salt, and pepper.
5. To serve, ladle soup into individual bowls; top each serving with Parsley Croutons. Garnish, if desired.

Parsley Croutons

MAKES 1 DOZEN CROUTONS
PREP: 5 MIN., BAKE: 5 MIN.

12 thin slices French baguette
3 tablespoons olive oil
2 garlic cloves, halved
½ cup (2 ounces) shredded Muenster cheese
¼ cup chopped fresh parsley

1. Brush both sides of baguette slices with olive oil; rub garlic halves over slices. Place slices on an ungreased baking sheet, and sprinkle evenly with cheese and parsley. Bake, uncovered, at 400° for 5 minutes or until golden.

Crab and Oyster Bisque

This rich seafood soup earned our Test Kitchens highest rating.

MAKES 8 SERVINGS
PREP: 15 MIN., COOK: 20 MIN.

¼ cup butter or margarine
4 garlic cloves, minced
2 shallots, finely chopped
3 tablespoons all-purpose flour
1 (8-ounce) bottle clam juice
1 cup dry white wine
1 tablespoon Worcestershire sauce
1 teaspoon Cajun seasoning
¼ teaspoon pepper
1 quart whipping cream
1 (12-ounce) container fresh oysters, drained
1 pound fresh lump crabmeat

1. Melt butter in a Dutch oven over medium heat; add garlic and shallot, and sauté until tender. Add flour; cook 1 minute, stirring constantly. Add clam juice and wine; cook 2 minutes or until thickened, stirring constantly.
2. Stir in Worcestershire sauce and next 3 ingredients. Cook until thoroughly heated, about 10 minutes. Stir in oysters and crabmeat; cook just until edges of oysters curl.

Beer-Cheese Soup

If you prefer a soup with more of a bite, we suggest using a dark beer, such as Michelob Honey Lager.

MAKES 4 TO 6 CUPS
PREP: 15 MIN., COOK: 16 MIN.

2½ cups milk
1 (12-ounce) bottle beer, divided
2 (5-ounce) jars processed cheese spread
1 (10½-ounce) can condensed chicken broth
½ teaspoon Worcestershire sauce
2 dashes of hot sauce
3 tablespoons cornstarch

1. Combine milk and ¾ cup beer in a Dutch oven. Cook over medium heat, stirring constantly, 2 to 3 minutes or until thoroughly heated.
2. Add cheese spread and next 3 ingredients. Cook over low heat, stirring constantly, 2 to 3 minutes or until thoroughly heated.
3. Combine cornstarch and remaining beer; add to cheese mixture. Simmer, stirring constantly, 10 minutes or until thickened (do not boil).
Note: For testing purposes only, we used Kraft Sharp Old English Cheese.

Black Bean Soup

MAKES 10 SERVINGS
PREP: 25 MIN.; STAND: 1 HR.; COOK: 3 HRS., 20 MIN.

1 (1-pound) package dried black beans with
    seasoning packet
1 medium onion, chopped
1 large green bell pepper, chopped
4 garlic cloves, minced
3 tablespoons vegetable oil
4 (14-ounce) cans beef broth
1 smoked ham hock
1 cup Mirepoix (recipe, page 303)
1 tablespoon ground oregano
2 teaspoons salt
2 teaspoons freshly ground black
    pepper
1 teaspoon ground cumin
1 teaspoon chili powder
2 bay leaves
1 pound hot smoked sausage, sliced
Salsa (optional)

1. Remove seasoning packet from beans, and set aside. Place beans in a Dutch oven; add water 2 inches above beans. Bring to a boil. Boil 1 minute; cover, remove from heat, and let stand 1 hour. Drain.
2. Sauté onion, bell pepper, and garlic in hot oil in Dutch oven 4 to 5 minutes or until tender. Add beans, beef broth, and next 8 ingredients; bring to a boil. Reduce heat, and simmer, stirring occasionally, 1½ to 2 hours or until slightly thickened.
3. Cook smoked sausage and contents of seasoning packet in a skillet over medium-high heat until sausage is browned. Add to soup; cook, stirring often, 1 hour or until beans are tender. Remove and discard bay leaves. Serve soup with salsa, if desired.

Bistro Onion Soup

Thick slices of crispy French bread underneath slices of bubbly, melted cheese make this French classic soup irresistible.

MAKES 4 SERVINGS
PREP: 20 MIN., COOK: 50 MIN., BROIL: 4 MIN.

4 medium onions, sliced (about 2 pounds)
¼ cup butter or margarine, melted
2 tablespoons all-purpose flour
3 (14-ounce) cans beef broth
½ cup dry white wine
½ cup dry red wine
2 bay leaves
½ teaspoon salt
½ teaspoon dried sage
¼ teaspoon pepper
4 (½-inch) diagonally sliced French bread slices,
    toasted
8 slices Gruyère cheese

1. Sauté onion in butter in a Dutch oven over medium heat, stirring often, 15 minutes or until golden. Stir in flour; cook 1 minute. Add broth and next 6 ingredients. Bring to a boil; reduce heat, and simmer, partially covered, 30 minutes. Discard bay leaves.
2. To serve, ladle soup into 4 individual ovenproof soup bowls. Place on a baking sheet. Add 1 bread slice to each bowl; cover bread with 2 slices cheese. Broil 3 inches from heat 4 minutes or until cheese is bubbly. Serve immediately.

Bistro Onion Soup

√Refried Bean Soup

Refried Bean Soup

This quick-and-easy soup is so filling, you need to add only tortilla chips and salsa, and supper's ready.

MAKES 7 SERVINGS
PREP: 10 MIN., COOK: 20 MIN., BAKE: 15 MIN.

1 small onion, chopped
2 garlic cloves, minced
1 tablespoon vegetable oil
1 (31-ounce) can refried beans
1 (16-ounce) can diced tomatoes, undrained
1 (10-ounce) can diced tomatoes and green chiles, undrained
1 (14½-ounce) can ready-to-serve chicken broth
2 tablespoons chopped fresh cilantro (optional)
6 corn tortillas
2 cups (8 ounces) shredded Monterey Jack cheese
1 (8-ounce) carton sour cream

1. Cook onion and garlic in hot oil in a Dutch oven over medium-high heat, stirring constantly, until tender. Add beans and next 3 ingredients, stirring until smooth; bring to a boil. Reduce heat, and simmer 15 minutes. Stir in cilantro, if desired.

2. Cut tortillas into thin strips; spread in a single layer on a baking sheet. Bake at 350° for 15 minutes or until browned, stirring every 5 minutes. Cool.

3. To serve, ladle soup into bowls; top evenly with tortilla strips, cheese, and sour cream. Serve immediately.

Baked Potato Soup

To bake potatoes in the microwave, prick each several times with a fork. Microwave 1 inch apart on paper towels at HIGH 14 minutes or until done, turning and rearranging after 5 minutes. Let cool.

MAKES 8 TO 10 SERVINGS
PREP: 30 MIN., COOK: 30 MIN.

5 large baking potatoes, baked
¼ cup butter or margarine
1 medium onion, chopped
⅓ cup all-purpose flour
1 quart half-and-half
3 cups milk
1 teaspoon salt
⅛ teaspoon ground white pepper
2 cups (8 ounces) shredded Cheddar cheese
8 bacon slices, cooked and crumbled

1. Peel potatoes, and coarsely mash with a fork.
2. Melt butter in a Dutch oven over medium heat; add onion, and sauté until tender. Add flour, stirring until smooth. Stir in potatoes, half-and-half, and next 3 ingredients; cook over low heat until thoroughly heated. Top each serving evenly with cheese and bacon.

Red Bell Pepper Soup

Sweet red bell peppers are showcased in this chilled soup laced with sherry and heavy cream.

MAKES 6 TO 8 SERVINGS
PREP: 12 MIN., COOK: 20 MIN., CHILL: 8 HRS.

6 red bell peppers, chopped
1 large onion, chopped
2 celery ribs, chopped
4 cups chicken broth
1 (7-ounce) jar diced pimiento, drained
2 teaspoons fresh lemon juice
1 teaspoon salt
½ teaspoon curry powder
½ teaspoon black pepper
1 cup whipping cream
2 tablespoons dry sherry
Garnish: chopped green onions

1. Combine first 4 ingredients in a Dutch oven; bring to a boil. Cover, reduce heat, and simmer 10 minutes or until vegetables are tender. Remove from heat; stir in pimiento.
2. Ladle half of vegetable mixture into a blender; process until smooth, stopping to scrape down sides. Repeat procedure with remaining half of vegetable mixture. Return mixture to pan; stir in lemon juice and next 3 ingredients. Bring to a boil; reduce heat, and simmer, uncovered, 10 minutes, stirring occasionally. Cover and chill at least 8 hours.
3. Stir whipping cream and sherry into chilled soup. Ladle soup into individual bowls; garnish, if desired.

Gazpacho

MAKES 8 TO 10 SERVINGS
PREP: 20 MIN., CHILL: 4 HRS.

2 large ripe tomatoes, cut into chunks
2 yellow onions, cut into chunks
2 medium cucumbers, peeled, seeded, and cut into chunks
2 garlic cloves, halved
1 (7-ounce) jar roasted red bell peppers, drained
½ cup chopped fresh cilantro
1 (46-ounce) can tomato juice
¼ cup lime juice
¼ cup red wine vinegar
2 tablespoons olive oil
1½ teaspoons salt
½ teaspoon black pepper
2 teaspoons hot sauce
Sour cream (optional)
Ground red pepper (optional)

1. Process first 6 ingredients in a food processor until smooth, stopping to scrape down sides.
2. Stir together vegetable puree, tomato juice, and next 6 ingredients.
3. Cover and chill at least 4 hours. Top gazpacho with sour cream, if desired, and sprinkle with red pepper, if desired.

Spicy Squash Soup

Spicy Squash Soup

MAKES 6 SERVINGS
PREP: 30 MIN., COOK: 45 MIN.

3 (14-ounce) cans chicken broth
1 large onion, chopped
½ to 1 teaspoon dried crushed red pepper
3 cups peeled, cubed acorn squash (about
    1¼ pounds)*
½ teaspoon salt
3 cups water
½ cup uncooked long-grain rice
¼ cup creamy peanut butter
Garnish: chopped fresh parsley

1. Bring ¼ cup chicken broth, onion, and crushed red pepper to a boil in a large saucepan; cook 5 minutes or until onion is tender. Add remaining broth, squash, salt, and 3 cups water; bring to a boil. Cover, reduce heat, and simmer 20 minutes. Add rice; cover and simmer 20 more minutes or until squash and rice are tender.

2. Process peanut butter and half of soup in a blender or food processor until smooth, stopping to scrape down sides; pour into a large bowl. Process remaining soup until smooth; add to bowl, stirring well. To serve, ladle into individual bowls. Garnish, if desired.

*Substitute butternut squash, if desired.

Cucumber Soup With Dill Cream

MAKES 4 TO 6 SERVINGS
PREP: 15 MIN., CHILL: 8 HRS.

2 cups half-and-half, divided
4 cucumbers, peeled, seeded, and chopped
2 green onions, sliced
1 tablespoon lemon juice
1 (16-ounce) container sour cream
½ teaspoon salt
½ teaspoon hot sauce
½ cup sour cream
1 tablespoon chopped fresh dill
Garnish: fresh dill sprig

1. Process 1 cup half-and-half and next 3 ingredients in a blender or food processor until smooth, stopping to scrape down sides.

2. Stir together cucumber mixture, remaining 1 cup half-and-half, container of sour cream, salt, and hot sauce. Cover and chill 8 hours.

3. Stir together ½ cup sour cream and chopped dill; dollop on each serving, and garnish, if desired.

Cucumber Soup With Dill Cream

Pot Liquor Soup

Pot Liquor Soup

A crusty skillet cornbread on the side is in order here.

MAKES 10 SERVINGS
PREP: 1 HR., COOK: 55 MIN.

2 pounds fresh collard greens
¾ pound smoked ham hocks
1 (1½-pound) ham steak, chopped
2 tablespoons hot sauce
3 tablespoons olive oil
3 medium onions, chopped
1 garlic clove, minced
6 red potatoes, diced
3 (14½-ounce) cans chicken broth
2 (15.8-ounce) cans field peas with snaps, rinsed
    and drained
2 (15.8-ounce) cans crowder peas, rinsed
    and drained
2 cups water
½ cup dry vermouth
1 tablespoon white vinegar
1 teaspoon salt

1. Remove and discard stems and discolored spots from collards; rinse with cold water. Drain; tear into 1-inch pieces.
2. Bring collards, ham hocks, and water to cover to a boil in a large Dutch oven. Remove from heat; drain. Repeat procedure once.
3. Toss together chopped ham and hot sauce; cook in hot oil in Dutch oven over medium-high heat 6 to 8 minutes or until browned.
4. Add onions and garlic; sauté until tender. Stir in collards, ham hocks, potatoes, and remaining ingredients. Bring mixture to a boil, reduce heat, and simmer, stirring occasionally, 45 minutes.
5. Remove meat from hocks; discard hocks. Return meat to soup.

Roasted Garlic-and-Basil Tomato Soup

A hot grilled cheese sandwich complements this savory soup quite well. Add a salad for a satisfying, complete meal.

MAKES 2 SERVINGS
PREP: 10 MIN., BAKE: 15 MIN., COOK: 5 MIN.

3 large garlic cloves, slightly flattened
1 (3-ounce) package shallots, peeled and halved
1 tablespoon olive oil
1 (14½-ounce) can Italian-style stewed tomatoes,
    undrained
1½ cups chicken broth, divided
½ teaspoon hot sauce
½ teaspoon balsamic vinegar
¼ teaspoon salt
⅛ teaspoon freshly ground black pepper
Pinch of ground red pepper
1½ tablespoons minced fresh basil

1. Place garlic and shallots in an 8-inch square pan lined with aluminum foil; drizzle with oil.
2. Bake at 450° for 15 minutes, stirring twice; cool.
3. Process garlic cloves, shallots, tomatoes, ¾ cup chicken broth, and next 5 ingredients in a blender or food processor until smooth, stopping to scrape down sides.
4. Cook tomato mixture and remaining ¾ cup broth in a medium saucepan over medium heat 5 minutes or until thoroughly heated. Stir in minced basil; serve immediately.
Note: To serve 4, double all the ingredients. Process half each of garlic, shallots, and tomatoes with 1 cup broth in blender; repeat. Heat tomato mixture and remaining 1 cup broth in a large saucepan for 8 minutes.

Chicken Soup With
Matzo Balls

Chicken Soup With Matzo Balls

You don't have to wait until Passover to enjoy matzo balls. These flavorful dumplings are made from unleavened bread meal and served in chicken broth or soup.

MAKES 16 TO 18 SERVINGS
PREP: 35 MIN., COOK: 1 HR.

8 carrots
2 parsnips
5 celery ribs
3 sweet onions
1 (2½- to 3-pound) whole chicken
10 cups water
8 chicken bouillon cubes
Matzo Balls

1. Cut first 3 ingredients into 2-inch pieces; cut onions in half. Place vegetables, chicken, water, and bouillon cubes in a Dutch oven; bring to a boil. Reduce heat, and simmer, covered, 1 hour or until chicken is tender. Remove chicken and vegetables from broth with a slotted spoon; cool slightly. Bone chicken, and cut into bite-size pieces; set aside. Process vegetables in a food processor until smooth.
2. Skim fat from broth. Stir vegetable puree and chicken into broth. Cook over medium heat, stirring occasionally, until thoroughly heated. Serve with Matzo Balls.

Matzo Balls:

MAKES 1 DOZEN
PREP: 15 MIN., CHILL: 30 MIN., COOK: 30 MIN.

4 large eggs, lightly beaten
1½ cups matzo ball mix*
¼ cup canola oil
½ teaspoon salt
6 cups water

1. Stir together first 4 ingredients; cover and chill 30 minutes. Shape mixture into 1-inch balls. (Do not exceed this size.)
2. Bring 6 cups water to a boil in a medium saucepan; drop balls into boiling water. Cover and simmer 30 minutes. Remove from water with a slotted spoon.
*During passover use kosher matzo ball mix.

New Year's Day Soup

This soup has all the ingredients you need to ring in a year of good luck.

MAKES 6 TO 8 SERVINGS
PREP: 20 MIN.; COOK: 1 HR., 30 MIN.

1 cup diced smoked lean ham
2 celery ribs, chopped
1 medium onion, chopped
2 carrots, chopped
2 garlic cloves, minced
2 (15-ounce) cans black-eyed peas, undrained
2 (14½-ounce) cans low-sodium fat-free chicken broth
2 (14½-ounce) cans stewed tomatoes, undrained
1 (14½-ounce) can diced tomatoes, undrained
1 (8-ounce) can tomato sauce
1½ cups chopped fresh spinach
½ cup chopped fresh parsley
½ teaspoon pepper
Chopped fresh spinach (optional)

1. Sauté first 5 ingredients over medium heat in a Dutch oven until vegetables are tender.
2. Stir in black-eyed peas and next 4 ingredients; bring mixture to a boil. Cover, reduce heat, and simmer 1 hour and 30 minutes. Stir in 1½ cups spinach, parsley, and pepper. Serve with additional chopped fresh spinach, if desired.

Sausage-Tortellini Soup

This tasty soup combines favorite ingredients from an Italian kitchen, including a variety of fresh vegetables.

MAKES 10 SERVINGS
PREP: 25 MIN., COOK: 50 MIN.

1 pound Italian sausage
1 large onion, chopped
1 garlic clove, pressed
3 (14½-ounce) cans beef broth
2 (14½-ounce) cans diced tomatoes, undrained
1 (8-ounce) can tomato sauce
1 cup dry red wine
2 carrots, thinly sliced
1 tablespoon sugar
2 teaspoons dried Italian seasoning
2 small zucchini, sliced
1 (9-ounce) package refrigerated cheese-filled
    tortellini
½ cup shredded Parmesan cheese

1. Remove and discard sausage casings. Cook sausage, onion, and garlic in a Dutch oven over medium-high heat, stirring until sausage crumbles and is no longer pink; drain.
2. Return mixture to pan. Stir in broth and next 6 ingredients; bring to a boil. Reduce heat; simmer 30 minutes. Skim off fat.
3. Stir in zucchini and tortellini; simmer 10 minutes. To serve, ladle into bowls; sprinkle each serving with cheese.

Meatball Minestrone

Frozen cooked meatballs are the speedy secret to this flavorful soup that tastes like you've been cooking it all day.

MAKES 16 SERVINGS
PREP: 10 MIN., COOK: 30 MIN.

3 garlic cloves, minced
1 tablespoon olive oil
3 (15-ounce) cans cannellini beans, undrained
    and divided
1 (32-ounce) container chicken broth
1 (1.4-ounce) package vegetable soup mix
60 to 64 frozen cooked meatballs
1 (14½-ounce) can diced tomatoes with basil,
    garlic, and oregano
½ teaspoon dried crushed red pepper
8 ounces uncooked rotini pasta
1 (10-ounce) bag fresh spinach, torn
Breadsticks

1. Sauté minced garlic in hot oil in a stockpot over medium-high heat 1 minute. Stir in 2 cans cannellini beans and container chicken broth, and bring mixture to a boil.
2. Stir in vegetable soup mix until dissolved. Add meatballs, tomatoes, and red pepper; return to a boil. Add rotini, and cook, stirring often, 15 minutes.
3. Stir in remaining can cannellini beans and spinach; cook 5 more minutes. Serve minestrone with breadsticks.
Note: For testing purposes only, we used Knorr Vegetable Soup Mix.

Old-Fashioned Vegetable-Beef Soup

Keep this hearty soup on hand for a quick soup and sandwich dinner.

MAKES 8 TO 10 SERVINGS
PREP: 35 MIN.; COOK: 2 HRS., 20 MIN.

⅔ cup all-purpose flour
1 teaspoon salt
1 teaspoon freshly ground pepper
2 pounds beef stew meat
2 garlic cloves, minced
3 tablespoons vegetable oil
2 (14-ounce) cans beef broth
1 cup Mirepoix
2 cups peeled, chopped potato
1 (28-ounce) can crushed tomatoes
1 (16-ounce) package frozen mixed vegetables, thawed
1 (16-ounce) package frozen white shoepeg corn, thawed
1 (15-ounce) can tomato sauce with garlic and herbs
1 tablespoon Worcestershire sauce

1. Combine flour, salt, and pepper in a large zip-top freezer bag; add beef. Seal and shake to coat.
2. Sauté garlic in hot oil 1 minute; add beef, and cook 8 minutes, stirring occasionally, until browned.
3. Add beef broth, Mirepoix, and remaining ingredients; bring to a boil. Reduce heat, and simmer 1½ to 2 hours or until beef is tender.

Mirepoix:

MAKES ABOUT 3 CUPS
PREP: 10 MIN., COOK: 15 MIN.

3 tablespoons butter
1 cup diced celery
1 cup diced carrot
1 cup diced onion

1. Melt butter in a large skillet; add vegetables, and sauté 10 to 15 minutes or until tender. Cool.
2. Store mixture in an airtight container in refrigerator up to 3 days, or freeze up to 2 months.

Old-Fashioned
Vegetable-Beef Soup

MIREPOIX *(mihr-PWAH)*

This magical medley of aromatic vegetables was originally used to enhance the flavor of braised meats and sauces. Consisting of equal parts celery, onion, and carrot, mirepoix was first created in France during the 18th century. Over the years, this classic French foundation has become a popular addition to many ethnic soups. Some folks add garlic and bell pepper to the flavorful basic blend.

Corn and Crab Soup

Corn and Crab Soup

Garnish this enticing soup with fresh parsley sprigs, if desired. Then watch your guests eat every bite.

MAKES 4 TO 6 SERVINGS
PREP: 10 MIN., COOK: 21 MIN.

¼ cup butter or margarine
¼ cup all-purpose flour
2 cups chicken broth
2 cups half-and-half
1 pound fresh lump crabmeat, drained
1 (11-ounce) can whole kernel corn, drained
½ teaspoon salt
¼ teaspoon garlic powder
¼ teaspoon pepper

1. Melt butter in a heavy saucepan over low heat; add flour, stirring until mixture is smooth. Cook 1 minute, stirring constantly. Gradually add broth, and cook over medium heat, stirring constantly, until thickened. Stir in half-and-half and remaining ingredients; cover, reduce heat, and simmer 20 minutes.

Seafood Gumbo

Instead of a traditional, oil-laden roux, this gumbo is thickened and colored with flour browned in the oven.

MAKES 36 SERVINGS
PREP: 20 MIN.; BAKE: 20 MIN.; COOK: 1 HR., 27 MIN.

2½ cups all-purpose flour
1 tablespoon olive oil
2 cups chopped celery
1 cup chopped green bell pepper
1 cup chopped onion
1 cup chopped green onions
5 garlic cloves, pressed
1 tablespoon filé powder
7 (14½-ounce) cans low-sodium fat-free chicken broth
1 tablespoon salt
½ teaspoon black pepper
½ teaspoon ground red pepper
1 tablespoon hot sauce
1 (10-ounce) package frozen cut okra
3 pounds unpeeled, large fresh shrimp
2 pounds fresh crabmeat
1 pound crawfish meat
2 (12-ounce) containers fresh oysters
Filé powder (optional)

1. Sprinkle flour evenly in a 15- x 10-inch jelly-roll pan.
2. Bake at 400°, stirring often, for 20 minutes or until caramel colored (do not burn); cool.
3. Pour olive oil into a 12-quart stockpot, and place over medium heat until hot. Add chopped celery and next 5 ingredients; cook, stirring constantly, 5 to 7 minutes or until tender.
4. Add toasted flour, broth, and next 4 ingredients; bring to a boil. Reduce heat, and simmer 30 minutes. Add okra, and simmer 30 minutes.
5. Peel shrimp, and devein, if desired. Drain and flake crabmeat, removing any bits of shell. Add shrimp, crabmeat, crawfish, and oysters to stockpot; cook 15 to 20 minutes or just until seafood is done. Stir in additional filé powder, if desired.

Seafood Gumbo

Mexican Chicken-Corn Chowder

Mexican Chicken-Corn Chowder

MAKES 6 SERVINGS

PREP: 20 MIN., COOK: 30 MIN.

3 tablespoons butter or margarine
4 skinned and boned chicken breasts (1½ pounds),
    cut into bite-size pieces
1 small onion, chopped
2 garlic cloves, minced
2 cups half-and-half
2 cups (8 ounces) shredded Monterey Jack cheese
2 (14¾-ounce) cans cream-style corn
1 (4.5-ounce) can chopped green chiles, undrained
½ teaspoon hot sauce
¼ teaspoon salt
½ to 1 teaspoon ground cumin
2 tablespoons chopped fresh cilantro
Garnishes: chopped fresh cilantro, Anaheim chile
      pepper

1. Melt butter in a Dutch oven over medium-high heat; add chicken, chopped onion, and minced garlic, and sauté 10 minutes.

2. Stir in half-and-half, shredded Monterey Jack cheese, and next 5 ingredients; cook, stirring often, over low heat 15 minutes.

3. Stir in 2 tablespoons cilantro. Garnish, if desired.

EASY FREEZING

Store a batch of soup in the freezer for a night when you're too busy to cook. It's best to let hot food cool before freezing to prevent it from standing at unsafe temperatures too long. For best results, pour hot soup into a large pan or baking dish; slightly cool. Spoon cooled soup into freezer-safe containers, or use small zip-top freezer bags for individual portions. Cover or seal, and freeze up to 1 month. Thaw overnight in the refrigerator, and reheat.

Mirliton-Corn Chowder

Mirlitons are squash about the size of large pears. They have delicate pale green skin, rather bland white flesh, and soft seeds.

MAKES 14 SERVINGS
PREP: 30 MIN., COOK: 1 HR.

2 tablespoons butter or margarine
4 large mirlitons, peeled, seeded, and chopped*
2 medium onions, chopped
1 red bell pepper, chopped
1 to 2 jalapeño peppers, seeded and chopped
2 garlic cloves, pressed
¼ cup all-purpose flour
1 (32-ounce) container chicken broth
1 (16-ounce) package frozen whole kernel corn
2 (4.5-ounce) cans chopped green chiles
2 cups milk
½ teaspoon salt
1 teaspoon ground cumin
½ teaspoon chili powder
2 tablespoons lime juice
Shredded Cheddar cheese (optional)
Chopped bacon (optional)

1. Melt butter in a Dutch oven over medium-high heat; add mirlitons and next 4 ingredients, and sauté 5 minutes or until onion is tender.
2. Sprinkle with flour, and cook, stirring constantly, 2 minutes. Gradually add chicken broth, stirring constantly.
3. Stir in corn and next 5 ingredients; cook, stirring occasionally, 45 minutes. Stir in lime juice. Ladle into bowls, and sprinkle each serving with shredded Cheddar cheese and bacon, if desired.
*4 large yellow squash or zucchini, seeded and chopped, may be substituted for mirlitons.

Wild Rice-Clam Chowder

Freeze the leftovers to eat later. See the Easy Freezing tip box on the opposite page for suggestions.

MAKES 10 TO 12 SERVINGS
PREP: 11 MIN., COOK: 50 MIN.

¼ cup butter or margarine
1 large onion, chopped (about 2 cups)
1 (8-ounce) package sliced fresh mushrooms
6 medium-size red potatoes, cut into ½-inch cubes
6½ cups chicken broth
1 tablespoon fresh lemon juice
½ teaspoon freshly ground pepper
1 bay leaf
2 (6½-ounce) cans chopped clams, undrained
1 (6-ounce) package wild rice, cooked (about 3 cups)
1½ cups half-and-half
⅓ cup all-purpose flour

1. Melt butter in a large Dutch oven over medium-high heat. Add onion and mushrooms; sauté 5 minutes or until tender. Add potatoes and next 4 ingredients; bring to a boil. Reduce heat to medium, and simmer 10 minutes or until potatoes are tender. Add clams and wild rice. Reduce heat to medium-low.
2. Whisk together half-and-half and flour. Gradually add flour mixture to wild rice mixture; cook 25 minutes or until slightly thickened, stirring occasionally. Remove and discard bay leaf.

Brunswick Stew

Brunswick Stew

This is a fast, delicious version of a Southern favorite.

MAKES 8 TO 10 SERVINGS
PREP: 5 MIN., COOK: 30 MIN.

3 cups chicken broth
2 cups chopped cooked chicken
1 (24-ounce) container barbecued shredded pork
1 (16-ounce) package frozen vegetable gumbo
    mixture
1 (10-ounce) package frozen corn
½ (10-ounce) package frozen petite lima beans
½ cup ketchup

1. Bring all ingredients to a boil in a Dutch oven over medium-high heat, stirring often. Cover, reduce heat to low, and simmer, stirring occasionally, 25 minutes or until thoroughly heated.

Three-Bean Chili

Add extra punch to this spicy chili with shreds of Monterey Jack-colby cheese.

MAKES 10 SERVINGS
PREP: 10 MIN., COOK: 30 MIN.

2 pounds ground chuck
1 large yellow onion, chopped
1 large green bell pepper, chopped
2 (14½-ounce) cans diced tomatoes with garlic
    and onion, undrained
1 (15-ounce) can tomato sauce
1 (15-ounce) can kidney beans, rinsed and drained
1 (15-ounce) can black beans, rinsed and drained
1 (15-ounce) can black-eyed peas, rinsed and drained
2 (1.6-ounce) envelopes chili seasoning
2 cups water
¼ teaspoon ground red pepper
1 tablespoon sugar (optional)
Toppings: shredded Monterey Jack-colby cheese,
    chopped green onions, sour cream, corn chips

1. Cook first 3 ingredients in a large Dutch oven over high heat 10 minutes, stirring until beef crumbles and is no longer pink. Drain. Return mixture to pan.
2. Stir in diced tomatoes, next 7 ingredients, and, if desired, sugar. Cook over medium-high heat 20 minutes. Serve with desired toppings.

Game-Day Chili

This spicy and flavorful chili tastes great on a cold day.

MAKES 10 SERVINGS
PREP: 25 MIN.; COOK: 3 HRS., 10 MIN.

2 pounds ground chuck
1 medium onion, chopped
3 to 4 garlic cloves, minced
2 (15-ounce) cans pinto beans, rinsed
    and drained
3 (8-ounce) cans tomato sauce
1 (12-ounce) bottle dark beer
1 (14½-ounce) can beef broth
1 (6-ounce) can tomato paste
1 (4.5-ounce) can chopped green chiles
2 tablespoons chili powder
1 tablespoon Worcestershire sauce
2 teaspoons ground cumin
1 to 2 teaspoons ground red pepper
1 teaspoon paprika
1 teaspoon hot sauce
Garnish: pickled jalapeño peppers

1. Cook first 3 ingredients in a Dutch oven over medium heat, stirring until meat crumbles and is no longer pink. Drain well.
2. Combine meat mixture, beans, and next 11 ingredients in Dutch oven; bring to a boil. Reduce heat, and simmer 3 hours or until thickened. Garnish, if desired.
Note: For testing purposes only, we used Sierra Nevada Pale Ale.

Chipotle Beef and
Butternut Squash Stew

Chipotle Beef and Butternut Squash Stew

MAKES 6 SERVINGS

PREP: 15 MIN., COOK: 1 HR.

2½ pounds top sirloin, cut into 1-inch pieces
2 teaspoons dried ground chipotle chile, divided
2 tablespoons olive oil, divided
1 medium onion, cut into 1-inch pieces
1 medium-size green bell pepper, cut into 1-inch
    pieces
1 (2-pound) butternut squash, peeled and cut into
    1-inch pieces
2 (10½-ounce) cans condensed beef broth,
    undiluted
1 (14½-ounce) can diced tomatoes
1 tablespoon brown sugar
½ teaspoon ground cumin
2 tablespoons all-purpose flour
Flour tortillas (optional)

1. Place beef in a bowl; sprinkle with 1 teaspoon ground chipotle chile, tossing to coat.
2. Brown beef in 1 tablespoon hot oil in a Dutch oven over medium-high heat, stirring occasionally, 10 minutes. Remove beef with a slotted spoon.
3. Add onion and bell pepper to Dutch oven, and cook, stirring occasionally, 3 minutes. Return beef to Dutch oven; stir in remaining 1 teaspoon ground chipotle chile, squash, and next 4 ingredients.
4. Bring to a boil. Cover, reduce heat, and simmer, stirring occasionally, 30 minutes.
5. Cook flour in remaining 1 tablespoon hot oil in a small skillet over medium heat, stirring constantly with a wooden spoon, 5 minutes or until golden. Add to stew, stirring well; cook 10 minutes. Serve with flour tortillas, if desired.

Frogmore Stew

This seafood stew is a hallmark recipe of the Lowcountry. It's a mix of sausage, potatoes, corn, and shrimp seasoned with a bagged spice mix and boiled until everything's tender.

MAKES 10 TO 12 SERVINGS

PREP: 5 MIN., COOK: 58 MIN.

10 quarts water
1 (5-ounce) package crab boil
2 large onions, quartered
3 pounds smoked sausage, cut into 1-inch pieces
3 pounds new potatoes
12 ears fresh corn, cut in half
3 pounds unpeeled, large fresh shrimp
Cocktail sauce (optional)

1. Bring water to a boil in a large stockpot. Add crab boil, onion, sausage, and potatoes; return to a boil, and cook 35 minutes or until potatoes are tender. Remove onion, sausage, and potatoes with a slotted spoon to a large bowl or platter; keep warm.
2. Add corn to stockpot; return to a boil, and cook 10 minutes. Add shrimp; cook 3 more minutes. Remove corn and shrimp with a slotted spoon to bowl with potato mixture. Serve immediately with cocktail sauce, if desired.

desserts

Pecan Pie Cake, page 314

Pecan Pie Cake

Prepare this cake for a fall get-together.

MAKES 1 (3-LAYER) CAKE
PREP: 35 MIN., BAKE: 25 MIN., COOL: 10 MIN.

3 cups finely chopped pecans, toasted and divided
½ cup butter or margarine, softened
½ cup shortening
2 cups sugar
5 large eggs, separated
1 tablespoon vanilla extract
2 cups all-purpose flour
1 teaspoon baking soda
1 cup buttermilk
¾ cup dark corn syrup
Pecan Pie Filling
Pastry Garnish (optional)

1. Sprinkle 2 cups pecans evenly into 3 generously buttered 9-inch round cakepans; shake to coat bottoms and sides of pans.

Pecan Pie Cake

2. Beat butter and shortening at medium speed with an electric mixer until fluffy, and gradually add sugar, beating well. Add egg yolks, 1 at a time, beating just until blended after each addition. Stir in vanilla.
3. Combine flour and baking soda. Add to butter mixture alternately with buttermilk, beginning and ending with flour mixture. Beat at low speed just until blended after each addition. Stir in remaining 1 cup pecans.
4. Beat egg whites at medium speed until stiff peaks form, and fold one-third of egg whites into batter. Fold in remaining egg whites. (Do not overmix.) Pour batter into prepared pans.
5. Bake at 350° for 23 to 25 minutes or until a wooden pick inserted in center comes out clean. Cool in pans on wire racks 10 minutes. Invert layers onto wax paper-lined wire racks. Brush tops and sides of layers with corn syrup, and cool completely.
6. Spread half of Pecan Pie Filling on 1 layer, pecan side up. Place second layer, pecan side up, on filling, and spread with remaining filling. Top with remaining layer, pecan side up.
7. Arrange Pastry Garnish on and around cake, if desired.

Pecan Pie Filling:

MAKES ABOUT 3 CUPS
PREP: 10 MIN., COOK: 7 MIN., CHILL: 4 HRS.

½ cup firmly packed dark brown sugar
¾ cup dark corn syrup
⅓ cup cornstarch
4 egg yolks
1½ cups half-and-half
⅛ teaspoon salt
3 tablespoons butter or margarine
1 teaspoon vanilla extract

1. Whisk together first 6 ingredients in a heavy 3-quart saucepan until smooth. Bring mixture to a boil over medium heat, whisking constantly, and boil 1 minute or until thickened. Remove from heat; whisk in butter and vanilla. Place a sheet of wax paper directly on surface of mixture to prevent a film from forming, and chill 4 hours.
Note: To chill filling quickly, pour the filling into a bowl. Place bowl in a larger bowl filled with ice. Whisk constantly until cool (about 15 minutes).

Pastry Garnish:

MAKES 16 TO 20 PASTRY LEAVES AND 12 PECAN PASTRIES
PREP: 1 HR., BAKE: 18 MIN., COOL: 10 MIN.

1 (15-ounce) package refrigerated piecrusts
1 large egg
1 tablespoon water
24 pecan halves

1. Unroll piecrusts, and press out fold lines. Cut 8 to 10 leaves from each piecrust with a 3-inch leaf-shaped cutter, and mark leaf veins using tip of a knife. Reserve pastry trimmings. Whisk together egg and 1 tablespoon water, and brush on pastry leaves.
2. Crumple 10 to 12 small aluminum foil pieces into $\frac{1}{2}$-inch balls. Coat with cooking spray, and place on a lightly greased baking sheet. Drape a pastry leaf over each ball; place remaining pastry leaves on baking sheet.
3. Bake at 425° for 6 to 8 minutes or until golden. Cool on a wire rack 10 minutes. Gently remove foil from leaves.
4. Pinch 12 pea-size pieces from pastry trimmings. Place between pecan halves, forming sandwiches. Cut remaining pastry into 2-inch pieces, and wrap around pecan sandwiches, leaving jagged edges to resemble half-shelled pecans. Brush with egg mixture. Place on a baking sheet.
5. Bake at 350° for 10 minutes or until golden. Cool on wire rack.

Buttermilk Layer Cake With Caramel Frosting

MAKES 1 (3-LAYER) CAKE
PREP: 22 MIN., BAKE: 24 MIN., COOL: 10 MIN.

1 cup shortening
2 cups sugar
3 large eggs
2½ cups all-purpose flour
½ teaspoon salt
½ teaspoon baking soda
1½ cups buttermilk
2 teaspoons vanilla extract
Caramel Frosting

1. Beat shortening at medium speed with an electric mixer until creamy. Gradually add sugar, beating well. Add eggs, 1 at a time, beating until blended after each addition.

2. Combine flour, salt, and baking soda; add to shortening mixture alternately with buttermilk, beginning and ending with flour mixture. Beat at low speed until blended after each addition. Stir in vanilla. Pour batter into 3 greased and floured 8-inch round cakepans.
3. Bake at 350° for 24 minutes or until a wooden pick inserted in center comes out clean. Cool in pans on wire racks 10 minutes; remove from pans. Cool completely on wire racks.
4. Spread Caramel Frosting between layers and on top and sides of cake as directed below.

Caramel Frosting:

MAKES ABOUT 3 CUPS
PREP: 18 MIN., COOK: 37 MIN.

3¾ cups sugar, divided
1½ cups whipping cream
¼ cup butter
¼ teaspoon baking soda

1. Bring 3 cups sugar, whipping cream, butter, and baking soda to a boil in a heavy saucepan. Remove from heat.
2. Sprinkle remaining ¾ cup sugar in a heavy 4-quart saucepan. Cook over medium heat, stirring constantly, 5 minutes or until sugar melts and syrup is light golden brown. (Sugar will clump before melting.) Remove pan from heat. Carefully and gradually stir whipping cream mixture into the syrup. (Mixture will bubble.) Stir until bubbles subside.
3. Bring caramel mixture to a boil over medium heat, stirring often. Wash down sugar crystals with a small brush dipped in hot water. Insert a candy thermometer, and cook, stirring often, 12 minutes or until candy thermometer registers 236° (soft ball stage). Remove from heat. Beat with a spoon until almost spreading consistency. Mixture will thicken slightly.
4. Pour about 1 cup of frosting on top of each layer of cake. Spread and work frosting with a small spatula until it firms slightly. Gradually add remaining frosting to top of cake and allow to drip over sides. Spread dripping frosting with a small spatula to cover sides of cake.
Note: For best results, apply frosting to cake as described above. Frosting is likely to harden too quickly if traditional techniques are used.

Best Carrot Cake

Best Carrot Cake

MAKES 8 TO 10 SERVINGS
PREP: 30 MIN., BAKE: 30 MIN., COOL: 15 MIN.

2 cups all-purpose flour
2 teaspoons baking soda
½ teaspoon salt
2 teaspoons ground cinnamon
3 large eggs
2 cups sugar
¾ cup vegetable oil
¾ cup buttermilk
2 teaspoons vanilla extract
2 cups grated carrots
1 (8-ounce) can crushed pineapple, drained
1 (3½-ounce) can sweetened flaked coconut
1 cup chopped pecans or walnuts
Buttermilk Glaze
Cream Cheese Frosting

1. Line 3 (9-inch) round cakepans with wax paper; lightly grease and flour wax paper. Set pans aside.
2. Stir together first 4 ingredients. Beat eggs and next 4 ingredients at medium speed with an electric mixer until smooth. Add flour mixture, beating at low speed until blended. Fold in carrots and next 3 ingredients. Pour batter into prepared cakepans.
3. Bake at 350° for 25 to 30 minutes or until a wooden pick inserted in center comes out clean. Drizzle Buttermilk Glaze evenly over layers; cool in pans on wire racks 15 minutes. Remove from pans, and cool completely on wire racks. Spread Cream Cheese Frosting between layers and on top and sides of cake. Store in refrigerator.

Buttermilk Glaze:

MAKES 1½ CUPS
PREP: 5 MIN., COOK: 5 MIN.

1 cup sugar
1½ teaspoons baking soda
½ cup buttermilk
½ cup butter or margarine
1 tablespoon light corn syrup
1 teaspoon vanilla extract

1. Bring first 5 ingredients to a boil in a large Dutch oven over medium-high heat. Boil, stirring often, 4 minutes. Remove from heat, and stir in vanilla extract.

Cream Cheese Frosting:

MAKES 4 CUPS
PREP: 10 MIN.

¾ cup butter or margarine, softened
1 (8-ounce) package cream cheese, softened
1 (3-ounce) package cream cheese, softened
3 cups sifted powdered sugar
1½ teaspoons vanilla extract

1. Beat butter and cream cheese at medium speed with an electric mixer until creamy. Add powdered sugar and vanilla extract, beating until smooth.

TIPS FOR A PERFECT CAKE

Make sure you evenly grease your cakepans all over, including into bottom edge. A zip-top plastic bag or sheet of plastic wrap works great to keep your hands clean.

Shake and turn the cakepan in several directions to get an even layer of flour on bottom and up sides. Turn cakepan over, and gently tap bottom to remove any excess flour.

Black Cake (A Kwanzaa Fruitcake)

This Jamaican cake is worth every minute of the time involved. It may become your holiday favorite.

MAKES 12 SERVINGS
PREP: 30 MIN.; CHILL: 8 HRS.; BAKE: 1 HR., 40 MIN.; COOL: 1 HR.;
STAND: 10 MIN., 48 HRS.

1¾ cups currants
1½ cups raisins
1½ cups pitted prunes
1 (8-ounce) package candied cherries
½ (7-ounce) package mixed dried fruit
2 cups dark rum
6 large eggs
⅛ teaspoon ground cinnamon
⅛ teaspoon ground nutmeg
½ pound butter
½ pound dark brown sugar
2 cups all-purpose flour
1½ teaspoons baking powder
¼ cup burnt sugar syrup
2 cups tawny port wine
Whipped cream (optional)

1. Combine first 6 ingredients in a large bowl; cover fruit mixture, and chill 8 hours or up to 1 week.
2. Process fruit mixture, in batches, in a food processor until smooth, stopping to scrape down sides; set aside.
3. Whisk together eggs, cinnamon, and nutmeg until foamy.
4. Beat butter and dark brown sugar at medium speed with an electric mixer until creamy. Add egg mixture, beating until blended. Add fruit puree; blend well.
5. Combine flour and baking powder; stir into fruit mixture. Stir in burnt sugar syrup. Spoon batter evenly into 1 greased and floured 10-inch springform pan.
6. Bake at 300° for 1 hour and 40 minutes or until a wooden pick inserted in center comes out clean. Cool in pan on a wire rack 1 hour; remove from pan, and cool completely on wire rack.
7. Pour 1 cup port wine evenly over top of cake, and let stand 10 minutes. Pour remaining 1 cup wine over cake. Wrap cake with cheesecloth; place in a covered container. Let stand 2 to 3 days. (Do not refrigerate.) Serve with whipped cream, if desired.
Note: Burnt sugar syrup is available by mail order from Eve Sales Corporation. Contact them at 945 Close Avenue, Bronx, NY 10473; or call (718) 589-6800.

Italian Cream Cake

Italian Cream Cake

MAKES 8 TO 10 SERVINGS
PREP: 25 MIN., BAKE: 30 MIN., COOL: 10 MIN., STAND: 10 MIN.

1 cup butter or margarine, softened
2 cups sugar
5 large eggs, separated
2½ cups all-purpose flour
1 teaspoon baking soda
1 cup buttermilk
⅔ cup finely chopped pecans
1 (3½-ounce) can sweetened flaked coconut
1 teaspoon vanilla extract
½ teaspoon cream of tartar
3 tablespoons light rum (optional)
Cream Cheese Frosting

1. Grease and flour 3 (9-inch) round cakepans. Line pans with wax paper; grease paper, and set aside.
2. Beat butter at medium speed with an electric mixer until creamy; gradually add sugar, beating well. Add egg yolks, 1 at a time, beating after each addition. Combine flour and baking soda. Add to butter mixture alternately with buttermilk, beginning and ending with flour mixture. Stir in pecans, coconut, and vanilla.
3. Beat egg whites at high speed until foamy. Add cream of tartar, beating until soft peaks form. Gently fold beaten egg whites into batter. Pour batter into prepared pans.
4. Bake at 350° for 25 to 30 minutes or until a wooden pick inserted in center comes out clean. Let cool in pans 10 minutes. Remove from pans; peel off wax paper, and let cool completely on wire racks. Brush each cake layer with 1 tablespoon light rum, if desired. Let stand 10 minutes. Spread Cream Cheese Frosting between layers and on sides and top of cake. Store in refrigerator.

Cream Cheese Frosting:

MAKES ABOUT 4 CUPS
PREP: 10 MIN.

1 (8-ounce) package cream cheese, softened
1 (3-ounce) package cream cheese, softened
¾ cup butter, softened
1½ (16-ounce) packages powdered sugar, sifted
1½ cups chopped pecans, toasted
1 tablespoon vanilla extract

1. Beat first 3 ingredients at medium speed with an electric mixer until smooth. Gradually add sugar, beating until light and fluffy. Stir in pecans and vanilla.

Fig Cake With Cream Cheese Frosting

MAKES 8 SERVINGS
PREP: 20 MIN., BAKE: 40 MIN., COOL: 10 MIN.

3 large eggs
1 cup sugar
1 cup vegetable oil
½ cup buttermilk
1 teaspoon vanilla extract
2 cups all-purpose flour
1 teaspoon baking soda
1 teaspoon salt
1 teaspoon ground cinnamon
½ teaspoon ground cloves
½ teaspoon ground nutmeg
1½ cups fig preserves
½ cup applesauce
1 cup chopped pecans, toasted
Cream Cheese Frosting

1. Beat first 3 ingredients at medium speed with an electric mixer until blended. Add buttermilk and vanilla; beat well.
2. Combine flour and next 5 ingredients; gradually add to buttermilk mixture, beating until blended. Fold in fig preserves, applesauce, and toasted pecans. (Batter will be thin.) Pour batter into 2 greased and floured 8-inch round cakepans.
3. Bake at 350° for 35 to 40 minutes or until a wooden pick inserted in center comes out clean. Cool on wire racks 10 minutes; remove from pans, and cool completely on wire racks.
4. Spread Cream Cheese Frosting between layers and on top and sides of cake. Store in refrigerator.
Note: For testing purposes only, we used Braswell's Pure Fig Preserves. Coarsely chop figs, if necessary.

Cream Cheese Frosting:

MAKES ABOUT 3½ CUPS
PREP: 5 MIN.

1½ (8-ounce) packages cream cheese, softened
5 tablespoons butter, softened
2 teaspoons vanilla extract
2 cups powdered sugar

1. Beat cream cheese, butter, and vanilla at medium speed with an electric mixer until smooth. Gradually add powdered sugar, beating at low speed just until blended. (Do not overbeat, or frosting will be too thin.)

Four-Layer Coconut
Cake

Four-Layer Coconut Cake

MAKES 8 TO 10 SERVINGS
PREP: 20 MIN., BAKE: 20 MIN., COOL: 10 MIN.

3 cups all-purpose flour
1 teaspoon baking powder
½ teaspoon salt
2⅔ cups sugar
1 cup shortening
½ cup butter or margarine, softened
1 cup milk
2 teaspoons coconut extract
1 teaspoon vanilla extract
5 large eggs
1 (6-ounce) package frozen flaked coconut, thawed
Coconut Filling
2 cups whipping cream
¼ cup powdered sugar
Garnish: toasted coconut shavings

1. Beat first 7 ingredients at medium speed with an electric mixer until well blended. Add extracts, beating well. Add eggs, 1 at a time, beating until blended after each addition. Stir in coconut. Pour batter into 4 greased and floured 9-inch cakepans.

2. Bake at 400° for 20 minutes or until a wooden pick inserted in center comes out clean. Cool in pans on wire racks 10 minutes; remove from pans. Cool completely on wire racks.

3. Spread Coconut Filling between layers. Beat whipping cream at high speed until foamy. Gradually add powdered sugar, beating until soft peaks form. Spread on top and sides of cake. Garnish, if desired.

Coconut Filling:

MAKES 5½ CUPS
PREP: 5 MIN., COOK: 15 MIN.

2 cups sugar
¼ cup all-purpose flour
2 cups milk
4 large eggs, lightly beaten
2 (6-ounce) packages frozen flaked coconut, thawed
2 teaspoons vanilla extract

1. Cook first 4 ingredients in a large saucepan over medium-low heat, whisking constantly, 12 to 15 minutes or until thickened and bubbly. Remove from heat, and stir in coconut and vanilla extract. Cool completely.

Coconut-Chocolate Cake

Treat yourself to a slice of this cake with a warm cup of coffee after a special dinner.

MAKES 1 (3-LAYER) CAKE
PREP: 20 MIN., BAKE: 30 MIN., COOL: 10 MIN.

1 cup butter or margarine, softened
2 cups sugar
4 large eggs
8 (1-ounce) semisweet chocolate squares, melted
2 cups all-purpose flour
1 teaspoon baking powder
½ teaspoon salt
½ cup cocoa
1 cup buttermilk
4 cups flaked coconut, divided
1¼ teaspoons vanilla extract
¼ cup cream of coconut
Butter Frosting
2 (1-ounce) semisweet chocolate
    squares

1. Beat butter at medium speed with an electric mixer until creamy; gradually add sugar, beating well. Add eggs, 1 at a time, beating until blended after each addition. Add chocolate, beating until blended.
2. Combine flour and next 3 ingredients; add to butter mixture alternately with buttermilk, beginning and ending with flour mixture. Beat at low speed until blended after each addition. Stir in 1 cup coconut and vanilla. Pour into 3 greased and floured 8-inch round cakepans.
3. Bake at 350° for 30 minutes or until a wooden pick inserted in center comes out clean. Cool in pans on wire racks 10 minutes; remove from pans, and cool completely on wire racks.
4. Stir together remaining 3 cups coconut and cream of coconut.
5. Spread Butter Frosting between layers, and sprinkle each layer with ½ cup coconut mixture. Spread top and sides of cake with remaining frosting; press remaining coconut mixture on sides and 1 inch from edge of top layer.

6. Seal 2 chocolate squares in a zip-top freezer bag, and place in hot water until chocolate melts. Snip a tiny hole in 1 corner of bag, and drizzle chocolate over top of cake. Store in refrigerator.

Butter Frosting:

MAKES 4 CUPS
PREP: 10 MIN.

1 cup butter or margarine, softened
8 cups sifted powdered sugar
⅓ to ½ cup milk
1½ teaspoons vanilla extract

1. Beat butter at medium speed with an electric mixer until creamy; gradually add sugar, beating until smooth. Add milk, beating until mixture reaches spreading consistency. Stir in vanilla.

Coconut-Chocolate Cake

Chocolate-Butter
Pecan Cake

Chocolate-Butter Pecan Cake

MAKES 12 TO 16 SERVINGS
PREP: 30 MIN., BAKE: 25 MIN., COOL: 10 MIN.

1¾ cups (11.5-ounce package) semisweet chocolate
   chunks
1 cup butter, softened and divided
2 cups sugar
4 large eggs
2½ cups all-purpose flour
¼ teaspoon baking soda
1¼ cups buttermilk
2 teaspoons vanilla extract
Butter Pecan Frosting

1. Microwave chocolate chunks and ½ cup butter in a microwave-safe bowl at HIGH 2 minutes or until chocolate melts and mixture is smooth, stirring every 30 seconds. Set chocolate mixture aside.
2. Beat remaining ½ cup butter and sugar at medium speed with an electric mixer until creamy. Add eggs, 1 at a time, beating mixture until blended after each addition.
3. Combine flour and baking soda; add to sugar mixture alternately with buttermilk, beginning and ending with flour mixture. Beat at low speed until blended after each addition. Stir in reserved melted chocolate mixture and vanilla. Spoon batter evenly into 3 greased and floured 9-inch round cakepans.

4. Bake at 350° for 23 to 25 minutes or until a wooden pick inserted in center comes out clean. Cool in pans on a wire rack 10 minutes. Remove from pans, and cool completely on wire rack.

5. Spread Butter Pecan Frosting between layers and on top and sides of cake. Arrange ½ cup chopped toasted pecans remaining from frosting recipe around outer edge on top of cake. Store cake in refrigerator until ready to serve.

Butter Pecan Frosting:

MAKES ABOUT 7 CUPS

PREP: 15 MIN., BAKE: 15 MIN.

2½ cups chopped pecans
¼ cup butter, melted
1 (8-ounce) package cream cheese, softened
1 cup butter, softened
2 (16-ounce) packages powdered sugar
3 tablespoons milk
2 teaspoons vanilla extract

1. Stir together pecans and ¼ cup melted butter in a 9-inch square pan.

2. Bake at 350° for 15 minutes or until toasted, stirring occasionally. Remove from oven, and let pecans cool.

3. Beat cream cheese and 1 cup softened butter in a large bowl at medium speed with an electric mixer until creamy. Gradually add powdered sugar alternately with 3 tablespoons milk, beating until light and fluffy. Stir in vanilla and 2 cups toasted pecans. Reserve remaining ½ cup chopped toasted pecans for garnish.

Mocha Torte

MAKES 8 SERVINGS

PREP: 25 MIN., BAKE: 18 MIN., COOL: 15 MIN.

1¼ cups water
¼ cup instant coffee granules, divided
1 (18.25-ounce) package devil's food cake mix with pudding
1 cup butter or margarine, softened
2 cups powdered sugar
2 tablespoons cocoa
2 tablespoons whipping cream
¼ cup coffee liqueur (optional)
Mocha Frosting

1. Stir together 1¼ cups water and 2 tablespoons coffee granules until dissolved.

2. Prepare cake mix according to package directions, substituting coffee mixture for water. Pour into 3 greased and floured 8-inch cakepans.

3. Bake at 350° for 18 minutes or until a wooden pick inserted in center comes out clean. Cool cakes in pans on wire racks 10 to 15 minutes; remove from pans, and cool on wire racks.

4. Beat butter at medium speed with an electric mixer until creamy; gradually add powdered sugar, beating at low speed until blended. Add remaining 2 tablespoons coffee granules, cocoa, and whipping cream, beating until blended.

5. Brush cake layers evenly with coffee liqueur, if desired. Spread cocoa mixture between cake layers. Spread Mocha Frosting on top and sides of cake.

Mocha Frosting:

MAKES 3 CUPS

PREP: 10 MIN.

3 cups powdered sugar
¼ cup cocoa
2 tablespoons instant coffee granules
½ cup butter or margarine, softened
1 tablespoon vanilla extract
1 tablespoon coffee liqueur*

1. Stir together first 3 ingredients. Beat softened butter at medium speed with an electric mixer until creamy; gradually add powdered sugar mixture, beating until spreading consistency. Stir in vanilla extract and coffee liqueur.

*1 tablespoon whipping cream may be substituted for liqueur.

TIPS FOR A PERFECT CAKE

Always add flour mixture to creamed butter and sugar mixture alternately with wet mixture, beginning and ending with flour.

Pecan Pie Cheesecake

Pecan Pie Cheesecake

This spectacular cheesecake was the grand prize winner in the first Southern Living Cook-Off. We know you'll think it's a winner too.

MAKES 16 SERVINGS
PREP: 15 MIN.; STAND: 1 HR., 30 MIN.; BAKE: 50 MIN.;
CHILL: 8 HRS.

1 (2-pound) package frozen pecan pie
2 cups graham cracker crumbs
½ cup granulated sugar
½ cup butter, melted
¼ teaspoon ground cinnamon
2 (8-ounce) packages cream cheese, softened
2 large eggs
⅔ cup sour cream
½ cup half-and-half
1 teaspoon vanilla extract
1 cup powdered sugar
1 tablespoon all-purpose flour
Garnish: Pastry Leaves (see box on opposite page)

1. Thaw pie at room temperature 30 minutes. Cut pie in half; reserve half of pie for another use. Cut remaining half into 10 wedges, keeping wedges intact, and set aside. (Pie will still be partially frozen after thawing 30 minutes; this ensures cleaner, easier-to-handle slices.)

2. Stir together graham cracker crumbs and next 3 ingredients; press mixture into bottom and 1½ inches up sides of a 10-inch springform pan.

3. Arrange 10 pecan pie wedges in a spoke design in prepared pan, placing 1 cut side of each wedge on crust with narrow end towards center of pan.

4. Beat cream cheese until smooth; add eggs, 1 at a time, beating after each addition. Add sour cream, half-and-half, and vanilla; beat until blended. Stir in powdered sugar and flour, stirring until smooth. Carefully pour cream cheese mixture evenly over pecan pie wedges in pan, making sure wedges remain in place.

5. Bake at 325° for 50 minutes. Turn off oven, and let stand in oven 1 hour. Remove to a wire rack, and let cool completely. Chill at least 8 hours or overnight before serving. Garnish, if desired. Store in refrigerator.

New York-Style Cheesecake

Don't overbeat the batter when adding the eggs. Beat only until blended.

MAKES 12 SERVINGS
PREP: 15 MIN.; BAKE: 1 HR., 15 MIN.; CHILL: 8 HRS.

1¾ cups graham cracker crumbs
⅓ cup butter, melted
¼ cup sugar
5 (8-ounce) packages cream cheese, softened
1 cup sugar
3 tablespoons all-purpose flour
1 tablespoon vanilla extract
3 large eggs
1 (8-ounce) container sour cream

1. Stir together first 3 ingredients. Press crumb mixture into bottom and 1½ inches up sides of a lightly greased 9-inch springform pan.
2. Bake crust at 350° for 10 minutes. Cool baked crust on a wire rack.
3. Beat cream cheese at medium speed with an electric mixer until smooth. Gradually add 1 cup sugar, flour, and vanilla, beating until blended. Add eggs, 1 at a time, beating until blended after each addition. Add sour cream, and beat just until blended. Pour into prepared crust.
4. Bake at 350° for 1 hour and 5 minutes or until center is almost set. Remove cheesecake from oven; cool on wire rack. Cover and chill 8 hours. Gently run a knife around edge of cheesecake, and release sides. Store in refrigerator.

German Chocolate Cheesecake

MAKES 12 SERVINGS
PREP: 30 MIN., BAKE: 45 MIN., CHILL: 8 HRS., COOK: 7 MIN.

1 cup chocolate wafer crumbs
2 tablespoons sugar
3 tablespoons butter or margarine, melted
3 (8-ounce) packages cream cheese, softened
¾ cup sugar
¼ cup cocoa
2 teaspoons vanilla extract
3 large eggs
⅓ cup evaporated milk
⅓ cup sugar
¼ cup butter or margarine
1 large egg, lightly beaten
½ teaspoon vanilla extract
½ cup chopped pecans
½ cup flaked coconut

1. Stir together first 3 ingredients; press into bottom of an ungreased 9-inch springform pan. Bake at 325° for 10 minutes. Cool crust.
2. Beat cream cheese and next 3 ingredients at medium speed with an electric mixer until blended. Add eggs, 1 at a time, beating just until blended after each addition. Pour into prepared crust. Bake at 350° for 35 minutes. Loosen cake from pan; cool. Cover and chill 8 hours.
3. Stir together evaporated milk and next 4 ingredients in a saucepan. Cook over medium heat, stirring constantly, 7 minutes. Stir in pecans and coconut; spread over cheesecake. Store in refrigerator.

PASTRY LEAVES

Pastry Leaves are one of our favorite garnishes. They can decorate both sweet or savory foods. One (15-ounce) package of refrigerated piecrust will make about 24 (2-to 3-inch) leaves. Leave the leaves their natural golden color, or tint them with egg wash for pretty fall hues. Here's how to make them:

Unroll piecrusts on a lightly floured surface. Cut leaves from piecrust using a leaf-shaped cookie cutter. Mark leaf veins using the tip of a small knife.

To make the tinted egg wash, whisk together 3 large eggs and 2 tablespoons of water. Pour into cups, tinting each with a few drops of liquid food coloring to create different colors. Brush leaves with egg wash, beginning with lighter colors first, and over-laying with areas of darker color. Use an artist's brush to add accents of bolder color with food coloring.

Crumple 2 (14-inch long) pieces of foil into 1-inch wide strips. Coat with cooking spray; place on a baking sheet lined with parchment paper. Gently drape pastry leaves over the strips of foil to give them a natural-looking shape; place several additional leaves flat on the baking sheet. Bake at 400° for 6 to 8 minutes or until golden. Cool on the baking sheet on a wire rack 10 minutes. Gently remove leaves; cool completely on a wire rack. Repeat procedure.

Two-Step Pound Cake

Two-Step Pound Cake

This cake requires a heavy-duty stand mixer with a 4-quart bowl and a paddle attachment.

MAKES 10 SERVINGS
PREP: 10 MIN.; BAKE: 1 HR., 30 MIN.; COOL: 10 MIN.

4 cups all-purpose flour
3 cups sugar
1 pound butter, softened
¾ cup milk
6 eggs
2 teaspoons vanilla extract

1. Place flour, sugar, butter, milk, eggs, and vanilla (in that order) in a 4-quart bowl. Beat at low speed with a heavy-duty electric mixer 1 minute, stopping to scrape down sides. Beat at medium speed 2 minutes. Pour into a greased and floured 10-inch tube pan.
2. Bake at 325° for 1 hour and 30 minutes or until a wooden pick inserted in center comes out clean. Cool in pan on a wire rack 10 minutes. Remove from pan; cool completely on wire rack.
Note: For testing purposes only, we used a KitchenAid mixer.

Traditional Method: Beat butter at medium speed with an electric mixer 2 minutes or until creamy; gradually add sugar, beating until light and fluffy. Add eggs, 1 at a time, beating after each addition. Add flour to butter mixture alternately with milk, beginning and ending with flour. Beat at low speed just until blended after each addition. Stir in vanilla. Pour batter into a greased and floured 10-inch tube pan. Bake as directed.

Cream Cheese Pound Cake

Serve this scrumptious Southern classic with whipped cream and a mixture of berries such as strawberries, raspberries, and blackberries.

MAKES 10 SERVINGS
PREP: 15 MIN.; BAKE: 1 HR., 40 MIN.; COOL: 15 MIN.

1½ cups butter or margarine, softened
1 (8-ounce) package cream cheese, softened
3 cups sugar
6 large eggs
3 cups all-purpose flour
⅛ teaspoon salt
1 tablespoon vanilla extract

1. Beat butter and cream cheese at medium speed with an electric mixer until creamy; gradually add sugar, beating well. Add eggs, 1 at a time, beating until combined.
2. Combine flour and salt; gradually add to butter mixture, beating at low speed just until blended after each addition. Stir in vanilla. Pour batter into a greased and floured 10-inch Bundt pan.
3. Bake at 300° for 1 hour and 40 minutes or until a wooden pick inserted in center comes out clean. Cool in pan on a wire rack 10 to 15 minutes; remove from pan, and cool completely on wire rack.

Extra-Rich Chocolate Cake

Extra-Rich Chocolate Cake

MAKES 24 SERVINGS
PREP: 20 MIN., COOK: 5 MIN., BAKE: 25 MIN., COOL: 10 MIN.

2 cups all-purpose flour
2 cups sugar
¾ teaspoon baking soda
½ teaspoon salt
½ teaspoon ground cinnamon
1 cup water
½ cup vegetable oil
¼ cup butter or margarine
3 tablespoons cocoa
2 large eggs
½ cup buttermilk
1½ teaspoons vanilla extract
¼ cup strong brewed coffee
Chocolate Frosting
Garnishes: whipped cream, chocolate curls

1. Stir together first 5 ingredients.
2. Bring 1 cup water and next 3 ingredients to a boil.
Add to flour mixture, and beat at medium speed with
an electric mixer until smooth.

3. Beat eggs and next 3 ingredients at medium speed until
blended. Stir into flour mixture. Pour into a greased and
floured 15- x 10-inch jelly-roll pan.
4. Bake at 350° for 25 minutes or until a wooden pick
inserted in center comes out clean. Cool in pan on a
wire rack 10 minutes. Spread Chocolate Frosting over
warm cake; cool cake completely in pan on wire rack.
Garnish, if desired. Store in refrigerator.

Chocolate Frosting:
MAKES 3 CUPS
PREP: 5 MIN., COOK: 5 MIN.

½ cup butter or margarine
3 tablespoons cocoa
1 (16-ounce) package powdered sugar
6 tablespoons milk
1½ teaspoons vanilla extract
¼ teaspoon salt

1. Melt butter with cocoa over low heat.
2. Remove from heat; stir in powdered sugar and
remaining ingredients until blended.

Cola Cake

Whip up this fun dessert with staple ingredients already in your pantry. Your children are sure to love it because it's extra yummy!

MAKES 15 SERVINGS
PREP: 20 MIN., BAKE: 35 MIN.

2 cups all-purpose flour
2 cups sugar
1 teaspoon baking soda
1 cup cola soft drink
1 cup butter or margarine
2 tablespoons cocoa
1 1/2 cups miniature marshmallows
1/2 cup buttermilk
2 large eggs, lightly beaten
1 teaspoon vanilla extract
Cola Frosting
1 cup finely chopped pecans

1. Combine first 3 ingredients in a large bowl.
2. Bring cola, butter, and cocoa to a boil in a saucepan over medium heat, stirring constantly. Gradually stir into flour mixture. Stir in marshmallows and next 3 ingredients. Pour into a greased and floured 13- x 9-inch pan.
3. Bake at 350° for 30 to 35 minutes or until a wooden pick inserted in center comes out clean. Spread Cola Frosting over warm cake; top with pecans.

Cola Frosting:

MAKES 2 1/4 CUPS
PREP: 5 MIN., COOK: 10 MIN.

1/2 cup butter or margarine
6 tablespoons cola soft drink
3 tablespoons cocoa
1 (16-ounce) package powdered sugar
1 teaspoon vanilla extract

1. Bring first 3 ingredients to a boil in a large saucepan over medium heat, stirring constantly, until butter melts; remove from heat. Add sugar and vanilla, stirring until smooth.

Quick Cola Cake: Omit first 10 ingredients. Beat 1 (18.25-ounce) package Swiss chocolate cake mix, 1 (3.9-ounce) package chocolate instant pudding mix, 1 (10-ounce) bottle of cola soft drink, 1/2 cup vegetable oil, and 4 large eggs at low speed with an electric mixer until blended. Beat at medium speed 3 more minutes; pour into a greased and floured 13- x 9-inch pan. Bake at 350° for 45 minutes.

Chocolate-Peanut Butter Frosting:
Substitute 1/2 cup peanut butter for 1/2 cup butter in Cola Frosting.

Milk Chocolate Bar Cake

MAKES 1 (3-LAYER) CAKE
PREP: 20 MIN., BAKE: 25 MIN., COOL: 10 MIN.

1 (18.25-ounce) package Swiss chocolate cake mix
1 (8-ounce) package cream cheese, softened
1 cup powdered sugar
1/2 cup granulated sugar
10 (1.5-ounce) milk chocolate candy bars with almonds, divided
1 (12-ounce) container frozen whipped topping, thawed

1. Prepare cake batter according to package directions. Pour into 3 greased and floured 8-inch round cakepans.
2. Bake at 325° for 20 to 25 minutes or until a wooden pick inserted in center comes out clean. Cool in pans on wire racks 10 minutes. Remove from pans, and cool completely on wire racks. Beat cream cheese, powdered sugar, and granulated sugar at medium speed with an electric mixer until mixture is creamy.
3. Finely chop 8 candy bars. Fold cream cheese mixture and chopped candy into whipped topping.
4. Spread icing between layers and on top and sides of cake. Chop remaining 2 candy bars. Sprinkle half of chopped candy bars over cake. Press remaining chopped candy along bottom edge of cake. Store in refrigerator.
Note: For testing purposes only, we used Duncan Hines Swiss Chocolate cake mix and Hershey's Milk Chocolate Bars with almonds.

Fresh Fruit Trifles With
Vanilla Custard

Fresh Fruit Trifles With Vanilla Custard

MAKES 8 SERVINGS
PREP: 30 MIN.

3 cups nectarines, peeled, seeded, and cubed
3 cups peaches, peeled, seeded, and cubed
2 cups plums, peeled, seeded, and cubed
2 teaspoons fresh lemon juice
2½ tablespoons chopped fresh mint
⅓ cup sugar
1 (16-ounce) frozen pound cake, thawed and cut into
    1-inch cubes (about 8 cups)
Vanilla Custard*
Garnish: fresh raspberries

1. Combine first 6 ingredients, tossing to coat.
2. Arrange half of pound cake cubes evenly in 8 (16-ounce) trifle dishes or glasses. Top evenly with half of fruit mixture. Repeat layers with cake and fruit mixture, and drizzle evenly with ½ cup Vanilla Custard. Garnish, if desired. Serve with remaining custard. Store in refrigerator.
Note: For testing purposes only, we used Sara Lee All Butter Pound Cake Family Size.

*Cook-and-serve vanilla pudding may be substituted. Prepare pudding according to package directions, adding 1 additional cup of milk.

Vanilla Custard:

MAKES 4½ CUPS
PREP: 10 MIN., COOK: 20 MIN., STAND: 1 HR., CHILL: 1 HR.

6 egg yolks
¼ cup sugar
2 cups whipping cream
2 cups milk
1 teaspoon vanilla extract

1. Whisk together first 4 ingredients in a medium saucepan. Cook over medium-low heat, stirring constantly, 20 minutes or until mixture thickens and a kitchen thermometer registers 170°. (Mixture should coat the back of a spoon.)
2. Pour mixture into a large bowl; stir in vanilla. Place plastic wrap directly over surface of mixture; let stand at room temperature 1 hour. Chill at least 1 hour.

Sweet Lemon Baby Cakes

MAKES 3 DOZEN
PREP: 6 HRS., BAKE: 33 MIN., COOL: 10 MIN., FREEZE: 30 MIN.,
STAND: 4 HRS.

1 (18.25-ounce) package white cake mix
3 large eggs
1¼ cups buttermilk
⅓ cup vegetable oil
3 tablespoons lemon juice
Lemon Glaze
Royal Icing

1. Beat first 5 ingredients at low speed with an electric mixer 1 minute. Increase speed to medium, and beat 3 minutes. Pour batter into a greased and floured 15- x 10-inch jelly-roll pan.
2. Bake at 350° for 28 to 33 minutes or until a wooden pick inserted in center comes out clean.
3. Cool cake in pan on a wire rack 10 minutes. Invert cake onto wire rack, removing pan; transfer cake to a large cutting board, and freeze, uncovered, 30 minutes.
4. Trim ¼ inch from cake edges on all sides; discard edges. Cut sheet cake into 36 (2¼- x 1½-inch) rectangles.
5. Place rectangles on a wire rack over parchment paper. Spoon a generous amount of Lemon Glaze over each cake. Spread and smooth glaze evenly over top and sides with a small icing spatula. Let stand 2 hours or until firmly set.
6. Fill a pastry bag fitted with a #1 or #2 plain tip with Royal Icing. Pipe monogram and decorations as desired on cakes. Let stand 2 hours or until dry.
To Make Ahead: Make cakes up to 1 day ahead, if desired. Cover loosely with aluminum foil, and let stand at room temperature.

Lemon Glaze:

MAKES 4 CUPS
PREP: 5 MIN.

2 (16-ounce) packages plus 2 cups powdered sugar
½ cup plus 2 tablespoons hot water
½ cup lemon juice
Red, blue, green, or yellow food coloring drops

1. Stir together powdered sugar, ½ cup plus 2 table-spoons hot water, ½ cup lemon juice, and desired amount of chosen food coloring in a large bowl until smooth. Use immediately.

Royal Icing:

MAKES 1¾ CUPS
PREP: 5 MIN.

½ cup cold water
¼ cup meringue powder
4 cups powdered sugar, sifted

1. Beat ½ cup cold water and meringue powder at medium-high speed with a heavy-duty stand mixer, using a whisk attachment, until stiff peaks form. Add sugar; beat until glossy.
Note: Meringue powder is found at cake-supply and crafts stores.

Lemon-Blueberry Ice-Cream Cupcakes

These cool concoctions can be stored in an airtight container in your freezer up to two weeks, so they're ready when you are.

MAKES 12 CUPCAKES
PREP: 20 MIN., FREEZE: 8 HRS.

12 foil baking cups
24 Danish wedding cookies, coarsely crushed
1 (21-ounce) can blueberry pie filling
1 (14-ounce) can sweetened condensed milk
1 (6-ounce) can frozen lemonade concentrate, thawed
1 (8-ounce) container frozen whipped topping, thawed
Multicolored candies and sprinkles

1. Place baking cups into muffin pans; sprinkle crushed wedding cookies evenly into cups. Spoon 2 teaspoons blueberry pie filling into each cup, reserving remaining pie filling for another use.
2. Stir together condensed milk and lemonade concen-trate; fold mixture into whipped topping just until blended. Spoon mixture over pie filling in prepared baking cups. Freeze at least 8 hours or until firm. Top with candies and sprinkles just before serving.
Note: For testing purposes only, we used Keebler Danish Wedding cookies.

Lemon Meringue Pie

Lemon Meringue Pie

Sealing meringue to the outer edge of crust over a hot filling ensures that the meringue topping will cook completely without shrinking.

MAKES 8 TO 10 SERVINGS
PREP: 25 MIN., FREEZE: 10 MIN., BAKE: 50 MIN.

1 (15-ounce) package refrigerated piecrusts
Lemon Meringue Pie Filling
6 egg whites
1/2 teaspoon vanilla extract
6 tablespoons sugar

1. Unroll and stack piecrusts on a lightly floured surface. Roll into 1 (12-inch) circle. Fit piecrust into a 9-inch pieplate (about 1 inch deep) according to package directions; fold edges under, and crimp. Prick bottom and sides of piecrust with a fork. Freeze 10 minutes.
2. Line piecrust with parchment paper; fill with pie weights or dried beans.
3. Bake at 425° for 10 minutes. Remove weights and parchment paper; bake 12 to 15 more minutes or until crust is lightly browned. (Shield edges with aluminum foil if they brown too quickly.)
4. Prepare Lemon Meringue Pie Filling; pour into piecrust. Cover with plastic wrap, placing directly on filling. (Proceed immediately with next step to ensure that the meringue is spread over the pie filling while it is still warm.)
5. Beat egg whites and vanilla extract at high speed with an electric mixer until foamy. Add sugar, 1 tablespoon at a time, and beat 2 to 4 minutes or until stiff peaks form and sugar dissolves.

6. Remove plastic wrap from pie, and spread meringue evenly over warm Lemon Meringue Pie Filling, sealing edges.
7. Bake at 325° for 20 to 25 minutes or until golden brown. Cool pie completely on a wire rack. Store leftovers in the refrigerator.

Lemon Meringue Pie Filling:
MAKES ENOUGH FOR 1 (9-INCH) PIE
PREP: 10 MIN., COOK: 10 MIN.

1 cup sugar
1/4 cup cornstarch
1/8 teaspoon salt
4 large egg yolks
2 cups milk
1/3 cup fresh lemon juice
3 tablespoons butter or margarine
1 teaspoon grated lemon rind
1/2 teaspoon vanilla extract

1. Whisk together first 3 ingredients in a heavy, non-aluminum, medium saucepan. Whisk together egg yolks, milk, and lemon juice in a bowl; whisk into sugar mixture in pan over medium heat. Bring to a boil, and boil, whisking constantly, 1 minute. Remove pan from heat; stir in butter, lemon rind, and vanilla extract until smooth.

Perfect Pumpkin Chess Pie

This pie is traditionally served around the holidays, but this version is so good you will want to serve it year-round!

MAKES 8 SERVINGS
PREP: 15 MIN.; BAKE: 1 HR., 10 MIN.; CHILL: 8 HRS.

½ (15-ounce) package refrigerated piecrusts
1 (15-ounce) can unsweetened pumpkin
2 cups sugar
½ cup butter or margarine, softened
3 large eggs
½ cup half-and-half
1½ teaspoons vanilla extract
¾ teaspoon salt
½ teaspoon ground cinnamon
¼ teaspoon ground ginger
¼ teaspoon ground cloves
Praline Sauce

1. Fit piecrust into a 9-inch pieplate according to package directions.
2. Beat pumpkin, sugar, and butter in a large bowl at medium speed with an electric mixer until smooth. Add eggs and next 6 ingredients, beating until blended. Pour into prepared crust.
3. Bake at 350° for 1 hour and 10 minutes or until almost set. Cool pie completely on a wire rack. Chill for 8 hours. Serve pie with Praline Sauce.

Praline Sauce:

Serve leftover sauce over ice cream or brownies.

MAKES 1¾ CUPS
PREP: 5 MIN., COOK: 1 MIN.

1 cup firmly packed brown sugar
½ cup half-and-half
½ cup butter or margarine
½ cup chopped pecans, toasted
½ teaspoon vanilla extract

1. Combine first 3 ingredients in a saucepan over medium heat. Bring to a boil over medium heat, and cook 1 minute, stirring constantly. Remove from heat; stir in pecans and vanilla. Cool completely.

Coconut Cream Pie

Look for cream of coconut near the piña colada and margarita mixes.

MAKES 8 SERVINGS
PREP: 25 MIN., BAKE: 8 MIN., CHILL: 2 HRS.

1⅔ cups graham cracker crumbs
¼ cup sugar
⅓ cup butter or margarine, melted
1 (8-ounce) package cream cheese, softened
1 cup cream of coconut
1 (3.4-ounce) package cheesecake instant pudding mix
1 (6-ounce) package frozen sweetened flaked coconut, thawed
1 (8-ounce) container frozen whipped topping, thawed
1 cup whipping cream
Garnish: sweetened flaked coconut

1. Stir together first 3 ingredients; press mixture evenly into bottom and up sides of a 9-inch pieplate. Bake at 350° for 8 minutes; remove to a wire rack, and cool completely.
2. Beat cream cheese and cream of coconut at medium speed with an electric mixer until smooth. Add pudding mix, beating until blended.
3. Stir in coconut; fold in whipped topping. Spread cheese mixture evenly into prepared crust; cover and chill 2 hours or until set.
4. Beat whipping cream with an electric mixer until soft peaks form, and spread evenly over top of pie. Garnish, if desired. Store in refrigerator.
Note: For testing purposes only, we used Jell-O Instant Pudding Cheesecake flavor.

Margarita-Key Lime Pie With Gingersnap Crust

MAKES 8 TO 10 SERVINGS
PREP: 25 MIN., COOL: 2 HRS., FREEZE: 2 HRS., STAND: 20 MIN.

4 large eggs
½ cup fresh Key lime juice
¼ cup orange liqueur
¼ cup tequila
2 (14-ounce) cans sweetened condensed milk
2 teaspoons grated lime rind
2 cups whipping cream
Gingersnap Crust
Garnishes: lime rind curls, sweetened whipped cream

1. Combine first 5 ingredients in a heavy saucepan over medium heat, stirring often, 20 minutes or until temperature reaches 165°; remove from heat. Stir in lime rind; cool 2 hours or until completely cooled.

2. Beat whipping cream at high speed with an electric mixer until soft peaks form. Fold into egg mixture. Spoon into Gingersnap Crust.

3. Freeze 2 hours or until firm. Let stand 20 minutes before cutting. Garnish, if desired. Store in refrigerator.

Gingersnap Crust:

MAKES 1 (9-INCH) CRUST
PREP: 15 MIN., BAKE: 8 MIN.

¾ cup sweetened flaked coconut, toasted
18 gingersnap cookies, crumbled
3 tablespoons unsalted butter, melted

1. Stir together all ingredients. Press into bottom and up sides of a 9-inch pieplate.

2. Bake at 350° for 8 minutes. Cool on a wire rack.

Classic Chess Pie

Chess pie commonly has a simple filling of eggs, sugar, butter, and flour. We've added three flavorful variations to this traditional recipe.

MAKES 8 SERVINGS
PREP: 23 MIN.; BAKE: 1 HR., 2 MIN.

½ (15-ounce) package refrigerated piecrusts
2 cups sugar
2 tablespoons cornmeal
1 tablespoon all-purpose flour
¼ teaspoon salt
½ cup butter or margarine, melted
¼ cup milk
1 tablespoon white vinegar
½ teaspoon vanilla extract
4 large eggs, lightly beaten

1. Fit piecrust into a 9-inch pieplate according to package directions; fold edges under, and crimp. Line piecrust with aluminum foil, and fill with pie weights or dried beans.
2. Bake at 425° for 4 to 5 minutes. Remove weights and foil; bake 2 more minutes or until golden. Cool.
3. Stir together sugar and next 7 ingredients until blended. Add eggs, stirring well. Pour into piecrust.
4. Bake at 350° for 50 to 55 minutes, shielding edges with aluminum foil after 10 minutes to prevent excessive browning. Cool completely on a wire rack.

Coconut Chess Pie: Prepare filling as directed above; stir in 1 cup toasted flaked coconut before pouring into piecrust. Bake as directed above.

Chocolate-Pecan Chess Pie: Prepare filling as directed above; stir in 3½ tablespoons cocoa and ½ cup toasted chopped pecans before pouring into piecrust. Bake as directed above.

Lemon Chess Pie: Prepare filling as directed above; stir in ⅓ cup lemon juice and 2 teaspoons grated lemon rind before pouring into piecrust. Bake as directed above.

Easy Pecan Pie

This pie will keep for a day well-covered at room temperature; then store it in the refrigerator.

MAKES 8 SERVINGS
PREP: 10 MIN., BAKE: 55 MIN.

1 (15-ounce) package refrigerated piecrusts
3 large eggs
1 cup sugar
¾ cup light corn syrup
2 tablespoons butter or margarine, melted
2 teaspoons vanilla extract
¼ teaspoon salt
1½ cups pecan halves*

1. Unroll and stack 2 piecrusts; gently roll or press piecrusts together. Fit into a 9-inch pieplate according to package directions; fold piecrust edges under, and crimp.
2. Stir together eggs and next 5 ingredients; stir in pecan halves. Pour filling into piecrust.
3. Bake at 350° for 55 minutes or until set. Serve warm or cold.
*Chopped pecans, a less expensive choice, may be substituted for the pecan halves.

Tiramisù Toffee Trifle Pie

Tiramisù Toffee Trifle Pie

This easy-to-make pie is elegant enough for the holidays yet simple enough for an "everyday" dessert.

MAKES 8 TO 10 SERVINGS
PREP: 30 MIN., CHILL: 8 HRS.

1½ tablespoons instant coffee granules
¾ cup warm water
1 (10.75-ounce) frozen pound cake, thawed
1 (8-ounce) package cream cheese or mascarpone, softened
½ cup powdered sugar
½ cup chocolate syrup
1 (12-ounce) container frozen whipped topping, thawed and divided
2 (1.4-ounce) English toffee candy bars, coarsely chopped

1. Stir together coffee granules and ¾ cup warm water until granules are dissolved. Cool.
2. Cut pound cake into 14 slices. Cut each slice in half diagonally. Line bottom and sides of a 9-inch deep-dish pieplate with pound cake triangles; trim around top of pieplate, if necessary. Drizzle coffee over cake.
3. Beat cream cheese, sugar, and chocolate syrup at medium speed with an electric mixer until smooth. Add 2½ cups whipped topping, and beat until light and fluffy.
4. Spread cheese mixture evenly over cake. Dollop remaining whipped topping around edges of pie. Sprinkle with chopped candy. Chill 8 hours.
To Make Ahead: This may be made the day before serving. Store in refrigerator.

Frozen Chocolate Brownie Pie

With a rich brownie crust and creamy ice cream filling, there won't be a scoop of this delectable dessert left.

MAKES 10 TO 12 SERVINGS
PREP: 30 MIN., BAKE: 15 MIN., FREEZE: 8 HRS.

¼ cup butter or margarine
⅔ cup firmly packed brown sugar
½ cup egg substitute
¼ cup buttermilk
¼ cup all-purpose flour
⅓ cup unsweetened cocoa
¼ teaspoon salt
1 teaspoon vanilla extract
½ gallon vanilla fat-free frozen yogurt, softened
1 quart chocolate fat-free frozen yogurt, softened
¾ cup chocolate syrup

1. Melt butter in a large saucepan over medium-high heat; whisk in brown sugar. Remove from heat; cool slightly. Add egg substitute and buttermilk, stirring mixture well.
2. Combine flour, cocoa, and salt; add to buttermilk mixture, stirring until blended. Stir in vanilla. Pour into a lightly greased 9-inch springform pan.
3. Bake at 350° for 15 minutes. Cool completely in pan on a wire rack.
4. Spread half of vanilla yogurt over brownie; spread chocolate yogurt over vanilla yogurt, and top with remaining vanilla yogurt. Cover and freeze 8 hours. Serve with chocolate syrup.

Strawberry Tart

Strawberry Tart

MAKES 8 SERVINGS
PREP: 20 MIN., CHILL: 5 HRS., BAKE: 18 MIN.

1 ½ cups all-purpose flour
½ teaspoon salt
⅓ cup sugar
⅓ cup cold butter or margarine,
      cut up
2 tablespoons cold shortening
3 tablespoons cold water
½ cup sugar
¼ cup cornstarch
2 cups half-and-half
5 egg yolks
1 teaspoon rose water or orange-flower water
      (optional)
3 tablespoons butter or margarine
1 teaspoon vanilla extract
1 quart fresh strawberries, sliced
Garnish: fresh mint sprig

1. Pulse first 3 ingredients in a blender or food processor 3 or 4 times or until combined.

2. Add ⅓ cup butter and 2 tablespoons shortening; pulse 5 or 6 times or until crumbly. With blender or processor running, gradually add 3 tablespoons water, and process until dough forms a ball and leaves sides of bowl, adding more water if necessary. Wrap dough in plastic wrap, and chill 1 hour.

3. Roll dough to ⅛-inch thickness on a lightly floured surface. Press into bottom and up sides of a 9-inch tart pan. Line dough with parchment paper; fill with pie weights or dried beans.

4. Bake at 425° for 15 minutes. Remove weights and parchment paper, and bake 3 more minutes.

5. Combine ½ cup sugar and ¼ cup cornstarch in a medium saucepan.

6. Whisk together half-and-half, egg yolks, and, if desired, rose water. Gradually whisk half-and-half mixture into sugar mixture in saucepan over medium heat. Bring to a boil, and cook, whisking constantly, 1 minute. Remove from heat.

7. Stir in 3 tablespoons butter and 1 teaspoon vanilla; cover and chill at least 4 hours. Spoon into prepared pastry shell; top with strawberry slices, and garnish, if desired. Serve immediately.

Lime Tart

MAKES 8 SERVINGS
PREP: 10 MIN., FREEZE: 1 HR., BAKE: 26 MIN., COOK: 5 MIN.,
CHILL: 8 HRS.

Pastry
1 cup sugar
¾ cup fresh orange juice
½ cup fresh lime juice
2 tablespoons cornstarch
½ cup whipping cream
6 egg yolks
2 large eggs
¼ cup unsalted butter

1. Roll Pastry into a 13-inch round on a lightly floured surface. Fit into a 9-inch round tart pan; trim edges. Cover and freeze Pastry 1 hour.
2. Line prepared Pastry with aluminum foil, and fill with pie weights or dried beans.
3. Bake at 400° for 10 to 12 minutes. Remove weights and foil; bake 14 minutes or until golden.
4. Whisk together sugar and next 6 ingredients in a medium saucepan until blended; add butter. Bring to a boil over medium heat, whisking constantly; boil 1 minute. Cool slightly; pour into Pastry shell. Place heavy duty plastic wrap directly on lime filling to prevent a film from forming, and chill 8 hours.

Pastry:

MAKES 1 (9-INCH) PASTRY SHELL
PREP: 10 MIN., CHILL: 30 MIN.

1¼ cups all-purpose flour
2 tablespoons sugar
½ teaspoon salt
½ cup cold unsalted butter, cubed
1 egg yolk
1 to 2 tablespoons cold water

1. Pulse first 3 ingredients in a food processor 3 or 4 times or until combined. Add cold butter, and pulse 5 or 6 times or until mixture resembles coarse meal. With processor running, add egg yolk and 1 tablespoon water; process until dough forms a ball and leaves sides of bowl, adding more water if necessary. Cover and chill 30 minutes.

Blackberry Pudding Tarts

MAKES 8 TARTS
PREP: 20 MIN., COOK: 25 MIN.

1 (10-ounce) package frozen tart shells
2 quarts fresh blackberries*
1 cup water
1½ cups sugar
½ cup self-rising flour
¼ cup butter or margarine
2 teaspoons vanilla extract
1 cup whipping cream
¼ cup sugar
⅛ teaspoon vanilla extract
Garnish: fresh blackberries, mint sprigs

1. Bake tart shells according to package directions, and cool completely.
2. Bring blackberries and 1 cup water to a boil over medium heat. Reduce heat, and simmer 5 minutes or until blackberries are soft.
3. Mash blackberries with a fork, and pour through a wire-mesh strainer into a 4-cup liquid measuring cup, using the back of a spoon to squeeze out 2 cups juice. Discard pulp and seeds. (Boil juice to reduce to 2 cups, if necessary.)
4. Combine 1½ cups sugar and flour in a saucepan; gradually add blackberry juice, whisking constantly until smooth. Bring to a boil over medium heat, whisking constantly. Reduce heat, and simmer 3 minutes or until thickened. Remove from heat. Stir in butter and 2 teaspoons vanilla.
5. Spoon filling into prepared tart shells. Cool tarts completely.
6. Beat whipping cream at high speed with an electric mixer until foamy; gradually add ¼ cup sugar, beating until stiff peaks form. Fold in ⅛ teaspoon vanilla. Dollop whipped cream over tarts; garnish, if desired.
*2 (14-ounce) packages frozen blackberries, thawed, may be substituted.

Nectarine Cobbler With Blueberry Muffin Crust

MAKES 8 SERVINGS
PREP: 30 MIN., COOK: 10 MIN., BAKE: 25 MIN.

4 pounds nectarines, peeled and sliced*
¾ cup sugar
2 tablespoons all-purpose flour
¼ cup butter
Blueberry Muffin Batter
Vanilla ice cream

1. Toss together first 3 ingredients in a large bowl.
2. Melt ¼ cup butter in a large skillet over medium-high heat. Add nectarine mixture to skillet; bring to a boil, and cook, stirring often, 5 minutes. Spoon hot nectarine mixture into a lightly greased 13- x 9-inch baking dish. Spoon Blueberry Muffin Batter evenly over hot nectarine mixture.
3. Bake at 400° for 25 minutes or until crust is golden. Serve with vanilla ice cream. Store leftovers in refrigerator.
*3 (21-ounce) cans peach pie filling may be substituted for nectarines. Omit sugar and flour. Melt butter in a large skillet over medium-high heat. Add peach pie filling, and bring to a boil; remove from heat. Proceed with recipe as directed.

Blueberry Muffin Batter:

MAKES ABOUT 4 CUPS
PREP: 10 MIN.

2 cups all-purpose flour
¼ cup sugar
1 tablespoon baking powder
½ teaspoon salt
1 cup milk
¼ cup vegetable oil
1 large egg, lightly beaten
1 cup fresh or frozen blueberries

1. Combine flour, sugar, baking powder, and salt in a large mixing bowl; make a well in center of mixture. Stir together milk, vegetable oil, and egg; add to dry ingredients, and stir just until moistened. Gently fold in 1 cup blueberries.

Blueberry Muffins: Spoon Blueberry Muffin Batter evenly into lightly greased muffin pan cups, filling two-thirds full. Bake at 400° for 20 to 25 minutes. Makes 1 dozen.

Pecan-Peach Cobbler

Two Southern favorites come together to create this delicious, deep-baked dessert.

MAKES 8 TO 10 SERVINGS
PREP: 35 MIN., STAND: 10 MIN., COOK: 15 MIN., BAKE: 43 MIN.

12 to 15 fresh peaches, peeled and sliced
       (about 16 cups)*
3 cups sugar
⅓ cup all-purpose flour
½ teaspoon nutmeg
1½ teaspoons vanilla extract
⅔ cup butter
2 (15-ounce) packages refrigerated piecrusts
½ cup chopped pecans, toasted
¼ cup sugar
Vanilla ice cream

1. Combine first 4 ingredients in a Dutch oven, and let stand 10 minutes or until sugar dissolves. Bring peach mixture to a boil over medium heat; reduce heat to low, and simmer 10 minutes or until tender. Remove from heat; add vanilla and butter, stirring until butter melts.
2. Unroll 2 piecrusts. Sprinkle ¼ cup pecans and 2 tablespoons sugar evenly over 1 piecrust; top with other piecrust. Roll to a 12-inch circle, gently pressing pecans into pastry. Cut into 1½-inch strips. Repeat with remaining 2 piecrusts, ¼ cup pecans, and 2 tablespoons sugar.
3. Spoon half of peach mixture into a lightly greased 13- x 9-inch baking dish. Arrange half of pastry strips in a lattice design over top of peach mixture.
4. Bake at 475° for 20 to 25 minutes or until lightly browned. Spoon remaining peach mixture over baked pastry. Top with remaining pastry strips in a lattice design. Bake 15 to 18 more minutes. Serve warm or cold with vanilla ice cream. Store leftovers in refrigerator.
*2 (20-ounce) packages frozen peaches may be substituted. Reduce sugar to 2 cups, flour to 3 tablespoons, and nutmeg to ¼ teaspoon. Proceed as directed.
To Make Ahead: Let baked cobbler cool; cover and freeze up to 1 month. Thaw in refrigerator overnight. Uncover, and reheat at 250° for 45 minutes.

The Best of Southern Living p6

p323 Mocha Torte

p324 Pecan Pie Cheesecake

p325 German Chocolate Cheesecake

p328 Extra Rich Chocolate Cake

p329 Cola Cake

p329 Milk Chocolate Bar Cake

p331 Sweet Lemon Baby Cakes

Pies

p337 Frozen Chocolate Brownie Pie

Cobblers

p340 Nectarine Cobbler with Blueberry Muffin Crust

p340 Pecan Peach Cobbler

p343 Blackberry Cobbler

Caramel-Apple Cobbler With
Toasted Pecan Ice Cream

Caramel-Apple Cobbler With Toasted Pecan Ice Cream

MAKES 8 SERVINGS
PREP: 45 MIN., COOK: 30 MIN., BAKE: 35 MIN.

½ cup butter or margarine
12 large Granny Smith apples, peeled and sliced
2 cups sugar
2 tablespoons lemon juice
1 (15-ounce) package refrigerated piecrusts
Toasted Pecan Ice Cream
Garnishes: finely chopped toasted pecans, decorative
    piecrust shapes

1. Melt butter in a large Dutch oven over medium-high heat. Add apples, sugar, and juice; cook, stirring often, 20 to 25 minutes or until apples are caramel colored. Spoon into a shallow, greased 2-quart baking dish.
2. Unroll 1 piecrust; cut into ½-inch strips. Arrange strips in a lattice design over filling; fold edges under.
3. Bake cobbler at 425° for 20 to 25 minutes or until crust is golden. Serve warm with Toasted Pecan Ice Cream.

Garnish, if desired. Store leftovers in refrigerator.
To make decorative piecrust shapes: Unroll remaining piecrust; cut apple shapes with a 1½-inch apple-shaped cookie cutter. Place on a baking sheet, and bake at 400° for 6 to 8 minutes or until golden.

Toasted Pecan Ice Cream:
For grown-ups, bourbon adds sweet, spirited flavor.

MAKES 2 PINTS
PREP: 5 MIN., FREEZE: 4 HRS.

2 pints homemade-style vanilla ice cream, softened
1 cup chopped toasted pecans
¼ cup bourbon (optional)

1. Stir together ice cream, chopped pecans, and, if desired, bourbon; freeze 4 hours.
Note: For testing purposes only, we used Blue Bell Homemade Vanilla Ice Cream.

Too-Easy Cherry
Cobbler

Too-Easy Cherry Cobbler

Save even more time by using crustless white bread for the topping.

MAKES 4 TO 6 SERVINGS
PREP: 15 MIN., BAKE: 45 MIN.

2 (20-ounce) cans cherry pie filling
1 (15-ounce) can pitted dark sweet cherries in heavy
    syrup, drained
1/4 cup all-purpose flour, divided
1/2 teaspoon almond extract
5 white bread slices
1 1/4 cups sugar
1/2 cup butter or margarine, melted
1 large egg
1 1/2 teaspoons grated lemon rind

1. Stir together pie filling, cherries, and 2 tablespoons flour. Stir in almond extract. Place in a lightly greased 8-inch square baking dish.
2. Trim crusts from bread slices; cut each slice into 5 strips. Arrange bread strips over fruit mixture.
3. Stir together remaining 2 tablespoons flour, sugar, and next 3 ingredients; drizzle over bread strips.
4. Bake at 350° for 35 to 45 minutes or until golden and bubbly. Store leftovers in refrigerator.

Too-Easy Peach Cobbler: Substitute 2 (16-ounce) packages frozen peaches, thawed and drained, for cherry pie filling and canned cherries. Omit almond extract and grated lemon rind. Proceed as directed.

Too-Easy Berry Cobbler: Substitute 1 (21-ounce) can blueberry pie filling and 2 (10-ounce) packages frozen whole strawberries, unthawed, for cherry pie filling and canned cherries. Omit almond extract; add 1 teaspoon vanilla extract and 1 teaspoon lemon juice. Proceed as directed.

Blackberry Cobbler

This recipe is a great excuse to go blackberry picking! Blackberries can be frozen for up to a year. However, you can use fresh or frozen blackberries in this down-home dish. (pictured on cover)

MAKES 8 SERVINGS
PREP: 10 MIN., BAKE: 45 MIN.

1 1/3 cups sugar
1/2 cup all-purpose flour
1/2 cup butter or margarine, melted
2 teaspoons vanilla extract
2 (14-ounce) bags frozen blackberries, unthawed*
1/2 (15-ounce) package refrigerated piecrusts
1 tablespoon sugar
Vanilla ice cream (optional)

1. Stir together first 4 ingredients in a large bowl. Gently stir in blackberries until sugar mixture is crumbly. Spoon fruit mixture into a lightly greased 11- x 7-inch baking dish.
2. Cut piecrust into 1-inch-wide strips, and arrange strips in a lattice design over blackberry mixture. Sprinkle top with 1 tablespoon sugar.
3. Bake at 425° for 45 minutes or until crust is golden and center is bubbly. Serve with ice cream, if desired. Store leftovers in refrigerator.
*5 (6-ounce) packages fresh blackberries may be substituted.

Clear-the-Cupboard
Cookies

Clear-the-Cupboard Cookies

MAKES 4½ DOZEN
PREP: 20 MIN., BAKE: 15 MIN. PER BATCH

1 cup shortening
1 cup granulated sugar
1 cup firmly packed brown sugar
2 large eggs
2 cups all-purpose flour
1 cup uncooked regular oats
1 teaspoon baking soda
1 teaspoon baking powder
1 teaspoon salt
1 cup flaked coconut
1 cup crisp rice cereal
1 teaspoon vanilla extract
1 cup chopped pecans, toasted (optional)

1. Beat shortening at medium speed with an electric mixer until fluffy; add sugars, beating well. Add eggs, beating until blended.
2. Combine flour and next 4 ingredients; gradually add to sugar mixture, beating until blended. Stir in coconut, cereal, vanilla, and, if desired, pecans. Drop by table-spoonfuls onto baking sheets.
3. Bake, in batches, at 350° for 10 to 15 minutes or until lightly golden. Remove to wire racks to cool.

Nutty Oatmeal-Chocolate Chunk Cookies

Chopped candy bars add a flavorful surprise to a traditional chocolate chip cookie recipe.

MAKES 6 DOZEN
PREP: 10 MIN., BAKE: 8 MIN. PER BATCH

2½ cups uncooked regular oats
1 cup butter or margarine, softened
1 cup granulated sugar
1 cup firmly packed brown sugar
2 large eggs
1 tablespoon vanilla extract
2 cups all-purpose flour
1 teaspoon baking powder
1 teaspoon baking soda
½ teaspoon salt
3 (1.55-ounce) milk chocolate candy bars, chopped
1½ cups chopped pecans

1. Process oats in a food processor until ground.
2. Beat butter and sugars at medium speed with an electric mixer until fluffy. Add eggs and vanilla; beat until blended.
3. Combine ground oats, flour, and next 3 ingredients. Add to butter mixture, beating until blended. Stir in chocolate and pecans.
4. Drop dough by tablespoonfuls onto ungreased baking sheets.
5. Bake, in batches, at 375° for 7 to 8 minutes or until golden brown; remove to wire racks to cool.

Soft Coconut Macaroons

If you're not preparing macaroons for Passover, use ¼ cup all-purpose flour instead of ¼ cup matzo meal.

MAKES 2 DOZEN
PREP: 10 MIN., BAKE: 20 MIN.

4 egg whites
2⅔ cups sweetened flaked coconut
⅔ cup sugar
¼ cup matzo meal
½ teaspoon clear vanilla extract*
¼ teaspoon salt
¼ to ½ teaspoon almond extract

1. Stir together all ingredients in a large bowl, blending well. Drop dough by teaspoonfuls onto lightly greased baking sheets.
2. Bake at 325° for 18 to 20 minutes. Remove to wire racks to cool.
*Using clear vanilla extract will keep the macaroons pearly white, but if you don't have it, use regular vanilla.

Pecan Squares

This recipe is adapted from The Silver Palate Cookbook *(Workman, 1982). We use salted butter and bring the filling to a rolling boil before pouring it over the crust.*

MAKES ABOUT 28 SQUARES
PREP: 20 MIN., BAKE: 50 MIN.

2 cups all-purpose flour
2/3 cup powdered sugar
3/4 cup butter, softened
1/2 cup firmly packed brown sugar
1/2 cup honey
2/3 cup butter
3 tablespoons whipping cream
3 1/2 cups coarsely chopped pecans

1. Sift together flour and powdered sugar. Cut in 3/4 cup softened butter using a pastry blender or fork just until mixture resembles coarse meal. Pat mixture on bottom and 1 1/2 inches up sides of a lightly greased 13- x 9-inch baking dish.

2. Bake at 350° for 20 minutes or until edges are lightly browned. Cool.

3. Bring brown sugar, honey, 2/3 cup butter, and whipping cream to a boil in a saucepan over medium-high heat. Stir in chopped pecans, and pour hot filling into prepared crust.

4. Bake at 350° for 25 to 30 minutes or until golden and bubbly. Cool completely in pan on a wire rack before cutting into 2-inch squares.

Walnut-Date Bars

Wrap these chewy treats in plastic wrap, and place them in a zip-top freezer bag; freeze up to three months, if desired.

MAKES 16 BARS
PREP: 20 MIN., BAKE: 35 MIN., STAND: 30 MIN.

1 (18.25-ounce) package yellow cake mix
²/₃ cup firmly packed brown sugar
2 large eggs
³/₄ cup butter or margarine, melted
2 cups chopped dates, divided
2 cups chopped walnuts or pecans, divided

1. Combine cake mix and brown sugar in a mixing bowl. Add eggs and melted butter, beating at medium speed with an electric mixer until blended. (Batter will be stiff.) Spoon half of batter into a lightly greased 13- x 9-inch pan; sprinkle with 1 cup each of dates and walnuts.
2. Stir remaining 1 cup each of dates and walnuts into remaining batter; spread over mixture in pan.
3. Bake at 350° for 30 to 35 minutes or until golden. Run a knife around edge of pan to loosen sides. Let stand 30 minutes before cutting. Cut into squares, and store bars in an airtight container.

Frosted Peanut Butter Brownies

MAKES 6 DOZEN
PREP: 20 MIN., COOK: 10 MIN., BAKE: 20 MIN., CHILL: 50 MIN.

1½ cups butter or margarine, divided
¹/₃ cup unsweetened cocoa
2 cups granulated sugar
1½ cups all-purpose flour
½ teaspoon salt
4 large eggs
1 teaspoon vanilla extract
1 (18-ounce) jar chunky peanut butter
¹/₃ cup milk
10 large marshmallows
¼ cup unsweetened cocoa
1 (16-ounce) package powdered sugar

1. Cook 1 cup butter and ¹/₃ cup cocoa in a saucepan over low heat until butter melts, stirring often. Remove from heat, and cool slightly.
2. Combine granulated sugar, flour, and salt in a large mixing bowl. Add chocolate mixture, and beat at medium speed with an electric mixer until blended.

Add eggs, 1 at a time, beating just until blended; stir in vanilla. Spread mixture into a greased 15- x 10-inch jelly-roll pan.
3. Bake at 350° for 20 minutes or until a wooden pick inserted in center comes out clean.
4. Remove lid from peanut butter jar; microwave peanut butter at MEDIUM (50% power) 2 minutes, stirring once. Spread over warm brownies. Chill 30 minutes.
5. Cook milk, marshmallows, and remaining ½ cup butter in a large saucepan over medium heat, stirring often, until marshmallows melt. Remove from heat, and whisk in ¼ cup cocoa. Gradually stir in powdered sugar until smooth. Spread over peanut butter; chill 20 minutes. Cut into squares.

Double-Chocolate Brownies

Two kinds of chocolate will lure you to try these decadent brownies.

MAKES 2 DOZEN
PREP: 10 MIN., BAKE: 35 MIN.

1 cup butter or margarine, softened
2 cups sugar
4 large eggs
1 cup unsweetened cocoa
1 teaspoon vanilla extract
1 cup all-purpose flour
1 cup chopped pecans
²/₃ cup white chocolate or semisweet chocolate morsels

1. Beat butter at medium speed with an electric mixer until creamy; gradually add sugar, beating well. Add eggs, 1 at a time, beating just until blended.
2. Add cocoa and vanilla; beat at low speed 1 minute or until blended. Gradually add flour, beating well.
3. Stir in pecans and chocolate morsels. Pour batter into a greased 13- x 9-inch baking pan.
4. Bake at 350° for 30 to 35 minutes or until done. Cool and cut into squares.

Crispy Peanut Squares (top),
Luscious Lemon Bars
(middle), and Layered
Apricot Bars (bottom)

Luscious Lemon Bars

MAKES 2½ DOZEN
PREP: 15 MIN., BAKE: 50 MIN.

2¼ cups all-purpose flour, divided
½ cup powdered sugar
1 cup butter or margarine, softened
4 large eggs
2 cups granulated sugar
⅓ cup lemon juice
½ teaspoon baking powder
Powdered sugar

1. Combine 2 cups flour and ½ cup powdered sugar.
2. Cut butter into flour mixture with a pastry blender until crumbly. Firmly press mixture into a lightly greased 13- x 9-inch pan.
3. Bake at 350° for 20 to 25 minutes or until lightly browned.
4. Whisk eggs in a large bowl; whisk in 2 cups granulated sugar and lemon juice. Combine remaining ¼ cup flour and baking powder; whisk into egg mixture. Pour batter over crust.
5. Bake at 350° for 25 minutes or until set. Let cool completely in pan on a wire rack. Cut into bars, and sprinkle evenly with additional powdered sugar.

Crispy Peanut Squares

This little melt-in-your-mouth bar cookie will remind you of a Rice Krispy Treat with a peanutty flavor.

MAKES 4 DOZEN
PREP: 10 MIN., CHILL: 1 HR.

1 cup sugar
1 cup light corn syrup
1 cup creamy peanut butter
1 teaspoon vanilla extract
6 cups crisp rice cereal squares
1 cup peanuts

1. Combine sugar, corn syrup, and peanut butter in a glass bowl; microwave at HIGH 3 to 4 minutes or until melted, stirring once. Stir in vanilla extract.
2. Fold in cereal and peanuts. Spread mixture into a lightly greased 13- x 9-inch pan. Cover and chill 1 hour or until set; cut into small squares.

Layered Apricot Bars

MAKES 1½ DOZEN
PREP: 25 MIN.; COOK: 20 MIN.; BAKE: 1 HR., 5 MIN.

1 (6-ounce) package dried apricots
½ cup butter or margarine, softened
¼ cup granulated sugar
1⅓ cups all-purpose flour, divided
2 large eggs
¾ cup firmly packed brown sugar
½ teaspoon baking powder
¼ teaspoon salt
½ cup chopped walnuts
1 teaspoon vanilla extract
Powdered sugar

1. Bring apricots and water to cover to a boil in a small saucepan. Reduce heat, and simmer, uncovered, 15 minutes or until tender. Drain and coarsely chop apricots; set aside.
2. Beat butter at medium speed with an electric mixer until creamy; gradually add granulated sugar, beating well. Stir in 1 cup flour, and press mixture into a lightly greased aluminum foil-lined 9-inch square pan.
3. Bake at 350° for 15 to 20 minutes or until lightly browned.
4. Beat eggs at medium speed until thick and pale; gradually add brown sugar, beating well. Add remaining ⅓ cup flour, baking powder, and salt, beating well. Stir in chopped apricot, walnuts, and vanilla; spread mixture evenly over crust.
5. Bake at 325° for 45 minutes. Let cool completely in pan on a wire rack. Cut into bars; sprinkle with powdered sugar.

Mocha-Chocolate
Shortbread

Mocha-Chocolate Shortbread

MAKES 50 TRIANGLES
PREP: 15 MIN., BAKE: 20 MIN., COOL: 30 MIN.

1¼ cups all-purpose flour
½ cup powdered sugar
2 teaspoons instant coffee granules
⅔ cup butter or margarine,
     softened
½ teaspoon vanilla extract
2 cups (12 ounces) semisweet chocolate morsels,
     divided
Coffee or vanilla ice cream (optional)

1. Combine first 3 ingredients in a medium mixing bowl; add butter and vanilla, and beat at low speed with an electric mixer until blended. Stir in 1 cup chocolate morsels.

2. Press dough into an ungreased 9-inch square pan; prick with a fork.

3. Bake at 325° for 20 minutes or until lightly browned. Sprinkle remaining 1 cup morsels over top of warm shortbread, and spread to cover. Cut shortbread in pan into 25 (about 1¾-inch) squares; cut each square into 2 triangles. Let cool 30 minutes in pan before removing. Serve with ice cream, if desired.

Pralines

MAKES ABOUT 2½ DOZEN
PREP: 10 MIN., COOK: 30 MIN.

1½ cups granulated sugar
1½ cups firmly packed brown sugar
1 cup evaporated milk
¼ cup butter or margarine
2 cups pecan halves, toasted
1 teaspoon vanilla extract

1. Bring sugars and milk to a boil in a Dutch oven, stirring often. Cook over medium heat, stirring often, 11 minutes or until a candy thermometer registers 228° (thread stage).
2. Stir in butter and pecan halves; cook, stirring constantly, until candy thermometer registers 236° (soft ball stage).
3. Remove mixture from heat; stir in vanilla. Beat with a wooden spoon 1 to 2 minutes or just until mixture begins to thicken. Quickly drop pralines by heaping tablespoonfuls onto buttered wax paper or parchment paper, and let stand until firm.

Cherry-Pistachio Bark

Lightly grease the cutter with cooking spray to make cutting easier.

MAKES 3½ POUNDS
PREP: 10 MIN., COOK: 5 MIN., CHILL: 1 HR.

1¼ cups dried cherries
2 tablespoons water
2 (12-ounce) packages white chocolate morsels
6 (2-ounce) vanilla candy coating squares
1¼ cups chopped red or green pistachios

1. Microwave cherries and 2 tablespoons water in a small glass bowl at HIGH 2 minutes; drain.
2. Melt chocolate morsels and candy coating in a heavy saucepan over low heat. Remove from heat; stir in cherries and pistachios. Spread into a wax paper-lined 15- x 10-inch jelly-roll pan.
3. Chill 1 hour or until firm. Cut with a 3-inch heart-shaped cookie cutter. Store in an airtight container.

Texas Millionaires

Store these candies in the refrigerator rather than the freezer because freezer temperatures can change the color of the chocolate.

MAKES 4 DOZEN
PREP: 25 MIN., COOK: 10 MIN., COOL: 5 MIN., CHILL: 1 HR.

1 (14-ounce) package caramels, unwrapped
2 tablespoons butter or margarine
2 tablespoons water
3 cups pecan halves
1 cup (6 ounces) semisweet chocolate morsels
8 (2-ounce) vanilla candy coating squares

1. Cook caramels, butter, and 2 tablespoons water in a heavy saucepan over low heat, stirring constantly until smooth. Stir in pecan halves. Cool in pan 5 minutes.
2. Drop mixture by tablespoonfuls onto lightly greased wax paper. Chill candies 1 hour (or freeze 20 minutes), or until firm.
3. Melt morsels and candy coating in a heavy saucepan over low heat, stirring until smooth. Dip caramel candies into chocolate mixture, allowing excess to drip off; place on lightly greased wax paper or parchment paper. Let stand until firm.

Strawberry
Meringue Parfaits

Strawberry Meringue Parfaits

If you're short on time, you can substitute store-bought meringues for homemade ones.

MAKES 6 SERVINGS
PREP: 15 MIN., COOK: 15 MIN., CHILL: 6 HRS.

1 quart fresh strawberries, sliced
1¾ cups sugar, divided
¼ cup cornstarch
4 egg yolks
3 cups milk or half-and-half
¼ cup butter or margarine
2 teaspoons vanilla extract
Meringues

1. Sprinkle sliced strawberries with ¼ cup sugar.
2. Combine remaining 1½ cups sugar and cornstarch in a large saucepan over medium heat. Gradually whisk in egg yolks and milk; cook milk mixture, whisking often, 12 minutes or until thickened. Bring milk mixture to a boil, and cook, stirring constantly, 1 minute. Remove mixture from heat; stir in butter and vanilla extract. Cover and chill 6 hours.
3. Spoon half of custard evenly into 6 parfait glasses; top with half of sliced strawberries and 3 Meringues. Repeat layers, ending with 1 Meringue on top of each serving. Serve remaining meringues with parfaits.

Meringues:

MAKES ABOUT 2½ DOZEN
PREP: 20 MIN., BAKE: 2 HRS., STAND: 8 HRS.

4 egg whites
1 teaspoon cream of tartar
¼ teaspoon almond extract
¼ cup sugar

1. Beat egg whites at medium speed with an electric mixer until foamy; add cream of tartar and almond extract, beating until blended. Gradually add sugar, beating until stiff peaks form and sugar dissolves.
2. Pipe or dollop mixture into small 2-inch cookie shapes or other desired shapes onto a parchment paper-lined baking sheet.
3. Bake at 200° for 2 hours. Turn oven off; let meringues stand in closed oven with light on 8 hours.

Two-Layered Ice-Cream Freeze

No one will guess that this version of spumoni, an Italian ice cream, is actually a light dessert.

MAKES 8 SERVINGS
PREP: 30 MIN.; FREEZE: 3 HRS., 30 MIN.

2 cups no-sugar-added, fat-free vanilla ice cream, softened
1 (16-ounce) container fat-free frozen whipped topping, thawed and divided
1 teaspoon almond extract
10 store-bought vanilla meringue cookies, crushed
2 cups no-sugar-added, fat-free chocolate fudge ice cream, softened
1½ cups fresh or frozen raspberries, thawed
¼ cup sugar
1 tablespoon lemon juice

1. Stir together vanilla ice cream, ½ cup whipped topping, and almond extract. Spoon mixture into a plastic wrap-lined 2-quart glass bowl, and freeze 15 minutes or until set.
2. Stir together 1½ cups whipped topping and cookie crumbs; spread evenly over vanilla ice-cream mixture, and freeze 15 minutes or until set.
3. Stir together chocolate fudge ice cream and ½ cup whipped topping. Spread over cookie crumb mixture. Cover and freeze 3 hours or until firm.
4. Process raspberries in a blender or food processor until smooth. Pour through a fine wire-mesh strainer into a small saucepan, pressing pulp with back of a wooden spoon; discard seeds. Bring raspberry puree, sugar, and lemon juice to a boil, stirring constantly; cook, stirring constantly, 2 minutes or until thickened.
5. Remove ice-cream mixture from freezer. Dip glass bowl in warm water 15 seconds. Invert onto a serving dish, discarding plastic wrap. Cut ice cream into wedges; serve with raspberry sauce and, if desired, remaining whipped topping.

Plum Ice Cream

Plum Ice Cream

MAKES 5 CUPS
PREP: 20 MIN., COOK: 5 MIN.

3 cups diced purple or black plums (about 6 plums)
1 cup sugar
3 cups whipping cream

1. Cook plums and sugar in a saucepan over medium heat 5 minutes or until plums are tender and sugar is dissolved.
2. Process plum mixture in a food processor until smooth; pour mixture through a wire-mesh strainer into a large bowl, discarding solids. Stir in whipping cream until blended.
3. Pour into freezer container of a 2- or 4-quart electric ice-cream maker. Freeze according to manufacturer's instructions. (Instructions and times will vary.)

1-2-3 Blackberry Sherbet

Our Test Kitchens awarded its highest rating to this three-ingredient dessert.

MAKES 1 QUART
PREP: 15 MIN., STAND: 30 MIN., FREEZE: 11 HRS.

4 cups fresh blackberries*
2 cups sugar
2 cups buttermilk
Garnishes: blackberries, fresh mint sprigs

1. Stir together blackberries and sugar in a bowl, and let stand 30 minutes.
2. Process blackberry mixture in a food processor or blender until smooth, stopping to scrape down sides. Pour through a fine wire-mesh strainer into a 9-inch square pan, discarding solids; stir in buttermilk. Cover and freeze 8 hours.
3. Break frozen mixture into chunks, and place in a bowl; beat at medium speed with an electric mixer until smooth. Return to pan; cover and freeze 3 hours or until firm. Garnish, if desired.
*2 (14-ounce) packages frozen blackberries, thawed, may be substituted for fresh blackberries.

Ambrosia Sorbet

Look for cream of coconut on the drink aisle of your supermarket, where cocktail mixes are found.

MAKES ABOUT 2 QUARTS
PREP: 10 MIN., COOK: 5 MIN., CHILL: 2 HRS., FREEZE: 20 MIN.

11 to 12 oranges
2 cups water
1 cup sugar
1 cup cream of coconut

1. Grate orange rind in a small bowl to equal 2 teaspoons; set aside. Cut oranges in half, and squeeze halves to equal 3 cups juice; set aside.
2. Bring 2 cups water and sugar to a boil in a large saucepan over high heat. Cook, stirring constantly, 3 minutes or just until sugar dissolves; remove from heat, and cool.
3. Stir in cream of coconut, juice, and grated rind; cover and chill at least 2 hours.
4. Pour mixture into freezer container of a 4-quart electric ice-cream maker, and freeze according to manufacturer's instructions. (Instructions and times will vary.)
Note: For testing purposes only, we used a Rival 4 quart Durable Plastic Bucket Ice-Cream Maker.

Watermelon Sorbet

MAKES 2½ QUARTS
PREP: 15 MIN., COOK: 5 MIN., CHILL: 2 HRS., FREEZE: ABOUT 30 MIN.

4 cups water
2 cups sugar
8 cups seeded, chopped watermelon
1 (12-ounce) can frozen pink lemonade concentrate, thawed and undiluted

1. Bring 4 cups water and sugar just to a boil in a medium saucepan over high heat, stirring until sugar dissolves. Remove sugar syrup from heat. Cool.
2. Process sugar syrup and watermelon, in batches, in a blender until smooth. Stir in lemonade concentrate. Chill 2 hours.
3. Pour mixture into freezer container of a 1-gallon electric ice-cream maker. Freeze according to manufacturer's instructions. (Instructions and times will vary.)

menus for
all occasions

Southwestern-Style Thanksgiving,
page 397

Parmesan-Pecan
Cheese Straws

Wine and Cheese Sampling Party

serves 8 to 10

Parmesan-Pecan Cheese Straws

Tropical Breeze Brie

Rosemary-Dried Tomato Goat Cheese

Assorted cheese and side items
(see suggestions, page 361)

Several wines for sampling

Parmesan-Pecan Cheese Straws

If your kitchen is warm, you may want to refrigerate the other half of the dough while rolling out the first.

MAKES 4 DOZEN
PREP: 25 MIN., BAKE: 10 MIN. PER BATCH, COOL: 3 MIN.

$2/3$ cup shredded Parmesan cheese
$1/2$ cup butter, softened
1 cup all-purpose flour
$1/4$ teaspoon salt
$1/4$ teaspoon ground red pepper
1 tablespoon milk
48 pecan halves

1. Process cheese and butter in a food processor until blended. Add flour, salt, and pepper; process 30 seconds or until mixture forms a ball, stopping to scrape down sides.
2. Divide dough in half; roll each portion into a 12- x 5-inch rectangle (about $1/8$-inch thick) on a lightly floured surface. Cut into 24 ($2\frac{1}{2}$- x 1-inch) strips. Place strips on an ungreased baking sheet; brush tops with milk. Top each strip with 1 pecan half.
3. Bake at 350° for 10 minutes or until lightly browned. Cool 3 minutes on baking sheet; remove to wire racks, and cool completely.

HOW MUCH TO BUY?

Figure out the quantities of cheese and wine you'll need with these tips.

Cheese: Select the number of cheeses to be sampled based on the number of guests. We offer five main choices in the Pairings Chart on page 361. For a group of 10 guests, select three cheeses. For example, you might opt for Brie, Parmesan-Pecan Cheese Straws, and Cheddar. Choose four cheeses for 15 guests; all five for 20 partygoers.

Estimate that each person will sample about 4 ounces of cheese total at the party. Multiply the number of guests by 4, and then divide by 16 to equal the number of pounds. (Round up to the closest pound.) Next, divide the total number of pounds by the number of cheeses you are serving—if you're serving 10 people, that's 40 ounces or $2\frac{1}{2}$ pounds. Round up to 3 pounds. If three cheeses are being served, buy 1 pound of each. (If you are making a recipe, double-check the number of servings with your guest count.)

Wine: Most resources say a 750-milliliter bottle of wine will pour about 6 glasses or about 12 samples. In theory, if you had 10 guests and three cheeses to serve (see example above), you would buy one bottle of wine to pair with each cheese. Those three bottles would allow about a glass-and-a-half per person. If you'd rather be safe than risk being short in supply, go up on the amount.

Tropical Breeze Brie

Tropical Breeze Brie

With its topping of papaya and kiwifruit, this appetizer offers a refreshing summer take on a cheese often served during the winter holidays.

MAKES 8 TO 10 APPETIZER SERVINGS
PREP: 25 MIN., CHILL: 1 HR.

2 kiwifruit, peeled and diced
1 large papaya, peeled, seeded, and diced
1 teaspoon grated fresh ginger
1 tablespoon lime juice
1 tablespoon honey
1 (13.5-ounce) Brie round
1 tablespoon sweetened flaked coconut, toasted
1 star fruit, cut into ¼-inch-thick slices
¼ whole fresh pineapple, cut into 2-inch pieces
Gingersnap cookies

1. Combine first 5 ingredients; cover and chill 1 hour.
2. Remove and discard rind from top of Brie, cutting to within ½ inch of outside edges. Place on a microwave-safe dish. Microwave at HIGH 1 to 1½ minutes or until softened but not melted.
3. Spoon fruit mixture over cheese; sprinkle evenly with coconut. Serve with star fruit, pineapple, and gingersnap cookies.

Rosemary-Dried Tomato Goat Cheese

This is a great recipe to take to any party.

MAKES 8 APPETIZER SERVINGS
PREP: 15 MIN.; STAND: 1 HR., 5 MIN.; BAKE: 8 MIN.

6 dried tomatoes
2 large garlic cloves, minced
4 tablespoons olive oil, divided
1 tablespoon chopped fresh rosemary
1 (16-ounce) French baguette
1 (10-ounce) package goat cheese

1. Place tomatoes in a small bowl; cover with boiling water, and let stand at room temperature 5 minutes. Drain and chop tomatoes. Combine tomatoes, minced garlic, 2 tablespoons olive oil, and chopped rosemary in a small bowl; cover tomato mixture, and let stand 1 hour at room temperature.
2. Slice baguette into ¼-inch-thick slices; place on baking sheets, and brush tops evenly with remaining 2 tablespoons olive oil.
3. Bake at 350° for 8 minutes or until lightly toasted.
4. Stir together 1 tablespoon tomato mixture and goat cheese in a serving bowl. Spoon remaining tomato mixture over top. Serve with toasted baguette slices.

Cheese or Recipe Selection	On the Side	Wine Suggestions	Wine Buzzwords
Brie (try Life in Provence or Supreme brands) OR Tropical Breeze Brie (facing page)	Strawberries, blueberries, green apple slices, grapes, water crackers, pecans Gingersnaps, fruit called for in recipe	Vinum Chenin Blanc, California (white) Rosenblum Vintners Cuvée Blanc IV, California (white blend) Edna Valley Chardonnay, California (white)	Fruity, dry (not sweet), fresh, uncomplicated Everyday, exotic, easy-to-drink, intense Bright lemon, green apple, mango, and vanilla
Spanish manchego (nutty, mild flavor, aged at least 3 months)	Pear slices, grapes, olive oil-brushed-and-toasted French baguette slices	Marqués de Cáceres Rioja, Spain (white) D.O. Calatayud Viña Alarba, Spain (red)	Light, user-friendly, hint of apple, silky, very crisp Sweet cherries and plums with a white pepper sauce
Parmesan-Pecan Cheese Straws (page 359)	Grapes	Michele Chiarlo Barbera D'Asti, Italy (red) Kris Pinot Grigio, Italy (white) Cline Red Truck, California (red)	Fruity, soft, great value for price Soft, flavor of pear, kiwifruit, almond, hint of honey Medium-bodied, complex with black pepper finish
Aged goat cheese (try California Humboldt Fog or French Bucherolle) OR Rosemary-Dried Tomato Goat Cheese (facing page)	Roasted red bell peppers, olives, French baguette slices Olive oil-brushed-and-toasted French baguette slices	Little James' Basket Press Red Table Wine, France Château Graville-Lacoste Graves, France (white)	Rustic, spicy, earthy, herbs, hint of apricot Ripe lush fruit, mineral element, crisp, old-school favorite
Cheddar (aged at least 6 months, cut from wheel shape, wax seal)	Fresh cherries, grapes, cashews (or with an English Cheddar serve pickles, olives, pickled onions)	Saintsbury Carneros Pinot Noir, California (red) King Estate Pinot Gris, Oregon (white)	Elegant, refined, dainty, hint of cherry or berry Lime, grapefruit, pineapple, apple with nutmeg and honey

Couple's Tool Shower

serves 6 to 8

Mexican Shrimp Cocktail

Great Guacamole   Chips

Texas Grilled Sirloin With Serrano Chile Salsa

Spanish rice and flour tortillas

Tangy Citrus Dressed Salad

Aztec Gold

Margaritas, beer, and soft drinks

Margarita Cheesecake

Bakery brownies and cookies

White Chocolate-Dipped Strawberries

PARTY OPTIONS

Whether they're green thumbs or all thumbs, many engaged couples dream of having an enviable garden. For them, a shower to stock the shed, held outside with casual food, would be like azaleas in full bloom—totally divine.

With a little ingenuity, you can turn some nitty-gritty tools into party decorations. Ask guests to drop off unwrapped shower gifts before the party. Add festive bows and gift tags; then display each present. Birdhouses and potted plants are naturals for table decorations, and a wooden fence makes a great gallery wall to display rakes, shovels, and hoes.

Mexican Shrimp Cocktail

MAKES 6 TO 8 APPETIZER SERVINGS
PREP: 30 MIN., COOK: 3 MIN.

2 pounds unpeeled, extra-large fresh shrimp
6 cups water
2 to 3 tablespoons fresh lime juice
3 garlic cloves, pressed
1/4 teaspoon salt
1/2 teaspoon pepper
1 cup ketchup
1/2 cup fresh lime juice
1/4 cup minced sweet onion
1/2 to 1 teaspoon hot sauce
1/2 cup chopped tomato
1/4 cup chopped fresh cilantro

1. Peel shrimp, leaving the tails on; devein, if desired.
2. Bring 6 cups water and next 4 ingredients to a boil in a large saucepan; add shrimp. Cook 2 to 3 minutes or just until shrimp turn pink. Drain shrimp, and chill, reserving 1/2 cup liquid.
3. Stir together reserved 1/2 cup shrimp liquid, ketchup, and next 3 ingredients. Stir in chopped tomato and chopped fresh cilantro. Chill sauce until ready to serve with shrimp.

Great Guacamole

MAKES ABOUT 5 CUPS
PREP: 20 MIN.

8 ripe avocados
1 medium-size ripe tomato, diced
1 small red onion, minced
2 to 3 tablespoons minced fresh cilantro
1 to 1 1/2 tablespoons lemon juice
1/2 teaspoon salt
1/8 teaspoon pepper
1 tablespoon hot sauce (optional)
Tortilla chips

1. Cut avocados in half lengthwise. Discard pits. Carefully remove avocado pulp, leaving shells intact, and place pulp in a large bowl.
2. Mash pulp with a fork until smooth; stir in tomato, next 5 ingredients, and, if desired, hot sauce. Serve immediately, or cover and chill up to 2 hours. Spoon into avocado shells. Serve with tortilla chips.

Texas Grilled Sirloin With Serrano Chile Salsa

MAKES 8 SERVINGS
PREP: 10 MIN., CHILL: 8 HRS., GRILL: 12 MIN.

2 pounds lean boneless top sirloin steak, trimmed
1/2 cup fresh lime juice
1/4 cup chopped fresh oregano
2 tablespoons chopped fresh rosemary
2 teaspoons pepper
2 garlic cloves, pressed
Serrano Chile Salsa
Flour tortillas

1. Combine first 6 ingredients in a large zip-top freezer bag; seal and shake well. Chill at least 8 hours, turning occasionally.
2. Remove steak from marinade, discarding marinade. Grill steak, covered with grill lid, over medium-high heat (350° to 400°) 5 to 6 minutes on each side or to desired degree of doneness. Cut diagonally across the grain into thin slices. Serve with Serrano Chile Salsa and flour tortillas.

Serrano Chile Salsa:

To make a milder salsa, use 2 or 3 serrano chile peppers. This salsa is also great served as a dip with tortilla chips.

MAKES 2 CUPS
PREP: 15 MIN., CHILL: 1 HR.

6 serrano chile peppers, diced
1 pound plum tomatoes, diced
2 tablespoons diced red onion
1/4 cup orange juice
2 tablespoons diced yellow or red bell pepper
2 tablespoons minced fresh cilantro
1 tablespoon rice vinegar
1/2 teaspoon salt
1/2 teaspoon sugar

1. Combine all ingredients; cover and chill 1 hour.

Tangy Citrus Dressed Salad

The dressing and tortilla strips can be made the day before the party. Let the tortilla strips cool thoroughly, and carefully seal them in zip-top plastic bags.

MAKES 6 TO 8 SERVINGS
PREP: 10 MIN.

1/2 pound romaine lettuce, torn
1 cup (4 ounces) shredded Monterey Jack cheese
1 red bell pepper, cut into thin strips
1/4 cup finely chopped fresh cilantro
Tangy Citrus Dressing
Frizzled Tortilla Strips (optional)

1. Combine first 4 ingredients; toss with Tangy Citrus Dressing. Top with Frizzled Tortilla Strips, if desired.

Tangy Citrus Dressing:

MAKES 1 CUP
PREP: 5 MIN., CHILL: 1 HR.

1/3 cup vegetable oil
1/4 cup fresh lime juice
2 tablespoons egg substitute
1 1/2 tablespoons tequila
1 1/2 teaspoons orange liqueur
1 garlic clove, minced
1 serrano chile pepper, seeded and diced
1/4 teaspoon salt

1. Whisk together all ingredients. Cover and chill at least 1 hour.

Frizzled Tortilla Strips:

MAKES 8 SERVINGS
PREP: 5 MIN., FRY: 2 MIN. PER BATCH

12 (8-inch) flour tortillas
Peanut or vegetable oil
Salt

1. Cut flour tortillas into 1/4-inch-wide strips. Pour peanut or vegetable oil to a depth of 3 inches into a Dutch oven; heat to 375°. Fry tortilla strips, in batches, 1 to 2 minutes or until golden. Remove from oil with a slotted spoon, drain on paper towels, and sprinkle with salt.

Tangy Citrus
Dressed Salad

Aztec Gold

We think you'll like this spiked apple drink with or without the vodka. For a sweeter drink, substitute lemon-lime soda for the tonic water.

MAKES 8 CUPS
PREP: 5 MIN., COOK: 5 MIN., CHILL: 1 HR.

2 (12-ounce) cans frozen apple juice concentrate, thawed and undiluted
6 whole cloves
2 tablespoons honey
1/2 teaspoon ground cinnamon
4 cups tonic water, chilled
3/4 cup chilled vodka (optional)
Garnishes: Granny Smith apple slices, cinnamon sticks

1. Cook first 4 ingredients in a small saucepan over medium heat, stirring occasionally, 5 minutes or until thoroughly heated. Remove from heat; cool. Chill 1 hour, or freeze 15 minutes. Stir in tonic water and, if desired, vodka. Serve immediately over ice, and garnish, if desired.

White Chocolate-Dipped Strawberries

To make White Chocolate-Dipped Strawberries, melt white chocolate morsels according to package directions. Rinse strawberries, and pat dry with paper towels. Dip in chocolate, allowing excess to drip. Place strawberries on wax paper until chocolate hardens. Place in a single layer in an airtight container, and store at room temperature. Strawberries can be dipped up to 4 hours in advance of the party.

Margarita Cheesecake

Show off this dessert by rubbing the rim of the cake plate with lime wedges and then rolling it in kosher or margarita salt.

MAKES 12 SERVINGS
PREP: 20 MIN., BAKE: 40 MIN., COOL: 30 MIN., CHILL: 8 HRS.

1 2/3 cups graham cracker crumbs
6 tablespoons butter, melted
2 tablespoons sugar
2 (8-ounce) packages cream cheese, softened
2 individual-size envelopes instant margarita mix*
3/4 cup sugar, divided
4 large eggs
1/3 cup tequila**
1 1/2 teaspoons grated lime rind, divided
1/2 teaspoon vanilla extract
1 (16-ounce) container sour cream
1 tablespoon fresh lime juice
Garnishes: lime slices, strawberries

1. Combine first 3 ingredients; firmly press into bottom and 1 inch up sides of a 9-inch springform pan.
2. Beat cream cheese at medium speed with an electric mixer until fluffy; gradually add margarita mix and 1/2 cup sugar, beating well. Add eggs, 1 at a time, beating after each addition. Stir in tequila, 1 teaspoon grated lime rind, and vanilla extract. Pour into prepared pan.
3. Bake at 375° for 25 to 30 minutes or until center is almost set.
4. Remove from oven; cool on a wire rack 30 minutes.
5. Combine sour cream, lime juice, remaining 1/4 cup sugar, and remaining 1/2 teaspoon lime rind; spread sour cream mixture over top of cheesecake.
6. Bake at 425° for 10 minutes. Remove from oven; run a sharp knife around edges of pan to loosen. Cool completely on a wire rack.
7. Cover and chill at least 8 hours. Place cheesecake on a serving platter; release sides of springform pan, and remove. Garnish, if desired.
*2 1/2 teaspoons lemon- or lime-flavored sweetened drink mix may be substituted for each envelope of margarita mix. In some areas the drink mix may be called lemonade or limeade.
**1/3 cup orange juice may be substituted for tequila.

Margarita Cheesecake, White Chocolate-Dipped Strawberries, and bakery brownies and cookies

Wedding at Home

serves 25

*Ham-Stuffed Biscuits With
Mustard Butter*

*Curried Chicken Salad
Tea Sandwiches*

*Boiled Shrimp With Rémoulade Sauce
and Spicy Cocktail Sauce*

*Steamed Asparagus and Green Beans
With Fresh Lemon-Basil Dip*

Ginger Tea

Strawberry Cooler

Tangy Limeade

Fruited Citrus Refresher

Apple Iced Tea

Bakery wedding cake

PARTY VARIATIONS
This menu offers lots of flexibility for any occasion. Replace the wedding cake with a cake to fit the theme. Serve the menu for a wedding or baby shower, an anniversary party, or a birthday bash.

Ham-Stuffed Biscuits With Mustard Butter

MAKES 5 DOZEN
PREP: 1 HR., STAND: 5 MIN., RISE: 1 HR., BAKE: 12 MIN.

1 (¼-ounce) envelope active dry yeast
½ cup warm water (100° to 110°)
2 cups buttermilk
5½ cups all-purpose flour
1½ tablespoons baking powder
1½ teaspoons salt
½ teaspoon baking soda
¼ cup sugar
¾ cup shortening
Mustard Butter
2 pounds thinly sliced cooked ham

1. Combine yeast and ½ cup warm water in a 4-cup liquid measuring cup, and let mixture stand 5 minutes. Stir in buttermilk.
2. Combine flour and next 4 ingredients in a large bowl; cut in shortening with a pastry blender or fork until mixture resembles coarse meal. Add buttermilk mixture, stirring with a fork just until dry ingredients are moistened.
3. Turn dough out onto a well-floured surface, and knead 4 to 5 times.
4. Roll dough to a ½-inch thickness; cut with a 2-inch round cutter, and place on lightly greased baking sheets. Cover and let rise in a warm place (85°), free from drafts, 1 hour.
5. Bake at 425° for 10 to 12 minutes or until golden. Split each biscuit, and spread evenly with Mustard Butter. Stuff biscuits with ham.

Mustard Butter:

MAKES ABOUT 1 CUP
PREP: 5 MIN.

1 cup butter, softened
2 tablespoons minced sweet onion
2 tablespoons spicy brown mustard

1. Stir all ingredients until blended.

Curried Chicken Salad
Tea Sandwiches

Curried Chicken Salad Tea Sandwiches

MAKES ABOUT 25 SERVINGS
PREP: 1 HR.

4 cups finely chopped cooked chicken
3 (8-ounce) packages cream cheese, softened
¾ cup dried cranberries, chopped
½ cup sweetened flaked coconut, toasted
6 green onions, minced
2 celery ribs, diced
1 (2¼-ounce) package slivered almonds, toasted
1 tablespoon curry powder
1 tablespoon grated fresh ginger
½ teaspoon salt
½ teaspoon pepper
48 whole grain bread slices

1. Stir together first 11 ingredients. Spread mixture evenly on 1 side each of 24 bread slices, and top with remaining 24 bread slices. Trim crusts from sandwiches; cut each sandwich into 4 rectangles with a serrated knife.

DECORATING TIPS FOR AN AT-HOME WEDDING

■ Add height to your tablescape by arranging food on tiered plates decorated with flowers or greenery.
■ For sparkle, hang flickering lanterns from ceilings or trees using monofilament line, available at crafts stores. Place mounted lanterns along steps and pathways.
■ Decorate walls and serving tables with sconces and candlesticks.
■ Mix and match your favorite heirloom crystal and silver pieces to create a unique look.
■ For added elegance, drape flowing fabric around columns, stair railings, tables, and window openings.
■ Accent silver or crystal wine goblets with shimmering ribbon.

Boiled Shrimp With Rémoulade Sauce and Spicy Cocktail Sauce

To save time, use peeled, large frozen cooked shrimp. Thaw according to package directions, and serve with sauces.

MAKES ABOUT 25 SERVINGS
PREP: 40 MIN., COOK: 15 MIN.

4 quarts water
½ cup Creole seasoning
2 large lemons, sliced
6 pounds unpeeled, large fresh shrimp
Garnishes: lemon and lime slices
Rémoulade Sauce
Spicy Cocktail Sauce

1. Bring first 3 ingredients to a boil in a large stockpot. Add shrimp; cook 2 minutes or just until shrimp turn pink. Drain and rinse with cold water.
2. Peel shrimp, and devein, if desired. Chill until ready to serve. Garnish, if desired. Serve with Rémoulade Sauce and Spicy Cocktail Sauce.

Rémoulade Sauce:

MAKES ABOUT 4 CUPS
PREP: 10 MIN.

4 cups mayonnaise
½ cup Creole mustard
1½ tablespoons paprika
2 tablespoons fresh lemon juice
1½ teaspoons ground red pepper
4 large garlic cloves, pressed
¼ cup chopped fresh parsley

1. Whisk together all ingredients until blended. Cover and chill until ready to serve.

Spicy Cocktail Sauce:

MAKES ABOUT 4 CUPS
PREP: 10 MIN.

1½ cups chili sauce
1 cup ketchup
¾ cup prepared horseradish
⅓ cup fresh lemon juice
1½ tablespoons Worcestershire sauce
2 to 3 teaspoons hot sauce
½ teaspoon salt
½ teaspoon pepper

Boiled Shrimp With
Rémoulade Sauce and
Spicy Cocktail Sauce

1. Stir together all ingredients until blended. Cover and chill until ready to serve.
Note: For testing purposes only, we used Heinz Chili Sauce.

Steamed Asparagus and Green Beans With Fresh Lemon-Basil Dip

MAKES ABOUT 25 SERVINGS
PREP: 20 MIN., COOK: 8 MIN.

1 cup chopped fresh basil
2 cups mayonnaise
1 (8-ounce) container sour cream
2 tablespoons grated lemon rind
¼ teaspoon salt
4 pounds fresh asparagus
2 pounds fresh green beans
Garnish: fresh basil sprig

1. Whisk together first 5 ingredients until blended. Cover and chill.
2. Snap off and discard tough ends of asparagus. Cook asparagus in boiling water to cover 2 to 3 minutes or until crisp-tender; drain. Plunge into ice water to stop the cooking process; drain.
3. Cook green beans in boiling water to cover 3 to 5 minutes or until crisp-tender. Plunge into ice water to stop the cooking process; drain.
4. Cover and chill vegetables until ready to serve with dip. Garnish dip with fresh basil sprig, if desired.

Ginger Tea

MAKES ABOUT 8 CUPS

PREP: 20 MIN., COOK: 10 MIN., STEEP: 5 MIN.

2 quarts water
½ cup grated fresh ginger
⅓ cup fresh lemon juice
¼ cup honey
4 regular-size green tea bags
1½ cups sugar

1. Combine first 4 ingredients in a large Dutch oven; bring to a boil, stirring often, over medium-high heat. Reduce heat to low, and simmer, stirring occasionally, 5 minutes. Remove from heat.
2. Add tea bags; cover and steep 5 minutes. Remove and discard tea bags; stir in sugar, and cool.
3. Pour tea through a wire-mesh strainer into a pitcher, discarding solids. Serve tea over ice.

BAKERY WEDDING CAKE

No time to bake? Order a plain iced cake from your local bakery. Carefully arrange fresh flowers on the top and sides for a pretty look. Check with your florist about which flowers are safe for contact with food and are in season.

Strawberry Cooler

MAKES ABOUT 9½ CUPS

PREP: 5 MIN.

1 (33.8-ounce) bottle ginger ale, chilled
1 (11.5-ounce) can frozen strawberry juice cocktail concentrate, thawed and undiluted

1. Stir together chilled ginger ale and thawed strawberry juice cocktail concentrate; serve over ice.
Note: For testing purposes only, we used Welch's Strawberry Breeze Blended Juice Cocktail Concentrate.

Tangy Limeade

This simple drink, ready in 10 minutes, will appeal to guests of all ages.

MAKES 8 CUPS

PREP: 5 MIN., COOK: 5 MIN.

1 cup sugar
6½ cups water, divided
¼ teaspoon lemon juice
1¼ cups fresh lime juice (about 6 to 8 large limes)

1. Cook sugar, ½ cup water, and lemon juice in a small saucepan over medium heat, stirring constantly, 2 minutes or until sugar dissolves. Bring to a boil over medium-high heat; cook, stirring occasionally, 3 minutes. Cool.
2. Stir together sugar mixture, remaining 6 cups water, and lime juice in a large pitcher; chill. Serve over ice, if desired.

Fruited Citrus Refresher

MAKES ABOUT 16 CUPS

PREP: 5 MIN.

2 cups Ruby Red grapefruit juice cocktail
1 (12-ounce) can frozen limeade, thawed and undiluted
1 (46-ounce) can pineapple juice
1 cup maraschino cherry juice
6 cups lemon-lime soft drink, chilled

1. Combine first 4 ingredients; chill until ready to serve. Stir in lemon-lime soft drink just before serving. Serve over ice.

Apple Iced Tea, Fruited Citrus
Refresher, Tangy Limeade,
Strawberry Cooler, and Ginger Tea

Apple Iced Tea

MAKES ABOUT 5½ CUPS
PREP: 10 MIN., STEEP: 5 MIN.

3 cups boiling water
4 cinnamon-apple tea bags
1 tablespoon sugar
1 (6-ounce) can frozen apple juice concentrate,
      thawed and undiluted
2 cups cold water

1. Pour 3 cups boiling water over tea bags; cover and
steep 5 minutes. Remove and discard tea bags. Stir in
sugar, juice, and 2 cups cold water. Serve over ice.

FESTIVE BEVERAGE BAR

Set up a festive beverage bar by placing a
variety of refreshing drinks in heirloom
crystal containers. Tie on sheer ribbons for
added elegance.

Dressed-Up Supper Club

serves 6

Hot Spiced Wine

Peanutty Party Mix

Warmed Cranberry Brie

*Pear, Jícama, and
Snow Pea Salad With
Basil-Balsamic Vinaigrette*

*Cajun Beef Fillets With
Parmesan Grits*

Asparagus With Lemon

Chocolate-Covered Cherry Pie

Hot Spiced Wine

To serve, use a tempered glass, heat-proof pitcher, a thermal carafe, or simply return the mixture to the Dutch oven, and ladle it into mugs.

MAKES 9 CUPS
PREP: 5 MIN., COOK: 20 MIN.

2 (750-milliliter) bottles red wine
2 cups apple juice
1 cup sugar
6 tablespoons mulling spices

1. Bring all ingredients to a boil in a Dutch oven; reduce heat, and simmer 15 minutes. Pour mixture through a wire-mesh strainer into a pitcher, discarding mulling spices. Serve wine hot.
Note: For best results, use a fruity red wine, such as a Beaujolais or Pinot Noir.

CHARMED WINE GLASSES

To help guests keep track of their wine glasses, tie strands of beads, one color for each guest, around wine goblet stems. Beads, tiny jingle bells, and thin ribbon or cording are available at local crafts stores.

Peanutty Party Mix

Peanutty Party Mix

Serve small bowls of Peanutty Party Mix for predinner nibbles. Then give guests a bag of this spicy treat to take home.

MAKES ABOUT 12 CUPS
PREP: 10 MIN., BAKE: 25 MIN.

1 (12-ounce) package chow mein noodles
2 cups dry-roasted or honey-roasted peanuts
2 cups uncooked regular oats
1/2 cup butter or margarine
1 tablespoon sesame oil
1/4 cup firmly packed brown sugar
1 (3/4-ounce) envelope hot-and-spicy fried rice
    seasoning mix
1 (6-ounce) package sweetened dried cranberries

1. Combine first 3 ingredients in a large bowl; set aside.
2. Melt butter with oil in a small saucepan over medium heat; stir in sugar and seasoning mix, and cook, stirring constantly, 5 minutes or until sugar dissolves. Pour sugar mixture evenly over peanut mixture in bowl; toss to coat. Spread mixture in an even layer in a lightly greased 15- x 10-inch jelly-roll pan.
3. Bake at 300° for 25 minutes, stirring twice. Remove from oven, and stir in cranberries. Cool completely in pan on a wire rack. Store in an airtight container.
Note: For testing purposes only, we used Sun-Bird Hot & Spicy Fried Rice Authentic Oriental Seasoning Mix.

Warmed Cranberry Brie

Try tossing pear and apple slices in pineapple juice to keep them from turning brown. It works as well as lemon juice and has a sweeter flavor.

MAKES 6 APPETIZER SERVINGS
PREP: 10 MIN., BAKE: 5 MIN.

1 (16-ounce) Brie round
1 (16-ounce) can whole-berry cranberry sauce
1/4 cup firmly packed brown sugar
2 tablespoons spiced rum*
1/2 teaspoon ground nutmeg
1/4 cup chopped pecans, toasted
French bread baguette slices, toasted
Apple and pear slices
Red grape clusters

1. Trim rind from top of Brie, leaving a 1/3-inch border on top.
2. Place Brie on a baking sheet.
3. Stir together cranberry sauce and next 3 ingredients; spread mixture evenly over Brie. Sprinkle evenly with pecans.
4. Bake at 500° for 5 minutes. Serve with toasted baguette slices, apple and pear slices, and red grapes.
*Substitute 2 tablespoons orange juice for spiced rum, if desired.

PLACE CARDS

For simple place cards, cut slits in the tops of small green apples, tuck berries, small pieces of curly willow, and name cards into slits. (Make sure guests know that the apple and place card holders are for display only and are not edible.)

Warmed Cranberry Brie

Kids' Birthday Bash

serves 8

Snuggle Dogs

Turkey Burgers

Taco Fries

Pink Cow Shakes
(double recipe)

Flowerpot Cakes

Bug Stick Cookies

Snuggle Dogs

MAKES 8 SERVINGS
PREP: 10 MIN., BAKE: 10 MIN.

16 individually wrapped processed American cheese
  slices
8 (8-inch) flat bread rounds
8 hot dogs
Toppings: chili, slaw, ketchup, mustard

1. Unwrap and arrange 2 American cheese slices in
center of 1 flat bread round; place 1 hot dog on bread,
and roll up, securing with a wooden pick. Place on a
baking sheet. Repeat with remaining flat bread, cheese,
and hot dogs.
2. Bake at 350° for 10 minutes or until cheese melts.
Remove picks before serving. Serve with desired
toppings.
Note: For testing purposes only, we used Kraft Singles
cheese slices and Toufayan Bakeries flat bread.

Snuggle Dogs and
Turkey Burgers

Turkey Burgers

Guests will love these little burgers served on kid-size buns.

MAKES 8 SERVINGS
PREP: 10 MIN., GRILL: 8 MIN.

1¼ pounds ground turkey
⅓ cup light mayonnaise
1 garlic clove, pressed
2 tablespoons chopped fresh basil
1 tablespoon Worcestershire sauce
1 teaspoon salt
8 small deli buns
Toppings: sliced tomato, mayonnaise, mustard,
     ketchup, shredded lettuce

1. Combine first 6 ingredients in a large bowl until
blended. (Do not overwork.) Shape turkey mixture
into 8 (2-inch) patties.
2. Grill, covered with grill lid, over medium-high heat
(350° to 400°) 4 minutes on each side or until turkey is
no longer pink. Serve on buns with desired toppings.

Taco Fries

*Serve these zesty fries with a side of Ranch dressing for a quick
dipping sauce.*

MAKES 8 SERVINGS
PREP: 5 MIN., BAKE: 45 MIN.

1 (26-ounce) bag frozen extra-crispy french fries
½ (1.25-ounce) package taco seasoning mix

1. Coat potatoes with vegetable cooking spray, and
place in a large zip-top plastic bag. Add taco seasoning
mix; seal bag, and shake to coat. Place in a single layer
on a 15- x 10-inch jelly-roll pan.
2. Bake at 425° for 30 to 35 minutes; stir and bake 5 to
10 more minutes or until golden.

Pink Cow Shakes

MAKES 5½ CUPS
PREP: 10 MIN.

4 cups vanilla ice cream, softened
1 (11.5-ounce) can frozen strawberry juice cocktail
     concentrate, thawed
½ cup milk

1. Process ice cream, strawberry juice cocktail, and milk
in a blender until smooth. Serve immediately.
Note: For testing purposes only, we used Welch's
Strawberry Breeze Blended Juice Cocktail Concentrate.

Pink Cow
Shakes

PARTY TIPS

■ Chill commercial juice boxes for a quick drink alternative. Embellish with festive or crawling critters. (photo 1)

■ Use galvanized pots in a garden stand to display easy-to-squeeze condiments. Reinforce the theme with toy bugs. (photo 2)

■ Paint guests' names on glass jars, and tie plastic wrap on top for personalized bug-collecting containers. These make great parting gifts.

■ Transform headbands into bug antennae for a fun activity that will keep kids busy as bees. Attach crafty pipe cleaners and fuzzy pom-poms for a buzzing effect (page 382).

Flowerpot Cakes and Bug Stick Cookies

Flowerpot Cakes

Buy unglazed terra-cotta pots at a discount superstore or garden center. Run them through the dishwasher (on the top rack) before using.

MAKES 8 SERVINGS
PREP: 15 MIN., BAKE: 30 MIN., FREEZE: 8 HRS.

8 (4-inch) unglazed, untreated terra-cotta flowerpots
1 (16-ounce) package pound cake mix
4 cups chocolate ice cream, softened
1 (16-ounce) container frozen whipped topping, thawed
Garnishes: chocolate cookie crumbs, chocolate sprinkles, Bug Stick Cookies (see below)

1. Cut out a circle of parchment paper to fit the bottom of each pot, and place inside to cover the drainage hole. Coat the inside of each pot with vegetable cooking spray.
2. Prepare pound cake batter according to package directions. Pour batter evenly into prepared pots. Place pots on a baking sheet.
3. Bake at 350° for 25 to 30 minutes or until a wooden pick inserted in center comes out clean. Cool completely. Spread ½ cup ice cream on top of each cake.
4. Cover each pot with plastic wrap, and freeze 8 hours. Top evenly with whipped topping. Garnish with cookie crumbs, sprinkles, and Bug Stick Cookies, if desired.

Bug Stick Cookies

Look for lollipop sticks at your local crafts shop or discount superstore. Decorating icing and gel can be found on the baking aisle of the grocery store.

MAKES 16 (3½-INCH) COOKIES
PREP: 1 HR., 15 MIN.; CHILL: 1 HR.; BAKE: 12 MIN. PER BATCH

1 cup butter, softened
1 cup sugar
1 large egg
1 teaspoon vanilla extract
3 cups all-purpose flour
1½ teaspoons baking powder
½ teaspoon salt
16 (8-inch) lollipop sticks
Decorations: red, yellow, pink, and white decorating icings; black decorating gel

1. Beat butter and sugar at medium speed with an electric mixer 3 minutes or until creamy. Add egg and vanilla, beating until blended.

2. Combine flour, baking powder, and salt; gradually add to butter mixture, heating until blended.
3. Divide dough in half, and shape each portion into 2 disks. Wrap each disk in plastic wrap, and chill at least 1 hour.
4. Roll dough to a ½-inch thickness on a lightly floured surface. Cut into desired shapes using bug-shaped cookie cutters; place cookies on baking sheets (photo 1).
5. Bake, in batches, at 350° for 10 to 12 minutes or until edges are golden. (Baking times may vary with different cookie shapes and sizes.) Slip a spatula under cookies to loosen; transfer to wire racks. While cookies are hot, carefully insert 1 lollipop stick into bottom of each cookie (photo 2). Cool completely on wire racks. Decorate cooled cookies with icing and gel in desired colors, using a decorator writing tip.
Note: For testing purposes only, we used Wilton lollipop sticks and Betty Crocker decorating icing and gel.

1 Roll cookie dough to a ½-inch thickness to ensure support of lollipop sticks, and cut out desired bug shapes.

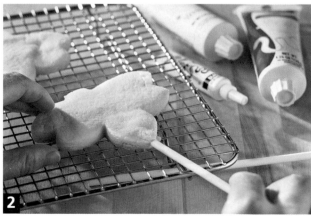

2 Center and insert sticks in the bottom of the cookies immediately after baking.

Game-Day Feast

serves 6 to 8

Hot Chile-Cheese Artichoke Dip

Sweet 'n' Salty Snack Mix

Miniature Reuben Melts

Hearty Chili

White Chicken Chili

Beer Rolls

Oatmeal-Fudge Bars

PARTY TIP

Colorful box containers hold napkins and flatware. They also make great carriers for guest favors.

Hot Chile-Cheese Artichoke Dip

Use light mayonnaise and light sour cream for fewer calories without losing any taste. Both versions rated highly with our staff.

MAKES 8 TO 10 APPETIZER SERVINGS
PREP: 10 MIN., BAKE: 30 MIN.

1 (8-ounce) package shredded mozzarella cheese
1 cup shredded Parmesan cheese
½ cup mayonnaise
½ cup sour cream
2 (6-ounce) jars marinated artichoke hearts, drained and chopped
1 (4.5-ounce) can chopped green chiles
½ teaspoon minced fresh garlic
Tortilla chips

1. Stir together first 7 ingredients in a medium bowl. Spread into a 9-inch round deep-dish pie plate
2. Bake at 350° for 25 to 30 minutes or until lightly browned. Serve artichoke dip immediately with chips.
To Make Ahead: Prepare dip as directed before baking. Cover and chill overnight. Let dip stand at room temperature 30 minutes before baking. Uncover and bake as directed.

Slow Cooker Chile-Cheese Artichoke Dip: Stir together first 7 ingredients in an 1½-quart slow cooker. Cover and cook on LOW for 3 to 4 hours or until cheese is melted and mixture is hot. Serve immediately with chips or hold on WARM for up to 2 hours.

Sweet 'n' Salty Snack Mix

Sweet 'n' Salty Snack Mix

MAKES ABOUT 12 CUPS
PREP: 15 MIN., COOK: 5 MIN., BAKE: 25 MIN., STAND: 25 MIN.

5 cups corn-and-rice cereal
2 cups bite-size pretzel sticks
1 cup honey-roasted peanuts
1 (6-ounce) can roasted salted almonds (about 1 cup)
½ cup firmly packed brown sugar
¼ cup butter or margarine
¼ cup light corn syrup
3 cups horn-shaped corn snacks

1. Combine 5 cups cereal, pretzel sticks, peanuts, and almonds in a large bowl; set aside.

2. Cook brown sugar, butter, and corn syrup in a small heavy saucepan over low heat, stirring until butter melts and sugar dissolves.

3. Pour sugar mixture over cereal mixture, stirring to coat. Spread evenly onto a lightly greased aluminum foil-lined 15- x 10-inch jelly-roll pan.

4. Bake at 325° for 20 to 25 minutes, stirring twice. Spread immediately on wax paper. Let stand to cool completely (about 25 minutes), separating mixture into individual pieces as it cools. Transfer to a large bowl, and stir in horn-shaped snacks. Store snack mix in an airtight container.

Note: For testing purposes only, we used Crispix for corn-and-rice cereal and Bugles for horn-shaped snacks.

Miniature Reuben Melts

Hearty Chili

If your Dutch oven isn't large enough to hold the meat in one layer, brown half of the meat as directed, remove, and drain. Brown the other half using an additional 1 tablespoon oil. This chili has a distinct chili powder taste. Start with the lowest amount of chili powder, and taste after cooking 2 hours. Add up to 2 more tablespoons, if desired.

MAKES ABOUT 9 CUPS
PREP: 25 MIN.; COOK: 3 HRS., 30 MIN.

1 large onion, chopped
1 tablespoon vegetable oil
1 (2½-pound) chuck roast, trimmed and cut into
    bite-size pieces
2 teaspoons minced fresh garlic
6 to 8 tablespoons chili powder
4 teaspoons ground cumin
1 teaspoon ground red pepper
1 teaspoon paprika
2 (14½-ounce) cans Mexican-style stewed tomatoes,
    chopped
2 cups water
1 (14-ounce) can beef broth
1 (6-ounce) can tomato paste
1 (15-ounce) can pinto beans, rinsed and drained
1 (15-ounce) can light kidney beans, rinsed and
    drained
Toppings: hot sauce, shredded Cheddar cheese,
    chopped green onions, sour cream

1. Sauté onion in hot oil in a large Dutch oven over medium-high heat 4 minutes. Add chuck roast pieces, and sauté 5 minutes or until browned; drain. Return to pan; add garlic, and sauté 1 minute. Add chili powder, ground cumin, ground red pepper, and paprika, stirring to coat meat evenly. Add Mexican-style stewed tomatoes, 2 cups water, beef broth, and tomato paste. Bring to a boil; cover, reduce heat, and simmer, stirring occasionally, 2 hours.
2. Stir in beans, and simmer, uncovered, stirring occasionally, 1 hour or until thickened. Serve with desired toppings.
To Make Ahead: Chili may be prepared ahead and frozen up to 1 month. Thaw in refrigerator overnight.

Miniature Reuben Melts

To make ahead, prepare mustard mixture and sauerkraut-cheese mixture in advance. Cover and chill separately until ready to assemble.

MAKES 16 APPETIZER SERVINGS
PREP: 20 MIN., BROIL: 7 MIN.

8 tablespoons Thousand Island dressing, divided
1½ teaspoons spicy brown mustard
1 cup refrigerated shredded sauerkraut
1 (4-ounce) block Swiss cheese, shredded
¼ teaspoon freshly ground pepper
16 cocktail-size rye or pumpernickel bread slices
6 ounces thinly sliced deli corned beef, coarsely
    chopped

1. Stir together 3 tablespoons Thousand Island dressing and spicy brown mustard; set aside.
2. Rinse and drain sauerkraut well, pressing between layers of paper towels to remove excess moisture. Stir together sauerkraut, shredded Swiss cheese, pepper, and remaining 5 tablespoons Thousand Island dressing. Set mixture aside.
3. Arrange bread slices on an aluminum foil-lined baking sheet. Broil 3½ inches from heat 1 to 2 minutes on each side or until lightly toasted.
4. Spread mustard mixture evenly over 1 side of each toasted bread slice. Top evenly with chopped corned beef; spread evenly with sauerkraut-cheese mixture.
5. Broil 3½ inches from heat 3 minutes or until lightly browned. Serve immediately.

White Chicken Chili

MAKES ABOUT 13 CUPS
PREP: 35 MIN.; SOAK: 12 HRS.; COOK: 2 HRS., 45 MIN.

1 pound dried great Northern beans
1 large onion, chopped
1 tablespoon vegetable oil
2 (4.5-ounce) cans chopped green chiles
2 teaspoons minced fresh garlic
2 teaspoons ground cumin
1½ teaspoons dried oregano
½ teaspoon black pepper
¼ teaspoon salt
⅛ teaspoon ground red pepper
1 (49-ounce) can chicken broth
1 bay leaf
5 cups chopped cooked chicken breasts
2 tablespoons chopped fresh cilantro
Toppings: shredded Monterey Jack cheese, salsa,
    sour cream, chopped fresh cilantro

1. Wash beans; remove any foreign particles and debris. Place in a Dutch oven or large bowl. Cover with water to 2 inches above beans; let soak 12 hours. Drain; set beans aside.
2. Sauté onion in hot oil in large Dutch oven over medium-high heat 5 minutes or until tender. Add green chiles and next 6 ingredients; sauté 1 minute. Add beans, chicken broth, and bay leaf. Bring to a boil; cover, reduce heat, and simmer, stirring occasionally, 2 hours or until beans are tender. Stir in chicken, and simmer, uncovered, stirring occasionally, 30 minutes or until thoroughly heated. Remove bay leaf, and stir in 2 tablespoons cilantro just before serving. Serve with desired toppings.
Kitchen Express: Substitute 3 (16-ounce) cans great Northern beans, drained, for the dried beans. Decrease chicken broth to 3 cups, and increase salt to ½ teaspoon. Sauté onion, chiles, and seasonings as directed. Add 3 cups chicken broth, bay leaf, chopped cooked chicken, and beans. Simmer 30 to 45 minutes or until thickened. Remove bay leaf, and stir in cilantro. Serve with desired toppings.
To Make Ahead: Chili may be prepared ahead and frozen up to 1 month. Thaw in the refrigerator overnight.

Beer Rolls

Use your favorite beer—ale or lager—in these slightly sweet rolls. We used Newcastle Brown Ale.

MAKES 1 DOZEN
PREP: 20 MIN., BAKE: 15 MIN.

3 cups self-rising flour
1 cup room-temperature beer
⅓ cup firmly packed brown sugar
1 egg, lightly beaten
4 tablespoons butter, melted and divided

1. Stir together first 4 ingredients and 3 tablespoons melted butter until moistened. Spoon about ¼ cup batter into each greased cup in a muffin pan.
2. Bake at 425° for 15 minutes or until golden. Brush rolls with remaining 1 tablespoon melted butter. Remove rolls from pan, and cool slightly on a wire rack. Serve warm.
To Make Ahead: Cooled rolls may be stored overnight in an airtight container. To reheat, brush rolls with melted butter, and bake at 425° for 4 or 5 minutes.

Oatmeal-Fudge Bars

MAKES ABOUT 2 DOZEN
PREP: 20 MIN., COOK: 5 MIN., BAKE: 25 MIN., CHILL: 1 HR.

1½ cups uncooked regular oats
1¼ cups all-purpose flour
½ teaspoon baking soda
½ teaspoon salt
½ cup butter or margarine, softened
1 cup firmly packed brown sugar
1 large egg
2 teaspoons vanilla extract, divided
1 (12-ounce) bag semisweet chocolate morsels
1 (14-ounce) can sweetened condensed milk
2 tablespoons butter
⅛ teaspoon salt
1 cup chopped walnuts

1. Combine first 4 ingredients.
2. Beat ½ cup butter and brown sugar at medium speed with an electric mixer until blended. Add egg and 1 teaspoon vanilla, beating until blended. Add oat mixture, and beat at low speed just until blended. Remove and reserve ¾ cup oat mixture. Press remaining oat mixture evenly into a lightly greased 13- x 9-inch pan; set aside. (Layer will be thin.)
3. Cook chocolate morsels and next 3 ingredients in a heavy saucepan over low heat, stirring often, until smooth. Remove from heat; stir in walnuts and remaining 1 teaspoon vanilla. Pour chocolate mixture evenly over oat mixture in pan. Crumble reserved ¾ cup oat mixture evenly over chocolate mixture.
4. Bake at 350° for 20 to 25 minutes or until lightly browned. Cool on a wire rack. Cover and chill 1 hour. Cut into bars.

Oatmeal-Fudge Bars

Pumpkin
Cheese Ball

Pumpkin Cheese Ball

A broccoli stalk serves as a realistic-looking stem for this edible pumpkin. Apple wedges make healthy accompaniments.

MAKES 16 APPETIZER SERVINGS
PREP: 30 MIN., CHILL: 4 HRS.

2 (8-ounce) blocks extra-sharp Cheddar cheese,
   shredded
1 (8-ounce) package cream cheese, softened
1 (8-ounce) container chive-and-onion cream cheese
2 teaspoons paprika
½ teaspoon ground red pepper
1 broccoli stalk
Red and green apple wedges

1. Combine first 5 ingredients in a bowl until blended. Cover and chill 4 hours or until mixture is firm enough to be shaped.
2. Shape mixture into a ball to resemble a pumpkin. Smooth entire outer surface with an icing spatula or table knife. Make vertical grooves in ball, if desired, using fingertips.
3. Cut florets from broccoli stalk, and reserve for another use. Cut stalk to resemble a pumpkin stem, and press into top of cheese ball. Serve cheese ball with apple wedges.
To Make Ahead: Wrap cheese ball in plastic wrap without stalk, and store in refrigerator up to 2 days. Attach stalk before serving.

Deviled Green Goblin Eggs

MAKES 1 DOZEN
PREP: 30 MIN., STAND: 1 HR.

6 cups hot water
1 (0.3-ounce) bottle yellow liquid food coloring
½ (0.3-ounce) bottle blue liquid food coloring
½ (0.3-ounce) bottle green liquid food coloring
2 tablespoons cider vinegar
12 large unpeeled hard-cooked eggs, with shells
    cracked
½ cup instant potato flakes
½ cup mayonnaise
½ cup sour cream
¼ cup minced fresh chives
½ teaspoon salt
½ teaspoon seasoned pepper

1. Stir together first 5 ingredients in a large bowl; add eggs, and let stand 1 hour. Remove and drain on paper towels. Peel eggs to reveal pattern on whites.
2. Cut eggs in half lengthwise; carefully remove yolks. Mash yolks; stir in potato flakes and next 5 ingredients until blended.
3. Spoon yolk mixture evenly into egg white halves. Attach 2 halves, gently pressing stuffed sides together.

Monster Eyes

Children will love these sausage balls that stare back at them.

MAKES ABOUT 6 DOZEN
PREP: 30 MIN., BAKE: 20 MIN. PER BATCH

3 cups all-purpose baking mix
1 pound ground hot or mild pork sausage, uncooked
1 (10-ounce) block extra-sharp Cheddar cheese,
    shredded
72 small pimiento-stuffed Spanish olives

1. Combine first 3 ingredients in a large bowl until blended.
2. Shape sausage mixture into 1-inch balls, and place on lightly greased baking sheets. Press 1 olive deeply in the center of each ball.
3. Bake at 400° for 20 minutes or until lightly browned and sausage is cooked.
Note: For testing purposes only, we used Cracker Barrel Natural Cheddar Extra-Sharp for cheese and Bisquick for all-purpose baking mix.

Wiener Worms

Wiener Worms

Cut bun-length hot dogs lengthwise into quarters. Place on grill rack crosswise, and grill, uncovered, until done. They'll curl into "worms" on their own as they cook. Serve alone or in buns with mustard and ketchup.

Harvest Moon Lollipops

These make a perfect party project for kids. (Help younger children insert the lollipop sticks.) Arrange lollipops in a container filled with florist's foam for a centerpiece, or give as party favors.

MAKES 1 DOZEN
PREP: 30 MIN.

12 (10- to 12-inch-long) lollipop sticks
1 (24-ounce) package Chocolate Flavor MoonPies
1 (14-ounce) package orange candy melts
Halloween candies
Halloween sugar cake decorations
Decorator icing
Ribbon (optional)

1. Insert 1 lollipop stick 2 to 3 inches into marshmallow center of each MoonPie.
2. Microwave candy melts in a glass bowl at MEDIUM (50% power) 1 minute or until melted, stirring once; spoon melted candy into a zip-top bag, and seal.
3. Snip a small hole in 1 corner of the bag; pipe melted candy around where sticks meet MoonPies to secure. Lay flat on wax paper, and let stand until firm.
4. Pipe a fun border of melted candy around edges. Attach candies and/or cake decorations with decorator icing. Tie ribbons around tops of sticks, if desired.

Harvest Moon
Lollipops

Southwestern-Style Thanksgiving

Smoked Pork

Ask the butcher to remove the chine bone for easier cutting.

MAKES 10 SERVINGS
PREP: 30 MIN., CHILL: 8 HRS., SOAK: 30 MIN., COOK: 5 HRS.

1 (7-pound) pork loin rib roast (10 ribs), chine bone removed, or 1 (7-pound) boneless pork loin roast
1 cup Cajun butter injector sauce
2 teaspoons salt
1 tablespoon pepper
2 tablespoons dried cilantro
Mesquite chips
Garnish: fresh cilantro sprigs

1. Trim fat from roast. Inject butter sauce evenly into pork. Combine next 3 ingredients; rub mixture over pork. Cover pork, and chill 8 hours.
2. Soak mesquite chips in water at least 30 minutes.
3. Prepare charcoal fire in smoker, and let burn 15 to 20 minutes. Drain chips, and place on coals. Place water pan in smoker; add water to depth of fill line. Place pork on lower food rack; cover with smoker lid.
4. Cook pork roast 4 to 5 hours or until a meat thermometer inserted into thickest portion of roast registers 160°. Slice pork, and place on a serving platter. Garnish, if desired.
Note: For testing purposes only, we used Original Cajun Marinade Injector for Cajun butter injector sauce.

Cranberry-Jalapeño Salsa

MAKES 2 CUPS
PREP: 10 MIN.

1 (12-ounce) package fresh cranberries
1 medium navel orange, unpeeled and coarsely chopped
3 tablespoons crystallized ginger
2 jalapeño peppers, seeded and coarsely chopped
¼ cup fresh mint leaves
1 cup sugar

1. Pulse cranberries in a food processor until minced. Transfer minced cranberries to a small bowl.
2. Pulse orange and next 4 ingredients in food processor 3 to 5 times or until mixture is finely chopped. Stir into cranberries; cover and chill, if desired.

Cornbread Dressing Cakes

Cornbread Dressing Cakes

MAKES 20 CAKES
PREP: 20 MIN., COOK: 28 MIN.

1 recipe Cornbread, crumbled
1 cup soft white breadcrumbs
4 ears fresh corn
2 tablespoons butter or margarine
2 medium-size sweet onions, diced
2 (4.5-ounce) cans chopped green chiles, drained
1/2 cup chopped fresh cilantro
2 teaspoons seasoned pepper
1 teaspoon garlic salt
3 large eggs, lightly beaten
1 cup mayonnaise
1 teaspoon ground red pepper (optional)
4 1/2 tablespoons vegetable oil

1. Stir together crumbled cornbread and 1 cup soft white breadcrumbs in a large bowl, and set aside.
2. Cut corn kernels from cob.
3. Melt butter in a large nonstick skillet over medium-high heat; add diced onion, and sauté 5 minutes or until tender. Add corn kernels, and sauté 5 minutes.
4. Stir together onion mixture, cornbread mixture, green chiles, next 5 ingredients, and, if desired, red pepper. Shape into 20 (3-inch) patties. Chill, if desired.
5. Cook one-third of patties in 1 1/2 tablespoons hot oil in a large nonstick skillet over medium heat 2 to 3 minutes on each side or until patties are golden brown, turning gently once. Repeat procedure twice with remaining patties and oil. Serve immediately, or remove to a wire rack to cool. If desired, cover and chill 8 hours. To reheat, place in a single layer on a baking sheet, and bake at 400° for 8 to 10 minutes.

Cornbread:

MAKES 1 (13- X 9-INCH) PAN CORNBREAD
PREP: 10 MIN., BAKE: 35 MIN.

1/2 cup butter
2 cups white cornmeal mix
1 cup all-purpose flour
2 tablespoons sugar
2 large eggs
2 cups buttermilk

1. Melt butter in a 13- x 9-inch pan in a 425° oven for 5 minutes.
2. Stir together white cornmeal mix, flour, sugar, eggs, and buttermilk in a large bowl.
3. Tilt pan to coat with butter, and pour butter into cornmeal mixture, stirring well. Pour cornmeal mixture into hot pan.
4. Bake at 425° for 30 minutes or until golden.

Steamed Vegetable Bundles

MAKES 10 SERVINGS
PREP: 20 MIN., COOK: 4 MIN., BAKE: 25 MIN.

¾ pound fresh green beans, trimmed
2 large carrots, cut into 40 strips
1 large red bell pepper, cut into 20 strips
3 large yellow squash
¼ cup butter, melted

1. Cook green beans with carrot strips and red bell pepper strips in boiling water to cover 3 minutes or until crisp-tender. Plunge into ice water to stop the cooking process; drain and set aside. Cook squash in boiling water to cover 1 minute or until crisp-tender. Plunge into ice water to stop the cooking process, and drain.
2. Cut squash into ½-inch-thick slices, and remove pulp from center of each slice with a round cutter or knife. Secure green beans, carrots, and peppers in bundles with squash rings, and place in a lightly greased 13- x 9-inch baking dish. Drizzle vegetable bundles with melted butter, and bake, covered, at 350° for 20 to 25 minutes or until thoroughly heated.
To Make Ahead: Cover and chill vegetable bundles 8 hours. Let stand at room temperature for 30 minutes before baking.

Roasted Sweet Potatoes and Onions

MAKES 10 SERVINGS
PREP: 15 MIN., BAKE: 30 MIN.

6 sweet potatoes, peeled and cut into 1-inch cubes
2 large sweet onions, cut into wedges
3 tablespoons olive oil
2 tablespoons fajita seasoning

1. Combine all ingredients; place on an aluminum foil-lined baking pan.
2. Bake at 450° for 30 minutes or until tender, stirring occasionally.

Cheese Biscuits With Chipotle Butter

MAKES 2 DOZEN
PREP: 10 MIN., BAKE: 12 MIN.

1 (7.25-ounce) package biscuit mix
1 (6-ounce) package cornbread mix
1 (8-ounce) container sour cream
⅓ cup buttermilk
1 cup (4 ounces) shredded Cheddar cheese
1 teaspoon fajita seasoning (optional)
Chipotle Butter

1. Stir together first 5 ingredients, and, if desired, fajita seasoning. Pat or roll dough out onto a lightly floured surface to a ½-inch thickness. Cut dough with a 2-inch round cutter, and place rounds on a lightly greased baking sheet.
2. Bake at 400° for 10 to 12 minutes. Serve with Chipotle Butter.

Chipotle Butter:

MAKES ½ CUP
PREP: 5 MIN.

½ cup butter, softened
2 teaspoons chopped fresh parsley
1 chipotle pepper in adobo sauce, diced
2 teaspoons adobo sauce

1. Stir together all ingredients. Cover and chill until ready to serve.

Cheese Biscuits With Chipotle Butter

Chocolate-Praline Pecan Cake

Chocolate-Praline Pecan Cake

This must be baked in two 9-inch square pans or ceramic baking dishes that are at least 2 inches deep.

MAKES 2 CAKES (ABOUT 9 SERVINGS EACH)
PREP: 30 MIN., BAKE: 40 MIN., COOK: 10 MIN.

1 recipe Chocolate Velvet Cake Batter
2 cups firmly packed brown sugar
⅔ cup whipping cream
½ cup butter
2 cups powdered sugar, sifted
2 teaspoons vanilla extract
2 cups chopped pecans, toasted

1. Prepare batter, and spoon evenly into 2 greased and floured 9- x 9- x 2-inch square pans or ceramic baking dishes.
2. Bake at 350° for 40 minutes or until a wooden pick inserted in center comes out clean. Cool cakes in pans on a wire rack.
3. Bring 2 cups brown sugar, whipping cream, and butter to a boil in a 3-quart saucepan over medium heat, stirring often; boil 1 minute. Remove from heat; whisk in powdered sugar and vanilla until smooth. Add chopped pecans, stirring gently 3 to 5 minutes or until mixture begins to cool and thicken slightly. Pour immediately over cakes in pans. Let cool completely. Cut cakes into squares.
To Make Ahead: Bake cakes and cool as directed. Cover and freeze up to 1 month. Thaw completely before pouring praline topping over the cakes.

Once the praline topping begins to thicken, immediately pour it over the cake, and spread evenly.

Chocolate Velvet Cake Batter:

The addition of hot water at the end of this recipe makes for an exceptionally moist cake.

MAKES ABOUT 8½ CUPS
PREP: 15 MIN.

1½ cups semisweet chocolate morsels
½ cup butter, softened
1 (16-ounce) package light brown sugar
3 large eggs
2 cups all-purpose flour
1 teaspoon baking soda
½ teaspoon salt
1 (8-ounce) container sour cream
1 cup hot water
2 teaspoons vanilla extract

1. Melt semisweet chocolate morsels in a microwave-safe bowl at HIGH for 30-second intervals until melted (about 1½ minutes total time). Stir until smooth.
2. Beat softened butter and light brown sugar at medium speed with an electric mixer, beating about 5 minutes or until well blended. Add eggs, 1 at a time, beating just until blended after each addition. Add melted chocolate, beating just until blended.
3. Sift together flour, baking soda, and salt. Gradually add to chocolate mixture alternately with sour cream, beginning and ending with flour mixture. Beat at low speed just until blended after each addition. Gradually add 1 cup hot water in a slow, steady stream, beating at low speed just until blended. Stir in vanilla. Use batter immediately.

A Southern Hanukkah

serves 6 to 8

Sweet-and-Sour Brisket

Asparagus With Orange Vinaigrette

Potato Latkes

Homemade Applesauce

Sweet-and-Sour Brisket

This unique and flavorful recipe received a high rating in our Test Kitchens.

MAKES 6 TO 8 SERVINGS
PREP: 15 MIN., BAKE: 4 HRS., STAND: 30 MIN.

1 (5-pound) beef brisket, trimmed
1 (1-ounce) envelope onion soup mix
½ teaspoon garlic powder
½ teaspoon Italian seasoning
½ teaspoon ground red pepper
1 (10-ounce) jar apricot preserves
1 cup water
1 cup chili sauce
2 (10-ounce) cans sauerkraut, drained

1. Place brisket in a lightly greased roasting pan. Sprinkle with soup mix and next 3 ingredients. Spread preserves on top of brisket. Add 1 cup water to pan. Cover tightly with heavy-duty aluminum foil.
2. Bake, covered, at 350° for 3 hours. Uncover and pour chili sauce over brisket; top with sauerkraut. Cover and bake 1 more hour. Remove from oven; let stand, covered, 30 minutes before slicing. Serve with sauerkraut and pan juices.

Sweet-and-Sour Brisket and Asparagus With Orange Vinaigrette

Asparagus With Orange Vinaigrette

If the asparagus are large or you prefer them to be more tender, increase the cooking time 5 to 10 minutes or to desired degree of tenderness.

MAKES 6 TO 8 SERVINGS
PREP: 30 MIN., COOK: 5 MIN.

3 pounds fresh asparagus
2 shallots, chopped
¼ cup white balsamic vinegar
1 teaspoon grated orange rind
2 large navel oranges, sectioned
⅛ teaspoon salt
⅛ teaspoon pepper
½ cup olive oil

1. Snap off and discard tough ends of asparagus; arrange asparagus in a steamer basket over boiling water. Cover and steam 3 to 5 minutes or until crisp-tender.
2. Plunge asparagus into ice water to stop the cooking process; drain.
3. Combine shallots and next 5 ingredients; gradually whisk in olive oil, blending well. Drizzle over asparagus. Serve immediately.

Potato Latkes

MAKES ABOUT 1 DOZEN
PREP: 30 MIN., STAND: 10 MIN., FRY: 8 MIN. PER BATCH

2 large baking potatoes (about 1½ pounds), peeled
    and shredded
2 large eggs
1 medium-size sweet onion, diced
½ cup all-purpose flour
1 teaspoon salt
¼ teaspoon baking powder
Vegetable oil
Homemade Applesauce

1. Combine shredded potatoes and water to cover in a bowl; let stand 10 minutes. Drain well.
2. Stir together potato, eggs, and next 4 ingredients, blending well.
3. Pour oil to a depth of ½ inch into a large heavy skillet; heat to 375°. Drop potato mixture by ¼ cupfuls into hot oil, and fry, in batches, 3 to 4 minutes on each side or until golden. Drain on paper towels. Serve with Homemade Applesauce.

Homemade Applesauce

Homemade Applesauce:

MAKES ABOUT 8 CUPS
PREP: 20 MIN., COOK: 50 MIN.

12 Rome apples, peeled, cored, and
    quartered*
3 cups apple juice
½ cup firmly packed brown sugar
½ cup granulated sugar
¼ cup lemon juice
2 (2-inch-long) cinnamon sticks

1. Bring all ingredients to a boil in a Dutch oven; reduce heat, and simmer, stirring once, 45 minutes. Drain; remove and discard cinnamon sicks. Coarsely mash apple mixture, using a potato masher. Store in the refrigerator up to 1 week.
*Other varieties of sweet red baking apples with a smooth bottom may be substituted.

Christmas Appetizer Buffet

serves 20

Cider Nog Punch
(double recipe)

Seasoned Pepper Beef Tenderloin

Creamy Spinach Dip

Bacon-Blue Cheese Dip

Cranberry Baked Brie
(double recipe)

Christmas Butter Cookies

Coffee bar

Cider Nog Punch

MAKES 12 CUPS
PREP: 15 MIN., COOK: 30 MIN., STAND: 1 HR., CHILL: 4 HRS.

4 cups half-and-half
2 cups milk
2 cups apple cider
4 large eggs
1 cup sugar
½ teaspoon ground cinnamon
¼ teaspoon ground nutmeg
¼ teaspoon salt
1 cup bourbon (optional)
1 quart vanilla ice cream, softened
1 cup whipping cream, whipped
Freshly ground nutmeg

1. Whisk together first 8 ingredients in a Dutch oven over medium-low heat; cook, stirring constantly, 20 to 30 minutes or until mixture thickens and coats a spoon. Remove from heat, and let stand at room temperature 1 hour to cool.
2. Stir in bourbon, if desired. Cover and chill at least 4 hours. Transfer chilled mixture to a chilled punch bowl or large bowl; stir in ice cream. Serve with whipped cream and ground nutmeg.

AT-HOME COFFEE BAR

■ Arrange your coffee bar on a countertop or sideboard easily accessible to a number of people. Plan enough room for cups, saucers, spoons, and flavoring ingredients.

■ Consider buying vacuum-insulated pump coffeepots. These thermal coffee dispensers will keep coffee fresh and hot for hours. You can choose from a variety of options and sizes. Best of all, they're relatively inexpensive, starting at about $30.
■ Bring the look of the season to your coffee bar with festive cups, jars, sugar and creamer bowls, and holiday decorations.
■ Include fun flavorings such as grated chocolate, cinnamon sticks, and shakers of ground cinnamon, cocoa, and nutmeg.
■ For spirited versions, offer guests a selection of liqueurs to add to their coffee. Include coffee-, almond-, orange-, hazelnut-, and praline-flavored liqueurs.
■ For a similar taste without the alcohol, use flavored syrups. Look for them in your grocery store on the coffee aisle or at coffee shops.

Seasoned Pepper Beef Tenderloin on rolls with Dijon-Horseradish Sauce; Bacon-Blue Cheese Dip with cut vegetables (page 406)

Seasoned Pepper Beef Tenderloin

MAKES ABOUT 20 APPETIZER SERVINGS
PREP: 15 MIN.; STAND: 1 HR., 10 MIN.; BAKE: 1 HR.

1 (4- to 5-pound) trimmed beef tenderloin
1 tablespoon olive oil
1 teaspoon salt
1½ tablespoons seasoned pepper
Dinner rolls
Dijon-Horseradish Sauce

1. Brush beef tenderloin evenly with olive oil; sprinkle evenly with salt, and rub with seasoned pepper. Place on a lightly greased rack in a roasting pan; let stand 1 hour at room temperature.
2. Bake at 500° for 15 minutes; reduce heat to 375°, and bake 40 to 45 minutes or to desired degree of doneness (145° for medium-rare). Remove from oven; cover tenderloin loosely with aluminum foil, and let stand 10 minutes before thinly slicing. Serve sliced beef on rolls with Dijon-Horseradish Sauce.

Dijon-Horseradish Sauce:

MAKES ABOUT 1¼ CUPS
PREP: 10 MIN.

1 cup mayonnaise
2 tablespoons whole grain Dijon mustard
2 tablespoons prepared horseradish
2 tablespoons sour cream
1 tablespoon chopped fresh chives

1. Stir together all ingredients until blended; cover and chill until ready to serve.
To Make Ahead: Store sauce in an airtight container in the refrigerator up to 1 week.

Creamy Spinach Dip

Creamy Spinach Dip

Serve the dip in a carved cabbage shell, if you'd like.

MAKES ABOUT 3 CUPS
PREP: 15 MIN., COOK: 10 MIN., CHILL: 1 HR.

2 (10-ounce) packages frozen chopped spinach
1 (8-ounce) container light sour cream
3/4 cup light mayonnaise
1/3 cup chopped green onions
1 tablespoon chopped fresh dill
1 teaspoon seasoned salt
2 teaspoons lemon juice
1/8 teaspoon ground red pepper
Assorted crackers or fresh vegetables

1. Cook spinach according to package directions; drain well, and stir together with sour cream, mayonnaise, green onions, chopped fresh dill, seasoned salt, lemon juice, and ground red pepper. Cover and chill at least 1 hour. Serve with crackers or fresh vegetables.
To Make Ahead: Store dip in an airtight container in the refrigerator up to 1 week.

Bacon-Blue Cheese Dip

MAKES 2 CUPS
PREP: 10 MIN.

1 (8-ounce) package cream cheese, softened
1 (4-ounce) package crumbled blue cheese
1/2 cup light sour cream
2 bacon slices, cooked and crumbled
3 tablespoons chopped green onions
1/2 teaspoon hot sauce
Assorted crackers or fresh vegetables

1. Beat cream cheese and blue cheese at medium speed with an electric mixer until creamy. Stir in sour cream and next 3 ingredients. Serve immediately, or cover and chill until ready to serve. Serve with crackers or fresh vegetables.
Note: For testing purposes only, we used Salemville Amish Crumbled Blue Cheese.
To Make Ahead: Store dip in an airtight container in the refrigerator up to 1 week.

Cranberry-Baked Brie

This recipe makes 2 baked Brie. As a serving idea, and because both are baked at the same time, you might consider putting them in two different rooms, especially for an open house-type gathering. They can also be baked separately.

MAKES ABOUT 10 TO 12 APPETIZER SERVINGS
PREP: 20 MIN., BAKE: 25 MIN., COOL: 10 MIN.

2 (8-ounce) Brie rounds
1 (16-ounce) can whole-berry cranberry sauce
⅓ cup chopped toasted pecans
2 tablespoons sugar
1 teaspoon grated lemon rind
2 teaspoons fresh lemon juice
1 (17.3-ounce) package frozen puff pastry sheets, thawed
Toasted French bread baguette slices
Granny Smith apple or pear slices

1. Trim and discard rind from tops of Brie; set aside.
2. Stir together cranberry sauce and next 4 ingredients.
3. Place one puff pastry sheet on a lightly floured surface; roll out fold lines. Spread half of cranberry mixture in a 5-inch circle in center of rolled-out pastry sheet. Place 1 Brie round, trimmed side down, on top of cranberry mixture.
4. Wrap puff pastry around Brie round, pinching edges and folds to tightly seal. Invert and place on 1 side of an aluminum foil-lined baking sheet. Repeat procedure with remaining Brie round, puff pastry sheet, and cranberry mixture. Invert and place on other side of foil-lined baking sheet.
5. Bake at 400° for 25 minutes or until pastry is golden brown. Cool on baking sheet on a wire rack 10 minutes. Serve warm with baguette slices and apple or pear slices.

Cranberry-Baked Brie

Christmas Butter Cookies

MAKES ABOUT 3 DOZEN
PREP: 20 MIN., BAKE: 13 MIN. PER BATCH

2 cups all-purpose flour
½ teaspoon baking powder
¼ teaspoon salt
¾ cup butter, softened
1 cup granulated sugar
1 large egg
½ teaspoon vanilla extract
Finely chopped toasted pecans (optional)
Red and green colored sugars (optional)

1. Combine flour, baking powder, and salt. Set aside.
2. Beat butter at medium speed with an electric mixer until smooth; gradually add granulated sugar, beating 5 minutes or until fluffy. Add egg and vanilla, beating until blended.
3. Reduce speed to low, and add flour mixture, beating just until combined.
4. Shape dough into 1-inch balls. Roll in chopped pecans or colored sugars, if desired. Place about 2 inches apart on lightly greased baking sheets.
5. Bake, in batches, at 375° for 12 to 13 minutes or until lightly browned on bottom. Remove to wire racks, and let cool completely.

Almond Spice Cookies: Add ½ teaspoon ground cinnamon, ⅛ teaspoon dried ground nutmeg, ⅛ teaspoon ground cloves, and ⅛ teaspoon dried ground ginger to flour mixture. Proceed as directed, stirring ¾ cup finely chopped toasted almonds into prepared dough. Omit pecans and colored sugars. Bake as directed. Makes about 4 dozen.

To Make Ahead: Cookies may be stored in an airtight container up to 1 month.